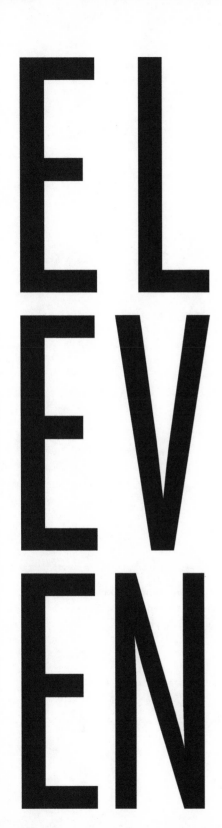

ELEVEN

by Paul Hanley

 **FriesenPress**

Suite 300 – 990 Fort Street
Victoria, BC, Canada V8V 3K2
www.friesenpress.com

ISBN
978-1-4602-5045-7 (Hardcover)
978-1-4602-5046-4 (Paperback)
978-1-4602-5047-1 (eBook)

1. Nature, Environmental Conservation & Protection

Distributed to the trade by The Ingram Book Company

Yann Martel, author of *Life of Pi*, recipient of the Man Booker Prize:

"Every concerned citizen of this planet needs to read this book. That means you, you there. If climate change, environmental degradation, population pressures and all the other ills of this planet induce in you a sort of fatalistic hunkering down, or, worse, nihilistic glee, then Paul Hanley's book shows a way forward. *Eleven* offers a glimpse of a world of eleven billion people that will not only be livable for all of us, but, surprisingly, *better* than the one we live in now.

"The book packs all the facts and parcels of knowledge that a solidly-argued work of non-fiction requires, but underpinning it is a spiritual argument that is even more convincing. At the heart of *Eleven* is an old-fashioned yet timeless and always radical emotional concept: love. A world packed with even more humans beings than there are now will be better, Hanley argues, because we will realize then what is of true worth: the connections we make with others. The fundamental unity of humankind, with all its emotional and existential consequences, is the guarantor of an authentically fulfilling life, rather than the clutter of objects with which we surround ourselves now or the mindless entertainment with which we fritter away our time.

"Read this book, plunge into it. It will blast away the facile inertia to which so many of us succumb. The way forward is scary, yes, but also exciting. A greater, simpler, healthier world awaits us. Prepare for it, work at it. And start by reading *Eleven*."

William E. Rees, originator of ecological footprint analysis:

"Paul Hanley's *Eleven* is the read for our times. Anyone still confused about the implications for global civilization of our gathering ecological and social crises—a number of politicians and policy-makers come to mind—should not be allowed out in public until s/he has read this book.

"*Eleven* provides a fluidly accessible and meticulously researched account of the modern human predicament, but Hanley's interpretation is uniquely buoyed above the usual tide of bad news by an ebullient confidence in *H. sapiens* as moral agent. The book is firmly rooted in the author's belief that, confronted with crisis, it is possible for the world community "to choose to move against the flow of history," that people have the capacity to change almost everything about the way they live in order to thrive with peace and justice on this finite planet. And the means are available for success—Hanley goes a long way toward demonstrating that virtually "everything that needs to be done to make the world just and sustainable is being done somewhere, successfully, already."

"This can only be encouraging to anyone swayed by Jared Diamond's treatise in *Collapse* that the modern world may well be headed toward the abyss. Indeed, reason for hope is couched even in Diamond's own sub-title: "how societies *choose* to fail or succeed." It seems the time has come for *us* to choose.

"And this is where *Eleven* comes in. Global society is teetering on the brink but Paul Hanley maps a feasible, albeit challenging, path back from the abyss."

Trevor Herriot, author of *River in a Dry Land* and *The Road is How*:

"Our bookshelves are full of volumes telling us how we arrived at our modern predicament, but in *Eleven*, Paul Hanley takes on the tougher task of meticulously describing the present moment and then weighing it against a future where we will be eleven billion. Astonishingly, brilliantly, and quite convincingly, he arrives at a balance that is more optimistic than you would expect.

"*Eleven* is an inspired map of the road ahead, drawn in lines of truth we turn our gaze away from every day. More than that, though, this sweeping book makes an audacious but coherent and thoroughly-researched case for the possibility that, by awakening to the reality of what we are doing to the earth and our own souls, we may already be getting ready to walk the road with our "better angels of our nature" fully in charge."

Wes Jackson, Founder of The Land Institute, recipient of the Right Livelihood Award:

"Paul Hanley has given us a blueprint for the future based on hope which would not be possible if we did not have the many good examples, both materially and in thought, that are outlined in his book *Eleven*."

TABLE OF CONTENTS

PREFACE

Eleven billion people will populate this marvelous planet by the end of this century. Adding almost 4 billion to an already overburdened world will force everyone to change everything. The sweeping changes that make an 11 billion-world work will wholly transform humankind, reshaping its inner life and external conditions. This process will result in the emergence of a new culture, a new agriculture, and ultimately a new human race.

One distinguishing characteristic of an intelligent person, observed Bertrand Russell, is that she or he can be "emotionally moved by statistics." If any statistic ought to move us it should be this: 11 billion people will crowd this planet by century's end, just one lifespan away. Truly absorbing its significance would move every one of us, not just emotionally, but to action.

Russell, an early proponent of population control, was frustrated by people's reluctance to think through the implications of population growth. "Mankind would rather commit suicide than learn arithmetic," he quipped 50 years ago.

We still avoid the topic today, though the Population Division of the United Nations has done the math for us.[1] It projects various scenarios for future growth, depending on the average global fertility rate. If, for example, fertility were to remain constant in each country at 2005-2010 levels, global population would exceed 27 billion by 2100. Fortunately, fertility is trending downward and that doomsday scenario will be avoided.

In the medium variant, considered the most likely scenario, world population is expected to increase to 8.1 billion in 2025 and 9.6 billion in 2050, before peaking just shy of 11 billion around 2100.

Some 40 high-income countries will actually see population decreases. Most of the world's 3.7 billion new citizens will be born in low-income countries; their combined population will rise from 5.9 billion to 9.6 billion in 2100.

By 2100, the populations of 35 countries—most in the lowest income range—are likely to triple. Among them, the populations of nine African nations are projected to increase at least five-fold. In 2100, Nigeria (174 million people in 2013) will be the third most populous country in the world, with a staggeringly high population of 914 million people. Nigeria is less than a tenth the size of China.

Ultimately, zero population growth is the only sane and sustainable option. It will be achieved sooner or later, but the strong likelihood is that it will not happen before some 11 billion souls are sharing this planet. That die is cast.

But population is just half the story. The human ecological footprint—the impact we have on the planet through resource use and emissions—is also rising. It currently exceeds Earth's carrying capacity by 60 percent. While the sheer volume of Earth's natural capital may allow us to carry on as is for some time, to do so with 50 percent more people would mean that our collective ecological footprint in 2100 would exceed Earth's carrying capacity several times over.

That alone would be untenable, but it gets worse. More nations—including the largest—have discovered the formula for affluence using an economic model that would dramatically deepen their footprint. More and more people will join the consumer class.[2] That said, extreme inequality is unlikely to disappear.[3]

As the table shows, projections based on a business-as-usual scenario would see the world population and economy, and consequently its ecological footprint, rising to levels that could only lead to a social and ecological catastrophe.

Despite mounting evidence of the gravity of the ecological threat and the arrival of hard consequences—floods, droughts, and fires—humanity persists in its strange slumber. But sleep will become impossible as we approach an 11-billion world. We are about to get a very loud wake up call.

Year	World Population	Annual % growth	Ecological Footprint (Earth equivalents)	Gross World Product (trillions of 1990 $)
1950	2,556,000,000	1.78	0.42	4
1960	3,039,451,000	1.91	0.62	7
1970	3,706,618,000	1.96	0.88	12
1980	4,453,832.000	1.78	1.06	15
1990	5,278,640,000	1.52	1.18	20
2000	6,082,966,000	1.22	1.29	30
2010	6,848,933,000	1.14	1.60	40
2020	7,716,749,000	0.93	1.90	55
2030	8,424,937,000	0.74	2.30	70
2040	9,038,867,000	0.59	2.60	85
2050	9,550,945,000	0.44	3.00	100
2100	10,900,000,000	0.11	4.80	250

Sources: Population: U.N. World Population Prospects: The 2012 Revision; GWP, various sources including IPCC; Footprint projections, various sources including Global Footprint Network.

Everything is going to change. As population and resource pressures mount, change will affect each of us at our core and will ultimately reshape our minds, our hearts, our values, our settlements, our homes, our work, our economy, our systems of governance. We are going to change so completely that future civilization will be barely recognizable. We are going to change because, faced with extinction, our "better angels" will prevail.

Cynics may find assurance in Buckminster Fuller's aphorism, that: "Human beings always do the most intelligent thing… after they've tried every stupid alternative and none of them have worked." Indeed, history shows that when we have to, we do change: sometimes radically, suddenly, and en masse. And the unprecedented pressure resulting from a 50 percent increase in the human population—equivalent to adding the current populations of China, India, the United States, Indonesia, Brazil, Pakistan, and Japan—will soon make it evident to everyone that we do "have to."

But let's be clear. The transformation that will ultimately bring about a new and better world order will occur concurrently with a terrifying disintegration of the old one, making the 21st century a most precarious period. Over the next 85 years we will see unremitting news of disaster and hardship as the old order crumbles, but simultaneously—slowly and quietly at first—news of positive change as a new one emerges.

This dual process of destruction and reconstruction will be more or less traumatic depending on the speed at which we drop outmoded worldviews and behaviours and adopt better ones.

Initially, progress will appear to be minimal or even nonexistent. For half the journey we will be closer to and look more like what we are leaving behind than what we are headed toward. Only in the latter part of the transformative process will we realize how much has changed.

To carry civilization forward in a full world, individuals, communities, and institutions will be forced by circumstance to transform themselves. That we will unite to meet this ultimate challenge is neither a utopian vision, nor even a matter of choice. It is the next, inescapable stage in human evolution.

A NEW CULTURE

Culture is the sum of all social processes that make the artificial (or human constructed) seem natural.
– Robert Welsch

CHAPTER 1

EVERYTHING. EVERYWHERE. ALWAYS.

It is difficult to change gods.
– Dostoyevsky

On September 28, 2009, Canada's Prime Minister Stephen Harper skipped a planned address to the United Nations General Assembly to make an appearance at a Tim Hortons media event.[4]

Why would a Prime Minister chose a doughnut shop over the world's assembled leaders? Presumably to align himself with the Canadian company's wildly popular brand.

It is also possible Mr. Harper just couldn't get by without his daily 'Tim fix.' After all, some Canadians are so addicted to their daily dose of Tim Hortons coffee that leaving the country can be a challenge. Canadian soldiers serving in Afghanistan, for instance, missed 'TiHos' so much that former Chief of Defense Staff General Rick Hillier personally requested a franchise for Canada's military base in Kandahar as a morale booster. The location opened on July 1—Canada Day—2006. In addition to training for the usual duties like making coffee and doughnuts, the Kandahar staff was instructed in nuclear and biological attack preparedness.

When Canada's military pulled out of Afghanistan, Tim Hortons was one of the last things to go. The Kandahar location closed in November 2011 after serving four million cups of coffee and three million doughnuts. One patron was none other than Prime Minister Harper, whose government had subsidized the location to the tune of $20 million over its five years of operation.

Prime Minister Stephen Harper enjoying his Tim fix at Tim Hortons' Afghanistan location.

For Canadians, Tim Hortons is not just a coffee spot. It has been described as a "national institution" and a "cultural icon." Such designations are not hyperbole. Started in 1964 by hockey star Tim Horton, the now ubiquitous chain had become so popular that by 2010 it commanded 76 percent of the Canadian market for baked goods; 62 percent of the country's coffee market (compared to 7 percent for Starbucks, its nearest competitor); and 25 percent of all fast food industry revenues, with sales over $2 billion. It had more than 100,000 employees at 3000 Canadian locations (twice as many as McDonald's). No wonder Canada has been called 'Timbit Nation,' after Timbits, the company's popular doughnut holes.

Interestingly, Canadians don't mind their national identity being associated with doughnuts. Not one bit. While it may be consistent with their self-deprecating sense of humour, the association is less funny when we consider the broader implications of a junk food-addicted consumer culture.

Given the chain's popularity, it's no surprise the rush hour lineup at the TiHo's drive-thru near my home often snakes through the cramped parking lot and onto the street, occasionally halting traffic in both directions. It's faster to park and walk in to pick up a coffee, but—winter or summer—patrons wait in a long line of idling cars and trucks for their daily fix.

Though known mainly for coffee and doughnuts, Tim's has an ever-expanding menu. If, as many do, a patron enjoys the popular large iced cappuccino and a frosted cinnamon roll on a coffee break, she or he would consume 940 calories, close to 40 percent of the recommended daily caloric intake for a man, and closer to 50 percent for a woman.

We all know that eating at Tim Hortons and the other fast food chains is not particularly good for us. What we may not realize is the full range of impacts that ripple out from our seemingly innocuous coffee breaks. Every snack embodies the energy that goes into the farm fuels, fertilizers, and pesticides required to produce the wheat, sugar, coffee, and other ingredients, to make the packaging, and to process and deliver the products. Preparation, refrigeration, cooking, and dishwashing at fast food outlets are said to consume more energy than any other aspect of the production system, while the consumer's drive to pick up a food item may use even more energy than producing the food.[5] In the United States—and the figure is similar for Canada—the agrifood system accounts for 10 percent of national energy use, with 80 percent of that amount used for non-agricultural components of the system.[6]

Tim Hortons' environmental report[7] shows the company uses the equivalent of 840,000 barrels of oil a year. Add in the energy used in producing, processing, and transporting the ingredients for its products, plus the consumers' drive to pick them up—including the energy used while idling their cars in the drive-thru—and Canada's Tim Horton's fixation requires well over 1 million barrels of oil. For just one fast food chain, that's not an insignificant portion of Canada's annual consumption of 650 million barrels.

And just as we thought there were no corners left without a Tim Hortons, the company announced it will open 500 new locations in Canada—plus another 300 in the US and 220 in the Middle East—as it targets compound annual profit-per-share growth of 11 to 13 percent by 2019.

CASCADING IMPACTS

High calorie baking used to be good for us, or at least necessary. Doughnuts, for instance, can be traced to New England's hardworking Dutch immigrants who valued them as a source of energy for long days of heavy farm labour. To increase energy content, they were deep fried in lard from the farm's hogs. Back then, energy inputs came from sunshine.

Today's industrialized production methods make high-calorie baking available 24/7/365 to people who rarely, if ever, engage in physical labour, triggering a public health crisis. And today, the energy supply comes mainly from non-renewable sources that emit climate-changing gases and pollutants.

Mass consumption of fast food unleashes a kind of trophic cascade of health, social, and ecological impacts. It is well established that the highly refined, high-carb Western diet typified by fast food is a key driver of rapidly escalating healthcare costs. Bad diets are a primary reason why Canadian spending on health care—more accurately illness care—increased from $39.7 billion to $137.3 billion (in 1997 dollars) between 1975 and 2009, while per capita spending went from $1715 to $4089. In 2009 dollars, health care spending reached $183.1 billion or $5452 per person in 2009, more than 10 percent of the country's Gross Domestic Product (GDP). Despite being a sign of deteriorating health, such expenditures are misinterpreted as positive when measuring GDP, our misleading metric of national well-being.

Fast food is even bigger in the United States, where highly processed foods generate $1 trillion in corporate revenues a year.[8] It is not surprising then that Canadian health care costs are dwarfed by US spending, which in 2009 hit $2.5 trillion, $8047 per person and 17.3 percent of GDP. A simple projection of historical growth rates shows US health care spending eventually exceeding total national income. Impossible, of course, but the Congressional Budget Office projects that in the absence of changes in federal law, total spending on US health care would rise to 25 percent of GDP in 2025, 37 percent in 2050, and 49 percent in 2082.[9]

What benefit does increased medical spending provide?

While wealthy consumer societies rightly boast high longevity, the other side of that coin is the rise of chronic illnesses. Canada is experiencing a "tsunami" of chronic disease according to one expert,[10] with more than nine million Canadians—a quarter of the population—suffering from heart disease, diabetes, and cancer. Chronic diseases account for about 50 percent of physician visits and about seventy percent of hospital stays, costing Canadians billions every year in medical costs. In my province of Saskatchewan, the North American birthplace of publicly funded medical care, the incidence and prevalence of essentially every health disorder monitored actually increased between 2000-2010 despite more than doubling health-care spending during that period.[11]

According to the US Centers for Disease Control and Prevention, genetics are responsible for only 10 percent of disease, environmental factors 90 percent.[12] Increased medical spending does little or nothing to improve health because the care model is not designed to promote health. It is designed to repair the damage caused by environmental factors, such as the foods we eat, pollution, insufficient exercise, accidents, and stress, rather than addressing causes. Yet very strong evidence shows that no–to-low cost solutions, all of which involve reduced consumption—mainly of food, harmful substance, and motorized transport—can dramatically reduce the incidence of chronic disease.

So can opting out of the high stress associated with maintaining a consumer lifestyle.

Yet a true health care system that mandated a healthy diet, better urban design with active transportation, and a safe environment would be seen as a radical imposition on personal freedom. We willingly accept manipulation by private, for-profit agrifood interests or carmakers or pharmaceutical companies, but we reject the notion that democratically elected governments can "dictate what we do."

Fast foods are more than a public health disaster. One study found that fully 50 percent of the ecological footprint of a major North American city resulted from supplying its food.[13] Estimates put the contribution of the agrifood system to climate change anywhere from 15 percent to as high as 50 percent when indirect impacts such as deforestation to increase the supply of farmland are included.[14]

Something as seemingly innocuous as waiting in line at a drive-thru intensifies the ecological footprint of our fast food addiction. Idling cars is not only a waste of time and fuel, it produces more pollutants than any other aspect of operating a vehicle. According to one estimate, if Canadian motorists avoided idling their vehicles for just three minutes every day—about half the time it takes to move through a busy drive-thru—they would reduce CO_2 emissions by 1.4 million tonnes annually and save 630 million litres of fuel, equivalent to taking 320,000 cars off of the road.[15]

Traffic congestion in cities, perhaps the worst drawback to urban living, costs Canadians up to $3.7 billion per year. More than 90 percent of this cost is associated with time lost, seven percent occurs because of fuel consumed, and three percent is from increased greenhouse gas emissions (GHGs).[16] In the worst travel corridors in large cities like Toronto drivers can spend 62 hours a year—a workweek and a half—idling in gridlock.[17]

That drive-thru at the busy street corner near my place—and thousands like it throughout North America and beyond—epitomizes life in the high-throughput consumer society, where something as simple as having a snack triggers a hydra-like calamity—one we can't see (or choose to ignore.) The illustration shows some social-ecological impacts of eating doughnuts or other fast foods.

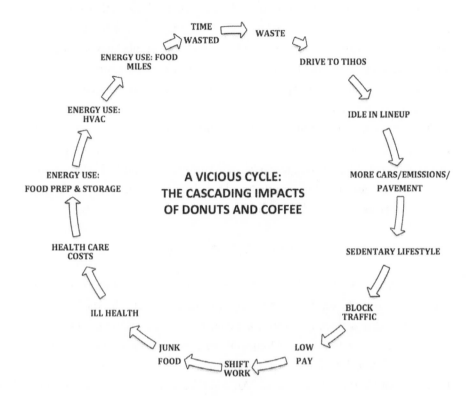

A VICIOUS CYCLE:
THE CASCADING IMPACTS
OF DONUTS AND COFFEE

This discussion is not intended as a targeted attack on Tim Hortons or its patrons (of whom I am occasionally one). In fact, the chain is exceptionally good at what it does, which is why it is so successful. Substitute any other fast food franchise you are familiar with; my point is that these ubiquitous fast food chains—with products scientifically designed to be irresistible—trigger uncounted ecological, physical, cultural, and economic costs that far outweigh benefits.

Does growth really make us richer, or is it making us poorer by increasing uncounted social and ecological costs faster than benefits?

Fast food joints are the pit stops of our illusory world, the consumer society. The world would be a better place if they did not exist. Yet North America's junk food culture is being exported worldwide as economic growth accelerates, countries like Brazil and China grow richer, and everyone aspires to the consumer lifestyle.

"The question is," says economist Herman Daly, "does further growth... really make us richer, or is it making us poorer by increasing the uncounted costs of growth faster than the measured benefits? That simple question is taboo among economists and politicians, lest we discover that the falling benefits of growth are all going to the top 1%, while the rising costs are 'shared' with the poor, the future, and other species."[18]

This discussion may paint a rather bleak picture, not only of our present but also our future prospects, yet it contains a key to solving the 11 billion conundrum. Ecological health is intimately linked to human health. Fostering collective human health will result in a healthy, balanced ecosphere and resolving ecological issues will foster human health.

THE GREAT WALL-MART OF CHINA

Plop someone down by the local Tim Hortons in my hometown and he or she could be in any city on our increasingly franchised planet. The mishmash of nondescript strip malls, chain stores, and pavement is ugly yet strangely alluring.

Put a Tim Hortons, Dunkin' Donuts, PetroCanada or ESSO here, a Safeway, Wal-Mart, Target, Jiffy Lube, or Bank of America there—or perhaps an East Dawning—it doesn't much matter. An interchangeable set of monotonous international chains and national equivalents is popping up everywhere. Aside from the branding that projects an illusion of choice, they are all much the same. Those companies that proliferate have triumphed in the struggle for corporate survival. They are the most efficient at moving product through the pipe and the most effective at delivering the consumer dream: *Everything. Everywhere. Always.* The winners push forward inexorably to claim every distant outpost, from Kandahar to Timbuktu to Beijing in a relentless campaign of consumer shock and awe.

As Tim Hortons plans a Far East expansion, there are already more than 4000 KFC and 1400 McDonald's outlets in China, where it is said there are now more public portraits of Colonel Saunders than Chairman Mao. The Chinese consume more and more processed foods and sugary drinks, and ever more animal protein. Between 1990 and 2009, per capita consumption in China of cereals, roots, beans, and pulses declined while consumption of cheese doubled, eggs tripled, chicken quadrupled, and beef increased five-fold. And with 100 million cars now on the roads, people walk and ride bicycles less.[19]

The health care industry is salivating. Loading up on hamburgers, fried chicken, pizza, and other high-fat foods—combined with more car travel—contributes to heart disease, obesity, diabetes, and cancer, the chronic conditions that result from a consumer lifestyle. Consistent with the North American experience, Chinese incomes and life expectancy will improve with the rise of consumer capitalism, but at a price. Roughly 92 million Chinese now suffer from Type II diabetes, a disease nearly unknown in their country until recently. A 2010 study by the Columbia University Medical Center estimates that heart disease and stroke rates in China will increase up to 70 percent by 2030.

Meanwhile, China's shift to an American-style diet is increasing the country's ecological footprint. Industrial-scale animal production to support increased meat consumption, for instance, has generated vast amounts of manure, resulting in increased GHG emissions and dead zones along the country's coast. Also consistent with the American model, food waste is growing. Restaurants and consumers throw away an estimated 55 million tonnes of food a year, enough to feed 200 million people.

As China reemerges as the world's economic superpower it has also become the largest source of climate emissions. While acknowledging the ecological implications of rapid growth, in a final speech to the National People's Congress in March 2013 retiring Premier Wen Jiabao nevertheless pledged to transform China into a consumer-driven economy.[20]

"We should energetically change the growth model and speed up structural adjustment of industry," Wen said. "We should enhance people's ability to consume and boost their desire to consume," he continued, signalling a shift from China's historic dependence on low-cost manufacturing and exports. The goals he announced are part of a long-range plan Xi Jinping, his replacement as general secretary, is expected to adhere to. Promoting consumer spending would support additional economic expansion and boost living standards for ordinary Chinese, who have been treated until now as a mere labour source while the elite siphons off most of the benefits of explosive growth.

So another country, the largest, is now officially committed to becoming a high consumption society, with India, the next largest, in the queue. The exponential growth and spread of consumerism over the past 70 years—over the course of a single lifetime—is *the most radical change the world has ever seen.* For one thing, it has pushed the global economy well past its ecological limits, sweeping ecosystems and cultures aside as it advances.

This particular formulation of society is not, however, an inevitable outcome of civilization building. It is the result of particular choices people have made, particularly those who benefit most from the current social-ecological order. The choices are made both consciously and unconsciously. Other choices would have led us to another kind of world. They still can.

THE BLISS POINT

What were the choices that resulted in a consumer society? Let's look at something as simple as the coffee break—a consumerist masterstroke—to illustrate the processes by which business interests engineered the consumer society and manufactured mass consent to this particular social-ecological model.

People have an instinctive attraction to sugar and fats. The coffee break—which is also a sugar break—taps these instincts while appealing to our need for social contact and stimulants to counteract workplace stress, boredom, and exhaustion. Providing a mild diversion from routine, stopping for a quick snack and coffee is a pressure release.

Some 2.5 billion people consume $70 billion in coffee products annually. That figure pales when compared to world sugar consumption at over 145 million tonnes per year, costing over $110 billion. Coffee and sugary treats are addictive; they make us feel temporarily satisfied and alert but, like most stimulants, are followed by a crash and the desire for another hit. Thus our need for regular coffee breaks, ever-larger cups sizes and Timbits by the dozen. It's a perfect consumer trap.

Coffee breaks did not appear out of nowhere. Short breaks began to be written into union contracts after World War II, providing workers with a moment's relief from a fast-paced routine.

The way the system works is that every threat to the status quo—from unionization to feminism—is converted into an opportunity to expand consumption and siphon off a little more cash. This concession to labour was quickly transformed into the *coffee* break following a very effective 1952 Pan-American Coffee Bureau ad campaign with the tag line "Give yourself a Coffee-Break—and Get What Coffee Gives to You." The influential behavioural psychologist John B. Watson also worked with the coffee company Maxwell House to popularize the notion. Coffee helped workers stay alert, increasing productivity, so the bosses came on board.

Coffee breaks became commonplace, but their full potential was yet to be realized. In the 1950s and 60s, watery coffee could still be bought for pocket change. In the 1970s, retailers struck on the idea of linking coffee choice to status and consumers responded by gravitating to higher quality, stronger or exotically-flavoured coffees that were also substantially more expensive. For retailers, it was a no-brainer: Coffee could be made for 10 cents and sold for a $1.00, or it could also be made for 25 cents and sold for $3.75.

People used to save up for vacations or splurge on occasional outings. Spending several dollars once or twice a day on high-end coffee offered a more immediate reward. It was also a new status symbol, sending out signals that you are a person with disposable income and the freedom to take time out from a busy schedule. Places like Starbucks were the epitome of a new coffee culture. From its original location opened in 1971, Starbucks expanded to 165 stores in 1992 then mushroomed to 17,000 locations in 50 countries by 2010. (Tim Hortons is a kind of everyman's Starbucks, although it too has gradually added high-cost coffee options.)

Our inclination to gather is at once served and exploited by the coffee franchise. Tim Hortons or Starbucks frequently involve lengthy queues, making the experience more akin to an assembly line than the convivial atmosphere of neighbourhood *third place* hangouts considered important to building community and reinforcing democracy and civil society.

Just as the coffee industry cleverly aligned their product with work breaks, the ascent of highly-processed fast foods was carefully engineered by the agri-food industry to align with the frenetic pace of the consumer economy.

Though most health experts would say that "adding value" to natural foods through processing actually reduces every value except profits, the financial incentive is massive. Turning fresh potatoes worth 15 cents, for example, into a bag of potato chips worth $3.00, a 2000 percent markup, is a huge incentive for food manufacturers, especially when the externalities—the costs to public health and the ecosphere—are carried by the public and the planet. Tipping the scales at 160 calories an ounce, the potato chip is considered the most egregious of junk food offenders: A long-term study[21] that followed 120,000 U.S. women and men determined that potato chip consumption was a greater contributor to weight gain than any other factor. And the salt content, which is legendary, is an important factor in hypertension, the cause of 400,000 deaths in the US per year.[22]

Food processing—the process of reducing food value to increase price—is a multi-trillion dollar industry. In 2005, worldwide processed food sales were $3.2 trillion, accounting for 75 percent of total food sales. In comparison, $400 billion was spent on fresh fruits and vegetables. Total US food sales are currently $1.35 trillion per year.[23] Sales of processed food sit at around $1 trillion while spending on fresh fruits and vegetables, at $65 billion a year, is actually declining.

One can't help but notice the large percentage of food sales that occur in one country. That the US, with less than 5 percent of world population, spends close to 20 percent of the global purchased food budget is an indication of how perverse consumerism has become in its place of origin.

That said, the annual growth rate of retail packaged food sales, at 2-3 percent, has all but peaked in high-income countries such as the US, whereas sales growth in the so-called developing countries ranges from 7 percent in upper-middle-income countries to 28 percent in lower-middle-income countries.[24] The global profit potential is huge, thus the move to build and capture consumer markets worldwide.

The deliberateness of the consumer revolution is well illustrated in *Salt, Sugar, Fat: How the Food Giants Hooked Us,* by Pulitzer-winning author Michael Moss. Moss explains how food manufacturers employ sophisticated food science to make their products irresistibly attractive to consumers. He shows us how products like potato chips and thousands of others are engineered to have just the right levels of sugar, salt, and fat—what he calls the unholy trinity—to be addictive. The food industry recoils at that word, preferring Newspeak terms like "crave-ability" and "more-ishness."

Speaking of addicting substances, it is interesting that the biggest player in the processed food industry in the US in the 2000s was none other than Philip Morris, the tobacco and alcohol company that then owned both Kraft and General Foods.

Critical to food research is the search for the *bliss point,* where taste test subjects report the most pleasure from various combinations of salt, sugar, or fats added to a product. (Without these additions, processed food tastes like straw, quite literally, reports Moss, who has sampled "bliss-free" versions in industry labs.) Scientists use consumer-testing results to tinker with recipes to save money and convert occasional customers into frequent buyers. Then the marketers take over. Appeals to customers are cooked up just as carefully as the flavors concocted in product development. Concerns such as health impacts are addressed with phony claims about "natural" content (everything in the universe can be considered natural, after all.) When manufacturers get the taste and marketing right, "products fly off the shelves."

It is no wonder. A brain imaging study[25] by a Boston Children's Hospital research team led by David Ludwig supports the notion that junk food addiction has more than a passing similarity to drug addiction. Researchers used MRI images to investigate how food intake is regulated by dopamine containing pleasure centres of the brain. High-glycemic foods appear to trigger the same brain mechanisms as addicting drugs. Consuming highly processed carbohydrates can cause excess hunger and stimulate brain regions involved in reward and cravings.

"Beyond reward and craving, this part of the brain is also linked to substance abuse and dependence, which raises the question as to whether certain foods might be addictive," said Ludwig. After study participants consumed a high-glycemic index milkshake they experienced an initial surge in blood sugar levels, followed by a sharp crash four hours later. This decrease in blood glucose was associated with excessive hunger and intense activation of the *nucleus accumbens*, a critical brain region involved in addictive behaviours.

Michael Moss reports that food companies are aware of the negative impacts of their products. (It's thought to be one reason Philip Morris left the food business.) In fact, many executives and scientists will not eat their own products. Yet they face unrelenting pressure from Wall Street to increase profits and share value. Says Moss, "They are profit-making entities and they are hooked on profits as much as we are hooked on taste." The industry is also boosted by government subsidies and other supports, such as campaigns by the US Department of Agriculture to increase consumption of cheese and red meat.

Engineering changes to food culture has been a critical ingredient in the recipe for higher consumption. The habit of mindless eating when not hungry, for example, was a significant cultural shift that coincided with the rise of TV viewing and aggressive advertising. Moss points out that when he grew up, his parents would say "Don't snack, you'll ruin your appetite," the idea being that only balanced meals, not snacks, provide a healthy diet. "That fell by the wayside and played into the hands of the food companies. At some point, it became acceptable to eat anywhere, any place, any time, and snacking became the norm.

The less you pay attention to what you put in your mouth, the less you're going to worry about what it is and the more apt you'll be to overeat."

And overeat we do. How much of the "holy trinity" do Americans, the biggest eaters of all, consume?

- On average, they consume 30 teaspoons per person per day of added sugars and sweeteners,[26] although the recommended limit is 8 teaspoons per day (an amount many experts find excessive.) Natural sugars such as those found in fruit are not included. Total annual consumption includes an average of 46 gallons per person of sugary soda and other sweet drinks, such as so-called 'vitamin waters,' equivalent to eating 14 sugar lumps a day.

- Estimates put daily salt consumption per person in the US at around 3500 mg,[27] though intake as high as 8500 milligrams is not unusual. Dietary guidelines for Americans recommend limiting sodium to less than 2300 mg a day and preferably 1500 mg, although less than 500 mg per day is actually needed for proper body functioning. The natural salt in food accounts for about 10 percent of total intake on average and the salt we add at the table or while cooking adds another 5 to 10 percent. About 75 percent of total salt intake comes from salt added to processed foods by manufacturers and salt added at food service establishments.

- In 2005, total added fats and oils available for consumption reached 86 pounds per person compared with 53 pounds per person in 1970.[28] The 2005 estimate translates into 71.6 grams of added fats and oils per person per day, about 32 percent of total caloric intake. This does not include dietary fats that occur naturally in foods, such as in dairy products and meats. Combined with dietary fats, added fats and oils take average consumption well beyond the recommended 20-35 percent of daily energy intake.

The fast food habit is not only a money multiplier for manufacturers. It also helps to reset society for more consumption in general. For a high-paced industrial society, easy-to-cook processed foods are critical time savers, allowing more people to work more. Housewives could now be drawn into the labour force en masse, increasing household disposable income and purchasing power. This transition allowed business to profit from a potential threat: the feminist movement.

MOTORDOM

Devaluing food to junk status and inducing consumers to gorge is just one way of concentrating wealth. The formula "de-value and excess" has been applied to every facet of life and is spreading rapidly worldwide. And critical to the success of the consumer model is excess and de-valued mobility.

The fast food industry and the rest of consumer society are fundamentally dependent on an addiction to automobiles. Automobiles so dominate urban landscapes it's hard to imagine cities any other way. But the car didn't always rule the road and its dominance was not achieved without a fight. It was another decision made by vested interests, with ultimate buy-in by the masses.

Until the 1920s and 1930s, city streets were the domain of pedestrians, trolley buses, horses-drawn wagons, bicycles, and kids at play. Emerging forms of transportation, cars and trucks were just one component of street traffic.

"In the 1920s," according to urban planner Gordon Price, "it was still unclear whether the public would accept private vehicles. There was a lot of carnage from traffic accidents and civic leaders were dubious about the large amount of space cars needed. Many thought curb parking should not be allowed." Price, who is Director of the City Program at Simon Fraser University, explains how "Motordom," an alliance of car dealers and manufacturers and motor clubs in the 1920s, created a popular notion of a utopian city redesigned for cars.

Referencing Peter Norton's book, *Fighting Traffic: The Dawn of the Motor Age in the American City*, Price points out that to accommodate automobiles, the city required not only a physical change but also a social one: before the city could be reconstructed for the sake of motorists, its streets had to be socially reconstructed as places motorists first belonged and then controlled.

Before the 1930s, children were free to play in the street and pedestrians crossed wherever they wanted. By the 1930s, Motordom managed to convince people that the pedestrian, not the car, was the interloper and had to be restricted. The pejorative "jay walker" was introduced and public safety programs "educated" pedestrians to use signals and crosswalks. In the process of creating "safe streets," Motordom gradually convinced the public that the automobile should be accepted as the street's dominant user.

Transportation engineers were instrumental in bringing this about. In 1942, the engineers consolidated Motordom's standards and codes in the

Transportation Planning Handbook, a kind of transport bible that created common professional standards.

"They introduced two powerful weapons: safety and liability," says Price. "If it didn't go along with professional standards for safety—which completely favoured automobiles—then a community would be liable for accidents. After the war, bylaws were put in place to ensure a big surplus of parking, which begins to shape urban form. By the 1950s, every city and town was built according to the standards of Motordom. The standards were not imposed, but gratefully accepted by the public. This was the era of cheap oil and life was as good as it had ever been. Automobile technology, standards, codes, money, oil, urban design, highway infrastructure: everything favoured the seamless use of automobiles."

As cars became the norm, cities sprawled and other ways of getting around become inconvenient or unavailable. New neighbourhoods eliminated sidewalks. Public transit became a kind of social service for students, the elderly, the poor; riding the bus or subway became low status. Besides, service in many areas was infrequent and often you couldn't get where you wanted to go.

This too was engineered. The famously poor transit system of a city like Los Angeles is no accident. Until the 1940s, LA had a well-used electric trolley system. It was bought and destroyed by Exxon, General Motors, and Firestone Tire. Big oil and the car companies similarly destroyed 100 electric railway systems in 45 major cities to cement their urban market. For this they were convicted of criminal conspiracy. The ringleader, a former treasurer of General Motors, was fined one dollar.[29]

Private vehicles of course represent a massive funnelling of wealth into the hands of the carmakers and dealers, oil companies, road builders, and other suppliers. The public expends untold trillions on building and maintaining infrastructure and absorbs externalities like health impacts, accidental injury and death, and ecological and climate impacts—whether they drive themselves or not.

Americans now devote an average of $9000 per year to own and operate a vehicle, according to the American Automobile Association,[30] and many families have two or more vehicles. The adjacent graphic, based on data from the Housing and Transportation Affordability Index, shows even higher transportation costs, equivalent to 27 percent of household income for moderate-income households.

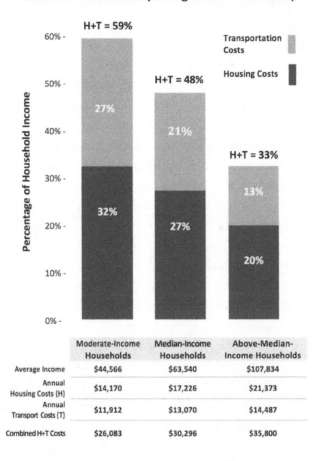

Combined cost burden for moderate-income homes vs. other income brackets (25 largest US metro areas)

	Moderate-Income Households	Median-Income Households	Above-Median-Income Households
Average Income	$44,566	$63,540	$107,834
Annual Housing Costs (H)	$14,170	$17,226	$21,373
Annual Transport Costs (T)	$11,912	$13,070	$14,487
Combined H+T Costs	$26,083	$30,296	$35,800

While cars are themselves among the most important consumer expenditures, their use also facilitates all other aspects of consumption, to the point that it is almost impossible to imagine modern consumers without vehicles. Would we go to Costco or Wal-Mart without cars? How much less would we buy if we had to carry our purchases home on foot or by bus?

The victory of Motordom is now so complete we can barely imagine a city not dominated by cars. In Canada, 67 percent of the population lives in suburbs, where it is near impossible to do without a car or two or three. In major Canadian cities, the proportion is even higher: 88 percent live in suburbs, most classified as *auto-suburbs*. Despite talk of increasing urban density, close to 95 percent of recent urban growth took place in suburbs; 1.5 million Canadians moved into these areas between 2006 and 2011, while city cores grew by just 90,000 people.[31]

Sticking with the status quo—a city increasingly spread out and dominated by cars—makes people "fat and vulnerable" says Price. Obesity, including childhood obesity, has become a huge problem: it is so difficult to get anywhere without driving that we effectively eliminate exercise as a normal component of our daily life. This undermines health and contributes to high medical costs, which is why I said transportation was *de-valued* when cars replaced active and public transportation. And in a community dominated by cars, congestion inevitably interferes with mobility, another example of economist Herman Daly's assertion that economic growth in consumer societies is now making us poorer, not richer, in any holistic sense of those words.

Motordom is predicated on a never-ending supply of relatively cheap oil, but the cost of supplying a non-renewable resource like oil eventually rises with higher demand and limited supply. The low cost oil gets used up and the remaining resource is more difficult and therefore costly to extract. It also takes ever more energy to find, extract, and refine the same amount of oil. This in turn results in more pollution and GHG emissions, which further undermines resilience.

Poor urban design is also closely linked to a cheap energy policy. Much to the determent of their citizens, cities are set up primarily to facilitate the consumer experience, the goal of which is to efficiently channel income to the rich. The outcome is inequality, which weakens social connectivity; undermines civil society and the democratic process; brings high ecological, energy, and infrastructure capital and maintenance costs; and undermines public health, with corresponding cost increases.

Cracks in the dominance of Motordom may be appearing, however. The spectres of expensive oil and climate change have entered public consciousness, traffic congestion is increasingly problematic, and by and large, people do not actually like an urban form that consists of congested arteries, strip malls, and parking lots. Due to cost and lifestyle choices, youth and young adults in large urban centres with good public transit are starting to abandon car ownership. US vehicle registration rates began to drop in 2006, suggesting that "Peak Car" may have hit the birthplace of Motordom.

That said, growth in the use of automobiles is shifting to new markets. According to London-based IHS Automotive, passenger-car production rose from 62.6 million in 2011 to 66.7 million in 2012, and was expected to reach 68.3 million in 2013. When cars are combined with light trucks, total light vehicle production rose from 76.9 million in 2011 to 81.5 million in 2012 and was projected to total 83.3 million in 2013. At 18.2 million units, China produced almost as many vehicles as the U.S. and Japan combined.[32]

A BET ON A DEBT AS AN ASSET

Consumer culture requires that consumption continuously expand. The chief stimulant of higher consumption is the economic caffeine known as debt. If not for easy credit, modern consumerism would not exist.

Credit is the power to obtain goods before payment, based on a belief that payment will be made later. Money itself is a form of credit, since it has no intrinsic value. While money used to be a proxy for gold, today's fiat money is essentially a consensus belief about exchange value. If that is not sufficiently abstract, actual money you can stuff in your pocket has been largely replaced with digital representations of money: the closest we come to money is often the image of our bank balance on a monitor. Even a tangible like gold may actually be an abstraction, a weak promise: it has been said that as little as 10 percent of the gold people own, in the form of certificates, actually exists.[33]

Like money, debt has become increasingly abstract. Local banks once lent money to people in their community so they could buy assets in that community which had real and usually appreciating value that could be recouped. Today, using credit derivatives, debt may be syndicated among thousands of investors unknown even to the bank, with little or no real assets backing it.

Decoupling loans from assets reached its apex with instant credit options like credit cards, the great facilitator of mass consumption. Between 1980 and 2013, revolving net credit card debt in the United States climbed sixteen-fold, from about $51 billion to over $846 billion. Similarly, instalment debt jumped from $297 billion in 1980 to $1.5 trillion in 2013. Overall, U.S. household consumer debt has soared from $351 billion in 1980 to nearly $2.9 trillion in 2013.[34] Currently, 46 million American households carry an average revolving credit card balance of over $14,000—which translates into more than $2,000 per household per year in finance charges and penalty fees.[35] Together with home mortgages, total US household indebtedness has crossed the $15.5 trillion mark—with the vast majority—about $13 trillion—in mortgage debt.

In a consumer society, debt is the name of the game for individuals, families, communities, and nations. The US Debt Clock[36] puts the scope of collective debt into perspective. While personal debt (circa 2012) now nears $16 trillion, total US debt is above $60 trillion. This amounts to $189,000 per person or $751,000 per family. By comparison, average savings per family is just $6600.

Most other nations are in equally bad shape, or worse. In 2013, global debt hit $223.3 trillion, including public-sector debt of $55.7 trillion, financial-sector debt of $75.3 trillion, and household or corporate debt of $92.3 trillion. (The figures exclude China's shadow finance and off-balance-sheet financing.) Per-capita indebtedness is $11,621 in emerging economies (and rises to $12,808 if you exclude the two largest populations, China and India). For high-income economies, it's $170,401.[37]

Mass indebtedness is, of course, a perfect way to maintain our mass addiction to consumption. We have to keep working harder and harder to pay off our debts. And if we stop buying the stuff that increases indebtedness, the economy is threatened with collapse. This is a treadmill that can never stop. It is no wonder that the United States, as the most consumption-dependent nation, elevates consumer spending and neglects saving. As Sheldon Garon, author of *Beyond Our Means: Why America Spends While the World Saves,* points out, eschewing saving over spending is closely identified with American patriotism.

The true nature of indebtedness came to an ugly head during the 2008 financial meltdown triggered by shady lending to consumers to buy and bid up housing. The fiasco amounted to "selling a bet on a debt [as] an asset," as Wendell Berry succinctly put it. According to the United States Senate's Levin–Coburn Report, "the crisis was not a natural disaster, but the result of high risk, complex financial products; undisclosed conflicts of interest; and the failure of regulators, the credit rating agencies, and the market itself to rein in the excesses of Wall Street." The house of mirrors was also a house of cards and would have collapsed had not the banks succeeded in obtaining bailouts from the public purse, a clever maneuver that further shifted the burden of debt onto the public.

At the heart of all this is a deep sense of entitlement and shameless greed on the part of the economic elites; this is coupled with a deep passivity among the public, a desire to be fed, to be seduced and led by whoever proves skillful at appealing to superficial dreams of more. As we examine it, we see the consumer culture as fundamentally defective, yet it succeeds by setting traps that appear inescapable.

The consumer society is a product of an economic model that requires continuous growth. But the promise of growth, which was to make some people very prosperous by making everyone a little more prosperous, is coming undone. Economist Herman Daly sums it up this way:

> Even though economies are still growing, and still put growth in first place, it is no longer economic growth, at least in wealthy countries, but has become *uneconomic growth*. In other words, the environmental and social costs of increased production are growing faster than the benefits, increasing "illth" faster than wealth, thereby making us poorer, not richer. We hide the uneconomic nature of growth from ourselves by faulty national accounting because growth is our panacea, indeed our idol, and we are very afraid of the idea of a steady-state economy. The increasing illth is evident in exploding financial debt, in biodiversity loss, and in destruction of natural services, most notably climate regulation. The major job...is to overcome this denial and shift the path of progress from quantitative growth to qualitative development, from bigger to better. Specifically this will mean working toward a steady-state economy at a sustainable (smaller than present) scale relative to the containing ecosystem that is finite and already overstressed. Since growth now makes us poorer, not richer, poverty reduction will require sharing in the present, not the empty promise of growth in the future.[38]

As Daly alludes to, the consumer economy based on an ethos of never-ending growth has become our false god. And as Fyodor Dostoyevsky put it in his novel *The Possessed*, "It is difficult to change gods."

FULL WORLD, EMPTY SELF

We have seen some examples of the ways economic elites constructed consumerism to advance their interests. The fuller impact of this effort on culture runs deeper: To create a new world order based on consumption, it was necessary to jettison once-revered ideals and values such as frugality, moderation, and humility, which interfered with unbridled consumption, while amplifying the acquisitive side of human nature. In a sense, we had to "change gods" and this was difficult; spiritual values, really a whole worldview, had to be abandoned and replaced with a materialist perspective.

In his book *Prosperity without Growth*, economist[39] Tim Jackson describes how consumer goods—from packaged foods and cars to electronics—have come to play a role in our lives that goes well beyond material functionality. One of the processes at play is what consumer researcher Russ Belk calls *cathexis*: "a process of attachment that leads us to think of (and even feel) material possessions as part of the 'extended self.'"

Our consumer goods come to define us and symbolize who we are, both to ourselves and to the world. They take on a significance equal to profound aspects of life such as our sense of meaning, ideals, values, and relationships, social and ecological. Belk notes that this kind of materialism even offers a kind of substitute religion. In a secular world, having hopes and ideals and goals, even when they are merely about material things, attempts to provide the vision religion offered in the past. They promise a kind of ideal world, a land of milk and honey and great coffee, the material version of the Promised Land.

Consumerism is the new "opiate of the people."

As Jackson points out, "It is precisely because material goods are flawed but somehow plausible proxies for our dreams and aspirations that consumer culture seems on the surface to work so well. Consumer goods…provide us with a tangible bridge to our highest ideals. They fail, of course, to provide genuine access to those ideals, but in failing they leave open the need for future bridges and so stimulate our appetite for more goods. Consumer culture perpetuates itself here precisely because it succeeds so well at failure!"

_____

Consumer culture perpetuates itself precisely because it succeeds so well at failure.

_____

Consumption is partly about survival, he continues, but it is also about the social and psychological process of identity, affiliation, aspiration, and self-expression. It is this social dynamic, rather than psychological flourishing, which serves to explain why our desire for material goods appears so insatiable. And why novelty matters to us.

Jackson references the psychologist Philip Cushman who argues that the extended self is ultimately an "empty self" that stands in continual need of being filled up with food, stimulants, consumer products, and celebrity gossip.

People are strongly influenced by social comparisons, thus the empty self is prey to powerful social forces and specific institutions given over to the pursuit of consumerism, on which the economic system comes to depend for its survival.

> Perhaps the most telling point of all is the rather too perfect fit between the continual consumption of novelty by households and the continuous production of novelty in firms. The restless desire of the empty self is the perfect complement for the restless innovation of the entrepreneur. The production of novelty through creative destruction drives and is driven by the appetite for novelty in consumers.
>
> Taken together these two self-reinforcing processes are exactly what is needed to drive growth forward. As the ecological economist Douglas Booth remarked, "The novelty and status seeking consumer and the monopoly-seeking entrepreneur blend together to form the underpinning of long-run economic growth."
>
> Restlessness creates a system driven by anxiety. The extended self is motivated by the angst of the empty self. Social comparison is driven by the anxiety to be situated favourably in society. Creative destruction is haunted by the fear of being left behind in the competition for consumer markets. Thrive or die is the maxim of the jungle. It's equally true in the consumer society. Nature and structure combine together here to lock us firmly into the iron cage of consumerism.
>
> It's an anxious and ultimately a pathological system. But at one level it works. The relentless pursuit of novelty may undermine well-being but the system remains economically viable as long as liquidity is preserved and consumption rises. It collapses when either of them stalls.[40]

Culture has been described as "the sum of all social processes that make the artificial (or human constructed) seem natural."[41] Our own hyper-consumer culture is so normal to us it doesn't appear constructed. It seems natural, the way things are meant to be. Consumerism has now so fully worked its way into most cultures—and is seducing the rest—that it seems to us an inevitable outcome of history and human nature. That it is just one possible version of reality, and one that was constructed for a purpose inimical to the public interest, generally escapes us.

As Erik Assadourian points out,[42] human behaviour may be rooted in nature but it is shaped primarily by cultural systems we are born into. Cultures are guided by dominant worldviews or paradigms, the shared ideas and assumptions that, over generations, are shaped and reinforced by leading cultural actors and institutions and by the participants in the cultures themselves. The elements of cultures—language and symbols, norms and traditions, values and institutions—have been profoundly transformed by consumerism. The word *consumer*, for example, is now used interchangeably with *person* in the 10 most commonly used languages.

Key to understanding the nature of consumer culture is to recognize its merger with the dominant economic system, the so-called free market economy—yet another social construct we are so immersed in we have come to see as conforming to the natural order. In fact, the modern growth economy is an illusion raised on a contradiction: it cannot be sustained without ever-accelerating growth on a planet that cannot sustain accelerating growth.

Growth is the monumental myth we live by.

AN UNLIKELY OPPORTUNITY

While the scenario presented here is hardly a positive one, it holds a key to an alternative future, one that can accommodate 11 billion people.

Much, even most, of what we do—from eating doughnuts to building car-dominated cities—lies on a continuum between unnecessary and destructive. Therein lies an opportunity. Not only would we be happier and healthier if we gave up many unnecessary and all destructive activities, letting go would free up resources to do things right.

How would this work?

Let's look at transportation as an example. The International Energy Agency[43] anticipates that global freight and passenger travel will double over the next forty years, increasing energy consumption in the transport sector 80 percent. This level of growth would require transport infrastructure investments of US$120 trillion, including new construction, reconstruction, upgrades, and annual operation and maintenance.

When parking requirements are included, an increase in transport infrastructure of this magnitude would pave over 350,000 km², roughly equivalent to the area of Germany. (If that amount of land were suitable for farming it would be sufficient acreage to feed 350 million people at average global grain yields.)

Combining vehicles, fuels, and infrastructure, the total cost of transport additions between now and 2050 would be—get this—$515 trillion. But this level of growth is consistent with a disaster scenario in which global average temperature rises by 4°C.

There's more. Nicholas Stern estimated the cost of a 2-3°C rise in average global temperatures at 5-20 percent of Gross World Product (GWP) per annum. The IEA estimates cumulative GWP to 2050 to be $6000 trillion. Assuming just 5 percent of this is lost due to climate change, the cost to the economy over 40 years would be another $300 trillion. Transport infrastructure, vehicle, and fuel increases would be 8.5 percent of GWP over this period, according to the IEA, so the extra cost to the economy from transport-related climate change would be approximately $25.5 trillion.

Now, what would the new transportation infrastructure facilitate? The lion's share of expansion would take place in emerging economies such as China and India. By further integrating world markets and extending the consumer lifestyle to everyone, the global economy would mushroom to double and triple its present size. The impact on the ecosphere would be catastrophic.

Let's say we come to our senses and decide not to expand transport infrastructure, at least not so much. *Avoid and shift* policies such as avoiding urban sprawl and switching from cars to public and active transport are consistent with a scenario where average global temperature rises just 2°C. The IEA reports that pursuing these policies would result in cost savings of $50 trillion by 2050, in addition to the costs avoided by reducing climate change.

What could that buy us? Nicholas Stern proposed spending just 1 percent of GWP by 2050 (approximately $60 trillion in total) to prevent catastrophic climate change. A 10 percent reduction in the growth of transport would free up most of the resources needed.

Let's do some "cowboy math" to get a rough measure of the potential savings possible from applying even moderate avoid and shift policies to the categories of consumer spending discussed in this chapter. A rough calculation is about all one can hope for given the size, complexities, and overlapping categories involved in assessing the global economy and the impact of avoid and shift policies. The following figures are based on a breakdown of global spending from the World Bank[44] and the other sources cited in this chapter.

Avoid and Shift Policy	Explanation	Current Cost	Cost Avoided
		Trillion $	
Reduce overconsumption of processed/fast food by top 20% of consumers by 50%	$7 trillion spent annually on food/non-alcoholic beverages; 75% of sales processed foods and $200 billion fast food; overconsumption of low quality food contributes to chronic illnesses	7	1.05
Reduce food waste by half	One third of all food wasted	2.3	1.15
Cut spending on transportation by 20%	Switch to bus rapid transit and active transportation	6.12	1.12
Reduce health spending 20%	Environmental factors responsible for 90% of illness; improving diet and activity levels, reducing pollution, would lower disease and medical costs	7.48	1.5
Reduce oil consumption 20% across each sector	Reduced spending in above categories also reduces energy consumption; food, health, and transport represent at least 25% of GWP; annual oil expenditures are approximately $750 billion for these sectors	0.75	0.15
Debt avoidance	Assuming average interest on total global debt of 5%, a 20% reduction of spending across three sectors could lower future interest by $.55 trillion per annum.	2.7	0.55
	Total potential cost avoided per annum		5.52
	Total potential cost avoided 2014-2050		200

Figures in constant 2012 international dollars

To reduce the human footprint to a sustainable level, spending would have to be reduced by even larger percentages. (How this can happen will be discussed in subsequent chapters.) The point of this exercise is simply to demonstrate that de-growth at this scale would free up substantial resources for civilization building activities, from reducing poverty to restoring ecosystems.

We can't ignore, however, the various side effects, negative and positive, of de-growth. Reducing spending by a trillion dollars doesn't mean a trillion dollars is available to "do good" with. As the economy shrinks, so do employment, income, profits, and taxes, reducing the amounts of money available to restore ecosystems, for example. By the same token, greenhouse gas emissions, pollution, and forest loss also decline, meaning less money is needed for restoration. And while people's income goes down, so do their expenses.

De-growth will result in a very different kind of culture, one in which human beings will no longer be defined as consumers. In a stable-state economy, time will be our greatest resource.

CHANGING GODS

Capitalism, said John Maynard Keynes, is "the astonishing belief that the nastiest motives of the nastiest men somehow or other work for the best results in the best of all possible worlds." Indeed, capitalism is often cited as the cause of the crisis in the social-ecological system. In this chapter, for example, it has been argued that contemporary culture has been consciously engineered by the corporate class to mold the masses into Pavlovian consumers. While this no doubt sounds like an anti-capitalist harangue, it is not capitalism that is the problem but *unregulated capitalism*, which Marx called "a machine for demolishing limits."

The capitalist system is unparalleled in its ability to supply things like refrigerators and washing machines that can make lives better. In this sense, capitalism has played a valuable role in advancing civilization. But because capitalism offers an effective way of meeting material needs is no reason to allow corporations to have their way with the world—and that is just what the public has allowed to happen.

Think about it. Is it fair to blame corporations for doing what they are designed and permitted to do: make money for investors? And wasn't building the consumer society just prudent business planning? The business class collaborated effectively to secure a bright future for itself, and why shouldn't it?

Isn't the real problem that the other protagonists in the social order—individuals, communities, and public institutions—have allowed themselves to be seduced by corporate promises to the extent that they have, in large measure, failed to protect their own interests or those of the ecosphere, which is a public trust?

The public, through the organs of the state and civil society, should establish the environment in which business operates in a manner that ensures that this important component of the social order serves not just its own but also the public interest. Just as the public must limit but not eliminate the power of the state, it must limit but not eliminate the power of capital. To achieve a healthy, just, and sustainable society, the interests of the public, business, and the state have to be more equitably balanced than is now the case. In those societies that achieve a more reasonable balance—the Nordic nations spring to mind—private business continues to play an essential role and it continues to be profitable. It simply pays a fairer share of the social and ecological costs of activities it profits from.

Capitalism is not, in itself, the problem. That said, unchecked, runaway capitalism that thrives on hyper-consumption is destroying the ecological balance of the planet. Neither is consumption in itself the problem; a reasonable level of consumption of goods and services is conducive to a becoming life. But basing the global economy on limitless, mindless consumption with no regard to social and ecological consequences is insane. We have allowed a monstrous "machine for demolishing limits" to take control of the planet. But as the seas rise and the glaciers melt, as the oil and the radiation spill into the oceans, as our cities are inundated with floods and fumes, as the bees disappear and the forests shrink, this machine is revealed for what it is.

It is critical then that we recognize that the contemporary social-ecological reality, based on the monstrous illusion of unlimited growth, is the product of choices. If the *way things are* is a product of choice then it *doesn't have to be this way*. Other choices could have been made, resulting in a different kind of world and better choices can still be made as we move to a world of 11 billion. We aren't doomed. In fact, different choices have been made in many places, leading to significantly better social-ecological outcomes.

An important question to consider is this: why are alternative approaches that have been proven on local, regional, and national scales not being pursued everywhere? And why—when world leaders and civil society have widely agreed on alternative approaches, such as Agenda 21, that would point us toward a fairer and more sustainable system—is inequity increasing, our ecological footprint deepening, and biocapacity decreasing? Why is it so difficult to take action? These questions point us to deeper issues we can only get to through cultural transformation.

It *is* "difficult to change gods." We should remember, however, that the monstrous idol of unrestrained growth we now worship is itself a relatively recent "change of gods." What we need now is a way to change gods again.

To make this change, what will be proposed in subsequent chapters is a systematic, comprehensive ethical educational movement, in every neighbourhood and village on the planet, involving children, youth, and adults in an experiential exploration of their purpose in being alive. It is not an easy solution, but it is the only approach that can sufficiently alter culture to make the world work for 11 billion people.

CHAPTER 2
THE MATERIALISTS' CRUSADE

Every inch of the existence of mankind, from birth to death, was to be a bargain across a counter. And if we didn't get to Heaven that way, it was not a politico-economical place, and we had no business there.
– Charles Dickens, *Hard Times*

"The tech juggernaut that revolutionized the consumer electronics industry is showing signs it is running out of steam," declared the business pages on January 23, 2013.[45] "Apple Inc., the corporate world's most remarkable growth story over the past few decades, posted earnings today that mark a stunning turn toward a new period of uncertainty."

Apple's Daily Stock Price July 2012 – June 2013

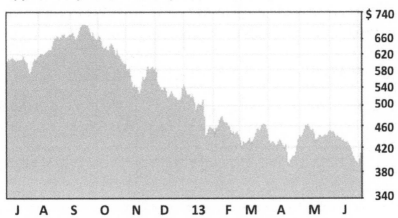

Apple shares tumbled a whopping 10 percent that day then kept falling. As the graph shows, the share price dropped below $460 from a September high of $705 and continued to decline in the following months, hitting lows around $385 in April and June.

Just how bad was Apple's performance? What were the disappointing results that made investors lose confidence?

Actually, the company had just announced record quarterly revenue of $54.5 billion and record quarterly net profit of $13.1 billion. Apple had experienced record sales: 47.8 million iPhones compared to 37 million in the year-ago quarter; 22.9 million iPads, compared to 15.4 million a year before; plus 4.1 million computers and 12.7 million iPods. For 2012 as a whole, the company had generated over $41 billion in net income and over $50 billion in operating cash flow.

For you or I that might seem a rosy picture, but it simply wasn't enough growth. Investors were spooked because Apple's gross margin had dropped to 38.6 percent compared with 44.7 percent during the same period in the previous year. Apple remained the third most profitable company in the world. Net profits were up. However, gross profits were no longer growing, sending a clear message: Abandon ship!

Apple's stock price illustrates the absurdity of the growth economy: Get to the top of the heap and you're no longer good enough because you can't climb any higher. At least not fast enough.

But wait. On August 12, 2013, two tweets by celebrity investor Carl Icahn resulted in Apple's stock surging $23 billion in a matter of hours, showing how capricious—and emotion-driven—investors can be. A month later, people camped outside Apple stores to be first to get the latest iPhones; 9 million sold on one weekend. Was Apple's "stunning turn" already over?

THE PRIMACY OF SHAREHOLDER VALUE

In 1970, the Nobel-prize winning economist Milton Friedman published an article in the New York Times that argued forcefully that the *only* social responsibility of a business was to serve the interests of its owners—its shareholders—by increasing its profits. Within a decade, academics and business leaders had bought into *shareholder value* as a primary business goal. One way to encourage a focus on shareholder value was to compensate executives with stock, thus encouraging them to focus single-mindedly on the company's—now their own—share value.

In 1986, Peter Drucker warned that, "Corporate managements are being pushed into subordinating everything (even such long-range considerations as a company's market standing, its technology, indeed its basic wealth-producing capacity) to immediate earnings and next week's stock price." Given their compensation now depended on it, many chief executives were succumbing to the pressure to boost short-term earnings at the expense of long-term value creation. Pressure also came from the bottom, as "under-performing" companies found themselves under siege from activist investors. The results could be disastrous: In the lead-up to the financial crisis—to take just one extreme example—financial institutions took on far too much risk in search of easy profits that would lead to a higher stock price.

In the decades since Drucker sounded the alarm, the problem of 'short-termism' hasn't abated. A 2013 global survey by the Canada Pension Plan Investment Board and McKinsey & Co. found that 63 percent of business leaders indicated that the pressure on their top executives to demonstrate strong short-term financial performance has increased in the past five years. Even companies like Apple, with a more balanced focus on employees, customers, products, and shareholders, can be influenced by the pressure to produce short-term results.

Of course this approach supports the kind of thinking that reinforces the propensity for business to ignore social responsibilities and to undervalue long term objectives such as the ecological sustainability on which resilience ultimately rests.

As the Apple story illustrates, our thirst for more—whether of goods or profits—is insatiable. Enough is not an option. Like an airplane, the economy stays aloft only when it moves forward. Fast. And the only way we know how to maintain that forward movement is for more and more people to buy more and more smart phones, food, clothes, stocks, whatever. Which is why our iPhone screens and websites, our fast food spots and shopping malls, our stock apps and financial service providers are the current staging grounds of a worldwide materialistic crusade. Launched by corporations, pushed by shareholders, abetted by governments, and cheered on by consumers, it is systematically commercializing every aspect of life, from procreation to cremation.

The crusade's ultimate goal is that every consumer can access *everything, everywhere, always,* ensuring a continuous flow of profits and an unending accumulation and concentration of wealth at the top of the economic heap. This is achieved through the rapid and continuous supply—and then oversupply—of any and every product or service imaginable; by anticipating every whim and desire and feeding it; by amplifying wants to the status of needs; by over-stimulating legitimate needs; by exploiting every potentially exploitable compulsion or yen; by feeding every addiction; by promoting a culture that revels in excess; by tapping people's instinctive and cultural desire for status; by demolishing all notion of limits.

The materialist crusade is advanced by cheapening goods and services to increase mass appeal or by inventing status-rich luxuries; by sending production to lowest-cost labour markets and by continuously refining manufacturing processes; by tapping into the full influence of mass media and by transforming shopping into entertainment; through the proliferation of retail outlets, convenience stores and shopping malls and by extending shopping hours 24/7/365; by commercializing the Internet and facilitating easy credit; by building ever-larger monopolies and ever more powerful brands; by generating arbitrary, ever-changing fashions to induce people to continuously update everything and by creating the mysterious concept of 'cool' which youth are especially anxious to attain; by elevating consumption to the *raison d'etre*, not just of economic sustainability, but of life itself.

Is this overstating the situation? Not at all. The creation of the limits-free consumer society was not an inevitable outcome of civilization. It was and is a deliberate, orchestrated, global campaign to reinvent culture to serve corporate interests. The materialist crusade is a coherent and open philosophy of corporations, marketers, and advertisers. It is not only *promoted* in media everywhere, it is the financial foundation of media everywhere.

The word *crusade*, with its religious and military connotations, is used here intentionally. Putting non-market relationships above commerce makes authentic religion anathema to materialism. It will be shown that the quasi-religious consumer crusade consciously aims to eclipse religious or spiritual values, that it is essentially violent, and that it is pursued along military lines.

OIKONOMIA OR CHREMATISTICS

The rift between the public good and private gain is a central problem of civilization. Aristotle long ago distinguished two economic motivations, *oikonomia* and *chrematistics*. Oikonomia, according to the economist Herman Daly, "is the science or art of efficiently producing, distributing, and maintaining concrete use values for the household and community over the long run. Chrematistics is the art of maximizing the accumulation by individuals of abstract exchange value in the form of money in the short run. Although our word 'economics' is derived from oikonomia, its present meaning is much closer to chrematistics. The word chrematistics is currently relegated to unabridged dictionaries, but the reality to which it refers is everywhere present and is frequently and incorrectly called economics."[46]

Although one can't deny that consumerism has *oikonomic* benefits, such as producing products that actually improve lives by reducing drudgery, it is quite clear that its primary objective is chrematistic: consumerism is designed to manipulate the masses to enrich the wealthy. In consumer societies, the working class is transformed into the consumer class by providing higher wages, which are recycled to buy goods from the capitalist class. Instead of hording it, mobilizing money by allowing it to flow through more hands further enriches the rich *and* staves off revolt.

Evidence of an intentional campaign by the chrematists to introduce extreme consumerism was identified by the end of the 19th century by Thorstein Veblen, the economist who first used the term "conspicuous consumption" in his classic *The Theory of the Leisure Class*. In it, he described a basic distinction between the productiveness of industry and the parasitism of its owners—the leisure class— whose chief activity was conspicuous consumption and whose economic contribution was waste activity that contributes nothing to productivity.

In the first half of the 20th century, business theorists began to prepare the ground for the consumer revolution that would gain ground rapidly after 1950. In the book *Consumer Engineering*, the influential ad man Earnest Elmo Calkins (1868-1964) proposed creating artificial demand for a product using design and advertising. In addressing the situation in 1929, where the speed of production had outstripped consumption, he rejected the obvious solution of reducing production, proposing instead that demand for products be maintained through *planned obsolescence*. He wrote, "Goods fall into two classes: those that we use, such as motor cars and safety razors, and those that we use up, such as toothpaste or soda biscuits. Consumer engineering must see to it that we use up the kind of goods we now merely use." He asked, "Does there seem to be a sad waste in this process? Not at all. Wearing things out does not produce prosperity. Buying things does."

The thinking articulated by Calkins was echoed by home economist Christine Frederick (1883-1970), who was a proponent of scientific management, or Taylorism, on the home front. Scientific management, developed by Frederick Taylor (1856-1915), used engineering practices to improve the productivity of both industrial machines and their operators. Frederick attempted to bring Taylor's ideas into the home by improving household efficiency; even the home could be a factory of sorts. Called an "evangelist" (note the religious connotation) for consumer ideology, her book *Selling Mrs. Consumer* argued for women's vital role as consumers in a mass-production economy, making the case for planned obsolescence to keep the economy humming. (Today, women make 85 percent of all consumer purchases.[47])

"The way to break the vicious deadlock of a low standard of living," she wrote in 1929, "is to spend freely, and even waste creatively."

> *Our economy demands that we make consumption our way of life, that we convert the buying and use of goods into rituals, that we seek our spiritual satisfactions, our ego satisfactions, in consumption.*

The materialist's crusade went into high gear with the publication of the seminal article *Price Competition in 1955*. It reads today like a consumer-capitalist version of the *Communist Manifesto*. In it marketing consultant Victor Lebow lays out the battle plan in clear, military terms. If you doubt the deliberateness with which business engineered the consumer revolution, this extraordinarily prescient article may persuade you. It merits lengthy quotations. Lebow begins by laying out the role of marketing, competition, and monopoly in military language:

> Marketing is concerned directly with the realities of competition. To use a military analogy, marketing involves the over-all strategy of distribution, while merchandising, advertising, promotion, and selling comprise the tactics. The costs of distribution actually represent the pressure needed to maintain

the high level of consumption. Our economy demands a constantly expanding capacity to produce.

Even the pattern of our employment shows this emphasis upon distribution. The great majority of all workers are employed in those sectors of our economy that are entirely outside of production. In fact, if we limit ourselves to the actual production and transportation of goods, this economy is like an inverted pyramid, with less than 30 percent of the labour force producing all of the economic values.

To the producer, competition is an irritant and a source of insecurity. Therefore, his drive is toward monopoly. Since every producer wants to remove the obstacles to the most profitable sale of the largest practical volume of his goods, his instinctive drive is to limit competition. The fact is that the essence of marketing strategy is to establish as many monopoly positions as possible. These may involve patents, trademarks, style leaderships, exclusive arrangements of all kinds, the size of dominance of advertising and selling efforts, and the extent to which the consumer's emotional attitude towards his consumption can become the captive of the producer.

Lebow now looks at the means and methods by which producers can take consumers captive, with the help of a then new technology. Note the religious language:

Television achieves three results to an extent no other advertising medium has ever approached. First, it creates a captive audience. Second, it submits that audience to the most intensive indoctrination. Third, it operates on the entire family.

The total result of the pressure is to change the pattern of living. The persuasive techniques for instilling new wants into the consumer may result in buying the new Hi-Fi set, or the new refrigerator, or the new car, and result also in displacing or postponing the purchase of clothes, or furniture, or vacation trips.

This leads to the third aspect of competition. It lies in the competition for the consumer's attention, for his confidence, for his response to new wants.

Our enormously productive economy demands that we make consumption our way of life, that we convert the buying and use of goods into rituals, that we seek our spiritual satisfactions, our ego satisfactions, in consumption. The measure of social status, of social acceptance, of prestige, is now to be found in our consumptive patterns. The very meaning and significance of our lives today is expressed in consumptive terms. The greater the pressures upon the individual to conform to safe and accepted social standards, the more does he tend to express his aspirations and his individuality in terms of what he wears, drives, and eats: his home, his car, his pattern of food serving, his hobbies.

These commodities and services must be offered to the consumer with a special urgency. We require not only "forced draft" consumption, but "expensive" consumption as well. We need things consumed, burned up, worn out, replaced, and discarded at an ever increasing pace. We need to have people eat, drink, dress, ride, live, with ever more complicated and, therefore, constantly more expensive consumption.

What becomes clear is that from the larger viewpoint of our economy, the total effect of all the advertising and promotion and selling is to create and maintain the multiplicity and intensity of wants that are the spur to the standard of living in the United States. A specific advertising and promotional campaign, for a particular product at a particular time, has no automatic guarantee of success, yet it may contribute to the general pressure by which wants are stimulated and maintained. Thus its very failure may serve to fertilize this soil, as does so much else that seems to go down the drain.

Having drawn an analogy between consumption and human waste that suggests Lebow himself recognized the cynicism of his philosophy, he now moves on to a discussion of how capital can mold the American mind through a "torrent of diverse pressures:"

> As we examine the concept of consumer loyalty, we see that the whole problem of molding the American mind is involved here. To take an analogy from modern physics, we can consider all of these various sales messages as impulses which build up until they produce a sale. The consumer is not only faced with a multiplicity of choices, he is also being bombarded with a torrent of diverse pressures.
>
> The consumer aspires to standards of eating, dressing, housing, and transportation which involve factors of prestige, social status, and the importance of the individual. Crude and obvious though their methods may be, nobody has better understood this nor more conscientiously sought this than the automotive industry. Particularly noteworthy has been the care with which each make of automobile has been symbolized, and the symbol maintained through many body changes and other alterations. The Big Three—and the smaller fourth—maintain a hierarchy of automobiles, corresponding to promotions in the consumer's social rank.

Next Lebow further acknowledges the symbolic and even religious quality of consumerism, which for the consumer supplies "the reason for his existence" and demands a loyalty that transcends consumer items themselves:

> This factor of symbol and significance has become partly obscured with the advent of television. Here we have a new and most powerful medium of communication. It creates a new set of conditions, impelling toward a monopoly of the consumer's attention. For the first time, almost the entire American consuming public has become a captive audience. Television actually sells the generalized idea of consumption. It promotes the goal of higher living standards.

The symbols by which the consumer lives are all subsumed in a larger and far more important symbol. For, regardless of the ambitions the manufacturer or retailer may have for products, the consumer's highest loyalty is actually towards his standard of living, toward the goals, aspirations, and wants which comprise the reason for his existence.

The drive to emulate the upper social strata still plays an important role in providing goals for the consumer's living standards. If the consumer's basic loyalty to his standard of living is understood correctly, it is clear that the family thinks only partly in terms of the individual items that satisfy its aspirations. The real goals are to *look* better, *live* better, *dress* better, *travel* better.[48]

MENTAL INFRASTRUCTURE

Victor Lebow's revealing article illustrates the extent to which the consumer world has been consciously constructed. In his fascinating, disturbing essay, *Mental Infrastructures, How Growth Entered the World and Our Souls*,[49] psychologist Harald Welzer delves deeper into this, describing the historical process by which economic growth and its chief tenet, consumerism, have not only captured the global political and economic agenda but also entered our souls as a kind of global state religion.

"The ascendancy of economic growth as the key concept of economic policy in industrial nations took place with astonishing speed," comments Welzer. "It is only a few decades ago that growth began to play a prominent role in economics, yet today, the position it holds in economic theory is quite disproportionate to the value policymakers ascribe to it as a virtual silver bullet for achieving general prosperity, reducing social inequalities, combating unemployment and the like. Today, no politician can afford to promote economic policies that would renounce the civil religion of growth…"

Even today's Green parties and prominent environmentalists largely hold to the growth model, believing it is possible to decouple growth from resource consumption. This would allow an economy based on renewable energies and more thoughtful consumption of "sustainable" goods and services. The green option, suggests Welzer, "serves above all to maintain the illusion that we can make a sufficient number of minor adjustments in order to reduce the negative environmental consequences of economic growth while leaving our present system intact. This illusion, which is neither scientifically nor economically sound, illustrates just how magically compelling growth has become…This is in odd contrast to the concept's period of historical prominence, thus raising the suspicion that the paradigm's preeminence has not only economic and political reasons but also a deeper, mental dimension, too."

Following are a few of Welzer's key observations about the construction of contemporary culture:

Inventing the future The perpetual growth paradigm came into its own only after the Second World War with policies that facilitated the reconstruction of Europe in a manner that aimed to create social peace through the widest possible participation in prosperity. It was at that time that "the economic growth paradigm became linked to the state's responsibility to safeguard it. The close coupling of the normative idea of social peace to continuous economic growth is probably most responsible for making limitless growth paradigmatic for today's economic and social policies. Institutional infrastructures regulate growth; the material ones manifest it; and mental infrastructures translate it into *lifeworlds*, equipping the inhabitants of growth societies with the associated biographies and notions of self."

By "lifeworld," Welzer refers to the shared assumptions, common understandings and values that develop over time in social groups, from families to communities. Assumptions derive their power from their "of course" or taken for granted quality; questions about the lifeworld—why you believe in the growth imperative, for example—can only be answered by some version of "that's just the way it is." (Importantly, and this will be returned to later, making lifeworld assumptions fully conscious explicitly destroys them.)

While the religion of growth/consumerism came into its full power after 1950, Welzer describes a number of historical factors that emerged with the Industrial Revolution that made its ascendency possible.

To begin with, the concept of growth is based on the idea that the future will be better than the present. As odd as it may seem today, any vision of *a future*, at least as an attainable alternative state of earthly existence, was largely nonexistent before the 17th century and the dawn of the industrial worldview.

Prior to industrialization, the order of things was static as far as the individual or the community could perceive. Change occurred over the course of centuries and millennia, quite unlike today when events and technologies change by the minute. The lack of a future in classical cosmologies is also attested by the fact that most grammars of that time did not have a future tense.

Inventing the individual The emergence of a growth paradigm also involved changes to the conception of the individual. In the pre-modern era people were tightly integrated in local and domestic contexts and only rarely could one's social position be changed through one's own efforts.

Only with the vast manpower needs of industrialization and the resulting dislodgement of labour from traditional relationships do we begin to speak of individuals with biographies or curricula vitae in the modern sense. Only in the modern period has the idea of people being locked into a divinely given lot and bestowed with an unchangeable personality been set aside. Sayings such as "life is what you make of it" would have been inconceivable prior to the modern period. Only with modernity could individuals "develop," "grow," "achieve something," or "make something of themselves."

Inventing self-constraint Among the changes that occur as a result of modernity are a progressive shift in the relationship between external and self-constraints. While feudal rulers maintained their power by force, modern societies are characterized by dwindling external constraints. At the same time, individual self-constraints increase. In European societies and their colonial offspring, the Protestant work ethic has played an important role in building self-constraints.

Inventing the workday The implementation of the industrial working day serves to illustrate this: During the early phase of industrialization workers were disciplined into putting in their 12 hours, six days a week, with the threat of violence. On Mondays in particular, workers frequently failed to show up and literally had to be rounded up and whipped to go to work. Eventually, the eight-hour industrial working day, which had been established after considerable struggle, became the seemingly natural standard that dictated the sleeping, waking, and recreational rhythms of all members of society, from toddlers to retirees. Today, the goal of our efforts is no longer to shorten working hours but to *maintain* jobs, something a 19th-century industrial worker trying to avoid gruelling labour would have found perverse. External constraint has evolved into self-constraint.

Inventing time Industrialization transformed the conception of time. Not only did it beget a vision of the future and establish the rhythms of the industrial workday and workweek, the harmonization of international railway time and the division of the world into time zones culminated in a standardized, worldwide, artificial time regime. This historically recent phenomenon has been internalized with such thoroughness that today we are hardly aware that in the modern era we no longer know the natural rhythms of real daily or seasonal time.

Inventing mobility Accompanying the transformation of time was the acceleration of movement in space that commenced in the 19th century with the adoption of motorized vehicles. Altering the perception of space and time has led to an ever-accelerating mobility, where gains in minutes over distances of hundreds of kilometres appear to warrant enormous investments.

Inventing a personal future A notion of *time gained* corresponds with increased life expectancy. In 1800, average life expectancy was 30 years. By 2000, it had risen to 67, with considerably higher figures for industrialized societies. This made it possible that something akin to a personal future could enter people's imaginations, making the planning of one's life conceivable and supporting the idea that human life, like the economy, is a process of continual growth.

No longer considering him or herself in a cyclical generational context, in which one's own lifetime is merely an episode in a succession of linked lives, Economic Man as an individual with a personal biography must make the most of the limited time allotted him or her—keeping track of time, saving as much time as possible, using it, or accumulating it. These trends toward greater open-endedness simultaneously make the present moment more important and more fluid: each station of the present is the transit point to what will come next. We are not *in* the present, just passing through.

Inventing infinite work Welzer also saw a transformation in the nature of work. For pre-industrial craftsmen and artists and their clients, for example, the objective of work was to create a specific object. The work was done once the product was completed and remuneration was based on that product. Industrial production, on the other hand, no longer involves the creation of a product as an end in itself.

It is a system in which continuous work generates an essentially infinite series of products for the creation of surplus value, capital that is immediately re-invested in the improvement of production or the expansion of the product range in order to push the system's horizons toward infinity. Nothing is ever finished; the work never stops. And accounting for the frenetic activity and endless production is paramount.

This model not only involves an inversion of means and ends—work and money become the ends, the products and their production mere means—but also the essential "incompleteness of action" and a fundamental "futility of production." This is not only the root of the idea of limitless growth, essential to furnishing the infinite universe of consumable objects, but also the source of the mentality of an individual that is never complete and always growing.

As a result, a notion of vocation is replaced with mere activity; rather than being a baker, one now works (for the time being) making bread.

Inventing productivity One result of the adoption of a growth model is "the astonishing transformation of substance into mere states of passage: Each manufacturing operation is only the precursor to the next; every product the predecessor of the following; each work step only a preliminary act in an endless chain of repetitions. Though no purpose will ever be reached, money can be multiplied infinitely, and productivity increased without limits. While work was previously seen as *molestia*, or toil, it is now ennobled as a *productive* activity."

As Joseph Vogl puts it: "According to this new understanding, wealth that exceeds the needs of all is 'productive,' as is work that does not cease when a need has been satisfied." This is the exact form in which work is understood in economic theory: as an unlimited, endless activity that does not have a specific, limited, product-related objective, but is dedicated to the ceaseless creation of value—consequently the never-ending production of "growth." Just as work becomes incessant, each moment in life, each stage in the sequence of life's events and every dollar in the bank becomes merely the preliminary stage of the next moment, the next stage, and the next dollar. So it is for the self: the self in every biography is only the predecessor of a self that has still more to accomplish.

Such a mode for the production of goods and the creation of value generates a constant self-transcendence in business as well as personality. In principle, both are geared toward overcoming the limits of the self, interminability and infinity, and thus systematically toward non-stop growth. A stationary economy is the exact opposite and thus completely unthinkable—it is immediately associated with a stagnation of social and personal development. The emotional note that always comes into debates whenever it is proposed that we could simply stop growing betrays the role growth has assumed within our emotional frameworks.

Inventing infinite energy The discovery of seemingly limitless forms of energy not only made industrialization possible, it also caused the societies that harnessed it to see themselves as *energetic* in comparison to the rest of the world, and thus superior, justifying colonization, racism, and militarism carried out with mechanistic precision.

Inventing industrial schooling Industrialization also influenced educational models. The invention of school as an institution for the upbringing and education of all members of a society is associated with the development of industrialized countries. In addition to imparting knowledge, the educational regime served to instill values such as punctuality, thoroughness, and orderliness with the aim to shape a social character capable of functioning with the synchronization required by a society marked by a clear division of labor. A further effect of schooling is the practice of instilling competitiveness, including measurement of individual performance using testing/grade systems. This process remains in effect today despite research showing it to be ineffective in supporting authentic learning. Similar to the accumulative consumer society it supports, schooling devolves to the mere accumulation and storage of ever more information.

Inventing consumerism In modern societies, social and mental infrastructures are not only determined by specific conditions of production but also by conditions of consumption. As previously noted, the role played by consumption in giving us a sense of meaning and purpose was identified early in the history of the consumer ideology. The individual that has been liberated from traditional and religious contexts has to be both the designer of his/her life and responsible for its purpose, and thus requires new external supports in order to define him or herself as someone leading a "successful life." In consumer societies, such supports consist of what one "can afford."

It is no coincidence, then, that shopping has now become a recreational activity, and that many products that are bought are no longer actually consumed. It is estimated, for example, that over 40 percent of all food purchased in some wealthy societies is thrown away. The sociologist Hartmut Rosa sees an overall shift from consumption toward buying, where the things acquired would be used only a few times at most—or not at all. If the items bought are no longer consumed, then buying itself becomes a meaningful act and increasingly one that forges community. So, modern malls become social places in which young people in particular gather to try on clothing, try out roles, and comment on one another's efforts. Often the clothing is of such poor quality it survives only a few wash cycles.

If the practical value—the dimension of quality—of a product disappears, then we are left with only its symbolic value, the quantitative dimension represented by its price.

WHY CHANGE IS SO CHALLENGING

People are typically unaware of the lifeworlds or paradigms that shape the culture in which they are immersed. It is exactly for the reason that paradigms are largely unconscious that they are so powerful. Becoming aware of paradigms that shape our culture and govern our behaviour makes changing them possible.

The fundamental cultural shift that occurred with the Industrial Revolution happened only slowly and for the average person unconsciously. People were not generally aware that a paradigm shaped the earlier way of life or that it was being replaced. Similarly, for people living today the consumer culture with all its trappings seems always to have been here; it governs our movements and is as natural a part of our daily lives as the invisible sewer system that ensures that our excreta disappear forever or the electrical grid that guarantees that the lights come on at the flick of a switch. The underlying paradigm is invisible.

But what if it fails to deliver the goods?

Because consumer societies realize meaning in consumption opportunities and growth, they face an existential crisis if they run out of resources as briefly seemed to be the case during the first oil crisis in the 1970s or the 2008 financial crisis.

Paradoxically, growth becomes more important as a society's material saturation progresses and its vital needs are fulfilled. The growth system perpetuates itself through extreme consumerism, and it is precisely this that constitutes the apparent limitlessness of growth societies. They can acknowledge a limit only when there is nothing left to consume, when all resources have been exhausted.

"And that is people's secret fear," writes Harald Welzer: "That everything they have established, everything they worked for, planned and believed in, could have been meaningless. The dimensions of meaning and identity that Western-style capitalist societies provide stand and fall with the functioning of the market."

Paradoxically, growth becomes more important as a society's material saturation progresses and its vital needs are fulfilled.

We can therefore write any number of narratives such as the Club of Rome's 1972 classic *Limits to Growth* or Jarod Diamond's *Collapse*—which show the precariousness of the growth economy—and modern societies will not change course. We are living a narrative that sees society solely in terms of progress, growth, and lack of limits. Before we can do anything to halt this narrative it has, again and again, unfolded. The catalogue of all things available is one that we browse every day. It is a self-evident universe and thus, to counter it with an alternative narrative based on an understanding of environmental limits is difficult, above all because the majority of mental structures are not the result of reflection or conscious decision. Growth is a massive world unto itself, one into which we are born and the story of which we ceaselessly repeat with our own consumer lifestyle.

The construction of the consumer society as the chief thrust of the economic growth imperative, argues Welzer, has resulted in psychologically different human beings from those in previous stages of civilization. The idea of growth is therefore not only enshrined in business and politics, but also in the psychological structure of the people who grow up in such societies.

When setting out to change the status quo it is essential to be aware of its mental structures, which are in a sense even more imposing than the material infrastructures that facilitate economic life. They have in fact been so thoroughly conditioned by the world as it is that they rarely allow a detached point of view. Whenever we observe our own actions, we get a close-up view of our conditioned selves, which never reveals the greater picture.

Ultimately, it will become apparent that the transformation to a post-growth, post-consumer society is not a project to be achieved by means of economic policy and technology so much as changing our mental infrastructure.

The processes that will make this deeper transformation possible are the main theme of this book.

GALLOPING CONSUMPTION

The materialistic crusade that slowly took shape after the Industrial Revolution became a juggernaut in the middle of the 20th century, when it was so clearly described by Victor Lebow. In 1955, when the world population was 2.7 billion, Gross World Product (GWP) was $5.4 trillion (in constant 1990 dollars). In 2012, population had increased 2.5 times but GWP had increased more than 8 times to $44.9 trillion ($71.8 trillion in 2012 US dollars.) The World Bank[50] puts *household final consumption expenditures*, i.e. the market value of all goods and services including durable products (such as cars, washing machines, and home computers) purchased by households in 2012 at 62 percent of GWP, or $44.5 trillion in 2012 dollars.

Consumption at this level has dramatically increased humanity's impact on the ecosphere. This impact can be assessed using the *ecological footprint* (EF), a measure of the productive ecosystem area required by a population to produce the renewable resources it consumes and to assimilate its wastes, including GHGs.

How much has increased consumption deepened the human ecological footprint since the mid-20th century?

The Global Footprint Network has estimated the historical growth of the total human footprint from 1961-2007.[51] In this instance, EF is expressed as the total demand placed on the whole ecosphere by humans, where a value of 1.00 means that demand is equivalent to *all* of the annual sustainable productive and assimilative capacity of the ecosphere. In 1961, EF was estimated at 0.63, meaning that the global economy used about 63 percent of Earth's sustainable capacity. If we use the rate of growth in EF for the early 1960s and push the estimate back a few years, global EF would have been 0.51 in 1955.

In 1976, operating the economy required all of Earth's sustainable productive capacity for the first time. As of 2007, the EF was 1.51, meaning the economy had exceeded the ecosphere's sustainable capacity by 51 percent. If we use the EF growth rate for the mid 2000s and push it forward, humanity's EF would be 1.61 today, meaning that our footprint has more than tripled since 1955.

There is actually some good news in that figure: that the economy increased eight-fold and EF only three-fold shows increasing resource-use efficiency. The good news is not good enough, given that EF now exceeds Earth's capacity by more than 60 percent.

How is it possible to use more than Earth's capacity?

Ecological capacity is often compared to capital. As long as humankind lives off the interest produced by Earth's natural capital, the economy is sustainable. Exceeding ecological carrying capacity means we are liquidating a certain amount of natural capital every year rather than living from the natural interest, which is ultimately unsustainable.

To illustrate this concept, let's imagine a grove of 1000 fast-growing trees, where 100 trees mature each year and 100 new trees are planted. A forester would be able to log 100 trees a year sustainably, without ever decreasing the stock of trees. If, however, he cuts 200 trees a year, his income doubles but the forest will disappear within 10 years, reducing his income to zero thereafter.

Given that Earth's carrying capacity has already been exceeded, the task before us is enormous. Humanity will somehow have to reduce its consumption of resources and emissions of waste by some 60 percent overall. That in itself would require a wholesale transformation of the economy. That we will have to achieve that goal while accommodating 50 percent more people suggests something more like a wholesale transformation of economy *and* culture.

Put another way, we have to create an economy that supports 11 billion people with an EF equivalent to that of the 4.1 billion people living in 1976, the last time our EF equalled 1.0. For that to work, we will need to be a very different kind of people, with more subtle habits and aspirations, than we are today.

Just how difficult it will be to turn the economy around is apparent when we look at the growth of consumption over the past hundred years and project it into the future. From 1900-1999, per capita resource consumption and waste output more than quadrupled; but taking the quadrupling of the human population over the same period into account, resource use and waste rose 16 times during the 20th century. Today, the high-throughput economies of wealthy countries require up to 80 tonnes of natural resources per person per year to supply the demand for goods and services.[52]

If we continue on this trajectory, humanity's annual impact on the ecosphere will have increased forty-fold between 1900 and 2050, and two thirds of this increase will have occurred in the 21st century. Consider that in the first decade of this century alone, the size of the global economy measured in GDP more than doubled, from $33.4 trillion in 2002 to over $70 trillion in 2012.

More and more people are moving up the continuum of consumption. If we don't turn the economy around, the resources and waste moving through the system each year will more than quadruple from present levels by the time the population hits 11 billion, which could quadruple the impact on the ecosphere, vastly exceeding the planet's carrying capacity. Even if the resource efficiency of the economy increases dramatically, efficiency gains per unit of production will be overwhelmed by growth in production. Only reducing consumption and renouncing the paradigm of continuous economic growth—only abandoning the materialists' crusade—offers hope.

While we rightly worry about the damage already done to the planet, we have to realize that most of the impacts from the expansion of population and economic activity are still to come. What this means is either that civilization smashes itself against the planet's ecological limits or humanity changes the way it does everything.

The premise of this book is that humankind will ultimately choose the latter course and change itself. But how will consumption be reduced and by whom? This question begs another: How much of our economic system is devoted to supplying legitimate needs that *cannot* be reduced—and will actually have to grow with the population—and how much to wants that *can* be reduced? Answering this question will help us understand how our ecological footprint can be lightened.

REVERSING GROWTH

Consumer goods and services include everything from necessities like nutritious food and education to frivolous expenditures like soda pop or luxury items. Obviously, each of us have certain legitimate needs that must be met; in fact, for the third of the world's population living on less than $2 a day, for whom consumption has risen only marginally from levels typical of 1900, consumption will have to increase to satisfy their needs.

On the other end of the scale, consumption by the richest consumers is exponentially higher than it was in 1900.[53] The 20 percent at the top of the global economic scale are mainly responsible for overshooting the planet's ecological capacity; they use about 80 percent of the world's resources and produce most of its GHG emissions.[54] This means that the turnaround must—can only—come by eliminating superfluous consumption by the top consumers. Here, Gandhi's famous aphorism—"Earth provides enough to satisfy every man's need, but not every man's greed"—comes into play.

A study by the consulting group A.T. Kearney,[55] which looks at the nature of global spending on consumer goods and services, will help clarify where the needed reduction in consumption must come from. The Kearney study, which defines consumer spending somewhat differently than the World Bank estimate previously cited, pegs consumer spending at about 40 percent of global GDP, or around $28 trillion. With a compound annual growth rate of 3 percent, Kearney expects consumer spending to rise 43 percent by 2020. Kearney's divides the world's consumers into four categories:

- **Basic Consumers:** For the 1.8 billion people in this group, consumer spending is concentrated almost entirely on necessities, such as food, travel to work, and items like shoes and clothing. Although this group is one-quarter of the world's population, their total spending on goods and services is just $1.4 trillion. Approximate average annual spending per capita in countries that make up most of this group is $4,000. However, approximately 1 billion basic consumers live on incomes between $1.25 and $2.00 a day. By 2020, this group will actually decrease in size as many migrate into the Emerging Consumer category. Obviously, we can't look to this group for any reductions in consumption. In fact, their increasing consumption will have to be compensated for by other consumers to achieve an overall decrease in EF.

- **Emerging Consumers:** For the 2 billion in this group, total consumer spending is $4.6 trillion. Their spending is still concentrated on food items, with more spending on clothing, footwear, and personal care products than the basic consumer. Approximate average spending per capita for countries currently in this group is $8,000. By 2020, this group is expected to expand to 3.4 billion, and their spending to rise to $10 trillion. It is unlikely that significant savings in consumption can come from this group.

- **Escalating Consumers:** The 600 million people in this group spend about $2.5 trillion on goods and services. At this level, a larger percentage of spending shifts to personal care, entertainment, and leisure items, as well as telecom spending. Approximate average spending per capita for countries currently in this group is $16,000. In 2020, this group is expected to be the same size, but spending will rise to $3.6 trillion. Some reductions in consumption and waste might be expected from the upper echelon of this group.

- **Established Consumers:** The 1.2 billion people in this group, about 17 percent of the world's population, spend about $20 trillion per year on consumer goods and services, about 70 percent of Kearney's estimate of consumer spending. For this group, necessities become a minor part of spending, which switches predominately to various services such as insurance and financial management, social protection, medical care, and leisure and entertainment. Approximate average spending per capita for countries currently in this group is $32,000. By 2020, the number of established consumers will rise slightly, to 1.3 billion, but spending will increase another 25 percent, to $25 trillion. Clearly, it is from this group that most reductions in consumption and waste, including GHGs, must come.

If you did the math, you no doubt noticed that only 5.6 billion people are included in Kearney's categories. The neglected 1.6 billion people are largely those living in extreme poverty, getting by on $1.25 a day or less. They spend almost all of their income on basic necessities such as food, leaving no discretionary income for consumer goods and services. This group would obviously benefit by increased consumption in areas such as food, housing, education, and heath.

On the other end of the spectrum are the *super rich* consumers. According to comprehensive calculations[56] of global income inequality conducted by World Bank economist Branko Milanovic, the top eight percent of global earners draw 50 percent of all income globally, revealing an astonishing inequality.

Average annual-income figures (circa 2011) range dramatically, from a low of $231 in Democratic Republic of Congo to $5,445 in China to $48,112 in the U.S. to a high of $171,465 in Monaco. But wealth inequality is higher than income inequality, and therefore a reasonable estimate of personal wealth throughout the world suggests that the wealthiest one percent own roughly half of all personal assets. And that top one percent—the "winners" in the economic globalization process—saw their real income rise more than 60 percent between 1988 and 2008 while the incomes of poorest five percent remained the same.

Both the proportion and total amount of superfluous consumption rises with income. The richest people within the Established Consumer group have the most disposable income and are responsible for most of the superfluous consumption, along with its ecological footprint. Income inequality and the protection of the ecosphere are thus intimately linked. To make the world work for 11 billion people, the richest segment of the population will have to dramatically reduce its consumption. Indeed, there is enough excess consumption in this segment of the population that moderating its consumption could dramatically reduce humanity's ecological footprint. More on that later.

Beyond that, the rich could play another pivotal role in change. Milanovic describes the super-rich upper echelon as a kind of club overwhelmingly composed of the old rich who pass their fortunes on to their children (tax-free in the many countries without estate taxes), send them to the most prestigious universities where they meet and make friends of others similarly situated, and then set them up in businesses of their own. Within this club, a tightly concentrated small core of top players form a "super-entity" that essentially controls the global economy.

While this may sound like classic conspiracy theory, it is simply fact. The extent of economic control by the super rich was quantified by a group of complex systems theorists at the Swiss Federal Institute of Technology who undertook a comprehensive study[57] of ownership patterns in the global economy. The researchers were not politically motivated; rather, they were using a study of the economy to better understand patterns in complex systems. They examined data on 13 million ownership relations in 43,000 transnational corporations (TNCs) and found that just 737 companies—mostly American and British financial institutions—control 80 percent of TNC value, while a core of just 146 top players control 40 percent of TNC value.

The researchers do not attribute this to collusion on the part of the super-rich; instead, it is consistent with the dynamics of any complex system, which favour ever more connectivity for the most highly connected nodes. In complex economic systems, money—and power—naturally flows to the most connected members, thus the highly connected super-entity of top economic players is a very small group with a very high degree of control over the economic system. Given their connections in the boardrooms of the corporate world, not to mention their political connections, their degree of influence is much greater than their actual share of the economic pie, which is already huge.

Another assessment, released by Oxfam in 2014, claims that the wealth of the world's 85 richest persons exceeds that of half of the world's population, the 3.6 billion poorest.[58]

While inequality and the concentration of economic and political power is obviously a central problem of civilization, it also contains a potential solution. The super-entity of plutocrats that controls the economy can be seen not only as the tip of a pyramid, but also as a fulcrum on which the whole social-ecological order is balanced. Shifting that fulcrum would rebalance the whole system.

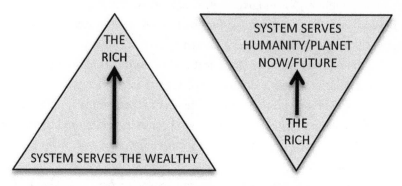

The rich can be parasitic or act as a fulcrum to leverage change

Setting cynicism aside for a moment, we can see that a shift in the values of a very small group of people—perhaps fewer than 150—could trigger a shift in the global economic order. The ultra rich are so rich that were they to adopt an ethic of giving they have the capacity to eliminate the gross inequality that is inimical to a sustainable civilization. And were they to embrace the steady state economy, they could play a lead role in reversing growth.

As already discussed, de-growth must be based largely on a reduction in consumption by the top 20 percent of consumers. Based on ecological footprint calculations, the ecological impact of the economy will have to be reduced by 60 percent to sustain the ecosphere, notwithstanding the 50 percent increase in population expected by 2100. Thus, if the top 20 percent of consumers— who are responsible for about 70-80 percent of consumption—reduced consumption by an average of 65 percent, global consumption would be cut by half, taking the world a good part of the way toward sustainability. Of course, reduction in consumption would be much higher for the richest segments of this group than for the middle class segments.

Given the excessive nature of consumption by Established Consumers, consumption at 35 percent of current levels on average, though dramatically reduced, would still be ample for a befitting life.

A complementary option that has to be pursued is improved efficiency. Buildings can operate on a fraction of the energy currently used; active and public transport can replace private vehicles; locally produced plant food can replace factory-farmed meat; green, renewable power can replace fossil fuels; products can be made from fewer inputs. There are endless opportunities to reduce the human footprint through improved efficiencies, yet growth can—and has—eclipsed these gains. Cars, for example, have become more fuel-efficient but fuel consumption—and carbon pollution—continues to rise due to the increasing number of automobiles.

Ecological footprint must be reduced by 60 percent, notwithstanding the 50 percent increase in population by 2100.

The human footprint must be reduced through efficiencies but cannot be sufficiently reduced through greater efficiencies alone; improved efficiencies must be accompanied by reduced per capita consumption by the heaviest consumers.

But can the richest 20 percent of consumers be persuaded to make drastic cuts in their consumption? Can the super rich be persuaded to give most of their money away? Or to transform the economic system that generates their wealth and power?

It does happen, even among the top plutocrats. Warren Buffett, for instance, continues to live in a home he bought in 1958 for $31,500, and to use public transit, after becoming one of the world's richest persons. He has pledged 99 percent of his fortune to philanthropic causes and has already contributed $31 billion to the Gates Foundation. (Whatever we may think of the Gates Foundation philanthropic priorities, philanthropy beats misanthropy.) Buffet also famously argued the rich should pay higher taxes, decrying the growing inequality in society. Billionaire philanthropist George Soros is well-known for his critique of *laissez-faire* capitalism and the encroachment of market values into all areas of life. Disillusioned by a materialistic lifestyle, Austrian businessman Karl Rabered gave away *all* of his fortune to a microcredit agency and now lives on $1350 a month, while wealthy American film director Tom Shadyac sold his Hollywood mansions and moved into a house trailer. It is a rarity, but if at least some of the super-rich can do it, there's hope the top 20 percent can voluntarily let go of some excess baggage.

ONE PLANET LIVING

Just how hard would it be for the top 20 percent of consumers to drastically reduce their ecological footprint? Very, is the short answer.

Jennie Moore and William Rees (Rees originated and co-developed ecological footprint analysis) examined how one wealthy Canadian city, Vancouver, could reduce its ecological impact.[59]

There are 11.9 billion hectares of productive ecosystem area on the planet. If this area were distributed equally among the 7 billion people on Earth (circa 2012), each person would be allocated just 1.7 global hectares (gha). Vancouverites, however, have an ecological footprint of close to 5 ghas per person, almost three times their fair share of global hectares. Moore and Rees report that 51 percent of Vancouver's EF comes from food consumption (and most of that from animal products), 19 percent from transportation, 16 percent from buildings, and 14 percent from consumer goods.

"Even if average Vancouverites followed a vegan diet; avoided driving or flying and only walked, cycled, or used public transit; lived in a passive solar house that used almost no fossil-based energy; and cut their personal consumption by half, they could only reduce their per capita Ecological Footprint by 44 percent (from 4.96 to 2.8 gha per capita)," observe Moore and Rees. "That seems like an impossible challenge already, and yet it is still a full global hectare beyond the one-planet threshold."

However, another 18 percent of a Vancouverite's footprint results from activities carried out on their behalf by provincial or national governments, from providing highway infrastructure and health services to subsidies to industry and operating the military. Things like demilitarization, switching to preventive health care, and reducing perverse subsidies to fossil fuel industries are additional ways of reducing EF that are beyond the scope of individual or municipalities.

In other words, successful planet-scale reduction in the ecological footprint would require concerted action to reduce all forms of consumption on the part of the top 20 percent of consumers in general, especially the richest segments; the full participation of all levels of government; as well as the focused action of the industries which supply the bulk of goods and services, particularly the largest TNCs that largely control the economy. As we will see in later chapters, there are also many contributions that can be made by those outside the wealthy segments of society, particularly in the area of land management, that will complement the process of reducing ecological impact.

In the first chapter, vicious cycles of negative impacts from excessive consumption were described. Fortunately, the opposite is also true: any effort to reduce consumption triggers *virtuous cycles* of social-ecological renewal.

Reducing the ecological impact of the food system, for example, results in improvements to human health. As the accompanying graphic shows, foods like vegetables, which have the lowest ecological footprint, have the highest benefits for human health. Shifting to a more ecologically-friendly diet high in vegetable content would thus reduce medical care costs, which are themselves another significant component of EF.

The Double Pyramid Model developed by the Barilla Center for Food and Nutrition:
The healthiest foods, such as fruits and vegetables, also have the lightest ecological footprint.

Such virtuous cycles have occurred on a large scale. When the Soviet Union collapsed in 1990, Cuba went into an economic tailspin from which it would not recover for half a decade. The biggest impact came from the loss of cheap petroleum that had been supplied by the Soviets. Gasoline quickly became unobtainable by ordinary citizens, crippling mechanized agriculture and food distribution systems. During the so-called "Special Period" (1991-1995), Cuba teetered on the brink of famine. Cubans survived by eating anything they could get their hands on, which was usually plants.

Unexpectedly, the health of Cubans improved dramatically during the years of austerity.[60] National health statistics show that during the economic crisis deaths from cardiovascular disease and Type 2 diabetes fell by a third and a half respectively. Strokes declined modestly. Overall mortality rates went down. The research indicates that weight loss due to increased walking resulting from a lack of transportation options and less food consumption, was responsible for the health improvement. Another factor was the switch to a diet largely based on fresh vegetables and fruits grown in community gardens and small farms. Furthermore, the lack of petroleum essentially eliminated the availability of petrochemicals, resulting in a wholesale adoption of organic farming methods and a decrease in chemical exposure. Unhealthy habits like smoking and drinking also decreased.

After 1995, when the economic situation "improved," vehicle transport was revived and old eating habits returned, the incidence of chronic illness shot back up to 1990 levels.

No one wants economic collapse and forced famine, but Cuba's Special Period provides surprising evidence that reducing consumption should not necessarily be viewed as negative; in fact, it can provide major population-wide benefits.

This result also supports the notion that economic metrics like GDP are inaccurate as measures of well-being. One alternate approach, the Happy Planet Index (HPI), measures the extent to which countries deliver long, happy, sustainable lives for their citizens using data on three metrics: life expectancy, well-being, and EF. National comparisons using HPI shows very different results than those using GDP: Wealthy countries with high GDP generally rank low on the HPI scale due to their heavy footprints.

While no country has "good" rankings in all three HPI measures, the 14 countries with the highest HPI ranking overall all manage good or middle range scores for life expectancy and well-being, with seven showing good EF rankings (of less than 1.78 gha/per capita, equal to the world's bio-capacity) and seven with an EF between 1.78 and 3.0 gha/capita).

Given its HPI standing, Cuba presents an interesting case. Although poor by international standards, and certainly much poorer than its neighbour the Untied States, Cuba's infant mortality and life expectancy rates, and several other measures of human progress, are the same as those of the U.S. Yet its EF (1.9 gha per capita) is less than a third the U.S. level (7.2 gha/capita). Even outside the "special period", Cuba is a model nation in terms of ecological impact; during the special period its ecological impact fell well below sustainable levels and health outcomes actually improved. And while Cubans experience a lower sense of well-being (5.4 out of 10 on the HPI scale) than Americans (7.2), it is still above the world average (5.28) for well-being.

It is noteworthy that most countries where the citizens say they experience high levels of satisfaction are wealthy countries with very high EFs. Denmark has the highest level of satisfaction, for instance, but its EF is 8.3 gha, 4.6 times the planet's biocapacity. On the other hand, the nations with the lightest EF almost always have low life expectancy and experience low levels of well-being. Afghanistan, for instance, has the lowest EF at 0.5 gha/capita but its life expectancy is just 48.7 and well being is 4.8.

Interestingly, of the nations with the highest HPI ranking, none is wealthy and almost all are in Latin America. Costa Rica, with the top HPI ranking has slightly higher life expectancy (79.3 years) and well-being (7.3) than the US (78.5 years and 7.2 for well-being.)

The Happy Planet Index shows it is possible to live long and well without overtaxing the planet. Even among the wealthy nations where people enjoy high levels of well-being and longevity there is a dramatic difference between EFs. Danes need 8.3 ghas to support their long and happy lives, while their Norwegian neighbours get similar results from 4.8 ghas. And the difference between the top countries and the mid-range in terms of wealth can be dramatically different in terms of EF. Venezuelans are just as happy from 3 gha per capita as the Dutch at 6.3, while Cubans live longer on 1.9 ghas/capita than the Danes at 8.3 ghas.

While low EF is usually related to low longevity and well-being, countries such as Pakistan and Zambia experience well-being at higher levels than average with less than half of what is considered a sustainable EF (0.8 ghas in both countries). Some countries with high ghas, such as Bahrain and Macedonia, experience low well-being, and some moderate-income countries, like Vietnam or Panama, with relatively low levels of consumption, also enjoy high levels of well-being.

The HPI demonstrates that there are many factors that result in a long and happy life—consumption is just one and not necessarily the most important. It seems reasonable, then, to draw this conclusion: Beyond a moderate level of consumption, which *is* conducive to a long and enjoyable life, increasing consumption is not responsible *in itself* for higher levels of well-being or longevity.

When we account for EF, the HPI shows it is possible to have a reasonably good and long life in a sustainable way. On the other hand, we know that a heavy EF threatens long-term sustainability for everyone—and ultimately longevity and well-being—given that a healthy economy ultimately depends on a healthy ecosphere. The present well-being of the wealthy nations is purchased from future generations.

Already the costs of maintaining the heavy EFs of wealthy nations are beginning to creep up when we consider levels of chronic illness and health care costs; indebtedness; decreasing ability to provide public goods like health care and education; the heightened levels of inequality; and the growing demand for military and police protection associated with extra- and intra-national inequality. As Herman Daly puts it, the wealthy nations are now increasing *illth* faster than wealth.

DISPELLING THE ILLUSION

As discussed in the previous chapter, pulling up to a favourite Tim Hortons in Saskatoon or KFC outlet in Beijing engages a largely invisible support system that results in a cascade of impacts affecting the climate, atmosphere, hydrosphere, soil systems, ecosystems, social systems, political institutions, ideologies, philosophies, and mythologies. Critical to change is that we understand our seemingly simple actions are not at all what they seem.

It has been shown that a vast and deliberate effort, led by vested interests and enthusiastically embraced by the masses, has constructed a version of reality as false as anything in science fiction.

Consumer culture is illusory in the sense that it appears to be one thing when it is in fact another. It purports to be the most effective system ever devised to meet human needs—and looks very much like it is. Instead, it is structured on inequality and overconsumption, putting it on a collision course with social and ecological limits that will in time make it impossible for the system to provide for human needs. The global expansion of consumer culture threatens humanity's ability to carry forward an ever-advancing civilization, which is an assault of the purpose of human life.

The good news from what we have looked at in this chapter is that a consumer culture is not the inevitable outcome of the civilization building process. Nor is it the natural result of the operation of an intrinsically selfish human nature. Those ideas are part of the illusion. This pathological system and its mythology are the product of decisions people have made, both deliberately and unconsciously, to construct a certain kind of reality that serves vested interests. Other better realities could have been constructed, and have been in many settings. Other better realities can still be constructed to make the world work for 11 billion people.

As population grows and the inevitable clash with our social and ecological limits intensifies humanity will be required to dispel these illusions and construct a new culture that better conforms to the reality of who we really are in the world as it is. The new culture will place meaning and value in non-material pursuits; turn our attention to higher goals in the areas of education, health, and the enhancement of relationships, both with our fellow human beings and the ecosphere; and reorient us from an unequal culture of power to an equal culture of service.

But first we will have to shed our addictions. Addiction has been defined as any behaviour associated with craving and temporary relief resulting in long-term negative consequences that a person is not able to give up. Excessive consumption is an addictive behaviour. And although addictions have an obvious solution—stop the consumption—for the addict, kicking the habit is the most difficult thing possible.

And second, we will have to revise our relationship to power and wealth. Power will come to be associated with an increased capacity to serve humankind. Wealth will be seen as a platform from which the capacity for service is amplified.

Breaking our addiction to consumption, and learning to use power and wealth in the service of others, will require an unprecedented change in culture, a change that transforms even our mental infrastructure. The ethical transformation called for can only be brought about through a mass-scale moral education movement that will reorient the minds and hearts of children, youth, and adults of every social class, in every nation. The nature of the needed educational process is the theme of later chapters.

CHAPTER 3

SPECTACULAR MATERIALISM

We are perishing for want of wonder, not for want of wonders.
– G.K. Chesterton.

It's July 5, 1994 and I have gone to bed at a home stay in Sophia, the capital of Bulgaria, blissfully unaware all hell is about to break loose.

Sophia circa 1994 is a quiet, cultured city of 1.2 million, peppered with attractive buildings, abundant public space, and sidewalk cafes. It even has a yellow brick road. But beneath its sophisticated exterior and despite the stylish clothes and jewelry worn by the young and attractive Sophians, many citizens are poor and depressed following the collapse of communist rule.

I find Bulgarians to be rather aloof; there is none of the natural interest shown in foreigners I had found in Albania earlier in my travels through the Balkans, or later in Turkey. So it's early to bed. But sometime during the night an explosion rattles my room, followed by screams. There is a series of great booms from around the city and the rumble of a great mob forming in the streets. Loud music and car horns are blaring from all directions. I don't have a clue what is going on and there is no one to ask. I can only assume the masses have risen up to overthrow an incompetent government of regrouped communists.

From the balcony of the apartment I see the city's lights are on. People have thrown open their doors and set up stereos on their balconies, which are blaring anthems into the night. The street below is full and looking down to the main street I see a throng marching with banners and flags.

This may be the only time I will see a revolution, so out I go into the streets and follow the crowd to the city's huge central square. The noise is deafening. (The next day I learn that close to a million people, almost the entire population of Sophia, had been in the square and the surrounding streets that night.)

A complete outsider, I have no idea what is happening or where all this is going. With the noise I can't find an English speaker to ask, but it gradually dawns on me that people are not angry but joyous, jubilant in fact. Booze is flowing. This is no revolution. It's a spectacular party on a scale I had never witnessed before or since. Finally I find an English speaker who explains: Bulgaria has defeated Mexico 3-1 in World Cup soccer.

In the early 1990s, soccer was still a minor sport for most native-born Canadians. I had not even known the World Cup was underway and certainly had no idea what World Cup football meant to its fans, i.e. most of the world's population. World Cup football was more than a game. It was a passion, almost a religion.

The 1994 series was the first time the Bulgarian team had won a World Cup match and that night was the first time it had defeated a major team. It was as if the nation itself had been validated. For the long oppressed citizens of Bulgaria, the victory seemed more than a revolution, it was a national vindication, a rapturous, near mystical collective experience.

I may have been ignorant about World Cup football, but being from Saskatchewan I know something about sports mania. Fast forward to Sunday, December 28, 2010. It is the final minute of Canada's football championship, the Grey Cup game. The Saskatchewan's Roughriders, behind by three points, have one last chance. Quarterback Darian Durant miraculously escapes being sacked and struggles valiantly to unload the ball onto the sidelines. From nowhere, Montreal Alouette defenseman Billy Parker picks it off, dashing Saskatchewan's championship hopes. Again.

Saskatchewan is a very big province (three times the size of the U.K.) with a very small population (around 1 million). Its most popular institution—by far—is the Saskatchewan Roughriders Football Club. People here are absolutely crazy about "the Riders." We call ourselves "Rider Nation." Our team's merchandise accounts for over half of all merchandise sales in the eight-team Canadian Football League.

Before the 2009 Grey Cup held in Calgary, Alberta—which Saskatchewan also lost to Montreal, on the last play of the game—local grocery stores were mystified by the huge demand for watermelons. Green is our team colour and Rider fans were buying watermelons to turn into helmets, a curious part of fan culture.

I don't have a television so I am watching the Grey Cup on the Internet. My stomach is tied in knots, armpits soaking wet, anxiety levels peaking—interesting given I neither like nor care about football. Spectator sports seem not only pointless to me but boring. The Saskatchewan Roughrider team is made up almost entirely of players not native to this area, including many American imports. It is not as if this is a real hometown team that might somehow be taken as representative of the community's talent. Nevertheless, this business venture that glorifies brute force, male aggression, and competitiveness has come to embody the hopes and dreams of the Saskatchewan people. When they do well, it's as if we all do well.

Oddly, I am caught up in the drama with everyone else. For the rest of the evening and the next few days I find myself thinking about the game and how close it was. It would have been great if "we" had won, if "we" were Canadian champions, as if my own identity would have been inflated by a company's ability to manage and market a competitive entertainment product. Such is the power of sports to manipulate emotions and dreams: they have us believing *they* are *us* and that it actually matters that *we* win. And, most important, that we pay to be part of the spectacle.

THE SOCIETY OF SPECTACLE

The Caesars preoccupied Rome with circuses; the Greeks had their Olympics; Jacobin England its masques; the Incas their *Capacocha*. Today, ever-larger sporting spectacles fuse with the endless stream of spectacular entertainments that preoccupy the masses as the forests fall, the climate cooks, and the rich rob them blind. The World Cups and Super Bowls and 3D blockbusters will not, cannot be ignored. These events consume us as much as we consume them.

Michel Foucault argued that antiquity was a "society of spectacle" while modern society is one of discipline, in which surveillance has replaced the pageant of power. But in his idiosyncratic and prophetic 1967 essay, *The Society of the Spectacle*,[61] Foucault's contemporary Guy Debord argued that, "In societies where modern conditions of production prevail, all of life presents itself as an immense accumulation of spectacles." Everything once lived directly recedes into representation. In this pseudo-world, where representative reality occupies the main part of non-working time, we are all passive spectators.

The spectacle cannot be understood as mere visual excess produced by mass-media, Debord argued. It is a worldview that has actually materialized. The spectacle is not a supplement to the real world, it is "the heart of the unrealism of the real society."

In its totality, spectacle is both the result and the project of the existing system of production. As information or propaganda, as advertisement or entertainment, the spectacle is the model of the social order; its form and content are the total justification of that order's conditions and goals; its creator-agent a ruling class whose mode of domination demands denial of its own existence. Yet elite power is at the root of the spectacle, which is the diplomatic representation of a hierarchic society where all other expression is effectively banned, if only by being overwhelmed by or absorbed into the spectacle. The spectacle is the existing order's uninterrupted discourse about itself, its laudatory monologue. It "covers the entire surface of the world and bathes endlessly in its own glory."

The spectacle is inseparable from the modern capitalist state with its structures of class domination, yet its appearance conceals the facts about actual relations among people. It also wormed its way into socialist states and succeeded in their subversion: as mentioned, portraits of Colonel Saunders now outnumber those of Mao from Shanghai to Beijing.

> The spectacle is the existing order's uninterrupted discourse about itself, its laudatory monologue. It covers the entire surface of the world and bathes endlessly in its own glory.

The Industrial Revolution subordinated humans to commodities and alienated them from the products of their labour. The subsequent development of capitalism, says Debord, alienated people from an advanced product of their labour, i.e. the representation of their own lives. At first capitalism cared only about work time, not leisure, but with the production of surplus goods, it began to seek the worker's cooperation as consumer, and here the spectacle comes into play. The economy can never eliminate privation; paradoxically, it can only nurture it, but the new privation is no longer material: "The real consumer becomes a consumer of illusions."

Economic growth freed industrial populations from a direct struggle for survival, but their liberator demanded a new dependency: providing for primary human needs was replaced by the primary need to provide for the economy's growth through an uninterrupted fabrication of pseudo-needs and an ever-expanding world-wide market.

The society of the spectacle has no aim other that its own existence, observed Debord. As the image of the dominant economy, its goal is nothing, its development everything. As an indispensable decoration, as the rationale of the system, spectacle is the main product of contemporary society.

The first phase of the domination of the growth economy over social life was the degradation of *being* into *having*. The current phase leads from having to *appearing*, with appearance itself the main commodity. Commodities no longer have intrinsic value in any functional sense, but only spectacular value, called brand. The spectacle, like money, is the abstract representation of value, which creates equivalence between things that are not comparable. Satisfaction no longer comes from the *use* of commodities, it is sought in the recognition of their value *as* commodities: the possession of commodities becomes sufficient unto itself. "The spectacle is the moment when the commodity has attained the total occupation of social life."

Although superficially satisfying, observing the spectacular leaves us isolated in the lonely crowd—and sleepy. As "the guardian of sleep," the spectacle is the means of maintaining our unconsciousness. It demands passive acceptance, obtained by its monopoly on appearance and by its capacity to manufacture consent. "It is the sun that never sets over the empire of modern passivity."

The spectacle is a modern material reconstruction of religious mythology that substitutes material aspirations for spiritual ones. Just as false religion creates external division, the spectacle has perfected interior separation. The spectacle is the technical realization of the exile of human powers into materialism. The institutionalization of the social division of labour, the formation of classes, gave rise to the mythic order with which power shrouds itself as a pseudo-sacred entity. The new sacredness justifies a cosmic order that corresponded to the interests of the elites, magnets that draw all wealth and power toward themselves.

Separation is the alpha and omega of the spectacle, which originates from a loss of unity. What binds its spectators also maintains their isolation. People trying to understand themselves through its representation lose hope of coherently living their own life. Thus, true community and critical thinking dissolve. Mass media, the most glaring superficial manifestation of the spectacular, are not neutral. If the administration of society and all human contact can no longer take place except through the intermediary of instantaneous communication, it is because this "communication" is essentially unilateral: even the open communication of "social media" is owned and operated by the powerful.

Each new product (think smart phones) promises to be the ultimate satisfaction of a need. By the time the consumer realizes it is not, a better product is promised. "That which asserted its definitive excellence with perfect impudence nevertheless changes." Thus, "every new lie of advertising is also an avowal of the previous lie."

The spectacle can make everything banal. The illusion of diversity masks the fact that everything is actually the same. There are "57 channels (And Nothin' On)" as Bruce Springsteen put it. There are 45,000 products on supermarket shelves; 44,500 are formulations of soy, corn, or wheat. The same for saleable human commodities, the politicians and stars that flare up to guide and distract us. The celebrity, "the spectacular representation of a living human being," is a commodity, a shallow spectacle of role and lifestyle. While appearing to have "made it," to have realized the promise of power or wealth or happiness, the celebrity—whether a president or superstar—in fact renounces autonomous qualities in order to identify with the general law of obedience to the spectacular.

Is there any way out of the society of the spectacle, when even rebellion is conducted within its terrain, when dissatisfaction itself becomes a commodity, and revolution is just another song or t-shirt image to be sold and bought? That is the big question, to be discussed in detail later. As Debord put it, "A critique seeking to go beyond the spectacle must *know how to wait.*"

For now, we can look at the components of the spectacular society. What are their impacts on people and on the ecosphere? What do they cost us in psychological, social, economic, and ecological terms? And what could we gain if we were able to "take the red pill" and exit this matrix of illusion?

SPECTACULAR IMPACTS

Billions of us watch sporting events—among the biggest spectacles of all—every year. Over 2 million Canadians, for example, go to a CFL football game each summer, paying a substantial $70 per ticket on average. Of course, these numbers are dwarfed by television viewership. Although some six million viewers watched the 2010 Saskatchewan-Montreal Grey Cup game on TV, football is not the main attraction for Canadians. Our most loved sport is hockey. It follows that the most watched television broadcast in Canadian history was the gold medal game of the men's ice hockey tournament at the 2010 Winter Olympics, where "Canada" beat the "United States;" 16.6 million Canadians watched the entire game, one-half the country's population and two million more than participated in the 2011 federal election.

The seriousness with which the true fan approaches sports is reminiscent of religious fanaticism. The word fan is an abbreviation of fanatic, i.e. a person filled with excessive and often misguided enthusiasm for something. Fanatic comes from the Latin *fanam,* meaning temple, which brings us to the fan's pseudo-religious zeal. Born as fora for ritualized aggression, with religious overtones, sports continue to fill this role; not infrequently, however, the vicarious aggression spills over into off-field violence. For the final game of the 2011 Stanley Cup series between the Vancouver Canucks and the Boston Bruins, for example, 155,000 fans crowded into Vancouver's downtown area to watch the spectacle on giant screens. Riots broke out, resulting in hundreds of arrests and injuries and millions of dollars in damage. In Canada, alcohol-fuelled hockey riots go back to the Richard Riots of 1955, when following the suspension of Montreal *Canadiens* superstar Maurice Richard angry fans wreaked havoc in Montreal.

Canadian rioters are comparatively mild mannered. In Britain, where hooliganism dates back to the 19th century, fighting is part and parcel of the football scene. Well-organized hooligan gangs, called *firms*, are formed for the specific purpose of antagonizing and physically attacking supporters of other clubs. But even the Brits are relatively mild by world standards. The worst riot in association football history occurred in Peru on May 24, 1964. When the fans rioted, police padlocked the stadium gates and fired tear gas into the crowd. Over 300 died, many from asphyxia. In Port Said, Egypt, on February 1, 2012, 79 were killed as Al-Masry Club fans using knives, swords, clubs, stones, bottles, and fireworks attacked Al-Ahly S.C. players. Still, today's fanatics are mild compared to those of antiquity: In the Nika riots of 532 AD, fans of rival chariot teams killed 30,000 and burned most of Constantinople. Fandom is not new but now it is ubiquitous.

Fans often invest more emotion in games than in their lived reality—plus a great deal of disposable income. Passions run high as millions throng to the arenas to take part in a particularly affecting experiences of the spectacular.[62] Every summer and fall, 17.5 million Americans attend NFL football games—at an average cost per ticket of $70, while another 37.5 million attend US college football, paying an average of $45 per game. Baseball attendance is much higher. In 2009, 100 million people attended major league baseball in the United States, Japan, and Canada. Meanwhile, 21.5 million attended pro basketball in the US and Canada, a similar number attended pro hockey, and more than 27 million attended college men's basketball.

These figures are dwarfed by soccer attendance. In 2010, 106.5 million people watched the Superbowl in the US, but 1.75 billion watched the World Cup final from South Africa. It was broadcast in more than 200 countries and regions around the world, included over 41,000 hours of programming and reached an estimated 28.8 billion aggregated television viewers.[63]

These are just the better-known spectator sports around the world: some of the most popular are indigenous to specific countries. Cricket is often considered the second most popular sport after soccer, mainly because of its immense support in India and Pakistan. Australia hosted the single most popular sporting event ever, judged by on-site attendance: The Australian-rules football championship in 2010 drew a crowd of 93,853 people.[64]

And today, fantasy sports, which are emerging as another billion-dollar industry, have taken illusion to a new level. In the US, more that 35 million people participate in on-line leagues made up of fantasy teams they create.[65]

Like other spectacles, sports amuse the masses and flood the coffers of the rich. The incentive for businesses such as football clubs to win and build a fan base is immense. One analyst estimates professional football revenues in the United States at $10 billion a year while world soccer rakes in $20 billion. In all, sports bring in something like US$63 billion in revenues worldwide annually, though this is likely a conservative estimate were amateur sports that charge admissions taken into account.

WHY SPORTS?

Few would question the value of participating in sports, especially for children and youth. Athletics provide healthy exercise, a sense of accomplishment, belonging, and, if you like sports and are reasonable good at them, fun. For adults, participation helps maintain a healthy body and mind. What, however, is the value of spectator sports, especially professional sports that are de-linked from one's neighbourhood or community? Such sports are mere commodities, mere spectacle that, arguably, distract us from a more profound experience of life.

Why then are they so popular? What is it that they represent that so many of us willingly dish out major cash, give them so much time, and invest them with such significance?

Most sports are variations on tag, a game used by animals to practice behaviours such as hunting, fighting, or escaping, all essential for survival. The fight or flight syndrome that guaranteed our survival in earlier stages of social development is thought to be behind our interest in sports. Sports tap into to our instincts, even as spectators.

In play, our instinctive fears as prey are experienced as pleasant: the preferred position in the game is offense, i.e. players generally prefer being the one chased. The hormonal reaction we get from responding to a threat or crisis makes us like to be scared. When threatened, we have increased strength, power, heightened senses, and intuition. We appear to be hard-wired to enjoy this feeling, which is older than we are as a species. Is it any wonder people like to experience this sensation, but within the comfort, security, and complete resolution of a football game?

On the other hand, hunter instincts come out in the defense position, where one is on the attack. Communal aspects of team sports have antecedents in hunting packs, offering participants and voyeurs—who identify with their team—camaraderie.

Critics may see watching others engaged ritualistically in an animalistic struggle for survival as a rather low-grade activity, but for billions of fans the passion for sports is intoxicating (the more so when it is involves consumption of intoxicants.) Teams like the Saskatchewan Roughriders and thousands of others become emblematic of the aspirations of a community, emblematic of some high ideal that cannot possibly find its full expression in this medium.

We sit and watch and drink beer and eat snack foods while professional athletes exercise for us. Perhaps there is nothing particularly wrong with being entertained by excellent athletic skills—although athletes often do great damage to themselves, literally sacrificing their lives for money and adulation—but to devote so much of our time to something essentially frivolous distracts us from life's purpose. Why do we focus ourselves on these things and often ignore the great issues of our time, the great opportunities of education and profound culture, and the intellectual, physical, and community activities that help us deepen our understanding of reality and elevate our perceptions and vision of what it means to be human?

A MULTI-TRILLION DOLLAR EXTRAVAGANZA

Spectator sports are, of course, just one facet of a vastly larger entertainment industry. The World Cup may have attracted 1.75 billion viewers, but the funeral of deviant pop star Michael Jackson—thought to be the largest television audience ever—drew an estimated 2.5 to 3 billion, some 40 percent of the world's population.

To what extent do we labour to generate wealth—with all the attendant resource consumption and waste production—merely to transform it into entertainment? And consequently, to what extent are we undermining the future of civilization merely to be amused? How much more amusement can the planet take? Is our obsession with this illusory world of entertainments worth it?

> *We spend almost as much on entertainment—about $3 trillion a year—as on our most basic need, food.*

What follows is an attempt to provide a rough estimate of the cost to society of our various forms of entertainment. The purpose of the exercise is simply to show how much of the economy is devoted to things that, while enjoyable, are unnecessary and often have deleterious effects on social well-being, health, and the ecosphere.

How much of the world's wealth is devoted to entertainment? It all depends how you define it. Using a broad definition that includes vices, economic analyst Elliott Morss[66] estimated annual worldwide revenues from entertainment at $3 trillion, about 4.5 percent of world GDP, close to what is spent worldwide on food. Though Morss's estimates are based on what he admits are "heroic assumptions," they are not far off a report from PricewaterhouseCoopers that puts global entertainment sales at $2 trillion, while excluding some of Morss's categories. A third estimate, from a European

Commission analysis of the global media and entertainment market,[67] including Internet access fees and advertising, TV fees and advertising, radio, recorded music, filmed entertainment, video games, and consumer magazine, newspaper, book, and B2B (business to business) publishing, put revenues at $1.4 trillion in 2009. The market for these sectors was expected to rise to $1.9 trillion by 2015.

Total worldwide sales by entertainment category are presented in the adjacent table, compiled from these sources and using a broad definition of entertainment.

Estimated Annual Global Spending on Entertainment	
Entertainment spending by category	Billions $US (circa 2010)
Condoned Vice	
Prostitution	400
Gambling	110
Pornography	97
Subtotal	**607**
Mass media	
TV subscriptions and license fees	200
Wired & mobile Internet access	188
Consumer magazines	43
Newspapers	72
Radio	14
Consumer books	50
Filmed entertainment	84
Recorded Music	23
Computer Games	54
Subtotal	**728**
Events	
Live performances	35
Sports	63
Subtotal	**98**
Dining & Travel	
Eating out	183
Tourism	2000
Subtotal	**2183**
Total	**$ 3,616**

The content of these categories is elaborated below.

Condoned Vice The broad definition of entertainment includes the commercialization of vices that while frowned upon in most societies are more or less condoned—and increasingly celebrated.

All three subcategories—gambling, prostitution, and pornography—capture a great deal of wealth by substituting thrill-seeking for authentic relationships.

At best, prostitution and pornography—prime examples of Debords' notion of the devolution of human relationships into mere representation—stand in for the genuine, sustained love that builds social unity. More often than not they involve the exploitation—often brutally—of women, as well as children and men. As a business, gambling necessarily means that almost all participants lose almost all the time, yet gamblers report that losing can be as thrilling—and addictive—as winning.

While the word "vice" implies a moral judgement, it is not my intention in presenting this information to judge others or to argue the *imposition* of a particular moral code. The point is that investing an inordinate amount of time, money, and resources in these activities has substantial social-ecological impacts. It can be argued that the focus placed on these addictive activities diverts attention from the purposes of life: to come to a full understanding of reality, to develop human potential, and to carry forward an ever-advancing civilization. Obviously, each of the activities is highly complex with multiple causes that cannot be trivialized. Freeing people from their grip is part of a transformation to a healthier society based on authentic relationships.

- **Prostitution** – Paid sexual services is one of the largest entertainment industries in the world but sales are hard to estimate due to the underground nature of the enterprise. A 1994 ILO study estimated revenues of more than $30 billion in Indonesia, Malaysia, Philippines, and Thailand, with income in Thailand alone at $22-24 billion at that time. Morss speculates that if prostitution were practised at the same rate per capita in the rest of the world, 1994 revenues would have been over $360 billion. And they most certainly have grown since 1994. Some other statistics demonstrate the size of this industry: in Japan, earnings from prostitution in 1998 were estimated at $3.1 billion. German prostitution revenues have been estimated at €8.4 billion; Spain is thought to have 500,000 prostitutes earning $54 billion annually; Iran is estimated to have 300,000 prostitutes. Putting all the available information together, Morss conservatively estimates 2009 revenues at $400 billion.

- **Pornography** - "My reaction to porno films is as follows," Erica Jong once quipped: "After the first ten minutes, I want to go home and screw. After the first twenty minutes, I never want to screw again as long as I live." Apparently, there are a lot of people who don't agree with Jong, evidenced by estimates that worldwide pornography revenues are approaching

$100 billion. In 2005, US producers alone released 13,500 new pornographic films. While the sale and rental of videos is still the top revenue generator, it will soon be eclipsed by online sales and pay-per-view. It has been estimated that 12 percent of all web sites are pornographic, while pay-per-view puts major hotel chains among the largest distributors of pornography.

- **Gambling** - According to a 2007 PricewaterhouseCoopers report, worldwide gambling revenue was expected to climb from $101.6 billion in 2006 to $144 billion by 2011. Morss estimated gambling revenues of $110 billion in 2009. Strangely, gambling is now promoted as an economic development model, but of course it produces nothing except revenues for those inside the industry at the expense of the gullible.

Entertainment Media This category is dominated by pop culture, but includes things like news and book publishing. Here the categories cross over considerably; film for example consumes a lot of TV time.

- **Television** – TV still reigns as the biggest moneymaker, with subscription and license fees earning $200 billion.

- **Film** – Approximately 3000 feature films are produced annually. Box office revenues in 2008 were $26.8 billion. Digital revenues from media and entertainment now exceed revenues from movie theatres and home video, leading to overall sales of $180 billion, but much of this revenue overlaps with TV and the Internet. This is taken into account in the estimates below.

- **Music** - According to the Recording Industry Association of America, US sales of music totalled $7.1 billion in 2008. That included physical sales of $5.5 billion and digital sales of $1.6 billion. The $23 billion global sales figure is from European Commission estimates.

- **Computer Games** - Computer games are one of the fastest growing amusements. Revenues from software sales were estimated at $34.6 billion in 2009 and hardware at $18.9 billion.

- **Internet Access** - 2.5 billion people use the Internet.[68] The cost of wired and mobile Internet access in 2012 was $250 billion. Let us assume that three quarters of this is entertainment related, i.e. social media use, chatting and texting, games, videos, news, and shopping.

- **News, Magazines, Books, and Radio** – The European Commission study puts total revenues at $179 billion. Are these media really entertainment? This is more and more the case, as media reporting becomes more a form of entertaining than informing audiences.

Events Commercial sporting events, with revenues estimated at $63 billion, have been discussed previously. In the live performance category, Morss includes music, theatre, opera, dance, and celebrity performances. While sales information is difficult to obtain, the estimate of revenues is $35 billion.

Dining and Tourism Much of eating out and travel is essentially entertainment.
- **Eating Out** - A recent estimate of global restaurant revenues was $550 billion. Morss puts the entertainment component of eating out at 50 percent of restaurant revenues and deducts another third for eating out done for convenience or necessity, such as getting lunch at work, resulting in an estimate of $183 billion for the entertainment value of restaurant eating.

- **Tourism** - The World Travel and Tourism Council's put world travel and tourism revenues in excess of $7 trillion in 2007, with revenues expected to rise above $13 trillion by 2017. Morss excludes travel, eating, and accommodation costs in his estimate of the entertainment value of tourism, reasoning that flying and accommodations are not entertainment. He puts the value of scenic and sightseeing transportation services and tourism-related entertainment at $25 billion. Nevertheless, the end-use value of tourism is impossible without getting to your destination and looking after yourself while you are there. Thus, it is quite reasonable to include at least part of transportation, accommodation, and dining in the costs of tourism. For this estimate, the entertainment value of tourism is set conservatively at $2 trillion.

If we combine the sources listed above, removing duplication wherever possible, we end up with a total of about $3.6 trillion, likely a conservative estimate.

Persona Adjustments "Everything once directly lived has receded into representation," said Guy Debord. Adopting a persona, an identity worn to represent oneself to others, or even to oneself, is an important element of the spectacle. While not suggesting that altering our appearance is entirely negative, such practices become negative to the extent that they distract us from authentic relationships. Altering personas through dress, hairstyles, makeup, scents, drugs, or even surgery—or watching other do this—is done largely to entertain oneself or others. Much of this behaviour is essentially frivolous. Let's look at the costs.

- **Fashion and luxury goods** - "Fashion," as Shaw put it, "is nothing but an induced epidemic." With total revenues of $3 trillion in 2011, the global textiles and apparel market,[69] including clothing, footwear, and luxury goods like jewelry, watches, and leather goods, including handbags, wallets, and luggage for all our travel needs, is a very large epidemic indeed. The performance of this market is forecast to accelerate, driving it to a value of $3.75 trillion by the end of 2016.

  While the clothing industry obviously meets legitimate human needs, it also creates an artificial demand for unnecessary and frivolous products. Let us be conservative and assume that two thirds of the demand is legitimate and one third frivolous, putting the frivolous market at $1 trillion.

- **Cosmetics, perfumes, and hair** - The global make-up industry generated close to $35 billion in 2010, according to the 2011 report, *Global Make-Up*.[70] Face cosmetics represented the leading market segment, with over $12 billion in sales revenue in 2010 accounting for more than 35 percent of overall market value. Market growth is expected to remain about the same until 2015, when the market is expected to reach $42 billion. Meanwhile, the worldwide facial care industry recorded almost 5 percent expansion in 2010 to exceed $50 billion.

  The world hair care products industry generated revenue of almost $49 billion in 2010.[71] The market is expected to reach almost $58 billion in 2015, an 18 percent expansion over five-years.

  Beauty salon revenue growth[72] is expected to grow to $49.3 billion by 2017, driven by an expected increase in per capita disposable income. Higher disposable incomes could also lead hair salon customers to spend more on higher-value services like manicures, pedicures, facials, hair modification treatments, and massages. The US beauty salon industry alone encompasses almost 750,000 spas, beauty salons, and barbershops.

World fragrance and perfume industry sales are around $27.5 billion and are expected to exceed $36 billion in 2017.[73] Market growth is fuelled by demand from emerging markets and consumer lifestyle trends granting an increasingly central place to grooming.

- **Cosmetic procedures** - More and more people are resorting to surgery to alter their persona. The International Society of Aesthetic Plastic Surgery[74] reports that liposuction represents 18.8 percent of all cosmetic surgical procedures, followed by breast augmentation at 17 percent, blepharoplasty (upper or lower eyelid lift) at 13.5 percent, rhinoplasty (nose reshaping) at 9.4 percent, and abdominoplasty (tummy tucks) at 7.3 percent.

Reflecting both advances in cosmetic surgery innovation and the desirability of less expensive treatments, the number of non-surgical procedures performed by plastic surgeons has surpassed surgical procedures. The top five non-surgical procedures are: toxin or neuromodulator injections, such as Botox and Dysport (32.7 percent), hyaluronic acid injections (20.1 percent), laser hair removal (13.1 percent), autologous fat injections (taking a patient's fat from one location and transferring it to another location) (5.9 percent), and IP laser treatment (4.4 percent).

The combined worldwide total of surgical and non-surgical procedures performed by certified plastic surgeons annually is 17.3 million. This figure does not take into account surgical and non-surgical procedures performed by non-surgeons. The cost of these procedures in the US alone is $10.7 billion, 21 percent of worldwide procedures. Assuming world costs average one half those in the US, that would put the world total to approximately $30 billion.

Of course, there is nothing wrong with being well dressed and attractive and one could debate at length about the value of such spending or how much of it is legitimate. The point here is that elaborate adjustment to persona are unnecessary and excessive in the context of an 11 billion world.

Estimated Annual Global Spending on Persona Adjustments (billions US$)	
Fashion	1000
Cosmetic surgery	30
Makeup	35
Facial care	50
Hair products	50
Hair dressing	45
Fragrance	30
Total	**$1240**

ADDICTION'S CASCADING IMPACTS

In Aldous Huxley's Brave New World—a fictional depiction of a society of spectacle—the populace is numbed with the ideal pleasure drug *soma* handed out freely by government. In our society, alcohol, tobacco, and various recreational and prescription drugs seem to fit soma's purpose, though unlike that perfect drug all have negative side effects, from hangovers and addiction to disease and dangerous behaviours. They also intensify the human ecological footprint.

Elliott Morss classes a number of drugs as forms of entertainment, including alcohol and recreational drugs, while excluding others like heroin and tobacco. Like alcohol, however, all such substances are used in the society of the spectacle as coping mechanisms; self-medication makes immersion in the spectacle bearable for hundreds of millions of people. As Shaw put it, "Alcohol is the anaesthesia by which we endure the operation of life."

The amounts currently spent on these anaesthetics are presented in the table below. A discussion of social and ecological impacts follows.

- **Alcohol** - Morss includes alcohol as a form of entertainment, which makes sense given its intimate association with parties, clubbing, sporting, and musical events. For 2008, industry groups estimated global distilled spirits sales at $299 billion, global beer sales at $614 billion, and wine sales at $250 billion, a total of $1.16 trillion.

- **Recreational drugs** - Like booze, recreational drugs like cannabis, cocaine, and Ecstasy are a form of entertainment and also associated with participation in other forms of entertainment. According to the UN Office on Drugs and Crime *2008 Annual Report*,[75] 3.9 percent of the world's population between 15-64 (166 million people) use cannabis. Worldwide, 41,000 tonnes of cannabis are produced annually. At $10/gram, that generates $410 billion. According to the same report, 16 million people use cocaine. Some 994 metric tons of cocaine valued at $122 billion were produced in Latin America, with most of the product probably sold in the US market. The UN report estimated global Ecstasy consumption to be 131 metric tons valued at $13.8 billion.

- **Prescription drugs** - Global sales of the legal antidepressants, stimulants, and anti-anxiety and anti-psychotic drugs that help people cope with stressful lives have reached more than $76 billion a year.

- **Other drugs** – These include so-called hard drugs, such as opium, heroin, and amphetamines. Tracking spending is difficult due to the illicit nature of the industry, but the UNODC estimates sales at $384 billion.

- **Tobacco** – Tobacco is a highly addictive stimulant that triggers the release of dopamine, resulting in a mild high. The main benefit derived from its use is alleviating unpleasant withdrawal symptoms caused by being addicted to it. Revenues from global tobacco sales are estimated to be close to $500 billion, generating combined profits for the six largest firms of $35.1 billion.[76] China accounts for about 40 percent of the global market for tobacco.

COMPILING THE SOCIAL COSTS

Direct expenditure is but one cost associated with alcohol, drugs, and tobacco. The use and abuse of the substances that buttress the society of the spectacle triggers a cascade of negative social, health, and economic impacts that waste trillions of dollars, with each dollar intensifying the human ecological footprint.

Estimated Direct Global Spending on Alcohol, Drugs, and Tobacco (billions of US$)	
Alcohol	**1,163**
Beer	614
Spirits	299
Wine	250
Entertainment Drugs	**546**
Cannabis	410
Cocaine	122
Ecstasy	14
Prescription drugs (antidepressants, etc.)	**76**
Other drugs (heroin, opium, etc.)	**384**
Tobacco	**500**
Total	**2,669**

Alcohol If alcohol—a causal factor in 60 types of diseases and injuries and a component cause in 200 others—were introduced today as a new product for human consumption it would be rejected on health impacts alone. Yet its use as a sop and a social lubricant is so ingrained in most cultures it would seem impossible to get rid of it, regardless of impacts.

With alcohol being "the cause of and solution to all of life's problems"—as Homer Simpson so aptly put it—its proponents and opponents are perpetually at odds. The first ruler known to prohibit alcohol was Yu the Great, the first ruler of China's Xia Dynasty (circa 2000 BCE), but his policy was overturned when his son assumed the throne. In the first half of the 20th century, religious moralists, the emerging women's movement, and others concerned about alcohol's deleterious influence helped usher in prohibition for considerable periods of time in a number of places, including the United States, Canada, the Nordic countries, Russia, and Hungary. However, the legal approach to prohibition consistently failed given criminalization of the alcohol trade actually worsened some social impacts.

However, prohibition has been fairly successful in the Islamic world, where alcohol is forbidden for religious reasons. Today, drinking is largely illegal in nine countries and parts of India with a combined population of 450 million, with rates of abstention estimated at up to 95 percent. The WHO[77] reports substantially lower prevalence of alcohol use disorders in Islamic nations, such as Iran (in 0.5 percent of the population), compared to neighbouring states where alcohol is accepted, such as Russia (16.3 percent). This demonstrates that it *is* possible to adopt value systems that result in reduced alcohol consumption.

Alcohol use and abuse results in a range of physical, mental, and societal problems:

- It is the world's third largest risk factor for disease and disability. In middle-income countries, it is the greatest risk.

- Alcohol ranks eighth among global risk factors for death. Booze results in approximately 2.5 million deaths each year, almost 4 percent of all deaths. Globally, 6.2 percent of all male deaths are attributable to alcohol.

- Alcohol-related disorders affect as much as 16 percent of the population in some countries, such as Russia, where use is very high.

- In the US, 25-40 percent of all patients in general hospital beds (i.e. not in maternity or intensive care) are being treated for complications of alcohol-related problems.

- The incidence of accidental death and injury is closely linked to alcohol use. In 2010 in the US, over 10,000 people were killed in alcohol-impaired driving accidents, accounting for nearly one-third of all traffic-related deaths.

- Alcohol is associated with serious social issues, such as child neglect and abuse. Recent data suggest that one child in every four in the US is exposed to alcohol abuse or dependence in the family.

- One of the clearest demonstrations of how alcohol use negatively impacts the family is the widely documented association between alcohol use and family violence. Other family issues likely to co-occur with alcohol problems include marital conflict, infidelity, jealousy, economic insecurity, divorce, and fetal alcohol effect.

- Alcohol problems affect the poor disproportionately. The lower the economic development of a country or region, the higher the alcohol-attributable mortality and burden of disease and injury per litre of alcohol consumed.

Total US social costs for health care, law enforcement, and other direct and indirect costs such as productivity loss related to alcohol have been estimated at $234.8 billion dollars a year.[78] Another study put the annual social cost of alcohol in Europe between €154 and €764 billion.[79] Non-drinkers—half the population or more in most countries—unfairly bear societal costs. The table below outlines some of the costs attributed to alcohol use in selected high- and middle-income countries in 2007.[80]

The average total social costs of alcohol are just over 2 percent of GDP for the high- and middle-income countries. If applied globally, the social costs of alcohol would be $1.4 trillion, assuming global GDP at $70 trillion.

Despite these problems and the costs to society, rates of alcohol use remain a low priority in public policy, including health policy, with many lesser risks given more attention.

Overview of economic costs attributable to alcohol in selected high-income and middle-income countries, 2007							
	High-income countries				Middle-income countries		
	Canada	France	Scotland	U.S.	Weighted Average	Korea	Thailand	Weighted average
Year	2002	1997	2001-02	1998	-	2000	2006	-
Population in study year (millions)	31.9	58.6	5.1	280.6	-	47.5	64.5	-
GDP (PPP) in study year (millions $US)	929 912	1 301 087	133 170	8 587 884	6 689 552	760 549	604 575	670 666
Direct healthcare costs	3045	3592	162	29 855	23 090	1516	344	841
Direct legal	2830	72	454	8049	6262	-	15	9
Other direct costs	966	7619	145	26	20 848	5459	49	2341
Indirect costs	6564	11 223	1052	170 707	129 659	17 938	7496	11 921
Total costs of alcohol	13 406	22 506	1813	234 854	179 859	24 914	7903	15 111
Costs per head (US$ PPP)	420	384	358	837	725	524	122	293
Total costs (%GDP PPP)	1.4	1.7	1.4	2.7	2.5	3.3	1.3	2.1

Source: Rehm et al. 2009

Illicit Drugs Though less prevalent than alcohol consumption, 5 percent of the world's adult population is thought to use illicit drug at least occasionally. Problem drug users number about 0.6 percent of the world adult population. Illicit drug use undermines economic and social development and contributes to crime, instability, insecurity and the spread of HIV and hepatitis.[81]

- There were between 99,000 and 253,000 deaths globally in 2010 as a result of illicit drug use, with drug-related deaths accounting for between 0.5 and 1.3 percent of all-cause mortality among those aged 15-64.

- Heroin, cocaine, and other drugs kill around 0.2 million people each year.

- One of the key impacts of illicit drug use is negative health consequences, which place a heavy financial burden on society. Expressed in monetary terms, some US$200 billion-250 billion (0.3-0.4 percent of global GDP) would be needed if adequate levels of drug treatment were available worldwide. The actual amount spent on treatment for drug abuse is far lower and fewer than one in five persons who needs treatment actually receives it.

- The impact of illicit drug use on a society's productivity, in monetary terms, seems to be even larger than the health costs. A US study suggested that productivity losses were equivalent to 0.9 percent of GDP, and studies in several other countries showed losses equivalent to 0.3-0.4 percent of GDP. A 2011 study estimated drug-related productivity losses in the US at $120 billion (0.9 percent of GDP) in 2007. Reduced labour participation and incarcerations were the main causes.

- Illicit drug use alone accounted for $181 billion in health care, productivity loss, crime, incarceration, and drug enforcement costs in the US.[82]

- Drugs other than alcohol are involved in about 18 percent of motor vehicle driver deaths. Drugs are often used in combination with alcohol.

- In 2009 alone, some 37,500 Americans succumbed to drug overdoses, many fuelled by prescription drug abuse or a combination of mixing medications, alcohol, or recreational drugs, more than from car accidents.

- In Canada, the social costs of drugs were 57 percent of alcohol-related social costs. If this ratio holds, global social costs of drugs would be approximately $800 billion.

Alcohol, Drugs, and Crime Alcohol and illicit drugs are significant factors in crime. Beyond hard costs associated with the criminal justice system, the social impact of alcohol and drug related crime is incalculable.

The UNODC estimates that in 2009 drugs represented about one fifth of global criminal proceeds. In the United Kingdom, for example, the costs associated with drug-related crime (fraud, burglary, robbery, and shoplifting) were equivalent to 1.6 percent of GDP, or 90 percent of all the economic and social costs related to drug abuse. While drug-related sales generate the highest proceeds in developed countries, those proceeds typically range from only 0.3 to 0.7 percent of GDP. Illicit drug markets are much more prominent in some countries, however. UNODC estimates suggest that the value of Afghan opiate-related sales was equivalent to slightly more than 60 percent of the country's

GDP in 2004. While this proportion decreased to 16 percent in 2011, this figure is still very significant.

Anecdotal reports from police and criminal lawyers—that almost every crime involves the use of alcohol and/or drugs—are borne out by statistics.

- In the US in 2006, for example, alcohol and other drugs were involved in 78 percent of violent crimes, 83 percent of property crimes, and 77 percent of public order, immigration, or weapon offences, and probation or parole violations, according to the National Center on Addiction and Substance Abuse at Columbia University.[83]

- About 4 percent of homicides were drug related.

- 32 percent of state and 26 percent of federal prisoners reported they had committed their current offence while under the influence of drugs.

- Nearly 4 in 10 violent victimizations involve alcohol; about 4 in 10 fatal motor vehicle accidents are alcohol-involved; and about 4 in 10 offenders, regardless of whether they are on probation, in local jail, or in state prison, self-report that they were using alcohol at the time of the offence.

Estimates based on a global survey by the United Nations put the cost of worldwide policing services at $223 billion in 1997[84] and $268 billion in 2005.[85] Factoring in inflation, policing costs today would be at least $300 billion. In Canada, policing related to drugs and alcohol was estimated at 40 percent of total policing costs. Using this ratio, the cost of drug and alcohol related policing costs is estimated at $120 billion. Spending on courts and prosecutions was $75 billion in 1997[86], so conservatively at least $100 billion today; at 40 percent of total costs, drug and alcohol-related costs would be $40 billion.

More than 10.1 million people are held in penal institutions throughout the world, as pre-trial detainees and remand prisoners or as sentenced prisoners. Almost half of these are in three countries: the United States (2.29 million), including 330,000 drug offenders; Russia (0.81 million); or China (1.65 million), plus more than 650,000 in Chinese detention centres. This brings the world total to more than 10.75 million.

As previously stated, drugs and alcohol are involved in most categories of crime. In the US, for example, more than half of federal inmates are in prison on drug-related convictions. In 2009 alone, 1.66 million Americans were arrested on drug charges and four of five of those arrests were for possession.

US federal and state governments spend about $74 billion a year on corrections.[87, 88] Assuming the global average for the costs of incarceration is 20 percent of the US rate, the total cost of incarceration for the world would be $107 billion. Conservatively, if 40 percent of incarcerations were drug and alcohol related, the cost would be around $43 billion.

This puts the estimate of drug- and alcohol-related costs in the criminal justice area at approximately $200 billion. These totals are included in the social costs for alcohol and drugs. This is likely conservative when we consider an additional area of spending: the large and often futile effort that goes into attempts to control the international drug trade. Over the past four decades, for example, the US has spent more than $1 trillion fighting a "war on drugs" that is demonstrably futile.[89]

Tobacco "The only consumer product proven to kill up to half its regular users," tobacco is responsible for about 6 million deaths worldwide every year.[90] Tobacco-related deaths have tripled in the last decade and now account for more than 15 percent of male deaths and 7 percent of female deaths.

Almost 80 percent of those who die from tobacco-related illnesses are from low- and middle-income countries, where cigarettes have become an average of 21.7 percent cheaper over the past decade. Tobacco is the number one killer in China, where smoking is said to cause 1.2 million deaths annually. It is also blamed for more than a third of male deaths in Kazakhstan and in Turkey, other major smoking nations.

Furthermore, more than 60 percent of all deaths are caused by non-communicable diseases (NCDs), for which tobacco use is one of the four greatest risk factors. Tobacco use is responsible for hundreds of billions of dollars each year in health-related costs.

Smoking also exacerbates poverty, with 10 percent or more of income going to tobacco in some low-income countries. Tobacco users who die prematurely deprive their families of income, raise the cost of health care, and hinder economic development. Tobacco also contributes to world hunger by diverting prime land from food production. Tobacco growing occupies 3.8 million hectares of farmland, enough to produce food for 36 million, sufficient for example to feed everyone in Algeria.

While the tobacco industry employs many people, it is an example of wasted labour, capital, and resources. It also reduces economic productivity due to illness.

A number of countries list health-related costs of smoking at more than 1 percent of GDP, including France, Poland, Indonesia, Australia, Philippines, Nepal, Bangladesh, Hungary, and Guatemala. In the US, cigarette smoking costs more than $193 billion (i.e. $97 billion in lost productivity plus $96 billion in health care expenditures). Japan lists its tobacco-related costs at an incredible $265 billion.

Tobacco is also a factor in accidental death. In 2000, fire caused by tobacco smoking caused 10 percent of all fire deaths, 300,000 deaths in all, and cost US$27 billion in damages.

A 2006 study by the Canadian Centre on Substance Abuse compiled the social costs of tobacco, alcohol, and illegal drugs in Canada circa 2002. The Canadian estimate put the total social costs of tobacco at 1.5 percent of GDP in 2002, or $16.9 billion. This percentage is not far off estimates for the US (with 9 times the Canadian population), where total annual social cost for smoking were estimated at $137 billion in 1999, 1.2% of GDP.[91]

If this rate held globally, the cost of tobacco to the world economy would exceed $1 trillion.

Another way to estimate costs is through health care spending. The Tobacco Atlas shows the percentage of health costs related to tobacco at a high of 11 percent in Egypt and a low of 0.8 percent in Finland, with a rate of 4.9 percent US and 4.6 percent for China and the UK. If the percentage averaged 4.5 percent worldwide, the cost would be $330 billion. (Total global spending on health care is 10.5 percent of GDP of $70 trillion.) Productivity losses related to tobacco were 2.8 times direct health costs in a study conducted in Canada. Extrapolated globally, this would put productivity losses as high as $1 trillion. The combined global health and productivity costs of tobacco using this approach would be $1.37 trillion. Conservatively, the social costs of tobacco are estimated here at $1 trillion.

COSTING THE SPECTACLE

My purpose in writing this is not to criticize or condemn those who participate in the spectacle or are plagued by its addictions. To the contrary, my point is that it is all but impossible not to. But *we will have to get free of this impediment*: in a full world, we simply can't afford to waste our time and energies on an illusion.

Together, the costs of entertainments, persona adjustments, drugs, and related components of the society of spectacle, all essentially unnecessary, useless, or actively destructive, stand at close to $11 trillion, or 15 percent of global GDP.

Costing The Spectacle	
Activity	Annual Cost (billions US$)
Gambling, prostitution and pornography	607
Mass media	728
Live Shows and Sports Events	98
Dining and travel (entertainment portion)	2183
Persona Adjustments	1165
Subtotal	**4781**
Alcohol	1163
Illegal Drugs	874
Tobacco	550
Tranquilizers, etc.	76
Subtotal	2663
Social costs of alcohol	1400
Social costs of drugs	800
Social costs of tobacco use	1000
Subtotal	**3200**
Total	**10,644**
Percent of Global GDP	**15.2%**

What this table does not include is the ecological costs of producing and consuming all the goods and services that together generate the society of the spectacle.

Assigning costs to ecological deterioration is difficult, and even misses the point by trying to place a monetary value on priceless ecological goods and services. Nevertheless, it can be useful to attempt to translate the value of ecological goods into measurable monetary terms, something most people understand.

In addition to assigning dollar amounts to externalities, impacts are often measured using the ecological footprint metric, which is a more holistic approach.

The following points provide a snapshot of some of the ecological impacts that can be attributed to various categories:

- **Sports** - Cardiff University researchers studied the ecological impacts of a 2004 soccer match held in Cardiff.[92] They converted the energy and resources used on the day of the match into an ecological footprint, the hypothetical area of land required to support the use of those resources. Energy consumed, for example, was converted into the area of forest needed to soak up the carbon dioxide generated in its production, while food consumption was represented as the amount of farmland needed to make it. This method gave the match a footprint of 3051 hectares. More than half the footprint came from transport. The 73,000 fans collectively travelled nearly 42 million km to reach the match. Fewer than half travelled by car, but car users generated 68 percent of the transport footprint. Food was the second-largest contributor, weighing in at 1381 hectares for the 36,500 snacks consumed. The impact of waste disposal was 146 hectares. A University of British Columbia study of another sporting event found similar impacts.

  No one has tried to estimate the global ecological impacts of sport, but extrapolating the Cardiff ecological footprint analysis for a limited range of potential environmental impacts, it would take 9.5 million global hectares to provide the resources and manage the waste of the 227 million on-site spectators at the major sports events listed so far in this section. (The area of biologically productive land and water on Earth is approximately 12 billion hectares.)

- **Beer** – An estimate of the climate impacts of beer consumption put average carbon dioxide emissions at 500g CO_2e per pint.[93] The global average cost of a pint was estimated at $2. Global spending on beer is $614 billion, equal to approximately 300 billion pints. This computes to 150 million tonnes of CO_2e, about 0.5 percent of all emissions, more than the emissions of Vietnam. According to the Stern report,[94] each tonne of CO_2 emitted causes damages worth at least $85, so a total of $12.7 billion.

- **Agricultural impacts** - A substantial amount of agricultural land is devoted to producing alcohol, drugs, and tobacco. A pesticide-intensive crop, tobacco is grown on 4 million hectares worldwide. At least 30 million hectares are devoted to raising crops for alcohol consumption, including grains, grapes, and hops. Illicit drugs—chiefly marihuana (420,000 ha is the mid-range acreage estimate); opium (190,000 ha); and coca (175,000 ha)—total 785,000 hectares worldwide.[95] The combined area (35 million ha) converted to cereal grain could produce food sufficient for some 350 million people.

British researchers reviewed a wide range of data sets to arrive at an estimate of the total costs of ecological impacts for UK agriculture circa 1996.[96] The research considered damages to water, air, climate, soil, biodiversity, and landscape, as well as pesticide, nitrate, microorganism, and disease impacts on human health. The aggregate of the cost of externalities amounts to about $343 per hectare per year. The study put the total value of the annual environmental cost of UK agriculture over a total area of 11.28 million ha at $3.86 billion. Applied to the 35 million ha used to produce alcohol, tobacco, and drugs, the costs would be $12 billion.

- **Marijuana** – Some of the ecological impacts of cannabis production have been studied in Nigeria, where production is booming. In 2012, the Southwest/Niger Delta Forest Project surveyed nine forest reserves to assess populations of the Nigeria-Cameroon chimpanzee, a subspecies that is considered the most threatened of the four subspecies and is listed as endangered on the IUCN Red List. During the survey, researchers had a first hand look at the effects of the marijuana boom. Half of the deforestation occurring in these reserves from 2010 to 2012 appeared to be the result of cannabis cultivation. Concealed within the forest, marijuana growers clear-cut and often burn large patches of land to plant their crop. Because the plants need a full twelve hours of sunlight, the canopy and any competing plants must be removed completely. Habitat is immediately lost and the surrounding forest is weakened by edge effects and increased foraging pressures from displaced wildlife. Additionally, crops often receive treatments of chemical fertilizers, herbicide, and pesticides, which can have deleterious effects on the surrounding ecosystem.[97]

- **Fashion** - The fashion industry has a major environmental footprint.[98] As of February 2012, for example, the China Pollution Map Database had 6,000 records of textile factories violating environmental regulations. The

Chinese textile industry, the largest in the world, creates about 3 billion tons of soot each year, a potent cause of climate change. A single mill in China can use 200 tons of water for each ton of fabric it dyes; many rivers run with the colours of the season as untreated toxic dyes wash off from mills. In 2010, the textile industry ranked third overall in Chinese industry for wastewater discharge amount, at 2.5 billion tons of wastewater per year. Typical of most industries, waste is a major issue. For example, millions of tons of unused fabric at Chinese mills go to waste each year when dyed the wrong colour. Waste is a major issue worldwide: consumers in the United Kingdom, for example, have an estimated $47 billion worth of unworn clothes lingering in their closets.

While no estimates of worldwide impacts of the activities discussed in this chapter are available, these five examples indicate several areas of ecological cost. Each aspect of the great spectacle can have similar impacts in terms of energy consumption, pollution, climate-changing emissions, resource consumption, and waste. These costs are largely externalized and not accounted for in standard economic metrics. Accounting for environmental impacts would show how bankrupt these activities are, not only in terms of the quality of our social experience, but also in terms of a sustaining civilization.

RE-INHABITING OURSELVES

He was among the world's top celebrities; the Jesse Owens Trophy winner as the World's Most Outstanding Athlete; four-time Associated Press Athlete of the Year (with more wins than any other man); four-time US Olympic Committee Athlete of the Year (with more wins than any other person); seven-time winner of the world's most famous race, a gruelling 21 days and 3500 km, an unheard of feat. His celebrity was vastly increased due to the fact that his greatest sporting achievements occurred *after* recovering from testicular cancer that had spread to his brain, almost ending his life—that and his legendary charity work that had raised $500 million for cancer education and research. By 2012, he had accumulated a fortune of $125 million from winnings, speaking fees, and product endorsements. He even had an asteroid named after him.

Then in June 2012, the high-flying cyclist crashed. The United States Anti-Doping Agency reported that Lance Armstrong had been operating "the most sophisticated, professionalized and successful doping program that sport has ever seen." It accused him not only of doping but also pressuring teammates to take unauthorized performance-enhancing drugs and trafficking them. Armstrong was banned from participating in sports sanctioned by the World Anti-Doping Agency. In January 2013, he publicly admitted to doping. By February 2013, when an unnamed Federal agent reported that Armstrong was being investigated for "obstruction, witness tampering, and intimidation," he was among the most reviled celebrities alive.

Why would Armstrong go to such extremes just to win a bike race? "Two things scare me," Armstrong once said, suggesting an answer to the question. "The first is getting hurt. But that's not nearly as scary as the second, which is losing."

Life in the society of the spectacle is portrayed as a competition; the super-stars are the winners, the top of the heap, the symbols of the potential of the human body and spirit. We look on vicariously as the Lance Amstrongs show us just how marvellous we could be if we would just buy the right bike, the right supplements, the right membership in the right gym—or take the right combination of drugs.

Celebrities, the sports stars, pop singers, and movie idols, are the "spectacular representation of a living human being" at the core of the spectacle, said Guy Debord. To realize the spectacle's promise of power or wealth or fame, the celebrity must sell his or her soul, becoming a medium through which the spectacle is expanded. The stars glamourize the high life, the alcohol and drugs, the excessive consumption, the fashion fetishes, the alterations to persona that prop up the spectacular society. In the process, they generate a payload of money for a lot of people, but to stay in the game, they have to keep on top of their game. Often, it takes drugs to keep them there. So along with their souls, they are often called on to sacrifice their body.

In time comes the exposé. Professional sports (or pop culture) is revealed for what it is: a drug-laced competition to rake in the most money. What a sad spectacle to see the transition of Michael Jackson into a 'freak' or, at the time of writing, the downward trajectory of Justin Bieber, another in the parade of teen idols. Yet even the fall of our celebrities—which not infrequently includes their death from drug overdose—and our disillusionment is simply absorbed into the spectacle. News of the idol's devolution from hero to demon cranks up the ratings. The fans gawk for a time, then raise up another star. And sometimes a star can generate more cash dead than alive.

The spectacle is both generator and product of the passions of the world—the admiration for power, the adoration of status, the love of luxuries, the attachment to frivolous pursuits, the glorification of violence, and the obsession with self-gratification. It must be realized that the isolation and despair from which so many suffer are products of this spellbinding environment, which is ruled by a pervasive materialism.

In the presence of the endless, invasive flow of the spectacular it becomes immensely difficult to live one's life *authentically*.

"Our relationship to any given category of existence is *authentic* to the degree that it is based on an accurate perception of the structure of reality," said philosopher William Hatcher.[99] "To interact authentically with reality is thus to interact in such a way that the intrinsic and universal values embedded in reality become known to us." Hatcher's concept of authenticity is a generalization of the notion of validity in science and logic, where "valid" means "in conformity with reality." While science can have a limited view of what is valid, Hatcher argues that authenticity involves the relationship between the totality of reality and the total person, including consciousness, mind, heart, and will.

The society of the spectacle generates an inauthentic perception of the structure of reality. It is an illusion that conceals what is really happening. It sells a false hope of happiness bought with power, status, and fortune, when in reality it reeks of fundamental injustice, gross inequality, festering violence, and a compromised ecosphere.

To live life authentically one has to continuously expand the life of the mind, heart, and soul. Finding space for this is difficult, especially for the young, when it means competing with the 3D Ultramax, surround-sound power of an omnipresent, 11 trillion-dollar spectacle. Waking to the simple, soundless, subjective experience of our inner lives; to direct relationships with our fellow human being; to the synergy of vital communities; or to the ecological reality that sustains us is profoundly challenging in this context.

This is not to say that all entertainments and recreational pastimes are bad and must be eliminated. Rather, that the time devoted and resources mustered toward these choices has become so excessive it puts civilization at risk. And we are about to increase the number of potential spectators by another 50 percent.

Moderation is called for. To make the world work for 11 billion people, the great spectacle must be sacrificed for a higher purpose: that we can carry forward an ever-advancing civilization, a civilization that exists not just for survival and entertainment but to foster universal enlightenment, enlightenment being a full understanding of the structure of reality. The wonder of the cosmos is, after all, the authentic spectacle, worthy of our full attention.

"We are perishing for want of wonder, not for want of wonders," said G.K. Chesterton. What the entertainment industry offers is but a weak facsimile. For all its dazzle, it cannot compare to the simplest, priceless pleasures. To gazing into your lover's eyes. To holding your child. To picking fresh, ripe strawberries. To swimming in a pond. To a moment's insightful meditation. This is the mystery of the sacrifice that will be required to sustain an 11 billion world: giving up the dazzle is no sacrifice at all.

Once again, the contemporary culture that concerns us also contains its own solution. To make the world work for 11 billion people, the creative energies that flow into creating this marvel can be diverted into building an authentic culture dedicated to unifying the human race, eliminating inequity, and restoring the ecosphere. And once again, this opportunity points to the necessity of launching a systematic public educational campaign to equip people to build this new culture, starting at the level of the village and neighbourhood.

CHAPTER 4
USELESSNESS

In December 1979, the Soviet Union invaded Afghanistan, ostensibly to back the communist regime in the country's civil war. At the time, the USSR was the largest federation in the world and one of two superpowers. Its "empire," encompassing half of Europe, all of northern Asia, and 400 million people, was among the largest the world had ever seen. Its wider sphere of influence included significant parts of the Middle East, South Asia, South America, the Caribbean, and Africa. The Afghan invasion was consistent with the Soviets' strategy to continuously expand its influence and further disseminate its ideology.

As expected, the USSR's 80,000 troops rapidly took control of the central government, major urban centres, military bases, and strategic institutions. However, the Soviets were not able to pacify the country despite overwhelming military superiority. Instead, their invasion triggered nationalistic and religious fervour, inflaming the rebellion. The Soviets found themselves drawn into battle against urban uprisings and an array of tribal armies, known as the *mujahedeen*. Despite increasing their force to over 100,000, they were ill prepared to fight a guerrilla war. The mujahedeen retained control over 80 percent of the country.

The Soviet military venture was further eroded by the involvement of various foreign powers, which provided over $1 billion a year in funds and arms to the *mujahedeen*. Direct interventions ranged from those of Arab fighters, including Osama bin Laden, waging *jihad* against the atheistic Soviets invaders, to terrorist activities led by CIA operatives.

With the rise of Mikhail Gorbachev to Soviet leadership in 1985 and a new approach to foreign policy, the Soviets were forced to accept the futility of their endeavour. By February 1989 they were able to complete a withdrawal of forces, nine years after the disastrous invasion often described as "the Soviet Union's Vietnam War" had begun.

It is estimated that more than 600,000 Soviet soldiers served in Afghanistan over the course of the demoralizing campaign. The official death count was 15,000, though unofficial estimates were as high as 50,000. A further 50,000 were injured and 10,000 were permanently disabled. More than 400,000 personnel became seriously ill due to local climatic and sanitary conditions.

Like America's Vietnam vets, the Afghan veterans, or *afgantsy*, returned to a country that deemed their sacrifice a mistake. Most of these soldiers suffered psychological trauma and not a few turned to a life of drugs and violence, with some becoming involved with local criminal gangs.

The war began in the era of broad Soviet influence, but also at a time when that influence was threatened by rapid political change, especially in the Islamic world. Designed to counter gains in American influence and further expand Soviet power in the region, the invasion had the opposite effect.

"A dead-tired man may stumble over a pebble and fall; but his weariness, rather than the pebble, is the cause." Referencing the American writer George Stewart's observation, Anthony Arnold has argued that the war in Afghanistan was the pebble that brought down a weary Soviet Union.[100] The failure in Afghanistan was one clear proof among others that its system was not working. The morale of three key institutions, the Communist Party, the military establishment, and the KGB, was badly damaged by the Soviet's failure to suppress the Afghans. While the war did not in itself create the weakness affecting these institutions, it revealed their deficiencies. A colossal military failure, combined with the Chernobyl nuclear disaster, gradually reduced public confidence in Soviet mythology. In addition to a general loss of confidence in the regime, other insidious effects of the Soviet involvement in Afghanistan included the expanding corruption, drug addiction, and crime radiating out from returning soldiers. The war thus became a catalyst for the internal collapse of the Soviet Union.

All this, as well as the cost of the war to the Soviet side, which has been estimated at $70 billion, had the effect of weakening the Soviet Union internationally. Instead of being perceived as anti-imperialist liberators, the Soviets were now seen as imperialistic oppressors of the worst order. Estimates of Afghan deaths in the war were as high as two million. As many as 10 million fled the country and another two million were displaced internally. In the 1980s, half of all the world's refugees were Afghans; millions were maimed or wounded; much of the country's infrastructure, including its crucial irrigation systems, was destroyed; fields were heavily bombed and as many as 15 million land mines were planted, mostly by the Soviets, crippling agriculture. The prolonged conflict left Afghanistan ranked at 170 out of 174 countries in the UNDP's Human Development Index; rather than liberating the Afghans, the Soviets had left the country one of the poorest in the world.

The impacts of the war were long lasting. It has been argued that it resulted in the destruction of shared Afghan cultural characteristics. The divisive divide-and-rule approach of the Soviets split the country along ethnic lines; with no language, religion, or culture in common, the divisiveness paved the way for the rise of the Taliban. The fact that America's interest in Afghanistan ceased once the Soviets withdrew did not help. After deciding not to assist with reconstruction, they handed over their interests to Saudi Arabia and Pakistan. Pakistan quickly took advantage of this opportunity and forged relations with Afghan warlords, and later the Taliban, to secure trade routes and other interests.

One legacy of the Soviet war, which can be traced to CIA training of the *mujahedeen* in car bombing and assassination and their backing of the Arab Afghans, was the rise of *al-Qaeda* and its international operations, including the attacks of September 11, 2001. This in turn triggered the American-led invasion and another decade of intense conflict that further weakened Afghanistan. The impacts went beyond human suffering. Decades of war also caused ecological destruction. Unregulated logging during the period, for example, reduced forest cover nationwide to just two percent.

In short, the legacy of the war has been destruction, not just of the Afghan nation but also the Soviet Union, which ceased to exist. The repercussions have radiated worldwide and include the indebtedness and subsequent weakening of the United States. Even now civil war continues with no end in sight.

TO THE VICTOR, THE SPOILAGE

The Soviet's Afghan war aptly illustrates a new reality: War has lost its utility. Once war achieved political and economic gains for its victors: *"To the victor, the spoils."* The riches of the great imperial powers were built on booty, territory, slaves, tribute, and trade won through conquest and colonization. Today, due to the changing realities of warfare, the victor is spoiled along with the defeated. Politically, economically, ecologically, and morally, all combatants lose.

Rising populations; the increasing sophistication of weapons of mass destruction; the development of international relations, communications, and commerce; and the emerging concepts of human unity, human rights, and national liberation progressively undermined the utility of conventional warfare throughout the 20th century. Yet we continue to devote trillions of dollars to it every year—more all the time—and more trillions are lost in the destruction of lives and property, the psychological trauma, the waste of resources, the ecological impacts and opportunities lost.

In *The Utility of Force: The Art of War in the Modern World*,[101] British general Sir Rupert Smith makes the case that conventional warfare is largely useless in the face of the real security threats of the 21st century. In fact, he argues this has been the case since the introduction of nuclear weapons at the end of the Second World War. Military thinking, however, is stuck in the 19th and early 20th century vision of "industrial conflict" involving massed armies. But war is "no longer a single massive event of military decision that delivers a conclusive political result," argues Smith. Conflicts today are waged for political advantage and public opinion as much as battlefield victory. The sides are often non-state actors. Conflicts are open ended. In these circumstances, even the vast might of a superpower, though highly destructive, is effectively useless.

In making the "business case" for the futility of modern warfare, Smith—whose military credentials include the command of the largest British armoured force deployed in action since World War II (in the Gulf War)—contends that conventional war has outlived its purpose and can no longer contribute to national interests, as the Soviets discovered in Afghanistan. He goes on to propose that:

> War no longer exists. Confrontation, conflict and combat undoubtedly exist all around the world...and states still have armed forces which they use as a symbol of power. Nonetheless, war as cognitively known to most non-combatants, war as battle in a field between men and machinery, war as a massive deciding event in a dispute in international affairs: such war no longer exists.

Smith points out, for instance, that the last real tank battle, one in which the armoured formation of two forces maneuvered against each other supported by artillery and air strikes, a battle in which tanks in formation were the deciding force, took place during the 1973 Arab-Israeli war. Tanks are still used in conflict, but the extensive use of tanks as industrial war machines that decide the outcome of wars has not occurred for 40 years. Nor is it likely to occur again.

> War as battle in a field between men and machinery, war as a deciding event in international disputes, no longer exists.

Despite their lack of utility, thousands of tanks have been built and purchased since 1973 at a cost to the public of between $1 million and $6 million each.[102] In 1991, when the Cold War ended, NATO had an inventory of 23,000 tanks, the Warsaw Pact 52,000. The world's inventory of tanks may now be as high as 100,000, having cost at least $100 billion and possibly as much as $200 billion. This is a huge commitment of resources for a technology that is no longer practical or effective in achieving military objectives, let alone political ones.

Smith says the introduction of nuclear weapons in 1945 was the beginning of the end of conventional warfare. The nuclear capability, with its logic of mutually assured destruction, made interstate industrial warfare on the scale of the World Wars untenable. Yet war planners continued to adhere to the old paradigm of industrial warfare even though the wars they were fighting, from Algeria to Vietnam, were of a new type. War had shifted from conflicts in which armies with comparable forces and weapons engaged in battlefields to strategic confrontations between a range of combatants, not necessarily armies, often involving improvised weapons.

The old paradigm of interstate industrial war had been replaced, Smith contends, by the new paradigm of "war amongst the people." In this new warfare people in the streets and fields and houses, all the people, anywhere, *are* the battlefield. Military engagements can take place anywhere, in the presence of civilians, against civilians, in defence of civilians. Civilians are the opposing force or the targets and objectives to be won over. And the combatant's own civilian population, perhaps not directly affected by war, as well as the public everywhere and the media, are additional and often critically important players.

Over the past several decades nation states send in their conventionally formulated military forces to do battle in the public battlefield and do not succeed.

Like Afghanistan for the Soviets or Vietnam for the French or Americans, these wars are spectacular failures to achieve the intended result, namely a decisive military victory that would in turn deliver a solution to the original, political problem.

Smith explains that the utility of the war effort is minimal: while the force may be massive and impressive—remember "Shock and Awe"—it does not deliver the goods. In wars like those starting in Afghanistan in 1979 or 2001 or Iraq in 2003, the initial military operation can be a success—remember U.S. President G.W. Bush's "mission accomplished"—yet the strategic problem remains.

Smith notes that force is often applied in a way that its method and purpose are difficult to explain to allies and the public at large.

War has also changed in sequence and timing, says Smith. It used to be a matter of peace-crisis-war-resolution-peace; now there is no predefined sequence, nor is peace necessarily the start or end. Conflicts have become time-less. The Korean War, the first major confrontation in the new era of conflict, may be the ultimate example: ostensibly, it ended in 1953 yet the confrontation remains unresolved to this day—and today a highly unstable North Korean regime wields nuclear weapons, making it more threatening than ever.

The adjacent table showing the loss of lives and the general outcome of selected wars since 1953, illustrates the new reality.

Conflict	Year	Deaths	Result
Korea	1950-53	3 million	Unresolved; 2011 N. Korea threatens to use nuclear weapons
Vietnam	1959-73	3 million	French and later US military defeat and withdrawal; massive ecological damage
Cambodia	1967-75	1.7 million	US incursion leads to regime change followed by genocide
Soviet-Afghanistan	1979-89	1.3 million	Withdrawal without resolution leading to ongoing civil war (and 400,000 additional deaths), a Taliban government, safe haven for al-Qaeda and the breakup of the Soviet Union
Iran-Iraq	1980-88	1 million	No winner, no territorial gains
Sudan	1988-2002	2 million	Ongoing, unresolved conflicts and famines
Somalia	1988-2004	550,000	Ongoing, unresolved conflicts and famines
Kuwait-Iraq	1990-91	85,000	Iraqi regime remained in power; prelude to the second Iraq war of 2003
Balkans	1991-95	260,000	Kosovo question unresolved
Rwanda	1994	900,000	Genocide, reestablishment of Tutsi regime
Congo	1998-2002	3.8 million	Most deaths result from famine and disease brought on by war; unresolved
Afghan war	2001-	40,000	Ongoing civil war and insurgency and resurgent heroin trade
Iraq	2003-	120,000	Ongoing civil war and insurgency

Whether you are morally opposed to war or not, it is difficult to deny this reality: war no longer delivers the goods. Logically, then, the use of war in an attempt to resolve conflicts should be on a decline as nations come to understand the new paradigm. And contrary to the impression conveyed by the daily news, this is exactly what has happened. Wars and other armed conflicts have decreased over the last 20 years. In 1993, as the Cold War came to an end, 53 substantial conflicts were underway. In 2009, that number had dropped to 37 and none were *interstate* conflicts.[103]

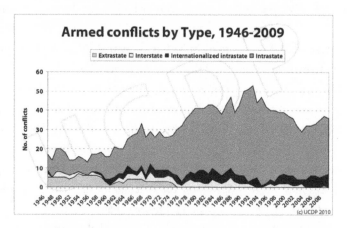

The intensity of these conflicts has also lessened: just 15 were classed as *major* and only five of these were considered to be *wars* as defined by the Department of Peace and Conflict Research at Uppsala University (see graphs). The vast majority of conflicts were *intrastate* with a smaller number of *internationalized intrastate* conflicts, i.e. conflicts that typically involved coalitions of nations versus armed non-state organizations. The ongoing Iraq civil war is an example.

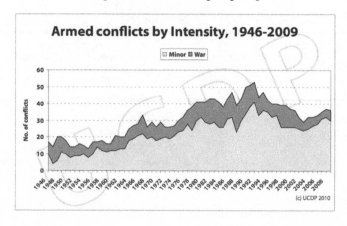

THE LONG PEACE

In *The Better Angels of Our Nature: Why Violence Has Declined*, psychologist Steven Pinker traces a steady historical decline in violence and the emergence, in the early 21st century, of the most peaceful period in human history. Pinker discusses several great processes that resulted in reductions of violence.

The first is the *pacification process*, which has seen a steady reduction of violent deaths. Forensic archeology has been used to estimate the percentage of deaths due to violent trauma in prehistoric societies. By examining skeletal remains, it has been estimated that violent deaths ranged as high as 60 percent of all deaths, with the average over many studies a little over 15 percent. For the 20th century, wrongly considered the most violent ever, with two world wars and several genocides, the violent death rate was 3 percent. In the first decade of the 21st century, it declined to 0.03 percent.

Ethnographic vital statistics allow us to estimate the rate of death by violence among people who have recently lived outside of state control, such as isolated groups of hunter-gatherers. The average is 500 per 100,000 per year. By comparison, violent deaths in 20th century Germany (among the most violent of places) were at 135/100,000; the world average was 60/100,000. By the 21st century, death by violence had dropped to 6.9/100,000 worldwide. For Western Europe, long the world's most violent region, it was now 1.2/100,000. For Germany it was just .84/100,000. The worst region is southern Africa, at 32/100,000, and the worst country is Honduras at 86/100,000, both well below the historical tribal average.

Pinker attributes the decline in violent deaths to the rise and expansion of state power. Think *pax Romana, pax Hispanica, pax Islamica*: a state or empire imposes hegemony over a territory and tries to stamp out tribal raiding and feuding, a nuisance to imperial overlords because it undermines their tax base. Hardly altruistic, but it worked.

Pinker next describes a *civilizing process* that helped reduce violence. Official homicide statistics date back to 1200 CE in some parts of Europe. The average homicide rate for Europe was close to 100/100,000 per year in 1000 CE. It is now 1/100,000. Why the reduction? It results in large part from the consolidation of centralized state power throughout Europe, including judicial systems. Warlording, feuding, and brigandage were replaced by *the King's justice*. Simultaneously, there was a growing infrastructure of commerce, the development of the institutions of money and finance, and of transportation technologies. The result was to shift the incentive structure from *zero-sum plunder* to *positive-sum trade*. In other words, commerce and exchange trumped fighting.

There has also been a *humanitarian revolution*, with a decline of institutionalized violence such as the death penalty and torture. In 18th century England, for example, there were 222 capital offences—from robbing a rabbit warren and consorting with gypsies to strong evidence of malice in a child as young as seven. Today, throughout most of the world, the only crime for which the death penalty is meted out is murder, and even capital punishment for murder is mostly abolished. The United States is the last Western country with a death penalty; even so, there are only 50 executions there per year despite there being 16,500 homicides.

Slavery has also been made illegal everywhere. Saudi Arabia banned it in 1962 and the last country to allow it, Mauritania, abolished it in 1980 (at least in principle).

The main cause for this transformation is literacy, according to Pinker. As Voltaire said, "Those who can make you believe absurdities can make you commit atrocities." Knowledge gradually replaced superstition and ignorance. Commonly held beliefs—Jews poison wells, heretics should go to hell, witches cause crop failures, children are possessed, and Africans are brutish—have generally disappeared.

Cosmopolitanism also built connections between diverse peoples and reduced ignorance. "It is plausible," notes Pinker, "that the reading of history, journalism, and fiction puts people into the habit of inhabiting other people's minds, which could increase empathy and therefore make cruelty less appealing."

Steady downward trends in violence and upward trends in human respect have yielded what Pinker calls *The Long Peace*, the period since the end of the Second World War. The idea that the 20th century was the most violent ever is simply wrong, says Pinker. While the first half *was* violent, the second was progressively less so, resulting in an overall historical low in violence. The 20th century's population explosion was a factor: war deaths may have been high, but as a percentage of total deaths they were down in the 20th century compared to previous periods.

Before 1945, an average of two new European wars occurred per year for 600 years. The percentage of time that the great powers were at war with each other after 1945 declined, eventually to zero. In fact, colonial wars have disappeared altogether and, as previously mentioned, interstate wars have also dwindled to zero while civil wars and internationalized intrastate wars increased until 1990 but have since decreased.

Deaths in war have also seen a long downward trend (with spikes along the way). Genocide statistics are down too; while the 20th century had big genocides, it was also the first period in which genocide was identified as a bad thing rather than something to boast about. Even Hitler tried to hide it.

As a result of the *rights revolution*, there has also been a reduction of systemic violence at smaller scales against vulnerable populations such as racial minorities, women, children, and those identified as homosexuals. In fact, affirmative action has become increasingly common: there are now more countries in the world that officially discriminate *in favour* of disadvantaged minorities than against them.

The higher levels of consciousness resulting from the women's rights movement has resulted in an 80 percent reduction in rape since the early 1970s, when it was put on the agenda as a feminist issue. There has also been a two-thirds decline in domestic violence, spousal abuse, or 'wife beating,' and a 50 percent decline in husband beating. Feminism, notes Pinker, has been very good to men who, like wives, are now much more likely to survive a marriage without getting murdered by their spouse.

There has also been an improvement in children's rights, with a decline in corporal punishment, child abuse, and fighting and abuse in schools. Hate crimes related to sexual orientation are declining, as lesbian, gay, bisexual, and transgendered people gain both legal rights and wider social acceptance.

Even animal rights have improved. Hunting is on the decline and vegetarianism on the rise, with more and more people concerned about the conservation and treatment of animals, as well as plants.

Pinker points out that human nature comprises inclinations toward violence *and* inclinations that counteract them, the latter being what Abraham Lincoln called "the better angels of our nature." Historical circumstances have increasingly favoured these peaceable inclinations: there has been an increase in human capacity for self-control, empathy, moral sense, and reason.

In summary, the main pacifying forces that counteract violent tendencies are:

- The *state monopoly on violence*: Only the state can use violence to enforce justice and, increasingly, state power is checked by democratic forces.

- *Gentle Commerce* is more effective in delivering prosperity than plunder; reciprocal altruism becomes most societies' *modus operandi.*

- The *Expanding Circle*: Our sense of community progressively expands beyond family to clan to tribe to nation to humankind—and even to the ecosphere.

- The *Escalator of Reason*: Literacy, education, and public discourse increase, allowing more people to think more rationally, abstractly, and universally.

If the world has indeed become as peaceful as Pinker suggests, it begs the question: Why do we have a sense that war and violent crime are on the increase? There are several likely reasons. First, violence of any kind seems much more abhorrent the more rare it is inside our circle of experience. Second, we have much more exposure to incidences of violence occurring outside our circle of experience due to media coverage. As actual incidence of violence goes down, our alarm about the incidents that still occur goes up. To put it another way, the brighter the light, the deeper the shadows.

But there is another factor to consider: Are we being manipulated by vested interests to believe that we live in a very violent society to justify investments in defence, policing, and prisons? The illusion that human beings are highly competitive and violent by nature is maintained by news and entertainment media seeking to capture our attention through ever more sensational content, including ever higher levels of violence. In our society of spectacle, violence is the main event. And the military industrial complex and prison industry like it that way.

THE GREAT BURDEN

The gradual decline in war ought logically to result in lower military expenditures, with a massive peace dividend available for human development and restoring the ecosphere. In fact, reductions in defence spending did begin in the late 1980s with the end of the Cold War. Official global military expenditures, which had risen to a peak of US$1.38 trillion in 1984, had dropped 42 percent to $804 billion by 1998.

Given ever-increasing global integration and the steady reduction in hostilities, it is more that strange then that military spending did not continue its downward trajectory. Instead, after 1998, spending started to rise. It again surpassed $1 trillion in 2004 before hitting $1.68 trillion in 2010.[104] To put this figure in perspective, $1.68 trillion is enough to give each of the 2 billion people who earn less than $740 a year, $840 dollars a year, more than enough money to eliminate abject poverty worldwide.

What is more, the defence burden is considerably higher than official spending figures would indicate.

It is well known that one nation, the United States, spends almost as much on defence as all other nations combined. Less well known is that traditional counts of US defence expenditures are misleading. Official metrics show US defence spending at $636 billion in 2009, for example, 43 percent of the world total. But these figures exclude many military-related expenditures. In one attempt to more accurately measure the public cost of the US military, Robert Higgs[105] combed through official budget documents and found military-related spending in excess of $1 trillion, close to 60 percent more than the stated amount. The following table breaks down the amounts.

US National Security Outlays in Fiscal Year 2009 (billions US$)	
Department of Defence	636.5
Department of Energy (nuclear weapons & environmental cleanup)	16.7
Department of State (plus international assistance)	36.3
Department of Veterans Affairs	95.5
Department of Homeland Security	51.7
Department of the Treasury (for Military Retirement Fund)	54.9
National Aeronautics and Space Administration (1/2 of total)	9.6
Net interest attributable to past debt-financed defence outlays	126.3
Total	**1,027.5**

Source: Robert Higgs' classifications and calculations; basic data from U.S. Office of Management and Budget, *Budget of the United States Government, Fiscal Year 2011* and U.S. Bureau of the Census, *Historical Statistics of the United States, Colonial Times to 1970*.

Higgs argues that a substantial portion of the government's interest expense on publicly-held debt represents current costs of defence outlays financed in the past by borrowing.

Finding out how much of the government's net interest payments on the publicly held national debt ought to be attributed to past debt-funded defence spending requires a considerable amount of calculation. I added up all past deficits (minus surpluses) since 1916 (when the debt was nearly zero), prorated according to each year's ratio of narrowly defined national security spending—military, veterans, and international affairs—to total federal spending, expressing everything in dollars of constant purchasing power. This sum is equal to 67.6 percent of the value of the national debt held by the public at the end of 2009. Therefore, I attribute that same percentage of the government's net interest outlays in that year to past debt-financed defence spending. The total amount so attributed comes to $126.3 billion.[106]

This general approach is confirmed in the following graph that shows the inflation-adjusted defence spending of the United States federal government from 1962 to 2014 (forecast).

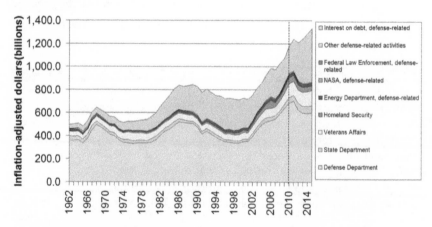

Source: Figures from the FY2010 "President's budget" Historical tables (Table 3.2 – Outlays by Function and Subfunction: 1962–2014), adjusted using CPI inflation data. Graph available at http://commons.wikimedia.org/wiki/File:InflationAdjustedDefenceSpending.PNG

Even Higgs' estimates may be conservative. According to an annual analysis of the Federal Budget by the War Resister's League,[107] when the cost of the Iraq and Afghan wars, veterans benefits, and the interest on the debt created by military spending are added to the current military budget, overall US defence spending equalled $1,372 billion in 2011, 100 percent more than designated in the official military budget and 48 percent of the total US federal budget. The official budget shows military expenditures at approximately 25 percent of total spending.

If Higgs' percentage was applicable to stated world military expenditure of $1.6 trillion in 2010, total world spending could be in excess of $3 trillion (4.2 percent of GWP), excluding hidden costs and costs by non-state combatants. This figure does not, of course, include various human, ecological, and wider economic costs of war, such as opportunity costs. While these costs are difficult to quantify, an attempt can be made to categorize and estimate them.

Broader economic impacts of the military

It is often said that war stimulates the economy, at least for the victors. While this can be the case in the short term, research indicates that longer-term net impacts have been negative. Joshua Goldstein[108] summarized the historical implications of war on economies as follows:

- The number one economic effect of war throughout history is to create inflation, reducing the standard of living. Wartime inflation typically follows a war, as when prices rose 30 percent in just two years in 1919-20 and again in 1946-47. The low inflation associated with current wars is an anomaly; some commentators however contend that, "inflation is baked into the cake" and will ultimately reveal itself.[109]

- Wartime conditions disrupt economic growth and affect financial markets, commodity prices, investment patterns, and unemployment in complex ways that are in whole more negative than positive.

- Although war is a net economic loss, not everyone loses or wins equally. War increased the inequality in a society and inequality has been shown to negatively impact all indicators of well-being.

Goldstein uses the impacts of the so-called War on Terror to illustrate the negative economic consequences of war and war preparedness. The attacks of September 11 and the security response that followed had a disastrous impact on the airline industry, for instance. In the US, Boeing laid off thousands of workers, pushing the company's job losses following 9/11 above thirty-five thousand. Boeing's CEO Phil Condit called it "the worst downturn since airplanes existed."

Job losses at Boeing reflected a broader malaise that settled across the American and ultimately the world economy during the first two years of the War on Terror. In the US, the uncertainties of wartime extended the economic slowdown of 2001 to early 2003. The worst job market in a generation—two million jobs lost in two years—accompanied a succession of corporate bankruptcies, from Enron to WorldCom to United Airlines. The US dollar dropped in value. World oil prices, a key economic variable, whipped up and down with the shifting risks related to war and perceived terror, resulting in instability. Spiralling federal deficits also reduced confidence, while budget shortfalls forced cutbacks in safety-net programs. The increased military spending and the costs of homeland security piled hundreds of billions of dollars onto the federal deficit.

Other countries have also poured billions into the War on Terror. Canada for example has spent $92 billion on post-9/11 security measures.[110] In 2009, partly as a result of increased military/security costs, it racked up its largest-ever deficit after more than 10 straight surplus years, wiping out substantial gains it had recently made in debt reduction.

Since September 2001, dozens of countries, including the US, have faced one economic crisis after another. The US deficit and debt reached dangerous levels, unemployment and bankruptcies rose, the dollar continued to shrink in value while the nation descended into partisan bickering unprecedented since the Civil War. And remember the US is the nominal *victor* in the so-called anti-terror wars in Afghanistan and Iraq. The economic damage to Iraq and Afghanistan themselves is incalculable.

Broader human impacts

What is a life worth? The US military actually has to quantify the value of a life to set the amount paid in death benefits and life insurance for personnel who die in service. In 2005, the payments increased from $12,240 to $100,000 for the death benefit and from $250,000 to $500,000 for life insurance. In other assessments, such as safety and environmental regulation, the US government values the life of a prime-age male at around $6 million.[111]

Given that approximately 4500 Americans have died in the Iraq war since 2003, the value of lives lost would be $27 billion dollars using the US military's metric. Assuming than an Iraqi life is as valuable as an American life, the loss of more than 100,000 Iraqi civilians[112] during the war could then be valued as high as $600 billion dollars.

Attempting to put a monetary value on a life may be bizarre, yet it is infinitely more difficult to quantify the emotional impacts of the loss of loved ones on spouses, children, parents, siblings, and friends. And there can be impacts of war that are in ways worse that death. The violence of war can permanently scar people, leading to traumas with long lasting personal, intergenerational, and culture-wide consequences. There is no way to begin to calculate the social costs of the full ramifications of war, their impacts on physical, emotional, and mental health, on political systems, and economies. Rape—just one horrific impact of war—will be used to illustrate social consequences.

War rape—like genocide, torture, refugee displacement, famine, disease, and other horrors associated with war—traumatizes the victim, their family, and community, undermining human progress in fundamental ways for multiple generations.

Rape, as with all terror warfare, is not exclusively an attack on the body—it has been described as an attack on the "body politic."[113] When rape is used as an instrument of war it is perpetrated against women, including pregnant and elderly women, infants, men, fleeing refugees, and the internally displaced. Yet its goal is not to maim or kill one person; it is to control an entire sociopolitical process by crippling it. It is an attack directed equally against personal identity and cultural integrity.

Rape has been used in war throughout history. Since the Second World War, however, it has assumed increased importance as a deliberate military strategy. Women are now not only raped but physically scarred and mutilated. In recent conflicts rape has been used as a reward for battle victory; a boost to troop morale; as punishment and humiliation for both men and women; to incite revenge in opposing troops; to eliminate or "cleanse" religious or political groups; and to destabilize entire communities by creating terror.

The prevalence of rape during war is unknown because no international detection or reporting system exists and because rape is often unreported for fear of further violence. Information on prevalence generally comes from focused studies in individual countries.

The 1998-2002 war in the Democratic Republic of the Congo—the most violent since the Second World War—resulted in the loss of 3.8 million lives. Since fighting broke out in 1998, tens of thousands of people have been raped, with the number of rape survivors estimated at 200,000. The use of war rape in the DRC has been characterized as a "cheap, simple weapon for all parties in the war, more easily obtainable than bullets or bombs." A 2010 study found that 30 percent of women and 22 percent of men in the eastern DRC reported conflict-related sexual violence. Men who admit to being raped risk ostracism by their community and even criminal prosecution since they may be considered homosexual, a criminal offence in the DRC.

The prevalence and intensity of rape and other sexual violence in parts of the DRC has been described as the worst in the world. However, in a 2005-06 Liberian survey, 92 percent of interviewed women reported they had experienced sexual violence, including rape.

During the Rwanda genocide, from April-June 1994, hundreds of thousands of women and girls were raped and/or became the victims of other forms of sexual violence. Compared to other conflicts the sexual violence in Rwanda stands out in terms of the organized nature of the propaganda that contributed significantly to fuelling sexual violence against Tutsi women, the very public nature of the rapes, and the level of brutality.

During the Bosnian war, Serb forces conducted a sexual abuse strategy known as "mass rape phenomenon" on thousands of Bosnian Muslim girls and women. No exact figures on how many women and children were systematically raped by the Serb forces in various camps were ascertained, but estimates range from 20,000 to 50,000.

The effects of rape and sexual torture on survivors are economically, physically, psychologically, and culturally devastating. Survivors can be left economically disadvantaged; they often contract sexually transmitted diseases; victims experience serious acute and chronic medical problems, forced pregnancy, higher maternal mortality, miscarriage, infertility, and chronic sexual dysfunction; because victims are often raped with a variety of objects they are at risk of fistula formation, cervical cancer, and recurrent infections. The psychological effects are also extensive; victims develop fear of intimacy, flashbacks, sleep disorders, and chronic psychosomatic problems such as headaches and gastro-intestinal disorders and may engage in self-injury. Rape is more likely to induce post-traumatic stress disorder than other events.

Significantly, the effects of rape extend to the family and community. It is common in some cultures for the family to struggle to accept the victim back into her home, or to abandon her completely, often leaving her children without property or support and leaving her in worsening poverty. Men whose partners or wives have been raped may feel humiliated and become violent towards their partner. Half of rape victims in Sierra Leone reported that their relationships with family and friends were deeply affected. Rape is also an attack on the culture and safety of the community and is often accompanied by other acts of terror that disrupt basic services such as education, farming, commerce, and access to health care.

Rape during armed conflict is not simply about military personnel, police, or terrorists. Before 2004, rape assailants in the Democratic Republic of the Congo were primarily military but after 2004 civilian rapes increased 17-fold while rapes by armed combatants decreased 77 percent. This pattern suggests a disturbing acceptance of rape among civilians following war.

Ecological impacts

The ecosphere is always a casualty of military conflict.[114,115] Obviously, active fighting destroys whole landscapes; throughout the history of warfare wells have been polluted, crops torched, forests cut down, soils poisoned, and animals killed to secure a strategic advantage, demoralize local populations, or subdue resistance. The United Nations Environment Programme has identified three main pathways by which war impacts the ecosphere:

- *Direct impacts* caused by the physical destruction of ecosystems and wildlife or the release of polluting and hazardous substances can last for decades. A range of examples include:

  - Bands of mercury in the soils of Slovenia are a continuing legacy of artillery barrages during the First World War.

  - Munitions dumped in and around the Caribbean island of Vieques by the US navy in the 1960s and 1970s are linked to locally high rates of cancer.

  - During the Vietnam War, 70 million litres of Agent Orange were sprayed over the country's forests, resulting in entire areas being stripped of all vegetation. Some are still unsuited to agriculture.

- Ecosystems have been deliberately targeted to achieve political and military goals. During its war with Iran, Iraq drained the marshes of the Euphrates-Tigris Delta. During the 1991 Gulf War, it set Kuwait's oil wells ablaze and discharged millions of tonnes of crude oil into waterways.

- During the 1999 conflict in the Balkans, the industrial complex at Pancevo—one of more than 50 such sites that were bombed—was hit 12 separate times, igniting 80,000 tonnes of oil. Black rain fell onto nearby towns, while toxic chemical compounds leaked into air, soil, and water.

- *Indirect impacts* result from the coping strategies used by local and displaced populations to survive the socio-economic disruption and loss of basic services. This often entails the liquidation of natural assets for immediate survival, or the overuse of marginal areas, which can lead to long-term ecosphere damage.

  - Deforestation rates soared during successive conflicts in Afghanistan, as Pakistani "timber mafias" looted valuable trees.

  - In the war torn Darfur region of Sudan, looting of natural resources by all sides has been widespread, including cutting high value timber, ivory poaching that decimated elephant and rhinoceros populations, and aggressive hunting for bush meat.

- *Institutional impacts* result from a disruption of state institutions, initiatives, and mechanisms of policy coordination, which result in poor management, lack of investment, illegality, and the collapse of positive ecosystem practices. At the same time, financial resources are diverted away from investments in public infrastructure and essential services towards military objectives.

  - A key example is the impact of the military on climate. The US Department of Defence (DoD) is the largest institutional user of fossil fuels in the world. In 2009, it emitted 73 million tonnes of CO_2. If compared to the consumption of fossil fuel by nations, the DoD would rank 34th in the world, at 400,000 barrels of oil a day, higher than Pakistan, a country of 187 million people. Assuming a similar rate of use, all the world's state militaries combined consume

930,000 barrels a day, equivalent to ranking 23rd among nations, higher than Venezuela.

- The ongoing conflict in Darfur provides an example of the consequences of the collapse of environmental governance due to military conflict. While environmental conditions were a root cause of the conflict, the breakdown of governance exacerbated the situation as the military and civilians took advantage of the anarchy to act with impunity in exploiting resources. The country was inaccessible for science-based data collection, further limiting rational resource management and conservation. The war economy created a funding crisis and provisions for sustainable management were cut from the government's budget.

Opportunity cost

Opportunity cost is the cost of any activity measured in terms of the best alternative forgone. For example, if it had not invaded Iraq—ostensibly to prevent the use of weapons of mass destruction, later found to be non-existent—what could the US have done instead? It might have provided universal health care and universal preschool, for example, with money to spare. The following graphic illustrates the point.

ANNUAL COST OF THE IRAQ WAR IN PERSPECTIVE

Iraq war*	Universal health care	Universal preschool	Security	Cancer research	Immunizations
	For all people in the U.S. without it	Half-days for 3-year olds and full-days for 4-year olds	Carrying out the 9/11 Commission recommendations	Annual budget	For the world's children against measles, whooping cough, tetanus, tuberculosis, polio and diphtheria
Annually $200 billion	$100 billion	$35 billion	$10 billion	$6 billion	$0.6 billion

*Includes $120 billion in annual military expenses plus the future cost of veteran medical care and disability payments, the cost of rebuilding the military post war and the increased cost of oil as a result of the war. *Source: The New York Times*

As discussed below, repurposing most of the money spent on the military would be sufficient to eliminate acute poverty worldwide, provide universal healthcare and education or ameliorate climate change.

WHAT IS WAR FOR?

Seen in the light of this argument, spending trillions annually on something that is not only profoundly destructive of human development and the ecosphere but also demonstrably useless—even by the reckoning of leading military figures—can only be described as both immoral and insane. Yet high military spending is broadly considered not just essential but synonymous with patriotism and a sign of national strength. Why does this contradiction persist?

Three things contribute to the ongoing dominance of the military: inertia; fear of *the other* coupled with the perception of security a robust military bestows; and the momentum of the military-industrial complex. This triple threat is aptly illustrated by Canada's plans to build new F-35 fighter jets and expand its navy.

Inertia

Although Canada is typically perceived as a peaceful nation it is in fact a major military spender, ranked 13th in the world in defence spending despite being 36th in population. Canada doubled its military budget between 2001 and 2010, spending $21 billion on defence in 2009-10, more than Israel (which actually faced military threats), Pakistan (a country of 174 million involved in a protracted territorial conflict with India), or Indonesia (with over 240 million people, the fourth most populous nation.)

The current government's policy is to massively expand military procurement. In 2011, for example, Irving Shipbuilding was awarded a $25-billion contract to build 21 combat ships. In announcing the contract, Defence Minister Peter MacKay said it was a very exciting day for the Royal Canadian Navy because the ships will help Canada "prepare for the challenges of the 21st century." The nature of these challenges was not stipulated.

At the same time, Canada was also planning to purchase 65 F-35 fighter jets. Costs per jet were projected at anywhere from $75 million (Canadian government estimate) to $110 million (US Government Accountability Office (GAO) estimate) to $148 million (U.S. defence specialist Winslow Wheeler.) Estimates of the total cost for all the jets, including service contracts, was set at $9 billion by government but was estimated at closer to $29 billion by Canada's Parliamentary Budget Officer Kevin Page. Department of National Defence documents later indicated the planes would be supplied to Canada by U.S.

manufacturer Lockheed Martin without engines.[116] The GAO has also warned about serious ongoing problems with the aircraft. Ultimately, when an audit by KPMG found the cost would be $45 billion—$600 million per plane—the government decided to "push the reset button."

As the cost estimate quintupled, it remained uncertain what the aircraft would be used for. When asked to clarify their purpose, all Minister McKay would say was that the aircraft "will allow us to face what future threats may exist." But it is entirely unclear what military threats Canada faces and which of these, if any, might require an arsenal of 65 sophisticated fighter aircraft—or 21 new combat ships.

What are the chances Canada will be threatened militarily? According to a Canadian government strategy document, Canada's only territorial disputes are with Denmark over Hans Island and the United States over the maritime boundary in the Beaufort Sea. The chance of a fight with either country is inconceivable.

A marginally more likely threat would come from Russia over control of the Arctic region, which is becoming more attractive for development as a consequence of climate change. Realistically, the chances of an armed conflict are next to zero. But if Canada had to defend its claims against Russia, would 65 planes be of much use against Russia's 7300 military aircraft, including 2000 fighter jets? Russia's northern naval fleet, headquartered on the Arctic coast, currently consists of 42 vessels, including aircraft carriers, destroyers, and submarines, as well as many more corvettes and smaller ships. Canada's comparatively tiny navy—even with the addition of the 21 new ships—does not even have a permanent presence in the Arctic.

While disputes with Russia may emerge, co-operation would obviously yield better results than confrontation. As Norway's Foreign Minister Jonas Gahr Store said, the West would benefit from "updating our mental maps, which are frozen in the Cold War" when dealing with Russia. And of course the same can be said for Russia in relation to the West.

While terrorism is a possible threat to Canada, the idea that any nation can protect itself from terrorists through conventional military preparedness is absurd. A terrorist threat could come anywhere, anytime. What could an expanded air force or navy do to prevent it? It is more likely that terrorists would hit a train, bus, subway, school, shopping mall, or public gathering, easy targets compared to, say, hijacking an aircraft. Indeed, the only terrorist threats in Canada that have resulted in arrests were land based and would not have required the use of the air force if they had been carried out. Even if threats come from hijacked aircraft, could aircraft be put in place in time to stop them?

Given that there are no conventional military threats against Canada, and likely no terrorist threats that can be prevented with conventional military methods, it is more likely that the purpose of the new aircraft is to support overseas missions such as the NATO involvement in Libya in 2011. Here again we come upon the issue of the utility of force: the record of military interventions in foreign countries in the last 50 years has in most cases been disastrous for all concerned, as previously described. While the Libyan air incursion by NATO was successful in helping rebels topple the government, there is no telling whether, left to their own devices, the Libyan revolution of 2011 could not have been accomplished, in due course, without force or foreign intervention, perhaps through non-violent or less violent means as was the case in Tunisia and Egypt. NATO airstrikes in Libya were highly destructive in lives and property. In general, such interventions are demonstrably ill advised. Will the foreign-supported revolution bring a more enlightened, democratic society, or merely a new dictatorship, rendering the intervention futile? What evidence is there that the former scenario is even likely?

The F-35 example is a perfect illustration of the persistence of outdated military mythology. As a result of an irrational attachment to this mythology, the government of Canada, like most governments, continues to subscribe to the old paradigm of interstate, industrial warfare that has repeatedly proven ineffective in dealing with contemporary security concerns. Resistance to change traps Canada and most other countries under the weight of military expenditures for no legitimate reason.

Fear of the other

To prop up the old paradigm it is necessary to cultivate an irrational perception of threats that come from some *other*, such as "Islamic extremists." Such fears can be easily reinforced through sloganeering. Politically, a robust military is perceived as necessary in order to appear strong in ways that appeal to small but influential political constituencies or segments of the electorate. And support for an unnecessarily large military in the general public is courted by appeals to outdated patriotism, support for the sacrifices of military personnel, and irrational fear of unknown others and slight dangers. If they are asked why we need the military, which is rare, politicians cannot identify genuine threats.

The military industrial complex

The persistence of the old military paradigm is, of course, cultivated by a military-industrial complex that would collapse without it. It appears that the sole beneficiary of heavy military spending is the military sector itself and in particular an arms industry experiencing rapid growth after a period of decline in the 1980s and 1990s. The top 100 arms-producing companies are raking in $250 billion a year in revenues, with earnings rising every year. They don't want to give it up. In Canada, billions are spent on arms by the Canadian government, but as much as $15 billion in arms are exported from Canada annually.[117]

As Andrew Bacevich argues in *Washington Rules: America's Path to Permanent War*, for want of a real threat, the military-industrial complex, which has penetrated into the corridors of power, has worked overtime to invent perceived threats where a mere hint of danger exists. Perhaps, he suggests, there are no significant threats at all: war today is merely a way for its chief beneficiary, the war industry, to justify military spending which is nothing more than an efficient means of concentrating an ever-larger portion of public wealth in the hands of its shareholders.

Is this too extreme a statement? Perhaps, but it appears that the contemporary arms industry precisely embodies the fear articulated by former US President (and top general) Dwight Eisenhower, who famously introduced the concept of a *powerful military–industrial complex to be feared* in his farewell address in 1961. It is instructive to review that speech.

Eisenhower made it clear that, while he favoured a strong military, the size and scope of the military presented a problem co-equal to any military threat. He pointed out that prior to the Second World War, "the United States had no armaments industry." Due to external threats, the country "has been compelled to create a permanent armaments industry of vast proportions" with millions employed in the defence establishment. "This conjunction of an immense military establishment and a large arms industry is new in the American experience. The total influence—economic, political, even spiritual—is felt in every city, every State house, every office of the Federal government." While recognizing the need for this development, "we must not fail to comprehend its grave implications. Our toil, resources and livelihood are all involved; so is the very structure of our society. In the councils of government, we must guard against the acquisition of unwarranted influence, whether sought or unsought, by the military industrial complex. The potential for the disastrous rise of misplaced power exists and will persist. We must never," he said, "let the weight of this combination endanger our liberties or democratic processes. We should take nothing for granted. Only an alert and knowledgeable citizenry can compel the proper meshing of the huge industrial and military machinery of defence with our peaceful methods and goals, so that security and liberty may prosper together."

Given the US has been unable to fully achieve its political goals in any major war since 1945, despite unprecedented power, it would seem likely that a major factor behind continuing this charade must be the political influence of the military industrial complex.

Elsewhere, Eisenhower spoke forcefully of the implications of military spending. "Every gun that is made, every warship launched, every rocket fired signifies, in the final sense, a theft from those who hunger and are not fed, those who are cold and are not clothed," with not so subtle reference to the Gospels. "We pay," he continued, "for a single fighter with a half million bushels of wheat," implying that that wheat is lost to the hungry. The former President could not have envisioned the vast inflation in armament costs. The fighter jet Eisenhower said represented a theft of a half million bushels of $2 wheat from the hungry cost around $1 million in his day. The contemporary lifetime cost is 250 times that amount (when servicing is included). In other words, one of Lockheed Martin's $600 million F-35 fighters would rob *120 million* bushels of $5 wheat from the hungry.

Speaking of the failure to achieve peace, in this case between the West and the Soviet Union, but surely applicable to the contemporary scene, Eisenhower said the *best* outcome of the arms race would be this: "a life of perpetual fear and tension; a burden of arms draining the wealth and the labour of all peoples; a wasting of strength that defies the American system or the Soviet system or any system to achieve true abundance and happiness for the peoples of this earth." This is exactly the situation in which we find ourselves today, with regard to the pointless and enervating arms race around the world.

THE PEACE DIVIDEND

The payoff for disarmament and demilitarization would be a boon unparalleled in human history. Usually called the *peace dividend*, it is comprised of the financial, human, and material resources liberated from war preparedness to be used for other purposes, from tax reduction to debt reduction to constructive public spending.

It was only following the Second World War that the practice of maintaining large standing armies and arms industries outside of wartime became customary. In 1939, Canada's total permanent armed force had dwindled to just 4,261 officers and men, with minimal equipment, from over 600,000 during World War 1. America's founding fathers were suspicious of a permanent military force and it was not until 1947 that a large standing peacetime army was officially established.

The exaggerated importance now assigned to the military in militaristic countries such as the United States is perhaps evidenced by the fact that some 19 countries have no armed forces or standing army at all, 28 spend less than 1 percent of their GDP on the military, compared to the world average in 2010 of 2.6 percent (and 4.7 percent in the US.) Some 33 countries spend less than $100 million and 81 less than $1 billion. Arguably, the countries with lower-cost defence preparedness are no less secure than the big spenders. There are no aggressive inter-state wars today; what is more, there is no way any nation can defend against interstate alliances such as NATO. Think Libya, Iraq, Serbia, Afghanistan—NATO completely overwhelms anything that can be thrown at it. Even so, neither can alliances like NATO prevail in the long run.

Having said all this, an 11 billion world will still need a military. Without force at its disposal, any state—even a world state—could become vulnerable to rogue elements capable of mounting a private militia. But legitimate military demand—to maintain internal order and defend against aggression—represents a fraction of current military supply.

Legitimate defence requirements justify perhaps 10 percent of the current investment. But more conservatively, reducing military spending to 1 percent of global GDP would provide $700 billion for defence and a peace dividend of more that $1 trillion annually, based on current stated annual military expenditures. (In fact, the saving would likely be much higher considering the full cost of all things military is likely closer to $3 trillion.)

To put this in perspective, a $1 trillion peace dividend would be sufficient to provide the 2 billion people who live on less than $2 a day, $500 each per annum, ending extreme poverty on a global scale. Or, it would be more than the amount estimated by the Stern report required to combat climate change, i.e. 1 percent of GDP or $0.6 trillion.

It is hard to imagine a successful transition to a world of 11 billion without disarmament and the rededication of resources from destruction to securing a sustainable, equitable civilization. But for all the benefits that would accrue it is tremendously difficult to break free of the military paradigm. The old paradigm, which emerged from a history of consistent military aggression may no longer be valid, but it has generated an entrenched political ideology that is intimately linked with national identity.

In popular mythology, for instance, a "true American" is someone who believes the United States must be the strongest country in the world militarily. Even to suggest that the country does not need a large military, because it has no utility and is sinking the nation in debt—or that it is immoral in Eisenhower's sense—is to face immediate rejection as being "un-American."

This makes it extremely difficult for a political leader—especially an American—to promote disarmament, no matter how strong the case in its favour. To begin with, a profound policy change requires a fundamental change in the national identity. On a political level, it requires the leader, and a major-ity of congress, to turn their back on powerful lobbies and political funders, as well as the army of constituents in the military-industrial complex who stand to lose their jobs. Essentially, it requires a fundamental change in the nature and structure of the political process. The reformers would have to explain and rally people behind a fundamentally different ideology using media that has effectively eliminated thoughtful debate. Opponents to change, including powerful and wealthy vested interests, can easily reinforce traditional American xenophobia through simplistic, repetitive sloganeering. Fostering a new ideol-ogy and new national identity requires painstaking effort over many years and the vehicles of learning, such as the media and the political system, do not admit this level of discourse. Change would require a restructuring of the political system, the media, and even the educational system.

I focus here on America because it is the most militaristic nation in the world, based on national spending. But militarism is not just an American pre-occupation: "peaceful" Canada is increasingly militaristic for no good reason.

"Xenophobia looks like becoming the mass ideology of the 20th-century fin-de-siècle," said the historian. Eric Hosbawn. "What holds humanity together today is the denial of what the human race has in common."[118]

The thing about contemporary xenophobia is that it is *fundamentally* illusory. In reality, humanity functions as one single social-ecological unit. The world is virtually one country and humanity its citizens, but we do not yet see ourselves that way. Therein lie both the problem and a unique opportunity.

The opportunity is a massive peace dividend worth more than $1 trillion a year, much more when we account for spin-off benefits. But an additional opportunity lies in transforming the vast capacity of the military toward peaceful reconstruction. The virtuous cycle of benefits that would ripple out from waging peace would be world changing.

SHIFTING VALUES

In this chapter and section we have seen that a set of values inimical to the public interest—from jingoism and militarism to materialism, consumerism, unregulated capitalism, and perpetual growth to obsession with entertainment and image and addictions—is undermining contemporary civilization and threatening to overwhelm the planet as humanity expands to 11 billion people.

While the accelerating economic momentum fuelled by these values is profoundly disturbing, the analysis presented in this section shows that the systems that arise from these values, like the values themselves, are not natural outcomes of the civilization-building process. They are constructed, often deliberately for private gain at public expense.

We have seen that much of what we value in practice, and the behaviours that flow from these values, lie on a continuum between unnecessary and destructive. Behaviours that are purely constructive, like reforestation, or necessary, like providing housing, actually occupy less and less of our time and attention. Meanwhile, those that are unnecessary (such as tourism), frivolous (various entertainments), useless (building stores of armaments), or destructive (addictions to tobacco or alcohol) are expanding, often dramatically.

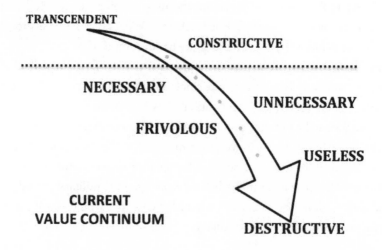

The good news is that much of what we are doing as individuals and as a society could be set aside since it is not constructive or necessary. We can eliminate destructive behaviours, such as the use of harmful and addicting substances, drop useless behaviours like expanding the military-industrial complex, reduce frivolous activities like obsessions with appearance or entertainment, and limit unnecessary activities like travelling. Decreasing these behaviours will reduce our ecological footprint, helping to make the world work for 11 billion people. And by liberating the time, energy, and resources that go into these pursuits and rededicating them to what is necessary, like providing people with adequate nutrition, and constructive, like restoring ecosystems, we can carry our civilization forward.

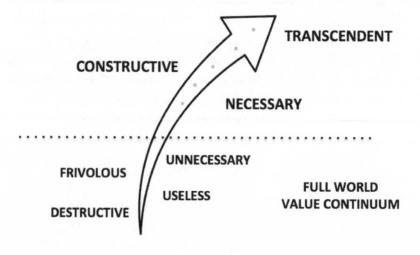

In subsequent chapters I will argue that the means of achieving this objective, this realignment of values and behaviours toward the necessary, constructive, and transcendent, is a mass educational campaign that involves the entire human race—children, youth and adults—in building a new culture designed for a world of 11 billion people.

CHAPTER 5

SEEDING A NEW CULTURE

In 1945, Germany was a place of despair. Crippled by its devastating defeat in the Second World War, its cities in ruin, it was occupied and divided among foreign powers. In its moral descent into fanaticism, genocide, and totalitarianism it had pulled much of Europe down with it, inflicting destruction on a scale unparalleled in human history. The resulting conflagration killed 40 million.

It is extraordinary to see what has happened since. Germany has been resurrected and is now among the most highly regarded nations in the world.[119] It has not been involved in a military conflict (aside from peacekeeping activities) since 1945. It is also among the least violent of nations, ranking 176th of 192 countries. The rate of violent deaths has dropped from 135/100,000 in the 20th century—with a spike to 2600/100,000 late in the Second World War[120]—to less than 1 per 100,000 today.

Violent conflict in Western Europe has been replaced with cooperation, resulting in the high levels of development and human rights typical of that region today. The solution was a gradual extension of instruments, from a common trading market to a common currency and parliament. A tradition of nationalistic conflict was subsumed in a shared continental identity. Europe discovered that unity and peace bring prosperity like nothing else, and Germany became a champion of the unification process.

The mostly gradual—but at times rapid—evolution of a united and peaceful Europe with world-leading economic, social, and conservation programs saw 20 countries willingly cede a measure of national power to a continental authority while remaining largely independent and culturally diverse. Even through the period of the Cold War, war was avoided. Ultimately, the East Bloc made peace with Western Europe after the Soviet Union voluntarily ceded control.

This is not to suggest that contemporary, materialistic Europe is now utopia, but compared to a past history of continuous warfare—an average of two new European wars per year for 600 years—the level of unity and peace it has achieved are just short of miraculous.

By 1945, the idea of a united Europe as a solution to near continuous warfare had been around for hundreds of years. Various forms of European union were proposed: by Bohemian King George of Podebrady in the 15th century; William Penn in the 17th; Abbot Charles de Saint-Pierre in the 18th; and Victor Hugo and Giuseppe Mazzinin in the 19th. The internationally-minded Tsar Alexander had suggested a kind of permanent European union at the Congress of Aix-la-Chapelle in 1818, and even proposed an international military force to provide recognized states with support against aggression. Such thinking intensified following World War I as a result of the massive loss of life it entailed. Richard Coudenhove-Kalergi, for example, started the popular Paneuropean Union in the 1920s. Leaders of thought such as Albert Einstein, Thomas Mann, and Sigmund Freud attended its first congress.

Yet it was only after World War II that real steps were taken to make the long-standing dream a reality. On one hand, we can ask why it had taken so long? On the other, why after 600 years of fighting and 500 years of proposals for change did the idea finally take hold? The answer may be found in an idea taken from ecology.

PANARCHY

Panarchy theory developed by the ecologists Buzz Holling and Lance Gunderson[121] helps us understand how complex systems of all kinds, from organisms to ecosystems to social systems, evolve, adapt, and sometimes experience sudden transformation.

The core idea is that all systems move through a four-stage *adaptive cycle*. The cycle's duration can range from seconds to years to millennia and may occur from the micro to the macro scale, from the level of soil bacteria to the whole ecosphere. The adaptive cycle shown in the illustration below involves:

- A stage of creative **growth** or **exploitation** in which the young system builds new capacity, is open and adaptive, and its resilience is high;

- A stage of **conservation**, in which the system gradually matures and accumulates capital; where components build capacity to efficiently perform functions; where connectivity increases and resilience decreases;

- A **release** stage where the ordered system, in its present form, may experience a sudden, even catastrophic crisis or collapse, which releases accumulated capital; and

- A stage of **reorganization** that involves a spike of creativity, innovation and new strategies, leading to a new growth stage.

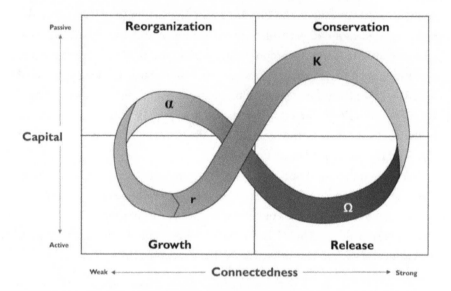

A forest is often used to illustrate the adaptive cycle.

During the forest's growth phase, the number of species and of individual plants and animals quickly increases, as organisms arrive to exploit all available ecological niches. The new forest is highly resilient: it thrives on change and adaptation. In this stage, connectivity among components is weak and capital is active.

As it evolves, the forest conserves natural capital (i.e. biomass and information) as it moves toward a more stable state, with high connectivity and multiple feedback mechanisms. Organic material in plants, animals, and soil increases and achieves a high level of organization. Every niche is exploited, with flows of energy, materials, and genetic information among the forest's organisms becoming steadily more numerous and complex.

As growth continues, the ecosystem's connectedness increases and more means of self-regulation and maintaining stability evolve. Nitrogen fixing plants and decomposers that break down organic matter increase, for example. Negative feedback loops among its various components keep temperature, rainfall, and chemical concentrations within a range best suited to maintaining the forest.

As the forest matures and passes into the conservation phase, the mechanisms of self-regulation become highly diverse and finely tuned. Species and organisms are progressively more specialized and efficient in using the energy and nutrients available in their niche. In the process, redundancies like multiple nitrogen fixers are pruned away. New plants and animals find fewer niches to exploit, so the steady increase in diversity of species and organisms slows and may even decline. Ever-greater connectedness and efficiency eventually result in diminishing returns by reducing the system's capacity to cope with severe shocks. The high connectedness helps any shock travel faster across the ecosystem. The forest ecosystem has become rigid, brittle, and lacking in resilience.

This stage eventually creates conditions conducive to a crisis, such as severe pest outbreaks or wildfire, which releases the natural capital accumulated in the biomass. Now there are opportunities for rapid change and innovation.

While the crisis may appear to be a disaster, in that the existing order is destroyed, the ultimate impact may be positive. A wildfire in a mature forest creates open spaces that allow new species to establish themselves and propagate; it destroys infestations of disease and insects; and it converts vegetation and accumulated debris into nutrients that can be used by plants and animals that reestablish after the fire. The organisms that survive become less dependent on their specific, long-established relationships. Most important, collapse also liberates the ecosystem's enormous potential for innovation and allows for novel and unpredictable recombination of its elements. Once-marginal species can now capture and exploit newly released nutrients, and once-problematic genetic mutations contribute to survival. Resiliency returns to the system.

The cycle of growth, conservation, release, and reorganization allows the forest to adapt over the long term by accommodating both growth and stability on the one hand and change and variety on the other.

As mentioned, every organism and community of organisms moves through adaptive cycles. The term *panarchy* refers to a hierarchy of adaptive cycles nested within each other, much like Russian dolls. Above a forest's cycle, for example, is the larger, slower adaptive cycle of the regional ecosystem. Above that is the even slower cycle involving global biogeochemical processes, where planetary flows of materials and elements such as carbon can be measured in time spans of years, decades, or even millennia. Below the forest's adaptive cycle are the smaller, faster cycles of sub-ecosystems that encompass, for instance, particular hillsides or streams. Adaptive cycles can be found all the way down to the level of bacteria in the soil, where activity happens on a scale of millimetres and take place in minutes or seconds.

The higher, slower-moving cycles provide stability and resources that buffer the forest from shocks and help it recover from collapse. A forest may be hit by wildfire, for example, but as long as the climate pattern across the larger region that encompasses the forest remains constant and rainfall is adequate, the forest will regenerate. Meanwhile, the lower and faster-moving cycles are a source of novelty, experimentation, and information. Together, the higher and lower cycles help keep the forest's collapse, when it occurs, from being truly catastrophic.

For this healthy arrangement to work, however, the various adaptive cycles in the panarchy must be at different points in the four-stage cycle. If they all peak at the top of their growth phases simultaneously, and all collapse at the same time, a much more devastating collapse can occur. Should a wildfire hit a forest at the same time as the regional climate cycle enters a drought phase, the forest may never regenerate, for example. It might convert to grassland.

THE SOCIAL-ECOLOGICAL PANARCHY

While panarchy theory is most often applied to ecosystems it has similarities with other theories of adaptation and change. Its core ideas recur repeatedly in literature, philosophy, religion, and studies of human history, as well as the natural and political sciences.

Holling proposes that panarchy theory and the four-stage adaptive cycle applies to all complex systems, and that human systems such as government, the economy, or culture are included with ecological systems in the stack of nested cycles that influence each other.

If we look again to the example of the forest, we see that people can be highly influential players in forest systems. The panarchy of adaptive cycles at work in the forest may include: one or more forest companies, each with its own agenda, along with the shareholders, company staff, and unions; government departments that both regulate the forestry company, controlling harvest and restocking rates, and encourage the growth of the forest industry; research and academic institutions involved in studying forest ecosystems or advising industry or government; conservation organizations, arguing for sustainable management or outright cessation of forestry activities; indigenous groups trying to protect their land and/or to take a share in development activities; recreational groups trying to improve access to the forest region; perhaps a mining, oil, or gas company seeking access to resources beneath the forest or a pharmaceutical company seeking to harvest a certain plant for drug production; local towns and cities dependent on forest jobs, but also tourism; and political institutions trying to sort it all out. Each of these players has its own adaptive cycles—such as financial or electoral cycles—that influence its involvement.

Human involvement in ecological cycles can have a positive or negative impact. We may, for example, attempt to extend the growth stage of a forest cycle to conserve timber production and recreational values by trying to prevent all forest fires. This may result in an unnatural build up of natural capital and ultimately a hotter, larger, and more destructive fire when it comes, including loss of life and property. On the other hand, good management of a forest could simulate the effects of fire, by selectively felling patches of older trees and replanting new ones, forestalling fires and disease. Intelligent forest management can play an important role in the mitigation of climate change.

Today, we are aware of the global impacts that the forest, as part of the larger boreal or tropical systems, has on climate, adding another level of complexity and connectivity. People in Germany or Vanuatu may feel they have a stake in forestry activities in Canada or Venezuela, since foreign forests are critical to climate stability in their region. The Germans might stop buying Canadian lumber if they disapprove of management practices. Vanuatu might raise their concerns before the international community, due to their vulnerability to sea level rise.

At the industry level, cycles in the prices of pulp and paper will affect the demand for lumber which impacts harvest rates, biodiversity, watersheds, soil quality, and local economies. Forest cycles, such as the increase in insect pests, may also affect timber supply and paper prices. Cultural or technological changes, like the use of the Internet or e-readers, affect paper demand. This can impact forestry practices, which are an important influence on climate change. In all then, the panarchy—with all the ecological and social processes at play—is remarkably complex.

The forest and the forest industry are nested within a range of ecological and social systems that impact each other. As Thomas Homer-Dixon points out, we can look at "humankind—including all our interactions with each other and with nature and all the flows of materials, energy, and information through our societies and technologies—as one immense social-ecological system." Humankind is a kind of ultimate adaptive cycle in which everything else is nested.

For people, accepting that adaptive cycles are part of our social-ecological reality seems to be a difficult thing to do: we are prone to become attached to things as they are and fear the release and reorganization stages of adaptive cycles. We are attached to the growth and conservation stages in forests, for example, because they provide a supply of products or recreational opportunities we depend on, while a renewal stage would destroy these, at least temporarily.

Humankind, including all social and ecological interactions and all flows of materials, energy, and information, is one immense social-ecological system.

Holling points out that our attachment to things as they are—which requires denial of the problems inherent in the current order—results in active efforts to extend the growth phase of the adaptive cycle of our global social-ecological system. A number of factors drive this effort, particularly the perceived need of companies, economies, and societies to maximize performance and productivity. Based on current trends, our obsession with growth will mean that global output of goods and services will quadruple from US$70 trillion to $240 trillion (in 2005 dollars) by 2050 if we continue on this path.

"The growth phase we're in may seem like a natural and permanent state of affairs," comments Homer-Dixon, "and our world's rising complexity, connectedness, efficiency, and regulation may seem relentless and unstoppable—but ultimately it isn't sustainable. Still, we find it impossible to get off this upward escalator because our chronic state of denial about the seriousness of our situation—aided and abetted by powerful special interests that benefit from the status quo—keeps us from really seeing what's happening or really considering other paths our world might follow. Radically different futures are beyond imagining. So we stay trapped on a path that takes us toward major breakdown."

As in all complex systems, resiliency declines as growth, complexity, and connectivity increase. According to Holling, the longer a system is "locked in" to its growth phase, the greater its vulnerability and the bigger and more dramatic its collapse will be. If the growth phase goes on for too long, "deep collapse" eventually occurs. Collapse in this case is so catastrophic and cascades across so many physical and social boundaries that the system's ability to regenerate itself is lost.

Holling thinks the world is reaching a stage of vulnerability that could trigger a rare and major pulse of transformation on the scale of the agricultural, industrial, and technological revolutions. "The immense destruction that a new pulse signals is both frightening and creative," says Holling. "The only way to approach such a period, in which uncertainty is very large and one cannot predict what the future holds, is not to predict, but to experiment and act inventively and exuberantly via diverse adventures in living."

> A major pulse of transformation on the scale of the agricultural, industrial, and technological revolutions is imminent.

DIVERSE ADVENTURES IN LIVING

European unity was such an experiment. Breaking from the old, aggressive nationalism became possible due to the catastrophic system collapse that was the Second World War. The "conservation stage" of Europe's adaptive cycle gave way to release and reorganization, clearing a niche for an innovative idea—the seed of which had already been planted by the pan-European movement—to flourish. It is highly unlikely such a profound change could have come about without the utter failure and collapse of the old approach. Yet the existence of an alternative approach, which had been partly thought out and developed during the conservation stage, made rapid regeneration possible.

While a world-scale "pulse of social transformation" far greater in scale than the Second World War is inevitable, we cannot predict when it will happen, how it will come about, or what the outcome might be—except that it will result in a different configuration of civilization than now exists. The two processes that are setting the stage for this transformation are happening simultaneously: the first, the breakdown in the existing order (an inevitable consequence of the overextended growth and conservation stage of the adaptive cycle); the second, the raising up of a new order (elements of which are already taking shape, often outside of our awareness.) There is no clear break when the old order ends and the new begins; the old order continues to dominate even as it disintegrates and the new order takes shape in its shadow. There may be defining moments—such as a major global financial or energy crisis—where the breakdown of the old order becomes apparent. The rise of the new order will be subtler.

In a sense, the old order collapses under its own weight. It happens with little regard to anything we do: even revolutionary activity will not necessarily change its fundamental characteristics. On the other hand, building the new order will require a concerted, universal effort, especially in the context of an 11 billion world.

So, how do we build it?

Here, Holling's prescription—to experiment and act inventively and exuberantly via diverse adventures in living—is instructive. It is not possible, or perhaps even desirable, to attempt a precise formulation of the culture of a future state of civilization. A new culture will unfold in response to a reading of our present reality. What can be done, however, is to begin to put in place *processes* of culture building. This can be done, on a small scale, at the local level, by initiating experiments in living that attempt to move people in desirable directions. These experiments are seeds and the seeds we plant now, during the growth and conservation stage of the planet's adaptive cycle, will find a niche in the release and reorganization stage that is coming.

Naturally, it is important that the soil is seeded with constructive ideas that are likely to contribute to an ever-advancing civilization. But what are the characteristics of constructive "adventures in living" that should be explored?

Adopting a posture of learning – First and foremost, our adventures should be seen not as ends in themselves but as part of a learning process based on experiment, involving a process of studying our reality, efforts toward constructive change, and reflection on results. While we have some ideas and principles to explore, no one knows with certainty exactly what will be needed to make the world work in the future. In fact, ideological certainty about what works and what doesn't makes the present system brittle and is something to avoid. Adopting a humble posture of learning will contribute to system resilience as we move forward. This humble approach—which recognizes that we are all equals moving forward on the same path of learning, all at different stages and speeds, each with different capacities and perspectives—is a key component of an emerging culture that will accompany the renewal of the social-ecological system.

Scripting a new cultural narrative – As William Rees, who popularized the concept of the ecological footprint, points out, we need to script a new, global cultural narrative. Says Rees, "We must learn to override our innate expansionist tendencies and abandon our perpetual growth myth. Instead of forcing the environment to conform to our demands we must learn to adapt our expectations to ecological reality. A good start would be a new global cultural narrative that shifts the values of society from competitive individualism, greed, and narrow self-interest, toward community, cooperation, and our collective interest in repairing the earth for survival."[122] Part and parcel of this process is a shift from short to long-term perspectives, or more accurately, to balancing the needs of present *and* future. We can script this narrative based on experiential learning that emerges from efforts to incorporate collective and ecological values in our adventures in living.

Building moral capacity – Creating a script that champions cooperative, collective values is one stage of culture building; the more difficult task is building the moral capacity to carry it out. "We need to increase our moral capacity," says Rees, "so we can choose between self-interest and the public good." "Our most 'human' qualities must prevail—our capacity for reason, our capacity for forward planning, our ability to make moral judgements, our compassion for other people and other species. If we use these qualities in a great expression of collective intelligence on both the local and global scales, humanity can become sustainable." As Rees

> We need to increase our moral capacity so we can choose between self-interest and the public good. Our capacity for reason and forward planning, our ability to make moral judgements, our compassion for people and other species, must prevail.

suggests, the values needed for an 11 billion world are already part of the human psyche, having incubated in our cultures throughout history; these higher values must be brought to the fore to supersede the self-interested values dragging down the current order.

Building capacity for resilience – A critical element of culture in an 11 billion world will be resilience. The hubris inherent in the present order—the triumphalist sense that ours is some ultimate form of civilization that finds itself at "the end of history"—is a significant factor in the present misguided efforts to prolong the growth stage of its adaptive cycle. A new culture will reject this notion, instead incorporating multiple processes for continuous reflection and adaptation that reinforce resilience in a full world context. This adaptation will necessarily involve new forms of political organization that replace a rigid ethic of power with a supple service orientation. This process will be fed by building moral capacity at the individual level.

A PARTICIPATORY EDUCATION MODEL

How can we encourage the development of the characteristics, qualities, and capacities needed for an 11 billion world? "Only unified learning, universally shared, makes accurate foresight and wise choice possible," writes E.O. Wilson in *Consilience*, his study of the unity of knowledge. In the course of building this knowledge, he continues, "…we are learning the fundamental principle that ethics are everything."[123]

The capacity to consistently make informed ethical decisions consistent with the full world scenario, on a scale ranging from the individual to institutions to communities, including the world community, is evidently beyond our current capacity. How can we hope to gain this capacity? William Rees points to a "need to initiate a…public education campaign on the severity of the crisis and the need for decisive action. It must be emphasized that global change is a collective problem requiring collective solutions." This awareness is essential, but the change process will have to move from awareness to the development of moral *capacity*, which implies the capacity to act effectively.

An educational process that aims to build foresight, wisdom, and a capacity for moral choices—choices that favour collective well-being over self-interest—will have limited results if it is based on traditional, industrial educational models designed to build the capacity of worker/consumers to contribute to the materialistic goals of the present order. What is needed instead is a global-scale learning process shaped by the same high-minded vision and values it hopes to evoke. It must be coordinated and focused, while also being inclusive, open to diverse approaches, and free of the fanaticism often associated with ideologies, including religious ideologies.

A number of promising alternative educational processes are already underway and much learning has taken place. One model that will be brought forward in this book, the Ruhi Institute,[124] exemplifies Hollings' prescription "to experiment and act inventively and exuberantly." Started in Columbia in the 1970s, the Ruhi approach has now spread to tens of thousands of communities worldwide.

Based on experiential learning from community development activities in rural Columbia, the institute gradually put in place a set of courses that aimed to build both vision and capacity in children, youth, and adults, with the goal of building resilient communities. The model uses a rational, scientific approach and also taps into spiritual wisdom, the mode of understanding reality from which a sense of individual and collective meaning and purpose is largely derived. Helping individuals develop a sense of meaning and purpose beyond immediate material survival has been of critical importance in the Ruhi experiment.

As will be explored in subsequent chapters, one's sense of meaning and purpose is critical in forming a long-term vision for the future of civilization. As E.O. Wilson points out, the search for "collective meaning and purpose is both urgent and immediate because, if for no other reason, it determines the environmental ethic."[125] Although Ruhi is not focused on ecological sustainability, that sensibility naturally emerges from an unbiased exploration of reality.

The Ruhi approach is participatory and experiential: participants use multiple modes of learning both to help them "read" their current reality and to try—from the outset—to change it for the better. As the Ruhi method has spread, processes have been established to collect—at the regional, national, and ultimately global levels—the learning about change that accumulates in local communities. Insights drawn from it are shared with all participating communities so that local approaches are continuously evolving based on collective experience and reflection.

The Ruhi methodology is a low-cost process of learning and capacity building that is continuously adaptive. What is more, it continuously generates new human resources to expand the learning process to more people in more villages and neighbourhoods. This approach has already proven its effectiveness by spreading to thousands of communities in every populated continent, without inputs and supports from government.

It is precisely this kind of approach—local, low-cost, low-key, non-confrontational, inclusive, self-generating—that is needed to bring about a cultural transformation at the grassroots level of society. As will be shown in a subsequent chapter, communities at the frontiers of learning using the Ruhi approach are already beginning to make fundamental cultural changes.

Importantly in the context of the issues raised in this section, the Ruhi approach offers a viable alternative to a materialistic worldview that is driving a social-ecological system based on unjust, unequal, and unsustainable economic activities. It promotes a balanced approach to development, understanding that happiness is achieved through the quality of one's inner life and relationships. The key components of this model are sketched here in brief:

- While important guiding principles are observed, the learning that drives the community-building processes emerges initially from small-scale development activities at the local level.

- Activities take place mainly at the grassroots level of the village or neighbourhood, where community building is most tenable.

- The learning process emerges out of local realities, using mainly local resources. Children, junior youth, and adults are all involved in transformational learning streams.

- The model is collaborative and consultative, rather than hierarchical.

- Small group learning is facilitated by one or more animators, who have taken part in previous training courses.

- The study begins with people "reading their reality" and proceeds from wherever the participants find themselves on the learning journey. The approach is applicable to poor, middle-income, or wealthy individuals and communities. The rich are understood to be as much—if not more—in need of "development" as the poor.

- Much of the learning emerges from action; starting with a series of conversations and reflections on guiding principles and practices, the participants propose ways of improving their communities—perhaps planting trees or starting activities for children. Initially, activities take place on a small-scale and are of short duration.

- Activities are service oriented. The goal is to build a community of purpose that aims to develop the capacity of an always-growing number of participants to understand their current reality and become positive change agents focused on the well-being of others.

- The participants reflect on what has been learned from their collective activities and formulate new activities that gradually grow in complexity and duration.

- Quantitative and qualitative data emerging from the local experience is pooled on the regional, national, and ultimately global level.

- While eschewing the dogmatic or fanatical elements of religion, learning is also drawn from humanity's collective spiritual wisdom and brought forward through the use of the arts, such as storytelling and songs.

- The participants strive to "be the change" they are seeking. Both outer, material and inner, moral development are important. Activities such as prayer, meditation, and contemplation help develop a balance of being and doing and attune individuals to a collective understanding of reality.

- A key objective is the continuous development of human resources through a self-generating training process, so that new people are always arising to facilitate a wider circle of participants and to walk with them on a common path of learning and service.

- A second objective is to move the community as a whole forward through acts of service and, as capacity develops, to engage in an ever-wider public discourse leading to social change on a larger scale.

Rather than prescribing a new cultural norm, the process outlined is one that, as the learning accumulates over time, begins to script the new cultural narrative needed for an 11 billion world. Meanwhile, moral capacity is being developed at the local level among a growing cohort of people who begin to build service-oriented communities capable of reading and responding to the realities of an 11 billion world. From the experiments, seeds are sown that can germinate and flourish in the renewal stages of adaptive cycles that will occur on the local, regional, national, and global scales as the old order crumbles, leading to the formation of a new, global culture.

Is a grassroots approach to building a a new culture that supports a just and sustainable global community really possible? Can people really develop the moral capacity needed to fuel change?

What choice do we have but to overcome our cynicism, to believe that profound change is possible, and that we can make it happen?

As Desmond Tutu so aptly put it, "I am a prisoner of hope."

A NEW AGRICULTURE

The ultimate goal of farming is not the growing of crops, it is the cultivation and perfection of human beings.

– Masanobu Fukuoka

CHAPTER 6
WELCOME TO WONDERLAND

The central place in every culture should be occupied by agriculture.
— Colin Duncan

Where did the food come from? Beyond a few wilted cabbages and dusty jars of pickles, the grocery stores were empty. Yet there was no evidence of hunger. On the contrary, Ukrainians appeared well fed.

In 1991, at the tail end of its communist era, I joined a small group of Westerners on a farm tour in Ukraine that also included a few days in Kiev. Eager to learn about the daily life of the average Ukrainian, we wandered about observing everything from city life to farm practices and, not infrequently given the legendary hospitality of Ukrainians, visiting their homes.

In my travel experience, food and drink vendors are ubiquitous in every busy town or city, especially in low-income countries where people have to hustle to make a living. Not so Kiev. For the traveller, something as basic as a drink of water was difficult to find. Obtaining a cup of coffee was an ordeal.

One morning I stumbled on an open coffee bar and took my place in the long queue. After 15 minutes I got to the front of the line, paid and was given a ticket which I took to the back of a second line where I waited another 15 minutes to get my coffee. The pointless double wait was typical of Soviet-era service seemingly designed to aggravate and denigrate the customer.

In Ukraine, I found any form of commercial service was provided with hostility and contempt. Yet on more than one occasion complete strangers offered home cooked feasts to my group of 10 foreigners. One stranger we met on the street spontaneously invited our party for dinner, for instance. When we arrived a few hours later, she met us at the door with bread and salt, a traditional welcome, and served up a multi-course dinner, free of charge. I expect the same person, in the uniform of a ticket agent or waiter, would have completely ignored us, or worse.

Culturally, the people seemed split in two; their private lives, space, and relationships governed by one ethic and their official, public life by another. One unexpected characteristic of the socialist countries I have visited was that social space was widely abused while private space was well cared for. Given the supposed socialist contempt for private property, it was more than interesting that apartments and houses and private yards were generally impeccable, whereas the care of lobbies and hallways and public parks was neglected.

Poking about in Kiev and other cities and towns, I discovered that not only were the food stores bare, the big department stores were empty of the goods people actually used. The stores sold clothes reminiscent of the 1950s. Outside, youth were dressed in cheap knock offs of contemporary designer jeans and tee shirts.

The big mystery then was, where did the food and clothes come from, if not commercial outlets? One Ukrainian I asked merely winked and said, "Welcome to Wonderland!"

Most of the Ukraine trip was spent on a collective farm near the city of Fostov getting to know community members and learning about farming practices. The collective included about 1500 residents whose main enterprise was a dairy herd. The experience did not readily answer the food source question, since the farm did not appear to produce anything.

We were billeted in homes, but gathered every noon hour in the farm's dining room for a meal that proved, beyond a doubt, that Ukraine had food and plenty of it. Our group of health conscious Westerners, all schooled in the avoidance of fat and other dietary excesses, were overwhelmed by the volume and caloric content of the food. Not even those of our group who were older, who had grown up on farms that required hard physical labour, could recollect meals as big and rich as these: platters of meats, plates of fat, bowls of fried potatoes and onions, fruit and potato pierogies smothered in sour cream, cabbage rolls, and bowls of vegetables, not to mention desserts.

We soon learned to leave a thin layer of food on the plate to prevent refills, for as soon as a space was opened, a server would reach over and refill it. For me, the forced eating was complicated by the fact that I was sick, likely from the water. Each day at the break of dawn I stumbled outside to vomit, but certainly not in the filthy outhouse. What, I wondered, did the milkmaids heading in for the early milking think of the foreigner puking, like clockwork, by the side of the road?

The women milked a herd of about 150 cows. I asked my New Zealand co-traveller, himself a dairy farmer, how many people it would take to manage a herd this size in New Zealand. He and his two sons could do it, he replied. Yet 1500 people worked this farm.

The main problem with the dairy, he said, was the cooler. On a dairy farm, milk is poured into a cooling vat where it is stored until it can be picked up for processing. On this farm the cooler didn't work so the milk was certain to sour before being collected. Essentially, what he was telling me was that the entire effort, supposedly the mainstay of 1500 people, was all but pointless.

The land itself was obviously excellent, with flat fields and rich black soil. There was plenty of rain. The landscape reminded me of southern Manitoba, though the climate was milder. The farm had modern equipment that didn't work due to a lack of parts. Instead, we saw people out in the massive fields with hoes, cultivating by hand. Needless to say, production was very low compared to the potential.

But how was it the farm could continue to operate with its main product unsalable and its secondary activities inoperative? It was simple: collective farms were state subsidized. Farm workers were paid wages by the state that were unrelated to their productivity. Consequently, there was no incentive to do productive work.

What then was the answer to the mystery of Ukraine's abundant food?

MYSTERY SOLVED

We soon discovered that each farm family had been allocated a small plot around their home for personal use, perhaps as little as a quarter-hectare. Whereas the collective farm was a disaster, the small plots were nothing short of miraculous, certainly the most productive pieces of land I have ever seen. In addition to vegetables of all kinds, they boasted abundant fowl, pigs, honeybees, small fruits and orchards.

I had heard that small plot agriculture was a very important source of food in Ukraine and elsewhere in the former Soviet Union. It was fascinating to actually see a small-scale agrifood system in action. Family gardens and peasant farms produced most of their own food and sold or bartered the surplus directly to extended family members and contacts in towns and cities, or through quasi-legal private farmer's markets.

Initially skeptical of the purported scale of small plot food production, I later found the numbers are born out in government and third party statistics. After the collapse of the Soviet collective farming system at the end of the communist era, the already high share of production from the small plot sector skyrocketed.

The situation in Russia was extraordinary.[126] In 1999, for example, more than 35 million families, including 105 million people or 71 percent of Russia's population, owned a dacha or a subsidiary plot; collectively, these people were cultivating more than 8 million hectares. This sector provided 91 percent of Russia's harvest of potatoes, 75 percent of its vegetables, 87 percent of berries and fruits, 58 percent of its meat, and 50 percent of its milk.

The following table shows that the output of these private households plots, each a maximum of 2 hectares, combined with those of peasant private farms ceded from former collectives, surpassed the production of larger agricultural enterprises in most categories. Even 20 percent of the country's grain was being grown on small plots.

RUSSIAN OUTPUT OF MAIN AGRICULTURAL PRODUCTS BY TYPES OF FARMS
(percent of total volume of production of all farms)

	Agricultural enterprises			Private household			Peasant private farms[1]		
	2000	2008	2009	2000	2008	2009	2000	2008	2009
Grains	90.8	78.1	78.2	0.8	0.9	0.9	8.4	21.0	20.9
Sugar beet	94.5	89.2	89.3	0.6	1.0	0.9	4.9	9.8	9.8
Sunflower seeds	84.3	70.7	70.7	1.2	0.4	0.4	14.5	28.9	28.9
Potatoes	7.5	11.4	13.1	91.2	83.5	81.1	1.3	5.1	5.8
Vegetables	22.9	19.2	18.4	74.7	70.7	71.3	2.4	10.1	10.3
Cattle & poultry	40.2	54.3	57.2	58.0	42.7	39.8	1.8	3.0	3.0
Milk	47.3	44.0	44.4	50.9	51.7	51.2	1.8	4.3	4.4
Eggs	70.8	74.6	75.8	28.8	24.5	23.4	0.4	0.9	0.8
Wool	37.8	18.4	...	56.8	55.4	...	5.4	26.2	...

1) Including individual entrepreneurs.   *Source: Russia in figures - 2010*

"When you look at the contribution of gardening to the national economy as a whole, it's even more stunning," comments agronomist Leonid Sharashkin. "In 2004, gardeners' output amounted to 51% (by value) of the total agricultural output of the Russian Federation. This represents 384 billion *rubles* (approx. US$14 billion), or 2.3% of Russia's Gross Domestic Product (GDP). This is greater, for example, than the contribution of the whole of the electric power generation industry (317 bn rubles), significantly greater than all of the forestry, wood-processing and pulp and paper industry (180 bn), significantly greater than the coal (54 bn), natural gas (63 bn) and oil refining (88 bn) industries taken together. The share of food gardening in national agriculture has increased from 32% in 1992 to over 50% by 2000."

While Sharashkin concludes that this likely represents the most extensive micro-scale food production system in any industrial nation, the situation in Ukraine was even more impressive. According to US AID,[127] the release of land parcels to rural inhabitants had spurred the formation of a massive small farming sector. In 1990, the share of agricultural land used by house plot owners (HPOs) and private family farms was 6 percent. This number later ballooned to 36.3 percent, of which HPOs represented 28.9 percent. At the same time, the share of small producers in total agricultural production topped 69.4 percent (of which HPOs produced 66.7 percent.)

The success of micro-food production in the former Soviet Union shows that even people living in virtually impossible circumstances can mobilize—en masse—to solve their problems.

It is fascinating to look back at the mythology created by the communist parties of the Eastern Block and how hollow that construct was in practice. Appearing to be a great, unassailable monolith, it browbeat and terrorized its own citizens, enforced farm collectivization, and imposed a complete monopoly of state enterprise, ultimately leading to social, economic, and ecological failure. Yet just under the surface another culture and economy operated, with people using whatever means at their disposal to survive. And when the day came that the great monolith of Soviet power and that of its allied states collapsed like a house of cards, the agrifood subculture—Ukrainian families' "diverse adventures in living"—rose to take its place. The success of micro-food production in the former Soviet Union shows that even people living in virtually impossible circumstances can mobilize—en masse—to solve their problems. To put it in the context of Holling's panarchy model, when the long *conservation stage* in Ukraine's adaptive cycle gave way to *release* and *reorganization*, the void left by the collapse of a hyper-authoritarian state exacerbated a crisis but also allowed greater freedom to address it.

That said, Ukraine and the other former socialist states have a long way to go to create an equitable, sustainable society; to a large extent, the ethos of power has not changed. Even as I write this, 23 years after my sojourn in Ukraine, Crimea has been invaded by Russia following the overthrow of its pro-Russian government.

"Experience of a totalitarian system of the communist type," said poet and politician Valclav Havel, "makes emphatically clear one thing which I hope has universal validity: that the prerequisite for everything political is moral. Politics really should be ethics put into practice...This means taking a moral stand not for practical purposes, in the hope that it will bring political results, but as a matter of principle."

The recent history of the former East Bloc states bears this out. When the paradigm of elite power remains in place societies don't really change, even after a revolution. Until a new ethos takes hold and shifts the nature of a society, injustices associated with the old models of governance reemerge and true progress stalls.

Their resilience allowed Ukrainians to cope, but they will not be able to transform their country until a new social-ecological paradigm is adopted. In this they are not unique; every nation is in need of a new approach to cope with the social-ecological reality of a full world, and nowhere is this more evident than in the agrifood system.

27.5 TRILLION CALORIES A DAY

Agriculture merits a separate section of this book because of its central role in civilization. If we are going to make the world work for 11 billion, among the most critical issues will be feeding people without destroying the land on which an ever-advancing civilization depends.

Currently, world agriculture produces about 19 trillion food calories daily. With a population of 11 billion, the agrifood system will have to generate more like 27.5 trillion food calories each day. Can we do this sustainably? As we consider how to adequately feed *all* of the current population—plus an additional 50 percent by century's end—the snapshot of the Ukrainian and Russian agrifood systems is instructive. A key point to be drawn from these examples is that agricultural production typically has less to do with physical restraints, such as soil quality or climate, and more to do with the way social-ecological systems are organized.

Communist countries suffered under an extreme form of authoritarian rule that placed economic decision making in the hands of the central government, eliminating local control of production and removing the kind of incentives that typically stimulate agricultural investment and productivity. In most cases the introduction of a communist system was accompanied by the rule of paranoid megalomaniacs—copies of the czars, emperors, and dictators they had overthrown. And in the case of the Soviet Union and Eastern Bloc states, the ongoing rivalry with the West fostered an arms race that sapped the region's wealth, leaving state agriculture in the sorry state I observed in Ukraine in 1991.

Looking at agricultural statistics, we can see that even two decades after the collapse of communism, with the exception of small plot agriculture, countries such as Russia and Ukraine are still producing food at yields well below the world average. In Ukraine in particular, low production has nothing to do with the land's productive capacity. The problem is a legacy of bad policies and oppressive rule that persist despite the change of regimes.

But the former communist states are not the only laggards. A substantial majority of nations produce less than the world average food yield. In some cases this can be linked to soil and climate limitations, but in most cases, even where physical constraints limit productivity, these constraints are closely linked to socio-economic and political factors.

Let's consider whether, in an ideal world where socio-economic-political systems and policies favour a strong agrifood system, there would be sufficient capacity to feed 11 billion people sustainably.

We begin by using "cowboy math" to provide a rough estimate of worldwide potential for food production. A useful tool for this analysis is average cereal yield in kilograms per hectare.[128] This is a crude statistic, given the variation in the nutritional value of cereals and the fact that cereals are not suited to every region, but for our purposes it provides a reasonable picture of relative productivity and capacity.

For this exercise, we will assume that each country produces cereal crops with nutritional values roughly equivalent to wheat or rice. The world average cereal yield (circa 2008) was around 2867 kg/hectare. Of 171 countries 76 produce more grain per hectare than the world average with some, such as Belgium (at 8576 kg/ha), producing close to three times that amount. The other 95 nations produce less than the world average with some, such as Zimbabwe (at 308.6 kg/ha), producing a mere fraction of the world average. Average cereal yields in Zimbabwe are 1/27th those of Belgium.

Assuming just one crop per year, an average cereal yield of 2867 kg/ha would provide 7.8 kg of grain per day per hectare, enough to provide the caloric needs of about 10 people.

As mentioned, there is a very substantial range of productivity across nations and many reasons for it, including climate and soil quality. However, physical factors alone cannot explain the variation. Why for example is the yield in Cambodia 2800kg/ha while next door, in Vietnam, it is 5064kg/ha? Why is the yield in the Dominican Republic 4245kg/ha while in Haiti, on the same island, it is 897 kg/ha. Clearly the political and social environment is highly significant.

A prime example is Zimbabwe. Due to its disastrous political regime the former "breadbasket of Africa" is now ranked last for cereal yield in Africa and the world, below even desert countries like Botswana. If we go back to 1980, yields in Zimbabwe were almost four times what they are today and very close to world average cereal yield at that time.

The average yield per hectare in Zimbabwe (308.6 kg/ha) would feed just over one person for a year. The average yield per hectare in nearby South Africa (3807 kg/ha) would feed some 14 people for a year. The main explanation for this difference is the degree of disunity and injustice found in Zimbabwe. Achieving a more unified society with freedom, good governance, sufficient investment, and access to markets would have a profound influence on productivity and thus the ability to feed ever-larger populations.

Ukraine provides a particularly good example of this observation. The total area of the country encompasses some 603,700 square kilometres. Forty million hectares are suitable for agriculture, equivalent to all the farmland in Canada, but Ukraine's farmland is generally of better quality than Canada's, plus Ukraine enjoys higher rainfall and milder weather. The relief of Ukraine is mainly flat: 95 percent of the land consists of plains, only 5 percent is mountainous. With one-third of the world's richest chernozem soils, Ukraine occupies a leading place among European countries by proportion of high-quality land. The deep black soil developed under grass vegetation has an enriched humus layer of between 40 and 50 centimetres. It covers 54 percent of the land.

Ukraine has 32,452,000 ha of arable land, the eighth largest agricultural land base in the world. From 2000-2010, cereal yields varied from 1800 kg/ha to 3500 kg/ha, with an average less than 2500 kg/ha, 13 percent below the world average.[129] Compare that to average production in Germany (6657 kg/ha), France (6957), Belgium (8414) or the average for the European Union (5257 kg/ha.)

Current total grain production in Ukraine is 40 million tonnes (2010) on 16.7 million ha. Hypothetically, if Ukraine's farms yielded like those in the European Union, it could produce 88 million tonnes of grain annually, enough to feed 317 million people. (One tonne of grain can feed 3.6 people for a year.) If grain was grown on all of Ukraine's arable land and produced yields comparable to the EU, it could produce up to 172 million tonnes, enough to feed 619 million people. But given its superior climate and soil quality, with the full deployment of modern agricultural techniques, there is no reason why yields like those in the highest producing countries would not be possible. In that case, Ukraine could theoretically produce more than 272 million tonnes of cereals, enough to feed as many as 980 million people.

Russia's potential production could be even greater due to its size. Russia with 121,781,000 ha of arable land produced an average of around 1850 kg of cereal grains per hectare from 2000-2010. If Russia could produce at the same average yield as Canada (3387kg/ha in 2008) on its arable land base, it could produce 400 million tonnes of grain, sufficient to feed 1.44 billion people. If it could produce closer to German levels, it could produce 800 million tonnes of grain, enough for 2.9 billion people.

Hypothetically then, Russian and Ukrainian agriculture, with full out deployment of modern agricultural technologies and policies on *all* its arable land, could theoretically feed all of the 3.7 billion people to be added to the world by 2100.

There are many countries with similar capacity, including a number of now independent countries that were part of the Soviet Union. Kazakstan, for example, has 22.7 million hectares of arable land producing an average 1020kg of cereal per hectare, less than half the world's average yield, despite soil and climatic conditions similar to those found on the Canadian prairies. Rain is a constraint but rainfall is higher than in Canada's prairie provinces, where production is higher than the world average. If Kazakhstan achieved yields at the world average on its arable land, it could produce enough grain to feed 230 million and if it could produce grain at the European average it would produce enough food for 450 million people.

HOW MANY PEOPLE CAN EARTH FEED?

In 2005, total world grain production was 2.3 billion tonnes, already enough to feed more than the current world population 2500 calories a day if equitably distributed. In the 99 countries that produced below the world average yield in that year, there were 720 million hectares of arable land, approximately half of the world's supply. The average cereal production per hectare on this area was 1826 kg/ha. If all arable areas in these countries were planted to cereals (or local foods of equivalent nutritional value), production would total 1.3 billion tonnes, enough to feed 4.7 billion people. And if production could reach the world average, total production would rise to just over 2 billion tonnes, enough to feed 7.2 billion people.

Bringing low yielding countries up to world average yield would obviously have great potential to feed many more people. And importantly, most of the new population expected by 2100 will be living in these lower-income countries, which have higher birth rates, not in the high-producing, industrialized nations with low birth rates. Increasing production in the low producing countries is clearly the highest priority for agriculture.

Having said that, there is also a large potential to increase yields in many countries that already experience yields above the global average. If all arable hectares in the 73 countries that yield above the world average for cereal in 2005 were seeded to grain and could yield 4500kg/ha, i.e. the average cereal yield for these countries, they could produce 3.2 billion tonnes, enough to feed 11.5 billion people.

And if all the world's arable acres were planted to cereals that yielded the global average of 2.8 tonnes/ha, the total world production in an average year would be 3.9 billion tonnes of cereals, enough to provide food for 14 billion people if eaten directly. If all the arable land could produce at the average production rate—4.5 tonnes/ha—for the 73 countries that produce more than the current world average, there would be sufficient food for more than 20 billion.

Whether it would make sense to apply the policies and practices of modern agriculture to all the world's arable land is another question that will be examined later, but this exercise suggests that the broad application of modern agricultural technologies and policies would, at least theoretically, make feeding 11 billion people technically possible.

You may question the use of cowboy math to draw that conclusion, but scholarly analyses of the potential for food production have yielded similar results. What is more, these analyses suggest that *it would not actually be necessary to increase agricultural inputs to feed 11 billion people.*

In 1994, the eminent environmental scientist Vacliv Smil answered the question *How Many People Can the Earth Feed?* in a journal article by that name.[130] The research was later expanded in his book *Feeding the World.*[131] Smil concluded there are no insurmountable obstacles to feeding at least 10 billion people, even without increasing agricultural inputs.

By far the most important outcome of his research was the identification of substantial inefficiencies throughout the food production and consumption chain. He concluded that a combination of improved agronomic practices (above all, more efficient use of fertilizer and water), lowered post-harvest waste, and healthier eating (mainly by reducing fat intake) could produce adequate nutrition for at least an additional 3 billion people without any increase in existing farm inputs. Furthermore, realistic mobilization of new productive inputs could secure enough food for another 2 billion people. *Agrimonde,* a more recent study of this topic from French researchers, came to similar conclusions.[132]

> By eliminating inefficiencies and waste, it would not actually be necessary to increase agricultural inputs to feed 11 billion people.

The socio-economic system currently in place denies access to food to a significant portion of the world's poor. This problem is likely to increase as the world struggles to accommodate 50 percent more people. But as we have seen, the problem of inadequate food supply is tied not so much to available supplies and resources as to the way in which the supplies and resources are managed—or mismanaged.

An analysis of the global potential for food production shows that better agrifood policies and practices could deliver the food needed for 11 billion people, one of the main concerns posed by rising population, even without tapping the increased production potential discussed in this chapter. What holds back the necessary change is mainly inefficiencies and ineffective policies and institutions, at the local, national, and international levels, compounded by a lack of ethical capacity.

The Ukrainian example illustrates these problems but also shows that people can adapt to enormous challenges—even the collapse of their state ideology and institutions—with surprising innovations that meet human needs. As we will see in subsequent chapters, examples of positive change on a large scale give us clear signs that humanity can rise to the challenge of feeding a burgeoning population if it adopts enlightened policies that are socially inclusive and ecologically sound.

A HOUSE BUILT ON SAND

While modern agriculture has in many ways been a boon by rapidly increasing the food supply to meet the demand of a rising population, this increase is built on a weak ecological foundation and will ultimately implode without profound change.

The main factor that has allowed agriculture to keep pace with population growth over the past few centuries has been the conversion of forests and natural grasslands to farms. Between farming and forestry, managed ecosystems now constitute half of the planet's ice-free land, while human-mobilized material and energy flows now rival those of the ecosphere itself.[133]

Now that the limits of agriculture's geographic expansion have been reached in most areas, the only viable way to increase food production has been to improve the productivity of existing farmland. In some regions, particularly in Asia, this has been achieved primarily by growing multiple crops each year in irrigated systems using new, short-duration crop varieties. The increased productivity of the last few decades is also closely linked to the use of fossil fuels to intensify mechanization and produce fertilizers and agricultural chemicals, as well as the adoption of crop varieties that respond well to these inputs.

Land-abundant countries, like Ukraine, Canada, or Russia, still possess the physical capacity to increase food production through various technologies that increase yield. These technologies have a significant ecological impact, however;

in addition, they are highly reliant on non-renewable and increasingly expensive fossil fuel inputs that contribute to climate change.

What is more, those countries and segments of their populations most in need of food could not afford to import it from the high producing, industrial nations. Thus the vast majority of new food supplies required to meet the needs of 3.7 billion new people will have to come from domestic production in low-income countries, many of which are already experiencing high population growth and significant stress on their agricultural resources.

As agriculture intensifies to meet demand, broad concerns emerge about related ecosystem impacts, especially in the low income nations. The key problems are:

Deteriorating land resources Soil erosion and other forms of land degradation rob the world of up to 7 million hectares of farmland every year. According to the study *Pilot Analysis of Global Ecosystems: Agroecosystems*,[134] 40 percent of the world's agricultural land is seriously degraded. Based on the most comprehensive mapping of global agriculture to date, the study indicates that almost 75 percent of crop land in Central America is seriously degraded, 20 percent in Africa (mostly pasture), and 11 percent in Asia. Although crop production can still grow on a global scale over the next several decades, the study warns that the underlying conditions of many of the world's agroecosystems are not good, particularly those in low-income countries. The added stress of feeding an additional 3.7 billion will certainly result in a downward spiral of degradation unless production methods and efficiencies are substantially altered.

Deteriorating water resources Some 40 percent of the world's food comes from irrigated cropland, but the productivity of these lands is in jeopardy. Water tables are dropping steadily in several major food-producing regions and farmers are racking up an annual water deficit of some 160 billion cubic meters. Meanwhile, the amount of irrigated land per person has dropped 5 percent since 1978 and one in five hectares of irrigated land is damaged by salt. In all, waterlogging and salinization have sapped the productivity of nearly half the world's irrigated lands; 30 million hectares have been severely damaged and an additional 1.5 million hectares are lost each year. Meanwhile, so much water is being diverted for irrigation and other uses that the lower reaches of several major rivers—including the Yellow in China, the Indus in Pakistan, the Ganges in South Asia, and the Colorado in the American Southwest—sometimes run dry for portions of the year. The number of people living in water-stressed countries is projected to climb from 470 million to 3 billion by 2025. In the swathe of countries from Morocco to Iran virtually every nation is facing water shortages. Given that it takes a thousand tonnes of water to grow a tonne of wheat, these countries import grain to meet their food needs. The water required to produce the grain and other farm products imported into the region is equivalent to the annual flow of the Nile.[135]

Agricultural chemicals Fertilizer and pesticide use has been another means of boosting productivity. Global use of nitrogen fertilizers went from 5 million tonnes in the 1940s to 100 million tonnes in recent years, and today about 40 percent of all the protein in the human diet is dependent on the application of nitrogen fertilizer. The global use of agricultural pesticides rose from about 50 million kilograms a year in 1945 to current application rates of over 2.5 billion kilograms per year. Excessive use of fertilizers and pesticides can pollute surface and groundwater sources, posing a health risk, especially for infants. In some countries, inadequate fertilization results in a form of soil mining that contributes to soil degradation.[136]

Genetic erosion The loss of genetic diversity in both wild and domesticated plant and animal species threatens future agricultural productivity. As monocultures replace natural ecosystems and traditional crop diversity, genetic resources useful for many purposes, including crop improvement, are disappearing. It is expected that 25 percent of the earth's biodiversity will disappear in this century.

Climate change Agriculture produces greenhouse gases linked to global warming. In addition to methane, some 30 percent of carbon dioxide emissions result from deforestation and land use practices such as burning rangeland. Global warming is already contributing to extreme heat, storms, drought and flooding, all of which negatively impact agriculture.

Overfishing Close to 1 billion people depend on fishing for most of their animal protein. About two-thirds of the world's marine fisheries are either overexploited, depleted, or at the limits of exploitation. About one half of all mangrove ecosystems, which are essential to the health of coastal fisheries, have been changed or destroyed, and coral reefs, another source of fish stock, are experiencing a massive collapse, probably as a result of climate change. Consequently, it is unlikely that we can look to the seas for additional food supplies.[137]

The impacts of these environmental factors are already being felt in the slowing of the rate of growth in productivity per person. For cereals, which occupy more than half of the world's harvested area, the slowdown in yield growth has been pronounced, dropping from 3 percent per annum in the 1960s to just over half that amount in the 1990s, before rising back to almost 2 percent in the last decade.[138]

In addition to environmental factors, an important reason for the slowing of growth in productivity may simply be that many major innovations, such as improved crop varieties, have already been widely adopted. Once in place, they can no longer increase but only maintain productivity. There may still be room for wider application of these practices, but those nations that have not already adopted them typically cannot afford to do so without significant outside assistance, yet levels of foreign aid in agriculture are declining. Official Development Assistance (ODA) decreased during the 1990s, for instance, from 0.33 percent to 0.25 percent of the GNP of OECD countries.[139]

Nevertheless, in the near term technical innovation is likely to succeed in offsetting the trends threatening food security for the majority of people; but the challenge of meeting human food needs is likely to grow ever more difficult over time as land and water resources deteriorate and population rises, mainly in the low-income nations that are already facing the most ecological challenges.

While aspects of modern agricultural policy and practice are beneficial and could be used more widely, modern agrifood systems are fundamentally unsustainable due to their heavy ecological and energy footprint. The planet-wide application of high-production, industrial agrifood systems—with low labour-inputs, high capital and energy intensity, and reliance on toxic chemicals—is not the only way forward, however. There are other options and adaptations to modern agriculture to consider as we develop sustainable ways to make good nutrition available to 11 billion.

As will be discussed in subsequent chapters, the ecological limitations presented by the current approach can be surmounted using a different mindset and accompanying principles and practices. Some of these will be specific to food producers, while others will be adopted mainly by food consumers, especially the heaviest consumers who draw a disproportionate share of resources.

The new ethos will have to be learned and incorporated into educational systems for children, youth, and adults, and translated into practice as rapidly as possible. This corresponds to the strengths of educational approaches exemplified by the Ruhi institute, which is particularly effective at the village level where fewer distractions and competing interests and opportunities exist than in urban settings. But new forms of experiential, moral education will have to become universal to lay the foundation of a just and sustainable agrifood system.

CHAPTER 7
RECLAIMING THE FUTURE

Sustained agriculture means maintenance first—attending to the health of soil, water, plants and animals—ahead of attention to yield and production.
– Stan Rowe

The cradle of Chinese civilization, the once-fertile, France-sized Loess Plateau has been in socioeconomic and ecological decline for centuries. Considered the most eroded area in the world, its land is largely ruined; consequently, many of its 50 million inhabitants face severe poverty. The impact of its ecological catastrophe has spread well beyond the region: at times, huge dust storms transport the eroded soil as far as Tokyo and Taipei; at others, rains wash away the soil and flood the Yellow River, wrecking havoc downstream.

The winds of change are now transforming the region long called "China's Sorrow." In 2005, China, supported by the World Bank, completed the largest watershed restoration project in world history on the upper banks of the Yellow River. The little-known, $500 million enterprise transformed 35,000km² (roughly the area of Taiwan) of the 640,000km² plateau from dusty wasteland to productive farms, wetlands, and forest.

Through terracing, watershed restoration, and replanting native trees and other vegetation, as well as restrictions on grazing, the rejuvenated land again supports a vibrant agricultural economy. The restored plant cover reduces flooding and dust storms by anchoring the region's soil, which is becoming a large carbon sink.

The hopeful practice of restoring degraded and desertified land has been under-publicized, according to journalist Paul Mozur,[140] perhaps because restoration processes are slow relative to short human attention spans. It can take decades for vegetation to fully return, and strict attention must be paid to matters like grazing and cultivation. Lack of awareness can block support for land restoration, which has huge potential for solving ecological and economic problems.

One antidote to the awareness gap has been John Liu's remarkable documentary film, *Hope in a Changing Climate*,[141] a film every despondent conservationist should see. Its jaw-dropping fades from the denuded landscapes filmed prior to the commencement of the restoration in 1995 to the lush fields and renewed forests that replaced them 10 years later cheer the heart.

The Loess Plateau Watershed Rehabilitation Project helped farmers reclaim steep slopes, control grazing, level fields, and diversify production. As a result, not only has the land been revived, per capita grain output has grown 62 percent, from 365 to 591 kilograms a year; the annual income of participant households increased from $70 to $200 per person; and perennial vegetation cover increased from 17 to 34 percent, reducing sediment flow into the Yellow River by more than 100 million tons per year.[142]

The restoration had a huge impact on the occupants of the plateau. Guo Sanren, a farmer born and raised on useless farmland in a mountain valley in Jungar Banner on the Loess Plateau, was astonished by it.[143] Like many locals, Guo used to do odd jobs in cities to feed his destitute family, which lived in abject poverty until the World Bank project was launched in his hometown in 1999.

Key to the success of the project has been the multiyear process of preparation, public consultation, and detailed efforts to establish property rights. Local people had to understand that shifting their longstanding farming practices to ensure that ecosystems were cared for would result in a better economic future. Importantly, local people were hired to undertake the massive ecological and watershed reconstruction.

"It'd be the same useless land if not for the World Bank loans," said Guo, who has returned home to farm again. In the past seven years, the watershed rehabilitation has improved ecosystems, planted trees, and built roads and other facilities in his hometown. Guo's family applied for a 35,000 yuan (US$4,375) loan to sink a well and build greenhouses to plant vegetables. They made 9,000 yuan ($1,125) in net income the next year. The following year the family made more than 35,000 yuan and had a new house built. He had never earned that much in the city.

The Loess Plateau project has benefited at least 3.2 million people and raised more than 1 million locals out of abject poverty. With terraced fields and new irrigation systems, the yield of wheat has doubled and farmers can make at least $190 dollars more annually than before on each hectare of cropland.

By the end of 2005, the number of needy households in the region affected by the project had been reduced from 256,000 to 66,000. Just 12 percent of local residents were still below the poverty line, compared to 39 percent reported in 1999.

The project has been praised by a former World Bank president as "one of the best projects ever implemented in the world." Indeed, there are few examples of land reclamation more dramatic than the Loess Plateau projects, which are an important model for worldwide land reclamation. The project proves it is possible to rehabilitate damaged ecosystems on a large-scale. What is more, this offers a major opportunity to both mitigate and adapt to climate change while reducing—even eliminating—abject poverty.

THE MAN WHO STOPPED THE DESERT

More modest but no less inspiring stories of ecological restoration and poverty reduction can be found around the world, and they often result from the leadership of individual farmers. Such is the story of Yacouba Sawadogo, who has shown that the most effective solutions often emerge from the grassroots, at the local level.

The Sahara is the world's largest hot desert. (The larger Antarctic and Arctic regions are cold deserts.) At over 9.4 million km², it covers most of Northern Africa and is comparable in size to Europe or the United States. To the south is the Sahel, a 3 million km² belt of semi-arid tropical savanna. Droughts, overgrazing, and deforestation are contributing to the desertification of this region.

The documentary film, *The Man Who Stopped the Desert*,[144] shows how Sawadogo, an illiterate farmer from Burkina Faso, has transformed the lives of thousands of people across Africa's Sahel by developing techniques to stop the spread of the Sahara.

During the 1970s and early 1980s, the Sahel was hit with drought after drought. Families abandoned their villages in search of food and water, but Sawadogo stayed and starting in 1980 pioneered techniques that halted the approaching desert. Together with Mathieu Ouédraogo, another local innovator, Sawadogo experimented with techniques for rehabilitating damaged soil, including simple approaches traditional to the region called *cordons pierreux* and *zaï holes*.

Cordons pierreux are thin lines of fist-sized stones laid across fields perpendicular to the flow of rainwater. As rain falls it pushes silt across the surface of the field. The silt then builds up against the cordon. Slowing down the flow of water gives it more time to soak into the earth. The accumulated silt also provides a relatively fertile spot for seeds to sprout. As plants grow they slow the water even further. Meanwhile, their roots break up the compacted soil, making it easier for water to soak in.

Zaï holes also catch water. Traditionally they were used in a limited way to restore barren land. Sawadogo increased the size of the holes and began filling them with manure and other biodegradable residues to provide a source of plant nutrients. The manure also attracts termites, whose tunnels break up the soil. Once established, the zaï holes are used to grow trees, sorghum, and millet.

Over a period of more than two decades, Yacouba Sawadogo created a forested area of approximately 20 hectares. Both Sawadogo and Ouédraogo have engaged in extension and outreach efforts to share the techniques, which have spread in the region. To promote the methods, particularly zaï holes, Sawadogo holds bi-yearly Market Days at his farm in the village of Gourga. Attendees from over a hundred regional villages come to share seed samples, swap tips, and learn from one another.

Countering the accepted wisdom of traditional land chiefs opposed to new farming techniques, Sawadogo's work was controversial. At one point, opposition turned to anger when jealous neighbours burned newly planted trees and millet fields. Later, government tried to appropriate the land for urban development. Sawadogo was undaunted by the opposition and today his name has become synonymous with reversing desertification, drawing the attention of governments and organizations such as the Gates Foundation, which has launched a multi-million dollar research and investment program for local solutions in Africa.

According to Chris Reij, facilitator of the African Re-greening Initiatives at the Centre for International Cooperation, who has followed desert reclamation work over the past 25 years, "Yacouba single-handedly has had more impact on…conservation than all the national and international researchers put together. In this region tens of thousands of hectares of land that was completely unproductive has been made productive again thanks to the techniques of Yacouba."

Interestingly, restoring vegetation has been shown to create climatic feedback loops that increase rainfall. Analysis of satellite images and rainfall in the Sahel between 1982 and 1999 show that 10 to 20 percent more rain falls where land is restored.

It has been estimated that 70,000 km² of forest is restored annually around the world, often in conjunction with agricultural restoration. Harnessing people's affinity for trees could be a key to launching large-scale reforestation schemes and fighting poverty, according to Reij. Indeed, he reports that African farmers are already taking to forest restoration in a big way.[145]

We rarely hear good conservation news from northern Africa, but farmer-managed natural regeneration of degraded land is taking hold in several areas. In part of Niger, for example, farmers have restored 5 million hectares of degraded land largely through tree planting in what Reij calls the largest environmental transformation in the Sahel region, if not Africa.

Such efforts have a great many positive social and ecological results that contribute to the sustainability of reforestation projects. Reij points out that trees reduce temperatures, wind speeds, and evaporation, sequester carbon, and increase biodiversity. They can produce both fodder for livestock as well as fruit and edible vitamin-rich leaves for people. Some species fix atmospheric nitrogen to enhance soil fertility. The social benefits include improved household food security due to the more productive, drought-resistant farming systems, and thus less hunger, poverty, and lower infant mortality, as well as sharply reduced firewood collection time for women.

Studies also indicate that investing in natural regeneration and agroforestry makes economic sense for farmers. One study, for example, showed an internal rate of return of 31 percent on investment in re-greening over 20 years. The African Re-greening Initiatives program, which is built on these local successes, eschews the big conventional project that require vast sums of money. In the African context, farmer-led reforestation appears to be much more successful than large-scale reforestation schemes because farmers themselves have a sense of ownership of their trees.

Whether restoration projects have emerged at the grassroots level, as with Yacouba Sawadogo's work in the Sahel, or through large-scale, government-initiated schemes like the Loess Plateau reclamation project, they clearly depend on the active participation of local farmers, as well as other stakeholders. Successful landscape restoration is less a technical problem than a social process, one that requires unity of thought and action.

IDEAS TRANSFORM LANDSCAPES

Filmmaker John Liu's involvement in documenting land restoration in China and East Africa led him to reflect deeply on his learning. Ecosystems rarely become dysfunctional on their own, he observed; they are disrupted when people place greater value on the products and services extracted from ecosystems than on sustaining their functions. Valuing *ecosystem functions* above production and consumption and making this the basis of their economic approach provides the rationale and impetus for stakeholders to mobilize to restore degraded land.

"We already have the knowledge necessary to do this and we certainly have the need given the enormous threat of climate change. What the Chinese came to realize on the Loess Plateau that allowed them to take the crucial step toward restoration was the theoretical understanding that '*Ecosystem function is vastly more valuable than the production and consumption of goods and services.*' This statement changes everything," asserts Liu.

> *Ecosystem function is vastly more valuable than the production and consumption of goods and services.*

Key to this understanding was an economic assessment that showed that the value of goods and services produced from the Loess Plateau was less than the value its ecosystem services could provide. That is, income drawn from the land was much lower than, for example, the benefit that would come from maintaining land cover to avoid downstream flooding. On top of that, it was determined that restoring ecological function would improve production and income, which was born out in experience.

The Chinese had understood what many have realized before, including economist E.F. Schumacher in his classic *Small is Beautiful* and ecologist Stan Rowe in his collection of essays, *Homeplace*:

> Carried over into agriculture, ecological concepts place the farmer, the horticulturist, the gardener, as overseer of an interrelated web of life whose organic bank of capital is the soil. The system will go on and on as long as the soil-capital is not degraded by taking more from it than is restored. Sustained agriculture means maintenance first—attending to the health of soil, water, plants and animals—ahead of attention to yield and production. Schumacher's rules for land use are profoundly ecological: guard the health, beauty and permanence of the land, and don't worry about sustained productivity. It is a derived benefit, a secondary quantitative benefit that will look after itself if the quality of land is preserved. The primary accent on health is well-placed because the health of humans (and their beauty and permanency) cannot be separated from the health of Nature....[146]

Ecosystem function first is an idea that can change the world, quite literally. John Liu's films show, for instance, parched landscapes completely denuded of plant cover and heavily eroded; exactly the same landscape is shown several years later, following ecological restoration, alive with productive fields and forests, with ponds and flowing streams. The restored land is an idea put into practice.

This is an example of how human consciousness shapes the physical world, not in an esoteric but in the practical sense, though philosophers may draw broader conclusions. We are continually shaping the world through our thoughts about our own reality in relation to the ecosphere. The thought that the physical world exists primarily to provide goods and services to be extracted and consumed by people engaged in a process of continuous economic expansion results in ecosystems being consumed. The ultimate outcome of this thought is a desert world and a collapse of civilization. The alternate thought, that the ecosphere must be carefully served and sustained by its inhabitants results in healthy ecosystems that provides goods and services in perpetuity. This in turn makes an ever-advancing civilization possible.

The Global Partnership on Forest Landscape Restoration has formalized Liu's observation on ecosystem function in its motto "Ideas Transform Landscapes." The Partnership and similar organizations envision the application of this idea as an opportunity for locally-based but planet-wide projects to restore billions of hectares of degraded land.

CREATING A NEW CONTINENT

Exactly how big is the problem—or opportunity—of degraded land? In 2011, the World Resources Institute working with the Global Partnership on Forest Landscape Restoration assembled available data to determine how much depleted land exists. They put the figure at over 2 billion hectares, more than the total area of South America. The analysis found that:

- One and a half billion hectares would be best-suited for mosaic restoration, in which forests and trees are combined with other land uses, including agroforestry, small-holder agriculture, and settlements.

- Up to half a billion hectares would be suitable for wide-scale restoration of closed forests.

- In addition to these two billion hectares, 200 million hectares of unpopulated lands, mainly in far northern boreal forests, have been degraded by fire. Such areas would likely be difficult to restore due to remoteness.

The distinguished soil scientist Rattan Lal of the Carbon Management and Sequestration Center, School of Natural Resources at Ohio State University, puts the area of depleted land even higher. He estimates that there are 3.5 billion hectares of degraded and desertified lands, close to one quarter of Earth's land surface of some 15 billion hectares.

Compare this area to total cropland of just 1.5 billion hectares (1.13 billion rain-fed and 407 million irrigated); global forest ecosystems with a total land area of 4.17 billion hectares; and grasslands covering 2.9 billion hectares globally, including 2 billion hectares of tropical grasslands or savannas and 900 million hectares of temperate grasslands. Most of the remainder is cold deserts, including Antarctica.

Given the vast area of degraded and desertified land, the potential for reclamation is equivalent to adding an entire continent to the planet's ecologically productive land.

GEOENGINEERING THROUGH LAND MANAGEMENT

Geoengineering is the deliberate large-scale intervention in the Earth's natural systems to counteract climate change. Proposals have been made, for example, to fertilize or increase the alkalinity of the oceans to increase carbon absorption or to release stratospheric aerosols to block sunlight. While such proposals are rightly met with skepticism—if not fear—we should acknowledge that burning fossil fuels, deforestation, and cultivation are inadvertent forms of *reverse* geoengineering.

Rattan Lal and others argue that restoring vegetation on degraded lands and increasing soil organic carbon (SOC) on existing farmland has the potential to sequester sufficient CO_2 to substantially mitigate climate change if done on a large scale. This form of geoengineering is a safe, win-win situation, since land restoration and soil improvement also restores watersheds, fosters biodiversity, improves productivity, and assists with rural poverty reduction.

Restoring vegetation on degraded lands and increasing soil organic carbon on existing farmland has the potential to sequester sufficient CO_2 to substantially mitigate climate change

The potential to reduce climate change by sequestering atmospheric CO_2 in soil and vegetation is huge. Photosynthesis converts 112 billion tonnes of atmospheric CO_2 into biomass annually. (By comparison, only 9 billion tonnes of carbon emissions are produced from fossil fuel combustion.) However, almost all of the CO_2 synthesized by plants is returned back to the atmosphere through plant and soil respiration. According to Lal, if 10 percent of what plants photosynthesize annually—about 11 billion tonnes—could be retained in the biosphere it would be possible to balance the global carbon budget.

Lal explains that the atmospheric concentration of CO_2 from fossil fuel combustion and land use changes has increased by 31 percent since 1750, resulting in gradual global warming.[147] Since the industrial revolution, global emissions of carbon are estimated at around 270 billion tonnes due to fossil fuel combustion and about 136 billion tonnes due to land use change and soil cultivation.

Emissions due to land use change include those from deforestation, biomass burning, conversion of natural ecosystems to agriculture, drainage of wetlands, and soil cultivation. Depletion of the SOC pool has contributed around 78 billion tonnes of carbon to the atmosphere. Some cultivated soils have lost one-half to two-thirds of the original SOC. The depletion of SOC is accentuated by soil degradation and exacerbated by land misuse and soil mismanagement.

Soil Sequestration Soil is the third largest carbon sink, after oceans and fossil fuels. Soil contains 4.5 times the sequestration capacity of all vegetation (including trees) and 3.3 times that of the atmosphere. While Rattan Lal estimates that 10-20 percent of annual greenhouse gas emissions could be removed each year by sequestering carbon in cultivated land, a study by the Rodale Institute was more optimistic, stating that "multiple research efforts verify that practical organic agriculture if practised on the planet's 3.5 billion tillable acres, could sequester nearly 40% of our current CO_2 emissions." Even by the more conservative estimate, carbon farming holds significant potential to mitigate climate change.[148]

The global potential of SOC sequestration through the application of recommended management practices on a large scale, at an average of 1 tonne/ha/year, is 1 billion tonnes of carbon per year, which would offset one-fourth to one-third of the total human-caused annual net increase in atmospheric CO_2, estimated at 3.3 billion tonnes per year. The cumulative potential of SOC sequestration over 25–50 years could be as much as 60 billion tonnes, close to half of all emissions from land use changes since 1750.

The potential of soil sequestration to mitigate climate change of course depends on the extent of the application of recommended practices. Some 1.5 billion hectares of land are currently under cultivation. There is an optimum range of SOC concentration of 2-3 percent in the root zone covering a wide spectrum of soils. Given that cultivation has generally led to substantial decreases in SOC, most soils can benefit from increased SOC formation. On top of that is the potential to increase SOC formation in billions of hectares of deforested, degraded, and desertified lands should they be reclaimed.

While soil sequestration could play a substantial role in ameliorating climate change, this should be seen as complementary to other measures to mitigate climate change, such as the progressive reduction of the use of fossil fuels through widespread energy efficiencies and conservation or the adoption of renewable energy sources.

REDD+ Deforestation and forest degradation, through agricultural expansion, conversion to pastureland, infrastructure development, destructive logging, and fires accounts for nearly 20 percent of global GHG emissions, second only to the energy sector and more than the entire global transportation sector. Eighty percent of these emissions stem from only 10 countries, mainly in the low-income bracket.[5]

Reducing Emissions from Deforestation and Forest Degradation, plus conservation, sustainable management of forests, and enhancement of forest carbon sinks (known as REDD+),[149] as well as afforestation (creating new forests), increases terrestrial carbon sinks, including SOC. Sequestering carbon in vegetation also enhances ecological functions and economic development.

Initially, the most important priority is preventing further deforestation. Currently, the clearing and degradation of forests adds almost 2 billion tonnes of carbon to the atmosphere each year. Progress is being made on reducing deforestation in some areas. Brazil, for example, has reduced the rate of deforestation by approximately 80 percent in recent years.[150]

Afforestation is often associated with REDD+. Over a 50-year period, it is estimated that adding 422 million additional hectares of forest is possible, a 10 percent increase in global forest cover. McKinsey and Company have estimated that by 2030, afforestation could potentially mitigate 0.27 billion tonnes of carbon per year; reforestation 0.38 billion tonnes of carbon per year; and improved management an additional 0.08 billion tonnes, a total of 0.73 billion tonnes, close to one quarter of the annual net increase in atmospheric carbon. It is thought that improved forest practices could mitigate up to 75 billion tonnes of carbon during the next 50 years.

Albert Bates has speculated that if 7.6 million people were employed full time planting trees, sufficient trees could be grown to absorb more that the world's annual carbon dioxide emissions.[151] The limitation is the amount of available land; a major area of opportunity is the reforestation of deserts, which now cover one third of the world's land mass.

Lal (see adjacent table) puts the technical potential of a range of measures to increase carbon sequestration in the terrestrial biosphere at approximately 3.8 billion tonnes, greater than the net annual increase in atmospheric CO_2. Over 50 years, these measures could mitigate up to 190 billion tonnes of carbon, more than all the carbon released from land use since 1750.

Technical potential of carbon (C) sequestration on land	
Activity	Technical Potential Billions of tonnes C/year
Afforestation, forest succession, agroforestry, peat land	1.2 – 1.4
Forest plantations	0.2 – 0.5
Savanna/grassland ecosystems	0.3 – 0.5
Cropland management	0.4 – 1.2
Restoration of salt-affected soils	0.3 – 0.7
Desertification control	0.2 – 0.7
Total technical potential	**2.55 – 4.96 (3.8)**

Source: Adapted from Lal in Bioscience, October 2010, Vol. 60 No. 9.

Expanding the Use of Wood as a Building Material Once a forest is mature the carbon sink no longer increases significantly, meaning that forest preservation is not the best strategy for maximizing carbon sequestration from forests. Selective harvesting, the use of forest products for durable goods such as building materials, and the subsequent replanting of trees results in higher levels of carbon sequestration. So long as the source forest is sustainably managed, replacing fossil-fuel intensive construction materials such as concrete, steel, aluminum, and plastics with wood can result in significant GHG emission reductions from the building sector. The building sector contributes up to 30 percent of global annual GHG emissions and consumes up to 40 percent of all energy. Given the massive growth underway in new construction in economies such as China, and the inefficiencies of existing building stock worldwide, unless a different approach is taken, emissions from buildings will more than double in the next 20 years.

Some 10 to 20 percent of the energy used by buildings is consumed in materials manufacturing and transport, construction, maintenance, and demolition.[152] It has been estimated that constructing buildings with wooden frames instead of concrete frames reduces net carbon emissions by 110 to 470 kg CO_2 per square meter of floor area on a lifecycle basis. Properly used, wood-frame construction can contribute to a superior building envelope from an insulation perspective due to lower rates of heat transfer, resulting in lower emissions from heating and cooling. Mitigation benefits can be optimized when wood construction materials are reused as a building material or fuel when buildings are demolished.

Incentives The technical potential for carbon sequestration from vegetation and soil is not the same as economic potential, the latter being highly dependent on the price of carbon. One important key to adopting climate-friendly agriculture and forestry practices is to establish a price for carbon emissions that makes *avoiding* deforestation as valuable as deforestation, or soil sequestration more valuable than the status quo.

Over the long-term, it has been estimated that pricing CO_2 at US\$27.2/ton could potentially eliminate deforestation, i.e. it would be more lucrative to maintain the ecological function of forests than to clear them. Other cost estimates show an effective price range of from US\$0.5 to US\$7/tonne of CO_2 for forestry projects in low-income countries to US\$1.4 to US\$22/tonne of CO_2 for projects in higher-income countries.

Even without a carbon price, Lal argues that soil carbon sequestration is a win–win strategy. It restores degraded soils, enhances biomass production, purifies surface and ground waters, and contributes to food security. Depending upon climate and other variables, Lal estimates that increasing soil organic carbon could increase cereal and food legume production in low-income countries by 32 million tonnes per year and roots and tubers by 9 million tonnes per year, food sufficient to feed well over 100 million people.

The Loess Plateau project shows that this kind of work can be done on a large scale. Lal argues that the key is to involve farmers, especially poor farmers, and to pay them to do restorative agriculture—which is what made the Chinese project successful.

More on that later, but first how realistic is it to think that land practices could actually ameliorate climate change? Historical evidence suggests that massive fluctuations in SOC and biomass, with corresponding impacts on climate, are not unprecedented.

THE AMERICAN CATASTROPHE
AND THE LITTLE ICE AGE

The 16th and 17th centuries witnessed what is likely the worst human catastrophe ever experienced when up to one fifth of humankind perished. The cause was the importation of disease into the Americas by European explorers, colonists, and their livestock.

Recent thinking from a number of archeologists summarized in Charles Mann's book *1491: New Revelations of the Americas Before Columbus* is that as many as 100 million people lived on the American continents circa 1491. Far from being a pristine wilderness, large parts of both continents were devoted to agriculture. The American "wilderness" was created when Europeans inadvertently—and intentionally—killed up to 90 percent of Americans, North and South. Most of them died before the colonists arrived in force.

When the British arrived on the east coast of North America they found the people particularly healthy and handsome compared to Europeans, who tended to have pocked skin from bouts of epidemic disease. The imported diseases wiped out most Americans for two reasons. Epidemic diseases like smallpox and measles originally jumped from herd animals to people. Since the people of the Americas did not for the most part have any livestock, they had not developed immunity to their diseases. Also, the genetic makeup of the American population made it particularly susceptible to epidemics.

Early European explorers travelling in the Mississippi basin found the area heavily populated, with towns and villages cheek by jowl along the riverfront. Archeologists have discovered the remnants of thousands of towns and one city of 50,000, its main mound larger than the pyramid of Giza, with homes reminiscent of the thatched houses of 19th century Japan. A second wave of explorers described the same place as an empty wilderness dominated by vast bison herds.

Archeological evidence and oral and written histories from indigenous Americans and early explorers shows that the Americans had developed some very sophisticated land management systems. America had a diverse population; some groups had non-sustainable systems while others had sustained their land base for centuries.

Mann describes what is now the eastern U.S. as a kind of well-tended forest-garden when the colonists arrived, composed mainly of nut trees and garden plots of corn, squash, and beans. The vast wild forests, celebrated by the likes of Thoreau, were actually a product of the collapse of agriculture after the human population had died back.

In western North America, people used fire extensively as a land management tool and hunted populations of bison, elk, and deer to prevent damage to cropland. Only after the mass human epidemics did buffalo populations reach the vast numbers recorded in the accounts of newcomers.

In what we think of as the world's last, best primeval wilderness, Amazonia, evidence indicates that a collection of heavily populated societies had discovered sustainable farming methods involving the use of charcoal and organic waste to create a soil type called *terra preta*.

Robert Dull of the Department of Geography and the Environment at the University of Texas reports that pre-Columbian farmers of the Neotropical lowlands numbered an estimated 25 million by 1491, with at least 80 percent living within forest biomes. The Neotropics include the tropical terrestrial ecoregions of both Americas and the entire South American temperate zone. Dull confirms that it is now well established that significant areas of Neotropical forests were cleared and burned to facilitate agricultural activities before the arrival of Europeans.[153]

Paleoecological and archaeological evidence shows that demographic pressure on forest resources—facilitated by anthropogenic burning—increased steadily throughout the Late Holocene, peaking around the time Europeans arrived in the late fifteenth century. The unprecedented population crash that occurred throughout the Neotropics following the arrival of Europeans was mostly complete by 1650, by which time it is estimated that about 95 percent of all indigenous inhabitants of the region had perished.

Dull and his colleagues reviewed fire history records from throughout the Neotropical lowlands and report new high-resolution charcoal records and demographic estimates that together support the idea that the Neotropical lowlands went from being a net source of CO_2 to the atmosphere before 1492 to a net carbon sink for several centuries following the European invasion. They argue that the regrowth of Neotropical forests following the Columbian encounter led to terrestrial biospheric carbon sequestration on the order of 2 to 5 billion tonnes of carbon, thereby contributing to the well-documented decrease in atmospheric CO_2 recorded in Antarctic ice cores from 1500 to 1750. This cooling trend was previously attributed exclusively to decreased solar irradiance and an increase in global volcanic activity. The scientists concluded that the post-Columbian carbon sequestration phenomenon was a significant forcing mechanism of the Little Ice Age.

The Little Ice Age, an exceptionally cold period between AD 1550 and 1850, brought significantly colder winters to parts of Europe and North America. Canals and rivers in Great Britain and the Netherlands were frequently frozen deeply enough to support ice skating and winter festivals. In the winter of 1780, New York's harbour froze, allowing people to walk from Manhattan to Staten Island. Sea ice surrounding Iceland extended for miles in every direction, closing harbours to shipping.

Cooling was not restricted to Northern Europe and North America. The southern section of the Bosphorus in Turkey froze in 1622, for example. In Ethiopia and Mauritania, permanent snow was reported on mountain peaks at levels where it does not occur today. In southern Africa, sediment cores retrieved from Lake Malawi show colder conditions between 1570 and 1820. Some evidence shows cooling and other climate disruptions in South America, Australia, and the South Pacific.

The cooler climate had a major impact on agriculture in some regions. Historians report that famines in France, Norway, and Sweden during this period claimed roughly 10 percent of the population of each country. In Estonia and Finland, losses have been estimated at a fifth and a third of the national populations, respectively. Grape production disappeared from some northern regions. In China, warm-weather crops such as oranges were abandoned in Jiangxi Province, where they had grown for centuries.

Most experts agree that the Little Ice Age had multiple causes, but human population decrease and subsequent decline in agricultural activity leading to increased forest and grassland regrowth, and therefore higher carbon sequestration, is increasingly cited as a significant factor.

Contemporary research adds further credence to the idea that climate change could be controlled in part through land management practices applied on a large scale. Research shows that increased plant growth as a result of the Green Revolution of the late 20th century helped to limit modern climate change. According to a report in the Proceedings of the National Academy of Sciences,[154] higher yields per acre since 1961 have avoided the release of nearly 600 billion tons of carbon dioxide to the atmosphere, about 20 years of fossil fuel burning at present rates. In other words, climate change would be substantially worse without the increased biomass that resulted from the Green Revolution.

These observations suggest that changes to agriculture and ecosystems can alter climate, supports the assumptions of Rattan Lal and others that a large-scale campaign to reclaim land, restore forests and grasslands, and adopt carbon sequestering farming methods could contribute significantly to the mitigation of extreme climate change.

SIX PROMISING ALTERNATIVES

The following sections looks at six practices that show promise in reducing the agrifood footprint and restoring agroecosystems while improving rural economies, particularly in low income countries.

Agroecology The potential of agriculture to sequester carbon is further supported in a report of the United Nations Special Rapporteur on the Right of Food.[155] Olivier De Schutter said that 45 to 50 percent of all human emissions of global warming gases come from the current form of food production, a much higher figure than is usually attributed to the agrifood system.

De Shutter reported that agroecology—the combination of agriculture and ecological principles—can put the agrifood system on the path of sustainability by de-linking food production from its reliance on fossil fuels. It contributes to mitigating climate change both by increasing carbon sinks in soil organic matter and above-ground biomass and by avoiding CO_2 and other GHG emissions from farms by reducing direct and indirect fossil fuel consumption.

The Intergovernmental Panel on Climate Change (IPCC) has estimated the global technical mitigation potential for agriculture at 5.5 to 6 billion tonnes of CO_2 equivalents per year by 2030. Most of this total (89 percent) can come from carbon sequestration in soils, something which can be achieved using the methods of agroecology.

Agroecology makes use of plants, trees, and animals to enhance productivity, harnessing local sources of nutrients and mainly human energy and appropriate, smaller-scale technologies. This reduces the need for expensive farm inputs, such as fuels, fertilizers, and pesticides, thus increasing net farm income.

De Schutter reports that agroecology already has a strong track record in improving food production and incomes in areas of low-income countries where it has been adopted. Because soils in many of these areas are seriously depleted, and yields are severely depressed, any effort to renew soils though the addition of SOC can have rather dramatic results. According to one report,[156] "Yields went up 214 percent in 44 projects in 20 countries in sub-Saharan Africa using agroecological farming techniques over a period of 3 to 10 years...far more than any GM [genetically modified] crop has ever done." Other recent scientific assessments have shown that small farmers in 57 countries using agro-ecology techniques obtained average yield increases of 80 percent. In Africa, average increases were 116 percent.

Agroecology is particularly suited to the needs of poor small farmers in the nations that will see the lion's share of population growth over the next 85 years. "Today's scientific evidence demonstrates that agroecological methods outperform the use of chemical fertilizers in boosting food production in regions where the hungry live," De Schutter said. While the industrial chemical approach can bring quick results, its high external input costs and dependence on aid and fossil fuels puts it out of reach of the mass of poor farmers, as well as being unsustainable.

> Evidence demonstrates that agro-ecological methods outperform the use of chemical fertilizers in boosting food production in regions where the hungry live.

Agroecology methods are comparable to the recommended management practices that have been proposed by Rattan Lal, including: appropriate afforestation of degraded/desertified lands; conversion of degraded croplands to pastures and tree cover; conservation agriculture with no-till farming and crop residue mulching along with cover cropping; integrated nutrient management based on appropriate use of organic and inorganic sources of plant nutrients; use of compost/manure and biochar in conjunction with other soil amendments; and complex crop rotations including tree crops. Some systems use small amounts of chemical fertilizers in the early stage of transition.

Another promising approach is the replacement of annual crops with perennial polycultures that mimic native ecosystems. Perennial systems would eliminate or reduce cultivation, which would increase SOC, limit erosion, and reduce energy consumption. The Land Institute in Salina, Kansas is pioneering an agricultural system that would have the ecological stability of native prairie with grain yields comparable to annual crops. The institute crosses annuals such as wheat, sorghum, and sunflower with perennial relatives to create perennial versions of these crops. It is also working to domesticate productive perennials, such as the high-protein Illinois bundleflower. Achieving productive and genetically stable perennial polycultures is expected to take several decades.

Regenerative Agriculture There is a widespread view that sustainable farming methods are not as productive as conventional agriculture, implying that conventional agriculture provides the best opportunity to feed a growing population. But a review of the literature that compares the results of sustainable and conventional methods confirms that sustainable methods are actually more productive and viable than conventional methods in regions where agricultural production is generally low and capital is difficult to obtain.

While some studies of organic and sustainable farming in North America and Western Europe indicate that these approaches can be somewhat less productive than conventional, industrial agriculture systems, at least over the short term, the opposite is true in low-income nations that have underdeveloped agricultural sectors.

Crop yields on farms that used sustainable methods increased an average of 79 percent over a four-year start up period, according to a major review of 286 farm projects involving 9 million farms on nearly 30 million hectares in 57 countries.[157] The study concluded that sustainable agriculture protects ecosystems while substantially improving the lives of farmers who adopt the resource-conserving practices. Working with colleagues in Thailand, China, Sri Lanka, and Mexico, Jules Pretty of the University of Essex found nearly all of the farm projects increased yields, and harvests of some crops like maize, potatoes, and beans increased as much as 100 percent. Sustainable agriculture practices, such as conservation tillage and integrated pest control, also reduced pesticide use and increased carbon sequestration. In addition, sustainable farming practices require less water, an important factor given predictions that by 2025 many countries will face substantial water shortages.

In another major study of the literature on organic farming, researchers from the University of Michigan concluded that when organic farming methods are applied to farms in low-income countries yields can be triple those of conventional farming.[158] The research also found that in higher-income countries, yields were almost equal on organic and conventional farms. In addition to equal or greater yields, the authors found that those yields could be accomplished using mainly on-farm sources of organic fertilizers and without putting more farm-land into production. It seems organic and sustainable practices are particularly effective in low-income countries because they allow low-income farmers to enhance yields using on-farm rather than purchased inputs.

Results from 30-year side-by-side comparisons of conventional and organic farming methods at the Rodale Institute in Pennsylvania showed that, contrary to conventional wisdom, organic farming can outperform conventional farming in every measure, in this case in the United States.[159]

The Rodale trials show that after a three-year transition period, organic yields equaled conventional yields. What is more, the study showed that organic crops were more resilient. Organic corn yields were 31 percent higher than conventional crops in years of drought, for example. Drought-year yields for organic crops are remarkable when compared to genetically modified (GM) "drought tolerant" varieties, which showed increases of only 6.7 percent to 13.3 percent over conventional (non-drought resistant) varieties. This is of particular interest considering that climate change is likely to bring drier conditions in many areas.

More important than yield, from the farmer's perspective, is income. Here organic is clearly superior. The 30-year comparison showed that organic systems could be almost three times as profitable as conventional systems. The average net return for the organic systems was $558/acre/year versus just $190/acre/year for the conventional approach. The much higher income reflects the premium organic farmers receive and consumers pay. But even without a price premium, the Rodale study found that organic is competitive with the conventional approach because of lower input costs.

The most profitable grain crop was the organically grown wheat netting $835/acre/year. Interestingly, no-till conventional corn was the least profitable, netting just $27/acre/year. The generally poor showing of GM crops was striking; it echoed a study from the University of Minnesota that found that farmers who cultivated GM varieties earned less money over a 14-year period than those who continued to grow non-GM crops.

Importantly, the Rodale study, which began in 1981, found that organic farming is more sustainable than conventional systems. They found, for example, that:

- Organic systems used 45 percent less energy than conventional.

- Production efficiency was 28 percent higher in the organic systems, with the conventional no-till system being the least efficient in terms of energy usage.

- Soil quality in the organic systems has increased over time while the conventional systems remain essentially unchanged. SOC increase was highest in the organic manure system followed by the organic legume system. The conventional system has shown a loss in carbon in recent years.

- Organic fields increased groundwater recharge and reduced runoff. Water volumes percolating through the soil were 15-20 percent higher in the organic systems.

A UN study cited in the Rodale report shows that organic farms create 30 percent more jobs per hectare than non-organic and that more money goes to paying local workers than to farm inputs.

Numerous independent studies cited by Rodale show that small-scale, organic farming is the best option for feeding the world now and in the future. In fact, agroecology farming methods, including organic farming, could double global food production in just 10 years, according to one UN report.[160]

No-till farming systems (NT) that make use of herbicides to control weeds have also been found to increase SOC. NT management is not effective in some soils and climates, however. Furthermore, the potential to mitigate global warming with NT management is highly variable and complex, and can be realized only when NT farming is practised over the long term.[161] In some soils, nitrous oxide emissions are higher under NT than under plough tillage, in others, tillage treatment has little effect on these emissions.[162] It has also been found that increasing SOC makes chemical fertilizers much more effective in raising yields. Without sufficient SOC, chemical fertilization can become ineffective.

The Biochar Option Biochar can be an effective tool in reducing or even reversing climate change.[163] Biochar is made by burning wood and other biomass with minimal oxygen. The process, called pyrolysis, burns the gases in the fuel leaving the bulk of the carbon behind.

Biochar is a highly porous substance that creates an ideal medium for the growth of bio-organisms like bacteria and fungi, which help to improve soil quality. *Terra preta*, a soil type that has been made using biochar for more than 1000 years, makes tropical and other light soils fertile and sustainable.

Biochar can be produced on an industrial scale or on farms on a small scale. Billions of people still use wood, straw, and dung as fuel for cooking and heating homes. Smoke from indoor fires is a cause of respiratory illnesses that cause more deaths than malaria. It produces black soot, an important factor in climate change. New types of cooking stoves are smokeless, much more efficient, reduce demand for firewood, and also produce biochar, which can be incorporated in gardens to improve productivity. Small farmers can also make biochar on a somewhat larger scale using crop residues.

On an industrial scale, there is considerable potential for projects that use forestry or farm byproducts to produce electricity and biochar. In Egypt, for example, it has been estimated that there is enough rice straw and husks to fuel 40 percent of the country's energy needs. In the boreal forest, the logging and pulp industry often has large stockpiles of wood chips and sawdust that could be converted to biochar, reducing their impact on climate as they decompose.

One research group led by Johannes Lehmann at Cornell University recently showed that 12 percent of GHG emissions could be offset with biochar produced from sustainably sourced biomass.[164] Over a century, Lehmann estimates the total offset at 130 billion tons. Darko Matovic, a professor of mechanical engineering at Queens University, contends that converting 10 percent of the world's biomass waste to biochar would sequester nearly five billion tons of carbon annually, more than the net GHG emissions added to the atmosphere each year by human activities.

The use of biochar is not without its detractors. For one thing, critics say that analyses of biochar only show technical potential; the logistics of actually converting 10 percent or more of the world's organic waste into biochar and burying it are, at this point at least, daunting. It is realistic, however, to see biochar as one of many options in the carbon farming toolbox.

The Brown Revolution While animal agriculture is generally less efficient in producing food calories than plant agriculture, some forms of sustainably managed animal production have potential to increase the food supply, improve sustainability and biodiversity, and ameliorate climate change.

The holistic management approach developed by biologist Allan Savory in Rhodesia (now Zimbabwe) in the 1960s, for example, is well suited in the world's historical grassland areas.[165] Savory recognized that Africa's grasslands evolved through a symbiotic relationship with large herds of grazing herbivores and that this was true of grassland around the world.

Savory observed that plant matter doesn't degrade easily on its own in arid areas and therefore contributes little to soil fertility and productivity. Large migratory animals break plants down in their rumen and stamp their manure into the ground, stimulating plant growth. Herbivores that travelled in large herds for safety from predators caused severe disturbance to the land but then moved on, giving plants time to regenerate. Holistic management uses this form of grazing as its model, but in the context of modern landholding systems. Instead of simply turning cattle into a large pasture, holistic ranchers will put a large number of animals in a small paddock, grazing the area briefly but heavily, then move the animals to a new paddock, letting the grazed land rest until the plants have regenerated.[166]

Counter intuitively, holistic management with its much higher stocking rates and therefore higher food production is actually a more sustainable, ecologically sound approach to livestock production than conventional low density approaches. It has strong potential for increasing both the productivity and sustainability of the 3.4 billion hectares currently devoted to grazing globally, and for increasing carbon sequestration on a large scale.

The widespread adoption of holistic management principles and other sustainable farming methods has been characterized as the Brown Revolution.[167] Whereas the Green Revolution focused on new plant varieties, fertilizers, and irrigation, the Brown Revolution focuses first on improving soil quality.

A group of American ranchers are applying this approach at Horse Creek ranch in South Dakota. The first year the group took over the ranch they stocked far more animals than the former owner—1,100 yearlings as opposed to the roughly 160 cows and calves of the previous year. The cattleman who sold them the yearlings was skeptical that the land could support that many animals, but after visiting their operation he conceded that the pastures grazed early that spring looked as if they hadn't been touched all year; indeed, they were ready to be grazed again. The increase was possible simply as a product of following the "bison pattern" of heavy grazing followed by sufficient rest.

The next year the ranchers more than doubled the herd to 2,250 head, and the land improved even further, with a greater diversity of grasses and forbs proliferating.

Techniques like holistic management can improve food production while offering a solution to climate change by increasing the ability to sequester carbon in rangelands. In *A Global Strategy for Addressing Global Climate Change*[168], Allan Savory estimates that increasing SOC by just 0.5 percent across the world's rangeland using holistic management could sequester sufficient carbon to reverse climate change.

Improved Water Efficiency Expanded irrigation, along with high yielding grain varieties and fertilizers, contributed significantly to a tripling of grain harvests since 1960. Irrigation is a key to high food production: While only 20 percent of the world's farmland is irrigated, it produces 40 percent of the food supply. But irrigation can have many pitfalls. For example, it is energy intensive, often depletes non-renewable fossil water, and causes salinity.

Among the technologies and practices suggested to improve irrigation efficiency, which allows more food production with less water inputs, are night irrigation, low-pressure sprinklers, low-energy precision application, and drip irrigation, all of which reduce losses by evaporation.

Farmers in India, Israel, Jordan, Spain, and the United States have shown, for example, that drip irrigation systems that deliver water directly to crop roots can cut water use by 30 to 70 percent and raise crop yields by 20 to 90 percent.

In the Texas High Plains, farmers using highly efficient sprinklers raised water efficiency to more than 90 percent while simultaneously increasing corn yields by 10 percent and cotton yields by 15 percent.

Israel is now reusing 85 percent of its domestic wastewater for crop production, freeing up additional freshwater for households and industry.[169]

A number of water management approaches that do not involve irrigation can also help to increase sustainable food production. Tree shelterbelts reduce evaporation from soil and transpiration from crops, while reducing wind erosion of soils by as much as 50 percent. One effective practice is intercropping with hydraulic lifter trees that draw moisture from deep in the soil at night and make it available to surrounding plants. Increased tree cover has also been shown to increase local rainfall.

A variety of proven methods allow producers to significantly improve the availability of water, which can contribute to more food production and the improvement of soil and biodiversity, including the increase in SOC with consequent climate impacts.

Urban Agriculture When I was a youth living in small town Saskatchewan, I was tutored in gardening and self-sufficiency by my elderly neighbours, George and Flossy Fowler, who operated a micro-farm on two lots next to mine. Long retired, they worked full time gardening, putting food by, and processing firewood from nearby forests, which they used to heat and cook. George showed me how to plant and maintain different vegetables and fruits and how to make compost and control pests. I learned that it was possible for a small family to be substantially food self-reliant on as little as two city lots, less than 1/10th of a hectare.

Having grown up in the city, I became fascinated with the idea that it was possible to grow one's own food. I developed the habit of walking the town's alleyways looking at gardens. One garden stood out distinct from all the rest, the masterwork of an elderly Chinese man. It was a marvel of industry, structural complexity, and intensive growth. I introduced myself and was given a tour.

Each vegetable had its techniques to maximize production, and every resource—including night soil—was used to feed the soil. Peas grew thick on a mesh of branches, the outside peas were picked fresh and the inside matured into cooking and seed peas. Squashes grew up from small pits bottomed with compost and manure, and hung from trellises. "Every day, one pail water," was his prescription for ideal growth of squash or cucumbers.

I acquainted myself with a mimeographed book, *How to Grow More Vegetables Than You Ever Though Possible On Less Land than You Can Imagine*, by the gardener John Jeavons. Using what he called the Biodynamic-French Intensive Method in the mountains of California, Jeavon's harvests were little short of amazing.[170] Per-acre yields of vegetables and fruits using his methods were between four and six times the average national yield. Jeavons says it would be possible for an urban, suburban, or rural gardener to net as much as $10,000 a year from the produce grown on a scant 1/10 acre.

In addition to high yields, the intensive system uses no polluting fuel, no toxic pesticides, and no energy intensive chemical fertilizers. It improves soil quality while using only 1/100 as much energy and 1/8 as much water as commercial agriculture. Intensive, small-scale growing techniques offer the possibility of vastly increased production where expertise and labour can substitute for space, mechanization, and external chemical inputs.

Intensive growing techniques are particularly well suited to urban agriculture, which has the potential to increase food supplies sustainably. Although the words "urban" and "farming" are not typically used together, the scale and scope of urban farming is far larger than commonly perceived.[171] Fifteen to twenty percent of the world's food is produced in urban and peri-urban areas, according to one study, and this percentage is on the rise. From balcony gardens to micro-farms, 800 million people worldwide are engaged in some form of urban agriculture. Of these, 200 million produce for the market and employ 150 million people full time.

Urban farming has a huge potential, judging from some Asian examples. Singapore—one of the most prosperous cities in the world—produces much of its meat and 25 percent of its vegetables within city limits. Even though it is the most densely populated large city in the world, Hong Kong produces 45 percent of its fresh vegetables, 68 percent of live poultry, and 15 percent of its pigs within the city. Shanghai, the largest city in China, produces 60 percent of its fresh vegetables, more than half its pork and poultry, and more than 90 percent of its milk and eggs from the urban and peri-urban area.

Large-scale urban farming is not limited to warmer countries. St. Petersburg, for example, has a tradition of urban farming that goes back to the 19th century. Up to 2.5 million people, half the city's population, are involved in agricultural activities. Some 560,000 hectares in and around the city are cultivated and 500,000 city residents spend their summers on garden plots on the outskirts of the city. In 1998, agricultural production in and around St. Petersburg exceeded production from the farms of the surrounding agricultural region.

Urban decay has stimulated urban agriculture in some American cities. After the race riots of 1967, 40,000 lots were vacated in downtown Detroit. Today, roughly one third of this 139-square-mile city consists of weed-choked lots and dilapidated buildings. In response, a network of urban farmers has turned 15 acres of idle land into more than 40 community gardens. One farm is more than 10 acres in size, scatted over seven parcels. It produces not only vegetables, but also hay, goat's milk, beef, honey, and eggs.

One of the main environmental advantages of urban farming is the elimination of distances between producers and consumers, and consequently the reduction of transportation-related energy consumption.

It is reasonable to assume that urban and peri-urban agriculture could feed up to 25 percent of the vegetable, fruit, and meat requirements of urban dwellers if it were widely adopted. Given that the urban population in 2100 is expected to be around 7.7 billion, urban agriculture could provide most of the nutrition for the equivalent of 2 billion people.

For this to be possible it will be necessary to utilize organic wastes effectively. When I visited Japan on an agricultural tour in 1995, my group visited a micro-farm in Tokyo. The farm contracted all its produce to a consumer food coop that was made up of members living in apartments immediately adjacent to the farm. Worn tatami mats used as a floor covering in the members' apartments were used to make compost for the farm, along with other food wastes, providing an ongoing source of organic fertilizer.

Organic wastes make up as much as 40 percent of the household waste stream. The average municipal waste generated per capita in the OECD countries is approximately 500 kg per year,[172] or about 200 kg of compostable organic waste per household. Assuming 2 billion urban households by centuries end, by rough estimate 400 million tonnes of compostable waste could potentially be available per year for urban agriculture, a considerable resource.

Human waste, currently a major source of water pollution, is another potential fertilizer source for urban agriculture. Though it has been used for centuries as a fertilizer, human waste can cause health problems due to pathogenic bacteria. However, there should be no serious obstacles to developing ways to divert this substantial waste stream into the production of energy and safe fertilizers. Between compostable food wastes and human waste, urban agriculture could become a closed loop food system.

A COMMON CAUSE

It has been shown that there are no insurmountable physical barriers to providing nutrition for 11 billion people. However, there are social, economic, political, and ethical barriers to providing food for *everyone* and in a *sustainable* way.

One of the key themes of this book is that the critical problems testing humanity—such as feeding 11 billion people on a deteriorating land resource under threat of climate change—are the very factors that will trigger the next stage of human evolution. Perversely, it appears the human psyche works in such a way that without these challenges transformations don't happen; the increasingly desperate struggle to deal with these fundamental crises will call forth the capacity needed to solve them.

Our efforts to respond to the threats facing civilization demand that we take the leap to a higher level of unity and cooperation. The threats are too big to deal with any other way.

Food is so fundamental that every person understands it. The agrifood crisis therefore provides common cause, furnishing the opportunity to transform science, politics, economics, ecology, and ethics, leading us forward to a new culture, a new kind of agriculture and a transformed, ethically-advanced, and united human race.

This will not occur by magic. Making it happen will be the greatest challenge humanity has ever faced, but the effort to meet the challenge will restore meaning to our lives.

The core proposal of this book is that the barriers to human progress can only be brought down using a comprehensive public educational approach that leads to profound social-ecological transformation, beginning at the village and neighbourhood level. While the big issues play out at the macro-level, fundamental change in the nature of society will take shape at the grassroots, and these changes will be directly linked to the agrifood systems devised to meet the needs of an 11 billion world.

CHAPTER 8
A NEW AGRICULTURE

The Proper Use of Land poses, not a technical nor an economic,
but primarily a metaphysical problem.
– E.F. Schumacher

In 1924, Richard St. Barbe Baker was appointed assistant conservator of forests for Nigeria and put in charge of an area the size of France. The forest was under pressure from a combination of heavy logging by foreign companies and clearing by indigenous farmers. Population pressure was beginning to accelerate the impact of the traditional slash and burn approach, as thousands of small tracts hollowed out the forest.

Unable to obtain funds or staff from the British Colonial Office to do the work required, Baker instead persuaded local farmers to participate in conservation activities, including a new farming approach he called *Igi Oko* (Tree Farms). Rather than cutting down and burning virgin forest, working the plot until the soil was depleted, and moving on, the participating farmers adopted what would now be called sustainable agroforestry or permaculture.

The participants first cleared an area of inferior bush that had grown up on previously cleared land. This was divided into half-acre plots, oil palms being planted first to mark the boundaries of each allotment. In between food crops they planted a selection of 300 of the most valuable trees, such as mahogany, as well as soil improvers that also provided useful timber. Then a variety of crops were sown among the trees, including nitrogenous types.

Each year new farms were allotted on deforested land so that in time they would create considerable areas of new forest for the benefit of the country.

This method provided a simple way to protect the land from soil erosion and ensure sustainable production. It ensured a food supply while at the same time providing for production of timber and fuel that would enrich the local economy perpetually. Baker pointed out that sustainable farming "was not a measure that could be enforced by law, but requires the voluntary co-operation of the people. I believe it should be introduced by farmers of their own race who should be trained cultivators and act as distributors of the young trees raised in local nurseries."

"It cannot be too strongly emphasized," continued Baker, "that the degree of rationalization even in forestry is determined by what is profitable—that is, by economic factors. 'Profitableness' as I use it here is considered from the point of view, not only of the individual, but the society and, of course, the fertility of the land, which is the very basis of human existence. The rhythm of growth must be manifested by approximating the conditions found in the natural forest...."

Baker envisioned a coordinated approach to development, centred on forestry but involving all aspects of the economic life of Nigeria. He proposed an innovative system of social organization: "I wished I could start a co-operative society among them. We must not try to impose worn-out methods in our African colonies. I should like to substitute co-operation for the wage system... This indeed might form the basis of an African co-operative movement, and follow on from afforestation to food production and the development of handicrafts. Many of the tropical and sub-tropical products would find ready sale in the home market. Labour would readily be derived from African pupils in co-operative schools of forestry and farming... At the close of each season when the books were made up, they, in company with those who had invested money for the establishment of the centre, would share in the profits made from their labour." The scheme would involve what would now be called "fair trade" arrangements for the sale of Nigerian products in London and other centres. Well ahead of his time, Baker also imagined developing ecotourism opportunities for the cooperative.

The methods were never fully employed. Instead, Baker was blackballed due to his sympathies with the Africans and never worked for the Colonial Office again. He went on however to become renowned as the "Man of the Trees," founder of one of the first international conservation organizations, the Men of the Trees, as well as a bestselling author and lecturer.

Nigeria developed along different lines. Today, it has the dubious distinction of having the highest deforestation rate for natural forests on the planet. Since 1990, the country has lost some 6.1 million hectares (35.7 percent) of its forest cover. Old growth forests are disappearing at an even faster rate.

Given the country is the world's 6th largest producer of petroleum and the 8th largest exporter, oil plays a major role in the Nigerian economy. While oil revenues provide the largest source of income, the country has become overly dependent on its oil sector while agriculture and forestry are in decline.

Although rich in natural resources, Nigeria's economy does not meet the basic needs of Nigerians. Disparity between the growth of GDP due to oil and increasing poverty is indicative of a skewed distribution of Nigeria's wealth. The majority of Nigerians are poor: 71 percent of the population live on less than one dollar a day and 92 percent on less than two dollars a day.

With the country's population projected to reach a staggering 914 million by century's end—on a land mass one tenth the size of China—it is hard to imagine a positive future without a profound transformation of culture and agriculture—not unlike that envisioned by Richard St. Barbe Baker 90 years ago.[173] But is such a change even possible?

A NEW AGRICULTURE

Though it may appear that the agrifood problem cluster is so complex and entrenched as to be insurmountable, I propose that not only is it surmountable, it contains an unparalleled opportunity to solve a number of the world's most pressing problems.

As we approach 11 billion, we will be compelled to invest in the agrifood system to ensure it is more productive and sustainable. By directing those investments to the right choice of macro and micro policies and appropriate practices, a new agriculture can help to regenerate soils, watersheds, and biodiversity; moderate a warming climate; revive and transform the impoverished rural communities where most of the world's poor live; and improve human health while reversing the upward spiral in health care costs.

Rather than viewing public spending on agriculture as a *cost*, appropriate spending on the agrifood system should be viewed as a long-term *investment*

with a high rate of return, one that will pay huge dividends for future generations through improved health, ecological resilience, and a stable climate. In
addition, this investment will generate sustainable forms of wealth and a wider
equity benefit, the social gain that results when extremes of wealth and poverty
are reduced. Importantly, social equity also translates into a reduction in the
birth rate.

Once again, the real problem is not technical solutions, it is building consensus around solutions and, even more so, acting in the public interest. But
the pressure from 11 billion will soon enough make maintaining the status quo
more difficult than taking the uncomfortable, revolutionary action needed to
solve the population-resource dilemma.

In the meantime, by following Buzz Holling's prescription—to experiment
and act inventively and exuberantly via diverse adventures in living—we can
spread seeds of change that will come into their own when the old world order
falls in on itself. We need tens of thousands of projects like Igi Oko in villages
and neighbourhoods throughout the world. But these projects cannot simply
be solely economic or even ecologically focused, they must also address the
moral dimension of the global social-ecological crisis.

A MORAL CRISIS

In 1996, the Food and Agriculture Organization of the United Nations assembled the world's Heads of State in Rome for the World Food Summit. The intention was to muster sufficient political will to set the world on a course to food
security. The Summit Declaration reaffirmed "the fundamental right of everyone to be free from hunger" and the leaders pledged their "political will and...
common national commitment to...an ongoing effort to eradicate hunger in
all countries...." Their declaration included commitments on peace, poverty
reduction, equality, sustainability, and fair trade.[174]

By 2001, the FAO frankly admitted that the political will necessary to end
hunger had not been mustered. The Committee on World Food Security noted
the *moral* implications of this failure:

> That some 792 million people in developing countries and 34
> million in the developed world remain chronically hungry in
> spite of the success of farmers in generating enough food to
> meet everyone's needs and that there is widespread evidence

of land degradation, imply that there are serious imperfections in the way in which we are handling our responsibilities to each other and exercising our stewardship over global resources. Inequity in access to food and technology, the damage to natural resources associated with some farming methods and scientific advances, erosion of biodiversity, threats to the sustainability of ocean fisheries and trade restrictions which prevent countries from exercising and benefiting from their comparative advantages all have important ethical dimensions. Looking at these issues from an ethical and human rights standpoint may contribute to the development of a consensus on how they can be better addressed in the common interest of humanity, capturing important considerations which may not be given sufficient weight when decisions are taken principally on technical or economic grounds or left to market forces alone.[175]

In recognizing "serious imperfections" in collective human behaviour, toward each other and the ecosphere, and in expressing its obvious frustration with the lack of political will to achieve food security, the committee was drawn to a moral argument. Linking food security to human rights and ethical values, and placing it in the context of "the common interest of humanity," is significant. In its frustration at the lack of progress on food security, the committee was identifying the moral bankruptcy inherent in the prevailing order.

Logically, the solution to the problems must be found in an approach built on a sound ethical footing. The committee hits on the ethical core of a development approach for the contemporary world: the core principle must be *the common interest of humanity*. Until we accept that all people, regardless of ethnicity, gender, class, or national status, are equal members of one human family, each with unalienable rights—and then act out of that belief—we are likely to overlook the obscene disparities that now divide humankind into a rich minority and a poor majority.

The well-being of mankind, its peace and security, are unattainable unless and until its unity is firmly established. Food security would be a consequence and a sign of achieving universal recognition of the fundamental principle of human unity. And achieving human unity in practice is dependent on another moral principle, justice. Justice is the one power that can translate the dawning consciousness of humanity's oneness into a collective will to achieve goals such as food security. Only the recognition of the oneness of humanity, demonstrated in the practice of fundamental justice, can ensure that everyone will be fed in an 11 billion world.

This idea is implied in the "The Right to Food" endorsed by the World Food Summit; the Committee of World Food Security notes that:

> The right to food is recognized in legally binding international instruments, including, most fully, the International Covenant on Economic, Social and Cultural Rights.... Under the Covenant, State parties are obliged to take all appropriate steps, to the maximum of available resources, to progressively achieve the right to food for all.... Under international law, the State is accountable for the enjoyment of human rights within its territory...it remains incumbent on the State to ensure that those who are unable to do so for themselves are adequately provided for, so that as a minimum, no one suffers from hunger.[176]

Economist and Nobelist Amartya Sen observed there has never been a famine in a democratic nation. His observation underlines the idea that food security is not so much a technical problem as an issue of justice. Extreme poverty and hunger result from the willingness, deliberately or through neglect, to permit inequalities within or between nations to be perpetuated. Hunger will be eliminated when people and governments embrace justice as an operating principle; when permitting poverty and inequality to degrade any human life is understood to be an assault on the dignity of the entire human race; when the oneness of humanity is the pivotal value around which human relationships are organized. Justice is also key to solving environmental problems associated with agriculture. As will be discussed in a later chapter, justice governs our relationship with the ecosphere: the circle of unity must be expanded to encompass the myriad species with which we cohabit this planet—and the planet itself.

The call to focus on lofty ethical principles may seem naïve, but given we have tried "every stupid alternative," as Buckminster Fuller put it, "and none of them have worked" it is time to do "the most intelligent thing." The future is calling forth our higher intelligence, which demands a second agricultural revolution, and this time it will also be an ethical revolution.

A NEW ETHICAL FRAMEWORK
GOALS FOR A NEW AGRICULTURE

Clearly, bringing about radical—i.e. fundamental and pervasive—change on a global scale is not a simple thing. Yet that is precisely what must be done to make the world work for 11 billion; one international research group studying agricultural problems put it this way: "The challenges facing agriculture today are unlike anything we have experienced before, and they require revolutionary approaches to solving food production and sustainability problems."[177]

Leaders of thought, from the FAO to sociobiologist E.O. Wilson, have concluded that an essential part of the transformative process is an ethical shift, which in turn will require a change in fundamental beliefs, attitudes, and values.

"Ethics is everything," says Wilson in the conclusion of *Consilience: The Unity of Knowledge*, his masterful synthesis of humanity's current understanding of reality. In the high-stakes world of 11 billion, the morality of everything we do is all-important. But as Wilson explains, the kind of shift required to make the world work for 11 billion runs counter to human genetic programming, which emphasizes the immediate survival needs of one's self and immediate relatives over the long term needs of the species, let alone the ecosphere. Consequently, the needed transformation will require fundamental change in what we perceive to be the determinants of human behaviour.

Humanity's childhood has ended; our future is being determined not by natural selection, the force that shaped us, but by our own decisions. Consequently, we must look deep within ourselves and decide what we wish to become.

This change is underway, says Wilson, the dean of evolutionary biologists. "*Homo sapiens*, the first truly free species, is about to decommission natural selection, the force that made us." He says humanity's childhood has ended; our future is being determined not by natural selection, the process that largely made us what we are, but by our own decisions. Consequently, "we must look deep within ourselves and decide what we wish to become."[178]

As a civilization, then, we have to do something that has never been done before; en masse, people have somehow to stand back from the immediate issues that they face, to take stock, and to engage in a broad and inclusive discourse about what they value. We have to consider, collectively, what human life is really about. Is it merely a matter of immediate economic survival and prosperity for oneself and one's family or immediate community? Can we transcend the power of the "selfish gene" and act for the well-being of humankind and the ecosphere, not just for now but for generations to come? Or, perhaps the better question is this: Can we learn to accept that our immediate survival needs are now subsumed in the long-term needs of humankind and the ecosphere?

To ensure an ever-advancing civilization, we have somehow to identify choices and agree to make decisions that will help us build a framework for action—based on appropriate values—to guide change. Even more challenging, we then have to overcome inertia and act!

In 1973, in his book *Small Is Beautiful*, the economist E.F. Schumacher wrote: "The Proper Use of Land poses, not a technical nor an economic, but primarily a metaphysical problem."[179] He went on to say that, "In the simple question of how we treat the land, next to people our most precious resource, our entire way of life is involved, and before our policies with regard to the land will really be changed, there will have to be a great deal of philosophical, not to say religious, change…If we could return to a generous recognition of meta-economic values, our landscapes would become healthy and beautiful again…"

There are five main meta-economic values that we must cultivate to make the shift to an ethically mature agrifood system.

Enlightenment Let's begin by posing the seemingly obvious question, "Why do we produce food?" Well, we need to feed our bodies to survive. And for people in the agrifood industry, food and the other products of agriculture are produced to earn an income, which is also about physical survival. But let's ask another seemingly obvious question, "Why do we want to survive?" "Why do we want to be alive, at all?"

As a brooding teenager I read depressing books by European existentialists, including Albert Camus' classic *The Stranger* and Jean Paul Sarte's *Nausea*. The main effect of these books was to make me feel more strange and nauseated than I already felt. Fortunately, life's joys—falling in love, having children, growing gardens, swimming in the river, basking in sunshine—dispelled the existential gloom. Yet when I think back to that period, I can agree in one sense with something that Camus said in in his influential essay, *The Myth of Sisyphus*: "There is but one truly serious philosophical problem, and that is suicide. Judging whether life is or is not worth living amounts to answering the fundamental question of philosophy."

It is a disturbing but useful point. Happily, most young people making their way through the serious introspection that often accompanies their coming of age conclude that life is worth living. But I would ask whether humanity is not in a sense asking this question of itself, right now, and effectively saying "no, life is not worth living."

Consider that our leaders have engaged panels of the world's leading experts, such as the Intergovernmental Panel on Climate Change (IPCC), to ask whether our way of life is sustainable. The panels have answered with a resounding NO! Our collective disregard for this information suggests to me that at some level we are not so sure life is worth living. Perhaps I am reading too much in to this and we are merely deluding ourselves or gambling that the white coats are wrong, and very much want to live. But the fact remains that we are in a period where our choice is either to maintain the status quo—which effectively means we die out or at least will be greatly diminished as a species—or to push the reset button on civilization and live on.

In defiance of the IPPC warning that civilization itself is threatened by climate change, humanity's overriding response has been to expand and accelerate all those things that cause climate change. Our response is to tap every facet of human ingenuity to expand the infrastructure to extract and distribute the remaining fossil fuels as fast as we can, and to gear up the global economy so that these fuels will be burned faster than ever. Are we not quite literally playing out the question of whether life, i.e. civilization, is worth maintaining or not?

Like Camus, are we not influenced in following this tack by the contemporary materialistic paradigm, which emerges in large measure from scientific enquiry? As biologist and Nobel laureate Jacques Monod puts it in his influential 1970 book *Chance and Necessity*, the end result of our scientific enquiry into the nature of life is that it has no meaning and purpose.

"The universe was not pregnant with life, nor the biosphere with man." We are an accident of the universe, the result of "pure chance" and have no particular significance. Monad fully understood the implications of the doctrine of chance. With it, he said, "The ancient Covenant is in pieces: man at last knows that he is alone in the unfeeling immensity of the universe, out of which he has emerged only by chance. Neither his destiny nor his duty have been written down." Science having led us to this bleak understanding of reality, we have no choice but to see life as *absurd*, that is, lacking any meaning that would give it purpose.

Logically, if this is the case, does it really matter if civilization continues or not? Nice if it does, perhaps, if one enjoys life, but what difference does it *really* make? Why should I care about the welfare of absurd beings I don't even know, living in the future? What would caring about them do for me?

Without a sense of meaning or purpose, where is the impetus to radically alter our way of life, indeed to sacrifice a degree of self-interest, in order that humanity can live on? Without a profound sense of meaning—something beyond material survival and being entertained while we wait to die—is the collective suicide implied in maintaining the status quo our unconscious answer to Camus's proposition? Without a higher purpose, a passive society is easily organized to serve the interests of individuals, which inevitably means that it serves those with money and a will to power; society becomes increasingly unequal, the masses feeling more and more like Sisyphus, the mythical character assigned to roll a rock up the hill only to have it roll down again, and to repeat that task forever.

The modern Sisyphus isn't rolling rocks, he's busy "keeping up with the global Jones," fulfilling his *raison d'être* in the consumer society. The futility of a life defined by competitive consumption reinforces the sense that life has no purpose beyond the mundane. Given this attitude, why would anyone care about anything beyond immediate concerns?

Traditional mainstays like religion, which have provided meaning in the past, seem bankrupt and out of synch with the modern world. The sense of ennui gripping the consumer preoccupies contemporary culture. In the hugely popular film, *The Matrix*, for example, the hero discovers that his consciousness is merely a character in a computer-simulated dream world, his real self one of billions of human cells feeding energy to the uncaring machinery that rules a world devoid of value. Such themes appear increasingly in entertainment media.

Our understanding of who we are, what we are doing on this planet and why is *causal*: it shapes our thought and thus our perception of reality and ultimately our behaviour—even our agricultural practices. As mentioned in the previous chapter, the problem of collective meaning and purpose is both urgent and immediate because, it determines the environmental ethic.[180] It also determines our social, economic, cultural, and political ethos.

If we believe that human beings are primarily *consumers*, that we exist merely to consume and wile away the hours, that our meaning and purpose is fundamentally *commercial*, then we lack a sense of meaning and purpose conducive to a sustainable, convivial civilization.

It does not take a lot of reflection to conclude, first, that little meaning can be found in a life focused on the consumption of goods and services, which our society is increasingly intent upon, and second, that profound meaning *can* be found by playing a constructive part in achieving a noble purpose, the ultimate noble purpose being to carry forward an ever-advancing civilization. This is the ultimate purpose because civilization provides the milieu in which human beings are able to independently investigate—and pool their understanding of—the nature of reality. This investigation is carried out using the human faculties of scientific and spiritual enquiry and refined through social discourse.

By spiritual, I do not mean the ignorant beliefs in outmoded ideas and practices that the many critics of religion rightly deride. I refer to our need and capacity to build an individual and collective sense of meaning and purpose through the exploration of the sacred. Even E.O. Wilson, the most erudite of positivists, acknowledges in his critique of religion that, "People need a sacred narrative. They must have a larger purpose, in one form or other, however intellectualized."[181]

It has been said, "religion is a faculty of human nature." Whether placed in us by God or a natural outcome of the evolutionary process (or both), this faculty compels us to investigate existential questions, using profound reflection, aided by insight, intuition, reason, and the study of humanity's collective spiritual wisdom; to systematize our answers; and to build communities around the great spiritual educators of humanity, the founders of enduring religions. Our covenant with the sacred allows us to imagine a larger realm of meaning that cannot be found through scientific investigation alone, and even experience a sense of transcendent oneness, a sense conducive to strong relationships with our fellow beings, human and otherwise, now and in the future.

Science independent of vested interests and authentic religion—i.e. religion true to fundamental spiritual values such as the independent and free search for truth, compassion for others, or justice for all—are partners in the pursuit of meaning and the definition of purpose. Religion may be "psychically full and rich" but without science it can devolve into superstition and fanaticism, as we are only too aware. On the other hand, science without religion "seems sterile and inadequate," as E.O. Wilson points outs.[182] It is easily, often willingly, subverted to serve vested interests seeking wealth and power. So in addition to authentic religion, we must also strive for *authentic science*, science that supports the goal of an ever-advancing civilization.

The goal of the combined scientific and spiritual enquiry is enlightenment, which, if we consider it deeply, is not simply to achieve the maximum possible understanding of reality. An accurate understanding of reality leads, necessarily, to enlightened action undertaken in a humble spirit of service to humankind. *Service* is indicative of the highest form of enlightenment. Thus, enlightenment need not take a lifetime of effort; engaging in service—something a four year old can do—is an indicator that one has achieved a degree of enlightenment.

A sense of higher meaning and purpose gives a direction to the way we organize society. The quality of our deep thought will influence our relationships, from those in the socioeconomic sphere to those with other species. If our purpose is mere existence, to eat, drink, and wile away the hours, we will create one kind of world; if it is service to the greater good of an ever-advancing civilization aiming for ultimate enlightenment, we will create another, better one.

With this sense of meaning and purpose in mind, we ask, "Why are we farming and producing food? What is the goal of the agrifood system?" A profound answer was proposed by the Japanese farmer and sage Masanobu Fukuoka: "The ultimate goal of farming is not the growing of crops, it is the cultivation and perfection of human beings."[183] Embracing this goal is a problem solver: with this high-level aspiration about human goals, the paradigm shifts from a merely socioeconomic or commercial approach—"How do we make more food and money?"—to an advanced, ethical approach—"What do we need to do to create a type of agrifood system that cultivates and perfects human beings?" This is the creative question we must retain and ask repeatedly at every stage in the process of creating a new agriculture.

Health What do we need to do to create a type of agrifood system that cultivates and perfects human beings? One creative answer is to establish health, not money-making, as a leading value. Money-making is a necessary element of the agrifood system, to be sure, but it should not be agriculture's guiding value.

To be effective, the concept of health must encompass people *and* the ecosphere. We cannot cultivate and perfect ourselves as human beings when we are burdened by illness, and as much as good food makes us well, a dysfunctional agrifood system motivated primarily by money-making undermines human health and ecological resilience. The unhealthy ecological impacts of the agrifood system have already been summarized, but the socio-economic failures of the system are similarly glaring. Some 925 million low-income people are underfed, while many more—from all income groups—are overfed yet malnourished. In fact, the number of obese and overweight people worldwide has now surpassed the number of underfed.

Poor nutrition is a worldwide problem affecting the poor, middle income and rich alike, though in different ways. Rich or poor, we tend to eat too many refined carbs, a main contributor to poor health and runaway health care costs.

As previously stated, uncontrolled health care costs—or more accurately the runaway costs of treating disease—constitute a major threat to the advancement of civilization. Wealthy countries, most notably the United States, are spending an ever-larger share of GDP on medical care, but this is doing nothing to improve health. As spending rises, most indicators of health are actually declining.

Aiming for the higher value of social-ecological health rather than wealth resets the goals for agriculture in ways that support the long-term viability of society. Ultimately, it also serves purely economic goals given that wealth is a benefit derived from looking after ecological function.

Unity and Social Equity The historian Eric Hobsbaum points to the anomaly that on the whole the countries with the largest agricultural population are the ones which have difficulties in feeding themselves, while the world's food surpluses come from a relatively tiny farm population in a few industrialized countries. Hobsbaum notes that advocates of economic growth are constantly surprised that they cannot replace the more inefficient farming systems of low-income nations with the industrial model. They fail to recognize that success usually comes from reform adapted to the specific conditions of regional farming.[184]

Even with a population of 7.2 billion, and total production (in grain alone) adequate to provide every human being with 2800 calories daily, close to 1 billion are chronically hungry. More than a third of our fellow human beings subsist on $2 a day or less and find it difficult to maintain an adequate diet. It is indeed ironic that most of the world's hungry and malnourished are poor farm families who, one would expect, could at least feed themselves, but whose capacity to do so is undermined by fundamental inequities built into the global economic order.

An agrifood system that has as its ultimate goal the cultivation and perfection of human beings must immediately grapple with the problem of exclusion. Is it just some human beings that deserve the benefits of prosperity? Or is our goal the well-being of all?

A net global increase in food production alone will not guarantee the end of hunger, since the poor cannot access food even when it is available. As we move to an 11 billion world, the question is not so much how to produce enough food as how to foster a more equal civilization. To make the world work for 11 billion, we have to move toward a global ethos in which no one would find it tolerable that anyone is hungry when there is plenty to eat.

This is the great task of civilization: to find ways to foster love and compassion, so that we place the well-being of others equal to or even above our own welfare. This task is supported by the recognition of *the oneness of humankind*, the notion that all human beings, regardless of category—gender, race, class, nationality, or any other—are members of one family, one race, each with unalienable rights to full participation in the commonweal. We are equal simply as a consequence of our birth into the human family.

While this value is acknowledged, at least superficially, by many people, it is far from being realized. To make the world work for 11 billion, it will be necessary to adopt human unity of as our leading value, for it to be universally promoted by all governments and organizations of civil society and taught to all children from the earliest age. Equity is a corollary of this principle.

One obstacle to realizing this vision is our habit of seeing humanity as an arena of competing interests, a world of them and us. So long as we think of humanity in that way, that is what we will be. But if we begin to read our reality without prejudice, we can see that humanity is actually one organic whole.

We have learned to see people as fundamentally competitive and self-interested; in fact, we have come to accept that competitiveness is a fundamental property of the natural order, the driver of evolution, including human evolution. Competitive self-interest may be an element of human nature, and an important factor in our evolution, but it is far from our totality. The fact is, cooperatively working for the common good is what almost all of us do, almost all of the time.

Mathematical biologist Martin A. Nowak contends that *cooperation* is the defining human trait.[185] He calls our species "super cooperators." People largely suppress competitiveness and self-interest, instead submitting to socially-beneficial restraints such as laws, conventions, and covenants every moment of the day (and night.) Self-restraint is required to create and sustain communities of various sorts. We work almost exclusively in collective endeavours for the common good; we play our part in maintaining the socioeconomic order, in marriages, families, networks of friends, workplaces, enterprises, and organizations of civil society. Even competitive entities such as corporations or sports teams are based on internal cooperation.

Human history is one of increasing inclusiveness. Generally speaking, we have learned to live together effectively in families, tribes, villages, city-states, and more recently nation states and federations of states. Despite our many spectacular failures, human beings have, through cooperation, progressively and successfully moved civilization forward. Logically, the next step in human evolution is to fully embrace a global civilization based on a universal recognition of the unity and oneness of humankind.

Recognizing the unity of humankind does not mean that we abandon other loyalties, such as national identities, any more than embracing national identities in the past meant that we turned our back on our existing communities. Generally speaking, national communities expanded our loyalties and our horizons. Larger scale federations, such as the United States, Canada, or the European Union have generally improved life for the federated partners.

The gradual emergence of a world economy and culture as a result of advances in technologies that bridge gaps of communications, travel, and trade is a reality, one that corresponds to the ecological reality of one planetary ecosphere. We inhabit one ecosphere, with impacts that ignore political boundaries. We share a global eco-commons and must learn to manage it in an equitable fashion.

Given that so many issues we face—agrifood issues or climate change being prime examples—are transnational, we need a more representative form of international governance. Many eschew the idea of global governance, seeing it as a threat to national sovereignty. They should recognize, however, that we already have a de facto global government made up of assemblies of national government officials, like the UN and the G20, as well as international organizations and corporations that have the capacity to exert an influence on a global scale. This virtual world government is currently unelected, unequal, and ineffective, and often dominated by vested interests. A better option would be to move to a world super-state that is elected, using a fully representative, non-partisan process.

Beyond this, humanity must take yet another revolutionary step by broadening its perspective even further to embrace the ecosphere in its circle of inclusion.

Centrality While agriculture has been in many ways marginalized in the modern world compared to activities that are ultimately non-essential or non-productive, the fact remains that civilization is entirely dependent on it. Agriculture is the basis of civilization.

Agriculture is fundamentally different than other economic activities because it deals with living systems. (Agriculture, in this context, includes activities that involve work with renewable resources, such as fishing and forestry.) Agriculture's products result from life processes and its means of production are living systems: soil, water, plants, animals, and people. Our other economic activities are, for the most part, man-made processes that deal with non-living materials or necessarily eliminate the life in living things. The ideal of industry is to eliminate the living factor, even the human factor, and to mechanize everything.

Both agriculture and non-agricultural industry are needed to support civilization, but in the final analysis, agriculture is primary and other industry secondary.

In *The Centrality of Agriculture—Between Humankind and the Rest of Nature*, environmental historian Colin Duncan contends that, "the central place in every culture should be occupied by agriculture."[186] While he acknowledges this will seem naïve or heretical to most living economists, Duncan argues that no sustainable human future can be conceived unless and until the centrality of agriculture is recognized.

A corollary to this is a 'farmers first' approach, in which agricultural development is focused around the requirements and concerns of farmers and farm labourers, especially those that are impoverished. We rebuild agriculture starting at the farm and village levels with the needs of rural people foremost. Currently, the system is built around the needs of consumers rather than producers. This order of things is typical of our society and is wrongheaded. Just as we concern ourselves with symptoms of disease and neglect the determinants of health, we concern ourselves with end products like food plants and animals and neglect producers and agroecosystems, placing emphasis instead on products and end consumers. Similarly, we concern ourselves with cities and neglect the village and countryside. An ethos for 11 billion demands we flip this.

RESTRUCTURING

These ethical principles—enlightenment, health, unity, equality, and central-ity—are the keys to restructuring the global agrifood system. To make the world work for 11 billion, we will have no choice but to create a civilization in which agriculture and farmers obtain a status commensurate with their impor-tance, and where the agrifood system is designed to serve the greater goal of the human project, i.e. enlightenment for all in a sustainable global civilization.

Motivated by this noble objective, we will want to make major changes, not just to the agrifood system, but in the way we do politics, organize economies, and manage international relations, themes dealt with in more detail elsewhere in this book. That said, the agrifood system can be a vehicle for a broader social-ecological transformation. In fact, refocusing society's priorities around agricul-ture, and particularly small farmers, has the potential to solve a number of the world's most pressing problems.

Approximately 2.6 billion people, close to 40 percent of the world's popu-lation, depend on agriculture for their livelihood.[187] Of the 525 million farms worldwide, 85 percent are operated by smallholders who cultivate plots of land no bigger than 2 hectares. An estimated 1 billion people are employed in the agricultural sector. In 2009, the agricultural sector accounted for 59.0 percent of total employment in sub-Saharan Africa, 53.5 percent in South Asia and 44.3 percent in South-East Asia and the Pacific. Although their share of total employment has declined over the past decade, the total number of workers in agriculture has grown.

Small farms produce half of the world's food—including 90 percent of the food grown in Africa and 40 percent of food grains in India—and cultivate around 60 percent of the arable land worldwide (about 1 billion hectares), often in soils that are of low fertility and insufficiently irrigated. Average yields are low, around 1 tonne per hectare (the world average is 3.3 tonnes.)

Although increasing in number, the percentage of small farmers relative to world population is getting smaller. The total area cultivated by smallholders has also been shrinking for years, thus explaining the decrease in average farm size in Asia and Africa.

Extreme poverty is largely concentrated in rural populations of small farmers and farm workers, who are increasingly neglected by government. Government spending on agriculture in the world's poorest countries averages just 4 percent of public expenditure. Governments in Africa spend around 6.6 percent of their national budgets on agriculture, a little more than US$15 per year for every rural inhabitant. In contrast, in the Green Revolution era, Asian governments allocated as much as 15 percent of their budgets to agriculture. Development aid to agriculture was 4.6 percent of all aid in 2007, compared with 18 percent in 1979.

On the other end of the scale, the size of industrial agricultural enterprises in Europe, the US, Canada, and Australia is increasing while their number is decreasing. Farming in the food exporting countries becomes increasingly capital, energy, and chemical intensive, and as rural populations dwindle the quality of rural community is diminished. Meanwhile, industrial farming contributes a host of ecological problems.

A global food system shaped to maximize efficiency gains and produce large volumes of commodities has failed to fully consider distributional concerns.[188] Increases in production far outstripped population growth during the period from 1960 to 2000. But these increases went hand in hand with regional specialization in a relatively narrow range of products, a process encouraged by the growth of international agricultural trade. The associated technological and policy choices concentrated benefits in the hands of large production units and landholders at the expense of smaller-scale producers and landless workers, resulting in the growth of inequality in rural areas and a failure to address the root causes of poverty.

The 1960s and 1970s were characterized by State-led agricultural development, under which governments, eager to provide urban populations with affordable food or to export raw commodities in order to finance import substitution policies, either paid farmers very low prices for the crops produced or supported only the largest producers who could be competitive on global markets, thus accelerating rural migration.

In the 1980s, the introduction in most low-income countries of structural adjustment policies resulted in a retreat of the State from agricultural development. It was anticipated that trade liberalization and the removal of price controls would encourage private investment, making up for the reduction of State support. However, overproduction in the highly subsidized farming sectors of high income countries put downward pressure on agricultural prices, discouraging the entry of private investors into agriculture in low income countries. If there was private investment at all, it went to a narrow range of cash crops grown for export markets.

Because small-scale farming was not viable under these conditions, many rural households were relegated to subsistence farming, surviving only by diversifying their incomes and migrating to cities. At the same time, the dependence of low-income countries on food imports grew significantly. Many of the lowest income countries are still primarily agricultural, yet, in part because they have to repay foreign loans in hard currency, they export a narrow range of commodities and therefore find themselves highly vulnerable to price shocks on international markets for these products. Their food bills have soared, the combined result of population growth and a lack of investment in local agricultural production and food processing to meet local needs.

When the prices of agricultural products suddenly increased in 2008 in the wake of higher oil prices and speculation, the lowest income countries found themselves trapped. The imbalances in the food system, which had been building up over the previous forty years, suddenly became visible, and the human consequences too important to ignore.

Indeed, many countries have succumbed to a vicious cycle. As they were confronted from the 1960s to the 1990s with strong population growth and rural-to-urban migration, their governments had no choice but to depend more on food aid or to import more food products. This made it even more difficult for their own farmers to make a decent living from farming, as they faced increased dumping of heavily subsidized foodstuffs on domestic markets. In effect, the import of low-priced food products functioned as a substitute for improved wages for workers in the non-agricultural sectors, and for the establishment of social protection floors for all. This was perhaps a convenient solution so long as the prices of basic food commodities remained stable or were declining. However, with higher and increasingly volatile prices, it results in new threats to the right to food of net food buyers and is a recipe for social and political instability. Furthermore, the increased reliance on food imports is a major cause of "nutrition transition" in low income countries, i.e. the shift to processed foods richer in salt, sugar, and saturated fats, foods that have a long shelf life and are attractive to urban populations and younger generations, but are often less nutritious and healthy.

Given that most of the 3.7 billion increase in world population by century's end will occur in the poorest countries, those with large rural populations, small farmers will be called on to supply the bulk of the local food supply. While many studies previously cited have shown that small farmers can dramatically increase productivity using sustainable farming methods, their ability to adopt these methods can be limited by lack of information, market access, and capital, even though the capital requirement may be very low.

On the surface, this scenario seems rather hopeless but the surface impression conceals a solution. When we think from the perspective of the five guiding principles for agriculture discussed in this chapter, a meta-solution emerges: *Pay farmers to restore ecosystem functions and mitigate climate change.*

The previous chapter detailed the potential to use a range of low-cost, sustainable farming methods, from agroecology to holistic management, to sequester atmospheric carbon in the soil and above ground vegetation. We learned that these methods provide many co-benefits: they help mitigate *and* adapt to climate change; improve soil structure and fertility; restore watersheds, water tables, and water quality; increase local rainfall; make clean water more accessible; reduce the incidence and severity of erosion, flooding, and drought; and increase biodiversity.

It is not possible to fix a degraded landscape without fixing the community that has degraded alongside it: ecological and socioeconomic transformation go hand in hand. Agricultural development is identical to community development.

Sustainable farming practices are often labour intensive and are particularly suited to smallholdings with degraded soils. Relatively small investments in small farms would achieve a number of public and private socioeconomic benefits, including: increased food production in areas where it is most needed; higher incomes for small farmers; reduced illness and health care costs for people and livestock as a result of improved nutrition; reduced birthrates and improved life outcomes for women and children; reduced social tensions from easing poverty; making rural communities more resilient and culturally vibrant; and removing the incentive to relocate to urban centres.

A big push to invest in small farmers could virtually eliminate extreme poverty over the course of the century and provide the food for the additional 3.7 billion people who will be mostly concentrated in these countries. On the ecological side, the potential is almost limitless, given the opportunity to extend sustainable agriculture and forestry beyond the billion hectares currently occupied by small farms to 3.5 billion hectares of degraded and desertified lands.

On the other side of the world, investment in small farms takes the pressure off large-scale, industrial agriculture to continuously expand production to "feed the world." Feeding the world can best be achieved by empowering producers everywhere to produce food, mainly to supply local and regional markets, not through the globalization of the capital, energy, and emissions intensive use of chemical fertilizers, pesticides, and mechanization, an approach that is more aimed at feeding corporate suppliers of farm inputs and credit than hungry people.

For the industrialized countries, de-growth is heretical, but reducing the pressure to continuously increase farm production presents new opportunities. For ecologist Stan Rowe, "The central question is whether mainstream agriculture on the industrial model can or will take an interest in *maintenance* and *sustainable production* when its tunnel vision is on *maximum yield and increasing production*. The record … so far is not good: loss of the soil's organic matter along with soil erosion, compaction, toxification, and salinization. If the unrecorded costs of production—the price Nature's bank has to pay for an exploitive system—were included with the costs of agribiz inputs, present crop prices would probably not cover the total." And although industrial farming methods "may be getting better, more conserving, more efficient, the direction is steadfastly toward the idiot's goal of growth, toward higher production, higher yields, greater profits, toward more and yet more. Few are willing to face martyrdom by voicing the thought that maybe, just maybe, good agricultural practice requires a decrease in production, not an increase."[189]

Relieving the pressure on big industrial farms to feed the world opens doors to a new role. Farmers can find an alternative income source in restoring land and watersheds and sequestering carbon.

GROWING INCENTIVES

Soil scientist Rattan Lal estimates that paying small farmers to improve soil is one of the most cost effective ways to ameliorate climate change.[190] He argues that adoption of best practices for restoration of marginal soils in low income countries has lagged because small landholders are cash poor and cannot invest in the inputs required, even though the cost is small. The only way to promote carbon farming is by incentivizing farming communities. The strategy would be to reward land managers through payments for ecosystem services, including carbon sequestration, green water credits, and biodiversity enhancement. This must be done by a fair, transparent, and just pricing process.

Paying for ecosystem services is a better strategy than subsidies and hand-outs, says Lal. While international development assistance is important, emergency aid and other knee-jerk approaches can create dependencies, kill initiative, ruin self-esteem, increase corruption, and distort values. Through payments for ecosystem services, small farmers are seen as preferred clients rather than aid recipients.

Most of the so-called costs of climate change mitigation or ecological protection are in fact investments with a high rate of return. Having said that, they do require the initial investment of capital that is hard to obtain from conventional capital markets. So, where can the investments come from?

According to Lal, the cost of carbon capture and storage (CCS) technology—often cited as a kind of ultimate solution to climate change—averages about US\$100/tonne of CO_2 (or US\$367/tonne of carbon (C)). In contrast, the costs of soil organic carbon (SOC) sequestration is between low and negative. In 2009, McKinsey and Company computed the greenhouse gas abatement cost curve and showed that tillage and residue management had a negative cost of about \$100 per tonne C compared with a cost of \$67 to \$80 per tonne C for CCS technology. The cost for SOC sequestration is low because costs are offset by increases in agronomic production and other co-benefits. In other words, investing in climate change mitigation through agriculture is the most intelligent option because it is the lowest cost approach.

Sequestration in above ground vegetation is another approach that small farmers can employ. A global analysis of land suitability as a carbon sink through afforestation and reforestation found that the total economic potential of C sequestration in the terrestrial biosphere is 1.25 billion tonnes C per year until

2030. Both relative cost and risks are lowest for C sequestration in biomass and highest with geoengineering, i.e. geologic and oceanic sequestration.

If farmers and land managers were compensated for C sequestration in soils and biomass at the rate equivalent to the cost of carbon capture and storage, Lal reasons, the payment for ecosystem services, even at the modest rate of soil C sequestration of 250 kg/ha/yr, would be about US$90/ha/yr. However, Lal believes most farmers would be pleased to adopt the required farming methods at about one-quarter the cost of CCS, i.e. US$25/ha/yr. Thus, payments to land managers for sequestering C in agricultural soils and agroforestry projects, not only as sink projects under the Clean Development Mechanism (CDM) of the Kyoto treaty but also for enhancing ecosystem services, would be an important strategy to alleviate poverty and advance regional and global food security.

Given that small farmers manage about 1 billion hectares, a universal rollout of best practices would cost a mere $25 billion a year, about $50 for the average small farm. This payment per farmer seems small, but consider that if the average yield per hectare on small farms is just 1 tonne, annual farm income would be in the neighbourhood of $500. A 10 percent income boost from carbon payments would allow farmers to introduce sustainable methods. According to the reports reviewed in the previous chapter, the application of these methods on small farms can increase production by as much as 100 percent after a few years, doubling farm incomes. Thus, after a few years of transition, the green payments could be phased out as farm incomes improve.

I say "a mere $25 billion a year" because it is a small amount relative to other expenditures relevant to this discussion. Efforts by a variety of organizations to quantify global subsidies for fossil fuels, for example, have generated estimates that range from $523 billion (International Energy Agency) to over $1.9 trillion (International Monetary Fund), depending on the calculation and what measures are included.[191] Most of these are consumption subsidies but at least $100 billion goes to fossil fuel producers, among the most profitable companies in the world.

From an emissions perspective, 15 percent of global carbon dioxide emissions receive $110 per ton in *supports*, while only 8 percent are subject to a carbon price, effectively nullifying carbon market contributions as a measure to reduce emissions. Accelerating the phase out of fossil fuel subsidies would reduce carbon dioxide emissions by 360 million tons in 2020, 12 percent of the emission savings that are needed in order to keep the increase in global temperature to 2°C.

Transferring less than 5 percent of current subsidies for fossil fuels (using the IEA figure) to ecological payments for small farmers (or 1.3 percent of the IMF figure) would be among the most cost effective ways to mitigate climate change, reduce extreme poverty, and increase food production where it will be most needed as we approach an 11 billion-world.

> Transferring less than 5 percent of current subsidies for fossil fuels to ecological payments for small farmers would be among the most cost effective ways to mitigate climate change, reduce extreme poverty, and increase food production in low-income countries.

At around $250 billion a year, farm subsidies in OECD countries have been criticized as a contributing factor to poverty in low-income countries, while at the same time intensifying the ecological impacts of large scale industrial farming. Switching production subsidies to ecological payments for farmers could reorient industrial agriculture, adding to the climate mitigation potential, while reducing negative impacts on farm incomes in low-income areas.

A version of a global fund of the kind proposed has already been established. The Global Agriculture and Food Security Program is a multilateral mechanism to assist in the implementation of pledges made by the G20 in 2009. The objective is to address the underfunding of agriculture and food security plans already being developed in consultation with donors and other stakeholders at the country-level. This would make aid contributions toward the achievement of Millennium Development Goal 1, to cut hunger and poverty by half by 2015, more predictable. Ten donors have pledged a total of US $1.4 billion. Of course a much larger amount is needed to make a substantive difference.

As I enumerated in the first section of this book, huge sums of money are associated with activities that range from unnecessary to destructive. There is no lack of squandered wealth in this world. Spending just 1 percent of the $2.5 trillion spent on alcohol globally every year (social costs included) could transform small farming worldwide. So would 1.5 percent of official military spending of $1.7 trillion. The money spent on any of prostitution, gambling, or pornography could essentially wipe out poverty and restore the ecosphere.

Relatively inconsequential tax measures could also raise the needed money. If, for example, each of 2.8 billion airline passengers per year was levied a carbon tax of just $10 per flight—an inconsequential amount to the average traveller—the income from this measure alone would pay for a universal small farm SOC program.

But this brings us back to the issue of ethics. There is nothing stopping us from solving our most important problems other than our lamentably defective global ethos.

A CONSUMPTION PROBLEM

We return now to the ethos of the consumer society discussed in the first section of the book, since the issue of overconsumption is also critical to the renewal of the agrifood system. The inadequacies of the agrifood system may demand higher production in some instances but also less—and smarter—consumption in others. Making the world work for 11 billion means we will have to stop wasting food, eat less of it, switch to different foods, and become much more efficient in our use of food producing resources. Solutions will come from consumers, not just producers.

It has been shown that it is technically feasible to feed a population of 11 billion people through *supply side* measures by producers, but this goal could also be accomplished through *demand side* measures, mainly by consumers. As Vaclav Smil put it: "We would not even have to increase the existing agricultural inputs in order to feed many more than ten billion people in a global economy guided by concerns about consumption equity and offering everybody frugal, largely vegetarian but nutritionally adequate diets."[192] On the other hand, says Smil, even today's population could not be fed if North America's current average per capita food supply—of which 40 percent is wasted—were to become the global norm.

Cutting Calories Diets typical of high-income countries and middle- and high-income earners in middle- and low-income countries are overloaded with calories. The National Academy of Sciences[193] makes the following daily calorie recommendations:

- 1,600 calories is about right for many sedentary women and some older adults.

- 2,200 calories is about right for most children, teenage girls, active women, and many sedentary men. (Women who are pregnant or breast-feeding may need somewhat more.)

- 2,800 calories is about right for teenage boys, many active men, and some very active women

Using this guide let's assume an ideal average intake of 2250 calories per person per day. Average caloric consumption for the world has been creeping up gradually, from an average of 2610 kcal/person/day in 1992 to 2780 in 2007, an increase of about 6 percent. Given the upward trend, we can safely assume that average consumption of calories is above 2800 kcal/person/day today. Average caloric intake is much higher (3420 kcal) in the high-income countries and higher yet in a few countries such as United States at 3770 kcal. At the other end of the scale, the average Eritrean consumes less than half the calories (1590) of an American.

The amounts cited here are actually calories available to the consumer; actual consumption is somewhat lower due to loses such as waste during food preparation.

Simply cutting calories to the average recommended daily intake of 2250 would then free up at least 550 calories per person per day. With a population of 11 billion, adopting this reduced calorie diet would free up sufficient food for more than 2.5 billion people.

The *longevity diet*, which replaces calorie-dense foods with calorie-sparse, nutrient-dense foods, has been shown in some studies to improve health and longevity. On this diet, adult males consume just 1,800 calories and adult women only 1,500. While this approach is not applicable to children and youth, pregnant and lactating women, or people who perform heavy physical labour or strenuous exercise, it may be quite appropriate in an increasingly sedentary world.

Lower calorie diets that rely heavily on nutrient rich vegetables would make substantially more food available for a growing population. Adopting a diet that averages 1650 calories would be more than 1000 calories lower than current diets. With 11 billion people, this would free up enough food to feed more than 6 billion people assuming an average caloric consumption of 1650 calories.

Toward Vegetarianism It is well established that a diet that uses less grain-fed animal products is more land efficient. One study[194] found a nearly fivefold difference (0.18–0.86 ha) in per capita land requirements between low-fat vegetarian diets and high-fat diets that included meat.

Another analysis[195] found that if all the grain currently fed to livestock in the United States were consumed directly by people, the number of additional people who could be fed would be nearly 800 million. With only grass-fed livestock, individual Americans could still get more than the recommended daily allowance of meat and dairy protein.

Nearly 35 percent of world grain, about 800 million tonnes, is being fed to livestock rather than being consumed directly by humans.[196] This would be sufficient to feed 2.6 billion people; using this grain to produce animal products feeds only 430 million.

While it is likely that a more vegetarian approach will be an important step in making the world work for 11 billion people, it appears that retaining some meat content can be sustainable. Incorporating small amounts of meat and dairy products in diets can, in some cases, be more land efficient than a vegetarian diet. Animals can make use of certain feeds that cannot be directly consumed by people and some land is better suited to grazing than cultivation. Approaches such as holistic resource management, described in the last chapter, could allow meat consumption without exceeding carrying capacity.

The Greens Revolution As mentioned, poor nutrition is a worldwide problem affecting the poor, middle income, and rich alike, though in different ways. The solution may be fairly simple: growing and eating more vegetables and fruits.

Writing in *State of the World 2011*, Abdou Tenkouano calls for a *Greens Revolution* to match the Green Revolution of the 1970s, which was really a *grain revolution*. Tenkouano, director of the World Vegetable Center in Africa, says that even if we provide enough calories from staple crops people will not be properly nourished until diets improve through diversification. Diseases related to imbalanced diets, especially from insufficient vegetable and fruit consumption, cause 2.7 million deaths worldwide annually and are among the top mortality risk factors.

Consuming more vegetables would also have broad social implications, reports Tenkouano. It would solve the problem of micronutrient deficiencies, including lack of Vitamin A, iron, and iodine, affecting some 1 billion people. These deficiencies lead to poor mental and physical development, especially among children, and cause poor performance at school and work, undermining communities already facing other health problems and poverty. Vitamin A deficiency, for example, can lead to permanent blindness in children and suppress the immune system, thereby predisposing children to respiratory tract infections, measles, and diarrhea. Inadequate intake of iron is also widespread, leading to chronic anemia. This condition is also linked to learning disabilities, mental retardation, poor physical development, and a reduced ability to fight infectious diseases, ultimately leading to premature death. Eating vegetables eliminates these problems.

Vegetables are also attractive from an economic viewpoint. Small farmers can earn much higher incomes from growing vegetables than staples. Yet very little work is being done on improvement of vegetable crops. In 2002, for example, the research centers that belong to the Consultative Group on International Agricultural Research invested $118 million on cereals research, but just $15.7 million on fruit and vegetable research. Improved vegetable varieties can have a big nutritional and economic impact. Better varieties of eggplant now developed for Africa, for example, can be harvested every week for seven months and produce for up to 15 months if pruned back at the end of the season. A typical farmer can harvest 10–20 bags of eggplant (30 kg each) every week throughout the seven-month growing season and earn $2,500 per hectare per year, several times the income possible from staple grain crops.

Vegetables are also something many people can grow in home gardens, vacant lots, or even on balconies. Adoption of a diet rich in vegetables is one way to feed the world, to feed it better, and with less environmental impact.

Meanwhile, health experts like Andrew Weil are calling for a fruit and vegetable revolution in high-income countries. Weil and others prescribe the adoption of a food pyramid approach built on a wide base of vegetables and fruits, with the next level as whole grains, and for the rest of our foods to be unrefined. The food pyramid incudes small amounts of animal products. Along with proper exercise, such a diet would eliminate the bulk of the health problems of over-fed and undernourished people and ameliorate the health care cost crisis. What is more, ecological impacts are lowest for the healthiest foods and highest for the least healthy foods. Vegetables and fruits are a win-win approach, for people and the ecosphere.

Improving Efficiency Improved efficiency comes up again and again as a standard first response to solving global problems. The agrifood system is a prime example.[197]

According to Vacliv Smil, the total edible crop at harvest on a typical farm yielding 4600 food calories per unit of production is reduced to 2000 useable calories though post-harvest losses, conversions to animal feed and animal protein, and waste in processing, distribution, and in households. This suggests that the first and most straightforward step toward feeding the additional 3.7 billion expected by century's end is to improve the efficiency of the food chain: reducing post harvest losses through improved food storage and handling; direct use of more food for human consumption rather than conversion to animal feeds and the consumption of animal products; and the reduction of waste in food processing and distribution, as well as in kitchens.

In general, harvest efficiency is an area where modern farming shines: under optimal weather conditions in wealthy countries, post harvest grain losses can be reduced to as little as .07 percent. In contrast, post-harvest losses of 15 percent are typical in low-income countries and losses of up to 80 percent are not unheard of given poor weather conditions. Food waste is most significant in countries that have insufficient investment in harvest equipment and in storage and distribution infrastructure. Smil estimates that annual post harvest losses amount to 136 million tonnes (enough food for 450 million people), six times what the FAO says would be needed to meet the food deficit of all the hungry people in low-income countries.

Reducing post-harvest cereal losses to 4 percent is considered reasonable. Improving grain storage would also maintain higher nutritional content, so that the same amount of a better quality grain feeds more people.

In higher income countries, food waste is more deliberate, and includes practices such as cosmetic trimming, discarding "imperfect" food, and waste of excess food. Food waste is epidemic in societies that push a cheap food policy that favours consumers, the vast majority, over producers, now a tiny minority with limited political clout. This policy effectively forces more and more farmers off the land, with those remaining required to adopt high-input, energy-intensive, high-producing industrial farming methods on an expanding land base. Cheap food is thus linked to unsustainable farming methods typical of high-income countries.

Crop Conversion A substantial amount of agricultural land is devoted to crops that can cause physical, emotional, and social harm. To recap figures presented in a previous chapter, the most significant of these is likely tobacco, which is grown on 4 million hectares worldwide. Illicit drugs—chiefly marihuana (420,000 ha is the mid-range acreage estimate); opium (estimated at 190,000 ha); and coca (estimated at 175,000 ha)—use 785,000 hectares worldwide.[198] In total, this acreage converted to cereal grain could produce sufficient food for up to 50 million people. Reducing tobacco and drug consumption would of course improve health and significantly reduce health care costs worldwide.

Alcohol is among the most destructive substances in widespread use, whether from a health, personal, emotional, economic, or social perspective. At least 30 million hectares are devoted to raising crops for alcohol consumption, including grains, grapes, and hops. If we assume that it would be beneficial to reduce consumption by 50 percent, this has the potential to free up 15 million hectares to grow food crops, enough to support up to 150 million people if sown to cereal grains.

Increasing evidence shows that high levels of sugar consumption are key to the global obesity epidemic and other negative health outcomes, including dental caries. Sugarcane is the world's most productive crop per hectare; 1.3 billion tonnes were produced in 2004, more than wheat and rice combined.[199] Some 29 million ha are devoted to sugarcane and sugar beet. The increasingly used sugar substitute high fructose corn syrup (HFCS) is even more insidious, according to some research. Some 107 million ha of corn are grown worldwide annually; if close to 10 percent of the crop is turned into corn syrups, as is the case in the US, some 10 million ha worldwide are devoted to producing unhealthy corn syrups. In total, then, as much as 39 million ha are given over to producing sugars. If sugar consumption were halved, this would free up 20 million ha for food, enough to feed up to 200 million people.

YES WE CAN. BUT WILL WE?

In this chapter we have looked at a variety of measures that would lead to a new agrifood system based on a higher set of ethical values than is currently the case.

We have also seen that an ethical approach would support increased production in lower income areas, higher food consumption for the undernourished, and lower consumption by the over-nourished. The following table provides a rough summary of the technically possible benefit of these measures, in terms of the ability to feed those who are currently hungry and the additional 3.7 billion that will be added to the world by centuries end.

Measure	Potential to feed
Decrease post harvest losses	0.33 billion
Lower calorie, high nutrient diets	2.40 billion
Divert grain from animals to people	2.10 billion
Convert tobacco/drug acreage to grain	0.05 billion
Reduce land devoted to sugar	0.20 billion
Reduce land devoted to alcohol	0.15 billion
Restore 200 million ha degraded land	1.90 billion
Increase average production by 50% on 50% of small farms	0.83 billion
Total potential	**8.0 billion**

These measures alone would provide almost double the food needed by the end of century. What is more, this approach could reduce poverty while restoring ecosystems and contributing to the mitigation of climate change. And it could all be achieved at no-to-low cost, since most of the measures actually have a negative cost or are only needed temporarily. Initial capital investments for other measures would require a minimum diversion of funds from anti-social activities, such as perverse energy subsidies.

This approach is feasible, if we want to do it.

The main obstacles to reforms of this type are entrenched habits and beliefs and a lack of moral capacity. The momentum of the current world order, its inequalities and blindness to ecological realities, will be impossible to change without an ethical transformation. Until an ethos built around *the material well-being of the individual in the present* shifts to one built around *the spiritual wellbeing of humankind throughout time* only limited progress will be made.

How do we achieve this advanced moral state? Through education. The core proposal of this book is that human beings are fundamentally virtuous, but these virtues only develop through effort by families and communities and institutions to foster them and by our own effort to attain them. Children, youth, and adults, we all need assistance to build our moral capacity and this assistance comes through education that is motivated by love. The moral education system can be combined with education that helps participants to understand and adopt the practical methods, practices, and lifestyle changes proposed in this chapter.

This educational process will require everyone's involvement. Many are already leading the way, and many more will become early adopters, but in time, the moral education process will come to involve whole villages and neighbourhoods and spread through whole countries. Ultimately, to make the world work for 11 billion people, we will be called to become what can only be described as a new human race.

SECTION 3
A NEW HUMAN RACE

*The historical mission of our times is to reinvent the
human at the species level.*
– Thomas Berry

CHAPTER 9

ETHICS ARE EVERYTHING

In 1975, as it was dawning on Norwegians just how rich they were about to become, journalist Solveig Torvik asked then Prime Minister Trygve Bratteli where Norway would be spending its newfound North Sea oil money. Better schools, perhaps? Roads? Medical services? Eldercare?

Bratteli responded with visible alarm. It would be impossible to spend Norway's wealth inside the nation without triggering inflation, he explained. And oil profits would have to be invested outside the country to maintain an income stream after the oil runs out in order to sustain the country's generous social benefits.

While this struck Torvik as high-minded and responsible, she says she couldn't escape the impression that the country's leaders were terrified of the oil money and couldn't get it out of the country fast enough. Perhaps, but Bratteli couldn't resist adding: "But we do have more money than the Swedes."[200]

They do indeed. To see just how much more, check out the Norges Bank home page (www.norges-bank.no), which shows the changing market value of the Norwegian Government Pension Fund. The fund is so massive that in a matter of minutes you might see its market value grow by one billion krone (NOK). As of July 17, 2014—at 3:05 pm CST—the fund was worth NOK 5.502 trillion (US$886 billion), making it the world's largest sovereign wealth fund (SWF).[201]

Norges Bank Investment Management, which handles the fund for the Norwegian government, anticipates it will grow to NOK 6.031 trillion (US$1.1 trillion) by 2020, by which time Norway's substantial oil production—which has already peaked—will have declined sharply. At a modest 4 percent return it would provide US$44 billion in revenues each year—in perpetuity, about what Norway currently earns from oil. Assuming Norway maintains near zero population growth, that's close to a $9,000 annual dividend per Norwegian citizen.

The designation "Pension Fund" is a bit of a misnomer, given income to the fund comes from the country's excess petroleum revenues rather than pension contributions. In 1969 oil was discovered in the North Sea. When the Norwegian government of the day determined to develop its share of the resource, it decided to do something unusual: use it with caution and prudence to maximize the benefits of a non-renewable resource for future generations. In 1990, to counter the effects of the projected decline in income anticipated after peak oil, and to smooth the disrupting effects of highly fluctuating oil prices, the Norwegian government passed legislation that established what was initially called The Petroleum Fund of Norway. In 1996 the fund began to collect parts of the large surplus from the Norwegian oil and gas sector, generated mainly from taxes on companies, payment for exploration licenses, and the country's interest and dividends from its partial ownership of StatoilHydro, a leading international energy and resource conglomerate.

The fund invests internationally in fixed income and equities and some real estate. It owns about 2 percent of all European stocks and about 1 percent of all equities in the world. If divided among its owners, the 4.9 million citizens of Norway, it could pay out about $181,000 per citizen (circa July 2014). The fund is considered the best-managed and most transparent sovereign wealth fund in the world. All investments are in line with ethical guidelines monitored by the Council of Ethics, which prohibits investment where there is a risk that corporate activities can contribute to violations of human rights, corruption, environmental damage, or other serious violations of fundamental ethical norms.

In contrast to the Norwegian model, major oil producing countries like the UK, Canada, and the United States have spent virtually their entire oil fortune on current needs and wants. Nothing has been set aside for future generations, for when the non-renewable resource peters out. Failing to preserve a portion of the wealth of the oil era will perhaps go down in history as the worst resource policy failure ever. As John Hawksworth of PriceWaterhouseCoopers argued in his essay *Dude, Where's My Oil Money?*, had Britain's North Sea oil wealth been set aside Norwegian-style, it could have financed a national fund far larger than Norway's. Instead, successive governments spent most of the cash to keep taxes "lower than would otherwise have been possible without rising debt levels or sharp cuts in public spending."[202]

Just one Canadian province has an oil fund, but Alberta's Heritage Fund, started in 1976, stopped collecting resource revenues after 1987 and has accumulated reserves of just $15 billion after 35 years. Since 1970, Alberta has earned some $200 billion in non-renewable resource revenues and taxes, mainly collected from oil and gas. Had a good portion of this amount been set aside and invested, the Heritage Fund would have rivaled Norway's.

The United States also has just one oil fund. Alaska's Permanent Fund was started in 1976 and has $40 billion in assets.

A number of other nations have set aside oil revenues. Abu Dhabi has accumulated more than $300 billion for example. Saudi Arabia's SAMA Foreign Holdings, although not strictly a SWF, holds $472 billion; huge, yes, but the Saudis earn $235 billion a year from petroleum. Iran has its Oil Stabilization Fund started in 1999 with $23 billion in assets. Nigeria's Excess Crude Account, started in 2005, has just $500 million. And the fact is, little is known about most of these funds: SAMA, for example, has a transparency rating of 2 on a scale of 10 compared to Norway's 10. (A 10 indicates the highest level of transparency.)

This discussion is not to suggest that Norway and its handling of resource revenues is beyond reproach. Norway has its own set of challenges—and critics. Still, it is close to unique in its management of non-renewable resources.

Why is that? Why does Norway use its windfall oil revenues so prudently, conserving their value for future generations—with absolute transparency in their dealings—while most other oil producing countries have done so little to sustain their non-renewable resource wealth? It is a profound question.

One thing we know is that Norway did not suffer economically as a result of its prudence. Following is a list of indices of comparative national wealth and other metrics, followed by Norway's ranking on that list as of 2011, compared to all other countries:

- UN Human Development Index - 1
- Democracy index - 1
- Legatum Prosperity Index -1
- Gender–related Development Index - 2
- Environmental Performance Index - 5
- Education Index - 7

- Global Peace Index - 9
- Corruption Perception Index - 10
- Competitiveness Index - 14

Norway also ranked 177th, i.e. last, on Foreign Policy magazine's Failed State Index, meaning it is considered the world's most functional and stable country. Norwegians enjoy the second highest GDP per-capita (after Luxembourg) in Europe and fourth highest GDP per-capita in the world. Today, Norway ranks as the second wealthiest country in the world in monetary value, with the largest capital reserve per capita of any nation.

Significantly, Norway is also among the most egalitarian of nations, in principle and practice. Along with its Scandinavian neighbours, Norway follows the "Nordic model" that includes a mixed market economy, high tax rates, and generous social benefits. With high levels of state ownership in certain sectors (including oil), the Norwegian government controls approximately 30 percent of stock value at the Oslo Stock Exchange. When non-listed companies are included, the state has an even higher share of ownership.

Public welfare provisions include universal health care, universal education, subsidized higher education, and comprehensive social security, all aimed at enhancing individual autonomy, ensuring the universal provision of basic human rights, and a stable society. The Nordic states are distinguished from other welfare states with similar goals by their emphasis on maximizing labour force participation; promoting gender equality; egalitarian and extensive benefit levels (parents have 46 weeks paid parental leave, for example); substantial wealth redistribution; and liberal use of expansionary fiscal policy. And Norway has an unemployment rate of just 3.1 percent (2011).

Norway's egalitarian ethic ensures that the wage difference between the lowest paid worker and the CEO of most companies is much smaller than in comparable western economies. This is evident in Norway's low *Gini coefficient*, a measure of inequality in income and wealth. The country has the third highest taxation level in the world; 30 percent of Norway's labour force is employed by the government, the highest in the OECD; 22 percent are on welfare and 13 percent are considered too disabled to work, the highest proportions in the world. Norway also has a high rate (53 percent) of trade union participation (compared, for example, to just 12.3 percent in the US.) Its hourly productivity levels, as well as average hourly wages, are among the highest in the world.

Perhaps the most notable sign of Norway's transparent egalitarianism is its annual publication of a tax list that includes every person in the country. The *skattelister* includes not only the taxes paid by fishermen or Sami reindeer herders or urban entrepreneurs, it also includes their income and total wealth. The searchable list is on line for anyone to view.

Despite being among the richest nations in the world, Norwegians tend toward frugality. It has been observed that they often walk to work, bring bag lunches, or drive older cars. Compared to other countries, Norwegians have, on average, lower disposable incomes and a very high cost of living. Lunch out costs an arm and a leg, consumer goods can be double the cost typical of other countries, gas is priced at $2.50/litre, double, for example, the price in Canada (despite plentiful domestic oil production.) But higher costs for goods and services make it possible to pay service workers a good wage; and service industry workers have to be paid well or they might head off to the oilrigs.

The average Norwegian puts in 26 percent less time at work in a year than an American. With more time off, better education, and better working conditions, productivity per hour worked is about 15 percent higher in Norway than the US. Plus, Norway has zero national debt.

Its frugality means Norway only draws 11 percent of its budget from oil, allowing it to continue to put money by in its Pension Fund and to spend just 4 percent of the fund's revenues each year. The unusual combination of frugality and wealth also allows close to one percent of national income to be spent on foreign aid annually, more than any other country.

Norwegians show that it is possible for a people to decide to defer their own wellbeing for the benefit of future generations. And exercising that decision has had a surprising result: *looking out for future generations enhances conditions for the current generation.*

WHY NORWAY?

All this is not to suggest Norway is perfect. Despite its green credentials, Norway has the 17th heaviest ecological footprint of any nation and ranks on the lower side (115th) of the Happy Planet Index, a measure of the amount of ecological capital a country spends to achieve happiness, longevity, and health. The ecological footprint of the oil industry is a factor in the country's low performance on these measures. But again, Norway is stepping to the head of the pack, with its decision in 2008 to become carbon-neutral by 2030, as well as a plan announced in 2010 to create the world's first "index of nature".

The Nature Index of Norway[203] uses 309 indicators to incorporate ecosystem services like pollination and forest growth into measures of prosperity, which amounts to a radical revision of conventional economic metrics.

Significantly, Norway's climate change policy involves a broad non-partisan agreement among all political parties, meaning that Norway can pursue a long-term climate policy regardless of changes in government. Government will use a carrot and stick approach to encourage more ecologically sound behaviour, including reduced GHG emissions. Billions will be allocated for efforts to promote renewable energy sources, strengthen public transport, and implement measures aimed at reducing emissions from the transport sector. At the same time, taxes on diesel fuel and petrol will be increased.

The Norwegian model shows that ethical conduct, both in terms of its egalitarian social order and efforts to enhance ecological sustainability, is not only possible on a national scale, it actually increases prosperity. But why has Norway adopted this enlightened approach while so many other nations have not?

Economist Jeffrey Sachs, referring to the work of economist Alberto Alesina, argues that social and racial cleavages in societies undermine social investments to reduce inequality and poverty.[204] Social spending tends to be highest where social and racial cleavages are the smallest. Nordic ethnic homogeneity has been an important enabling social factor in the success of the social welfare state. In the United States or Britain, in contrast, ethnic and racial divisions are major factors that undermine a sense of unity and concern for the commonweal. This disunity can also impact fundamental social attitudes and political models. Regarding the situation in the United States, Alesina comments:

> Our bottom line is that Americans redistribute less than Europeans for three reasons: because the majority of Americans believe that redistribution favors racial minorities, because Americans believe that they live in an open and fair society and that if someone is poor it is his or her own fault, and because the political system is geared toward preventing redistribution. In fact, the political system is likely to be endogenous to these basic American beliefs. [205]

Sachs puts it this way: "In the end, the social-welfare model relies on a form of trust. It seems people are more willing to withstand high rates of taxation if they know that their taxes are paying for programs that help people like them. Because poor people in the social-welfare states are of the same cultural and ethnic background as the rest of the population, it is easier to promote programs that support the poor."

Americans, notes Alesina, tend to believe that the poor are lazy, while Europeans see them as unlucky or unfortunate, so more deserving of social supports. And in welfare states, political systems are often more representative; measures such as proportional representation strengthen the position of parties with unconventional platforms or those representing lower income classes and minority groups.

One might argue that some of the same factors tend to support a sustainability ethic as well. Proportional representation has helped to legitimize parties such as the Greens in Europe, for instance. The ethic of generous social welfare for all can create a mindset where people are more concerned for the long-term welfare of society and future generations, which inevitably encourages more forethought in caring for the ecosphere. What is more, social inequality heightens competitive consumption, while equality reduces it.

Social equality and ecological sustainability go hand in hand.

THE SPIRIT LEVEL

The Spirit Level: Why Equality is Better for Everyone may be among the most important books ever written. The gist of it is that the most equal societies—those where disparities in average incomes are lowest—are better in almost every way than societies with large income disparities.

The authors, Richard Wilkinson and Kate Pickett, applied their skills as epidemiologists to study almost every social measure—from mental and physical health to violence and educational attainment, from social relations and teen pregnancy to imprisonment and longevity—and correlate it to income disparity in every

> The most equal societies—those where the disparities in average incomes are lowest—are better in almost every way than societies with large income disparities.

nation that makes sufficient statistics available to do so. In all cases, where there is a smaller gap between the average incomes of poorer and richer strata of the society, people are generally healthier, happier, better adjusted, better educated, and more cohesive.

Though it is among the wealthiest nations, the United States is riddled with social ills. Japan and Scandinavia, though equally wealthy, have significantly fewer problems. For instance, in the US 576 people per 100,000 are in prison compared to 40 per 100,000 in Japan and around 50 in Scandinavian countries. In the US, 30 percent of people are obese compared to 2.4 percent in Japan. A similar pattern holds for almost every social ill. Why?

The authors make the case that the cause of social problems is not poverty so much as disparity in income. Compared to Japan or the Scandinavian countries, the US has a much wider gap in incomes between the top 20 percent of income earners and the bottom 20 percent. The richest 20 percent are more that 8 times as rich as the poorest 20 percent in the US, whereas the difference is just 4 times in Japan or Scandinavia.

The issue seems to be that people are highly social beings who care deeply about their *relative* status. When people are poor relative to others, their self-esteem is affected, which results in a cascade of problems. On the other hand, when people have similar incomes, they are more at ease about status and social cohesion builds. Levels of trust are higher and problems like crime and mental illness decrease.

Interestingly, poorer societies that are relatively equal can be as successful as rich societies. An interesting example previously cited is Cuba. Although a poor country by international standards, and certainly much poorer than its neigh-bour the United States, Cuba's infant mortality and life expectancy rates, among other measures of human progress, are the same as in the US.

Even in the area of environment the inequality standard applies. More equal countries emit less GHG, for example. Sweden and France generate a fraction of the emissions of the US. Similarly, the ecological footprint of equal societies is generally lower than that of unequal societies. Again, Cuba is both above the UN threshold for high human development and has an ecological footprint that is close to sustainable.

"The fact that one country manages to combine acceptable living standards with a sustainable economy," observe Wilkinson and Pickett, "proves that it can be done." This is not to suggest that Cuban socialism is a better economic system than capitalism. More equal societies include capitalistic, socialistic, and mixed economies; what is common is that each has found a way to spread social benefits.

Wilkinson and Pickett argue that equality is actually better for the rich too. Wealthy people in more equal societies enjoy better physical and mental health and higher security than the rich in unequal societies.

For Wilkinson and Pickett, there are clear limitations to the benefits wealth can deliver. Statistics clearly show that past a certain point—whatever the typical average income is for a given society—there are few benefits to having more money. People with incomes above that level are not happier or healthier, they just have more stuff.

This suggests that the mainstay of the economy of most wealthy nations—economic growth through consumerism—is a chimera. Analyses of human wellbeing indicate that, once basic needs are met, more consumption causes more harm than good, socially and environmentally. Inequality and a high physical-throughput economy result in more *illth* than *wealth*.

ILLTH VS. WEALTH

Ecological economist Herman Daly tells an interesting story from his time as a senior economist at the World Bank. He was involved in the production of a document titled *Development and the Environment*. An early draft contained a diagram entitled, "The Relationship Between the Economy and the Environment." It consisted of a square labeled "economy," with an arrow coming in labeled "inputs," and an arrow going out labeled "outputs," nothing more.

Daly commented that a diagram about the physical environment should show the environment. He suggested it be redrawn with the same diagram of the economy inside a larger box representing the environment. Then the relation between the environment and the economy would be clear—specifically, that the economy is a subsystem of the environment and depends upon the environment both as a source of inputs and as a sink for outputs.

The next draft included the same diagram and text, but with an unlabeled box drawn around the economy like a picture frame. Daly commented that the larger box had to be labeled "environment" or else it was merely decorative, and that the text should explain that the economy exists within the environment and is subject to ecological limits. Instead, the next draft omitted the diagram altogether.

This, says Daly, illustrates the standard frame of reference of economists. No doubt they are aware of the existence of the physical environment, i.e. the ecosphere; they behave, however, as if the economy is *the whole* and not a part of a larger whole, namely an ecosphere that is not limitless.

Daly and other ecological economists, a small, unpopular subset of their profession, say that traditional economic problems (poverty, overpopulation, unemployment, unjust distribution) are all thought to have a common solution, namely an increase in wealth. All problems are easier if we are richer. The way to get richer is through economic growth, usually measured as GDP.

Daly accepts that richer is better than poorer, but questions whether what is labeled "economic growth" is, any longer, making us richer. He says that physical throughput growth is reaching its limit and has begun to increase *illth* faster than *wealth*, thus making us poorer rather than richer. *Illth* is the opposite of wealth, although it is not synonymous with poverty. It is a kind of "bad wealth." An example might be having so much wealth that people buy so many cars that it becomes impossible to move through traffic.

The impacts of a growing economy on the ecosphere—such as depletion of natural resources, climate change, loss of biodiversity—or on social conditions—such as health or the growing disparity between the rich and poor—can mean that traditional economic problems actually become worse with further growth. The ultimate example is climate change, where growth increases emissions to the extent that climate begins to undermine key industries like agriculture and forestry.

In wealthy places, what we conventionally call *economic* growth in the sense of growth of the economy can, ironically, become *uneconomic* growth in the literal sense of growth that increases costs—like deterioration of ecosystems or social wellbeing—more than it increases benefits.

Our commitment to an economy that fosters ever-increasing social inequality and at the same time undermines the wellbeing of future generations by damaging the ecosphere ought rightly be seen as a symptom of a state of disunity. That is, it places more value on some people than others—both in the present and in the future—rather than seeing all human beings—now and in the future—as equally important and deserving of the benefits civilization can bring. The principle-based solution to inequality and ecological degradation is an infusion of the unity principle into the collective consciousness.

THE UNITY DIVIDEND

Inequality is a product of disunity. Corollary to the unity principle—that the level of unity a society experiences is the ultimate determinant of wellbeing—is the principle of equality. To have a unified society, and enjoy the benefits thereof, it has to be an equal society. Not everyone has to have exactly the same standard of living; that is not the point. But the smaller the gap between high- and low-income strata, the better.

What this suggests is that the higher the state of unity of a society—the stronger the sense that every citizen is of equal value or status—the more that society will concern itself with social wellbeing, both in the short and over the long term. The concern for the long-term welfare of society logically translates into concern for the ecosphere.

The ethnic uniformity of states like Norway has contributed to their unity (in a uniform society it is easier to see everyone as having equal standing.) Their unity has contributed to Norwegians' social conscience (which is developed through equal access to education and high levels of transparency and public discourse.) Importantly, the development of social conscience has, in the modern era, facilitated the extension of their concern to non-ethnic Norwegians, through the extension of social benefits to immigrants and contributions to international development.

This is not to idealize Nordic societies; after all, they are progressive in part because they have not had to deal as extensively with issues of diversity characteristic of societies that have historically depended on colonization and immigration (including forced immigration, i.e. slavery.) It is ironic that the sense of inclusiveness that characterizes the Nordic states is born initially out of their racial homogeneity. It is remarkable then that this has developed into a wider sense of concern for all human beings and, beyond that, the ecosphere.

In more diverse societies such as the US, which has large African and Latino minorities, it will be critical to enhance an ethic of unity to bridge racial-ethnic-cultural divides. This will pay dividends in terms of social equity and the improvement of all social performance measures. Ultimately, it will also contribute to the foresight that allows people to look into the future and concern themselves with future generations through ecosystem sustainability, which is necessary for the welfare and resilience of an ever-advancing civilization.

Countries that have managed to achieve higher states of equality and sustainability show that a unified, sustainable society is not only possible, it is successful. Such examples help break down the entrenched notion that self-interest and greed are immutable human characteristics.

> *Rather than assuming we are stuck with levels of self-interested consumerism, individualism, and materialism which must defeat any attempts to develop sustainable economic systems, we need to recognize that these are not fixed expressions of human nature.*

"Rather than assuming that we are stuck with levels of self-interested consumerism, individualism and materialism which must defeat any attempts to develop sustainable economic systems," comment Wilkinson and Pickett, "we need to recognize that these are not fixed expressions of human nature. Instead they reflect the characteristics of the societies in which we find ourselves and vary even from one rich market democracy to another. At the most fundamental level, what reducing inequality is about is shifting the balance from divisive, self-interested consumerism driven by status competitions, towards a more socially integrated and affiliative society. Greater equality can help us develop the public ethos and commitment to working together which we need if we are going to solve the problems which threaten us all."[206]

Striving for unity is a virtuous cycle. Recognizing the principle of human unity helps to increase equality and sustainability, but increased equality and sustainability also reinforce unity. Importantly, the experience of unity helps to root out ingrained prejudices and vices that feed disunity.

A fundamental requirement of the change needed to sustain a world of 11 billion is to develop an ethic of unity, one that sees all citizens of a nation as equal and deserving of equal social, political, and economic rights and opportunities. We need to look at the globe in the same way, since we are all members of one human race. Ideally, we can consider Earth as one country. This is the sure ethical foundation for human transformation and for righting humanity's relationship to the ecosphere.

EXPANDING THE CIRCLE OF UNITY

"Only unified learning, universally shared, makes accurate foresight and wise choice possible," writes E.O. Wilson in *Consilience*. In the course of building this knowledge, he continues, "...we are learning the fundamental principle that ethics are everything."[207] I share this quote again to emphasize that it is primarily our choice of ethics—the personal and social system of moral principles governing appropriate conduct—that will determine whether we make the world work for 11 billion people.

Of course it is not so much a question of *stated* ethics as *lived* ethics, since often-unconscious values determine actual conduct. We may agree that everyone has a right to food, for example, yet our collective behaviour results in denial of that right to hundreds of millions, implying our operating ethics are weaker than our stated ones.

Shared ethics are agreements about how to view the world and our role in it. Based on our understanding of our reality, we build social contracts concerning the conduct that makes communities of different kinds possible.

"Human social existence, unlike animal sociality, is based on the genetic propensity to form long-term contracts that evolve by culture into moral precepts and laws," writes Wilson. "We...have discovered which covenants are necessary for survival, and we have accepted the necessity of securing them by sacred oath."[208] Ethical systems are *trust bonds* necessary to ensure, at least minimally, the various levels of human unity, from marriages, families, friendships, and organizations, to villages and neighbourhoods, to cities, nations, and global alliances. Trust allows us to let down our guard sufficiently that we can work toward a purpose that transcends self-interest, or at least that we can enhance self-interest through collaboration rather than conflict.

The future will stand or fall on whether we can identify and then live by those covenants necessary to ensure an ever-advancing civilization. Reading our current social-ecological reality, it is evident that we must accelerate the rate of our moral development, the glue that cements our covenants; the nature of our problems indicate that our ethical capacity is at present too limited to support the current social-ecological order let alone one that is substantially more burdened and complex, i.e. a full world of 11 billion.

While it may seem that a higher standard of moral conduct has and will continue to elude us, a review of history shows that, despite ebbs and flows, moral capacity has gradually increased, indicated by our ability to form increasingly more inclusive communities that transcend traditional barriers such as race or ethnicity. The concept of human rights, and its expression in the Universal Declaration of the Human Rights, is the hallmark of this positive trend. Yet few would be satisfied that this standard has been met in practice.

While our ecological ethic appears to have worsened, this appearance may be more a result of increased population pressure, added technological capacity, and greater awareness than a deteriorating ethic itself. Almost every nation now has environmental legislation and standards that would be sufficiently robust to ensure sustainability if rigorously adhered to.

The rapidly increasing human population demands an unprecedented increase in moral capacity in order to achieve an ever-advancing civilization, i.e. one in which human rights are increasingly met and the quality of the ecosphere is respected and enhanced. The case of the Nordic states shows that nation states have the capacity to form ethically sophisticated social contracts in which millions willingly yield their immediate self-interest to the longer-term interest of the whole community, including future citizens.

BOOSTING MORAL CAPACITY

Developing highly ethical habits of thought and action may not be as big a leap as it appears. The fact is, most of us live according to a reasonably high ethical standard most of the time. The world works as well as it does because of the ethical base we operate from. We are not in a constant state of war; we are in a constant state of peace punctuated by conflicts, which occasionally lead to violence. Most of us fail frequently to live to a high ethical standard, and some of us are very bad at it, but for the most part—wherever we go in the world—things work because people hold to the covenants by which their society operates.

If we look at the operation of a modern city, for example, it is a result of millions of ethically-guided interactions. For the most part, traffic flows, food arrives at markets, telephones work, neighbours and families get along. We can go out into the street knowing that there is a very high likelihood that our fellow travellers will follow the rules of the road and we will reach our destination. Most people work hard, pay taxes, observe laws, are respectful of others, and generally contribute to the commonweal. The international rate for murder—considered the most heinous of breaches in the social covenant—is

7.6 intentional homicides[209] per 100,000 people, which means that 99,992.4 per 100,000 are not murdered. Most places are relatively safe and free from severe violence. The point being that we already live according to a strong set of ethics.

There are of course anomalies; states fail and general breakdowns do occur in the social contract. But these are limited in time. Lebanon was embroiled in a horrific civil war in the 1980s, but its murder rate had fallen to 0.57 per 100,000 as of 2006, among the lowest in the world. It is the grave contrast with typical ethical behaviour that makes unethical behaviour so apparent.

The point is that, in general, we live morally, according to our current moral code. So it is not unrealistic to think that we can intensify and further mobilize this evident ethical commitment, that we can become aware of the wider ethical implications of our behaviour, deepen our ethical understanding, and reinforce our commitment to live ethically in a world of 11 billion. Fortunately, it is possible to increase the supply of virtues through education and social design. Many communities and societies have already achieved many of the ethical standards required in a full world.

The path toward a more ethical system will require each of us to give up certain habits of thought and action and adopt new ones; this will be difficult, for some of us more so than others, but we have no alternative if we are to build a global community with 11 billion fellow citizens.

Institutions will also have to change their habits. You can't have an institution that is so good that people do not have to *be* good. Yet good institutional design helps people to be good. It is easier to be good in a society that supports moral behaviour by, for example, providing universal education, the rule of law, fair institutions, economic opportunities, and so on. On the other hand, it is difficult to create a good institution without its being populated by reasonably good people.

Solving the world's problems calls on humanity to change in some fundamental ways. Fortunately, we are not starting at the beginning. We already have basic agreement on what proper values are; every society has a basic set of values, and acknowledges virtues like honesty. We have already codified universal values in internationally agreed upon declarations such as the Universal Declaration of Human Rights or the Universal Declaration of the Rights of the Child. We have assembled documents such as the Earth Charter, Agenda 21, and the Millennium Development Goals. These are the highest products of our culture to date. But most would agree that many societies fall well short of achieving them in practice, and even the best of societies are imperfect in their application.

Perhaps an initial reaction to this proposal is a cynical one: why should we think we can reshape the world according to these high principles, when we have so often failed to put them into practice. I counter that we have no choice; without the near universal deployment of these values—not just as the superficial ideals that they often are today, but as firmly held personal and communal values that actively govern our behaviour—the advance of civilization is endangered.

CHAPTER 10

THE WEIGHT OF TRAUMA

"How can I get to Albania?" That question could be easily answered today—Albania is now a *Lonely Planet* top travel destination—but in 1995 Google didn't exist and Albania remained a strange, foreboding land.

The travel agent in Thessoloniki was taken aback. "You can't go there!" she barked. Albanian immigrants were an unpopular underclass in Greece and the idea of voluntarily going to the place they came from was apparently unthinkable. Plus, she couldn't make a commission on a ticket to Albania: there was no such thing. The most she would or could do was point me to an obscure bus terminal in an empty lot. As I walked away she muttered something in Greek. "They'll slit his throat," maybe?

At the terminal I went from bus to bus asking, "Is this the bus to Tirana?" The Albanian driver shook his head side to side. In preparing for the trip I had read that shaking one's head side to side is a *no* gesture everywhere except Albania; in practice, it is strangely difficult to accept it as *yes*. I turned away but the driver caught my arm and took my bag. "Yes, yes. Tirana. Good, good. You are American? Bill Clinton, George Bush, very good! Fifty dollars, please."

The bus to Tirana wound its way through the plains of Kentriki Makedhonia and then the hilly Dytiki Makedhonia to the west. At the Albanian boarder, a handwritten sign listed varying prices for visas. As a Canadian I paid $20 but the fees were all over the map, depending, I wondered, on the border guards' feelings about various nationalities? Americans paid $100, Bulgarians $5, Russians $50; I had a sense the penciled-in price might switch at a moment's notice, depending on immediate cash requirements.

Ominously, our bus broke down shortly after crossing the boarder. We spent an hour or two by the side of the road as the driver replaced the fuel pump.

Albania was, and still is, the poorest nation in Europe. Passing through the drab and lifeless towns en route to the capital, Tirana, the people loitering in the dusty streets looked a little worse for wear. Boys ran up to the bus with sticks braided with cream-coloured cherries, hoping to make a little cash. Little Roma women and their children, looked down on by the Albanians, stared at me, unblinking, as if I was an alien. Contrary to the predictions of my travel agent back in Thessoloniki, however, I found no one wanted to slit my throat. To the contrary, Albanians were quite friendly and many went out of their way to help me on my way.

I had heard there were bandits on the roads; I doubt that was true, but travelling alone by car would have been difficult. How would one know where to go without road signs? Or maps. Come to a fork in the road and you had no way of knowing whether you were headed to Ballsh or Han I Hotit.

But why bother with road signs when there are no travelers? Albania had cut itself off from the world. Foreign visitors to the country numbered fewer than 300 annually in the "time of Hoxha" and were still few and far between in 1995. Furthermore, I discovered that Albania had no private vehicles prior to 1990 (which today might be considered an enlightened policy.) Italy had since found a market there for its clunkers, but in 1995, cars were still something of a rarity.

Albania had just come up for air after a long period of oppressive Stalinist rule that ended in 1992, most of it under Supreme Leader Enver Hoxha. He died in 1985 after 40 years of murderous dictatorship. Hoxha was, as they say, "so Left there's no Left left." To Hoxha, European and Chinese and Cuban communists were "running dogs of US imperialism". In his mind, the only true communists and allies left, now that Joe Stalin was gone, were Kim Il-sung and the North Koreans. As a result, Albania under Hoxha had become completely isolated.

Though previously largely Muslim, Albania had become the world's sole constitutionally atheistic state. Yet by 1995, Islam was on the rebound and copies of the Qur'an were common on the dashboards of buses and cars. Mosques were springing up here and there, financed by the Saudis.

At the time of my visit, Albania's commercial sector consisted mainly of kids selling *Carella* cigarettes, gum, and other odds and ends spread on a sheet of newspaper on the ground. Occasional street markets offered cheap consumer goods from China. There were no food stores, no retail stores of any kind. Where one obtained food or other necessities was not apparent to an outsider. The sole modern commercial ventures that had sprung up since 1992 were bars and coffee houses financed with Kosovo money.

Albania had taken no part in consumer culture during its communist era. But whatever the old economy might have looked like, it had collapsed. After the fall of the communist regime, people had wrecked the factories, sacked the armories, and then given up on work altogether, at least in the formal economy. They then waited for their former capitalist enemies to pour in aid. Only Italy had stepped up to the plate in a significant way. Along with its old cars, it was apparently providing what food was available, since Albanian agriculture had largely ceased to function. Farmers, like other workers, had given up.

The national diet consisted of imported eggplants, tomatoes, cucumbers, and peppers; a cheese used to make *bourek*, the national dish; meat butchered on street corners; and coarse but adequate local bread made from imported wheat.

Perhaps this was just as well; like the people, the land itself seemed exhausted.

Whether culturally, economically, psychologically, or ecologically, late 20th century Albania was at its nadir—almost. The survivors of the time of Hoxha were demoralized, confused, and passive: With no work, no industry, no functioning institutions, no civil society to fall back on, they wore a constant look of "what now?" on their faces.

Have we already gone too far to save ourselves and the planet? Is the kind of change needed to salvage civilization even possible? Can we overcome inertia and passivity? Can people be mobilized for profound change?

The personal and intergenerational trauma people carry as a result of oppression and abuse are a significant obstacle in the way of building a positive vision of the future, of forming the volition needed to achieve that vision, and of mobilizing for change. Can we have faith in human nature when we have experienced abuse? Can we be expected to change the world when we are demoralized by emotional and psychological pain from our own or our ancestors' past experiences?

Perhaps if places like Albania can overcome deep trauma and raise themselves up the rest of us can too?

ROTTEN CHERRIES

When I arrived in the small Albanian town of Peshkopia, where I stayed several weeks, the main occupation of the townsfolk was their daily long and leisurely promenade up and down the lovely Linden-lined main street. For an Albanian town, having a treed street was a rare and unusually effective effort to create an attractive social space.

It was not clear who, if anyone, was in charge of the town. Around the time of my arrival, I happened to notice a big puddle beside the main street, which seemed strange given the dry weather. As the days of my visit stretched on the puddle grew and soon a little fountain appeared. By the end of my stay the water, apparently coming from a broken pipe, was shooting a couple of metres into the air. No one bothered to fix it.

In the large hotel I stayed in on my first night in town, it was a similar story. Water puddled in the hallways and dripped through to the floors below. Apparently the only guest, my room was selected on the basis of dryness. Walking to the toilet down the hall, I wished for rubber boots. Later on I was able to meet many locals and moved in with a family who had a nice apartment. I spent time in the coffee houses chatting and hiked around the countryside, dropping into mysterious walled villages where I would be invited in for potent coffee and sometimes a meal.

At one point I met a young woman, a schoolteacher, who took me to visit her family's farm. We found her mother wandering her terraced hillside orchard, her apron filled with the same marvelous cherries I had bought earlier from the entrepreneurial boys at the bus window. There was no one to pick her fruit, however, and no market for it. It fell to the ground as it ripened and rotted.

Statistics for that period confirm my casual observation: agriculture had largely ground to a halt. Wheat production had dropped 50 percent after 1991; it never recovered. Instead, imports rose 50 percent.[210] Cotton production dropped 97 percent and never recovered. Independent sources[211] suggest that up to 25 percent of the population and more than 35 percent of the Albanian labour force had migrated, with close to two thirds of these working in Greece, primarily in construction, agriculture, and services.

Albania was a failed state. Expat remittances and foreign aid had become its main sources of income. On their own, Albanians could not even feed themselves.

How had this happened? It is a long story.

Albania, ancient Illyria, had been subjugated by foreign powers for millennia: First Rome, then Byzantium, Macedonia, and Bulgaria; from the 15th century to 1912 the Ottoman Turks; next, briefly, the French; and lastly the Italian and German fascists. All had their way with the country. Each subjugated the people and looted their resources. Over time its once vast mountain forests were thinned to a remnant. Its soil was eroded. When independence finally came, in 1945, it was ushered in by a paranoid communist regime noted even among Stalinist states for murderous repression and paranoia. Ultimately completely isolated from the world the Albanian people came to believe, at least on some level, the propaganda that theirs was its lone utopia. The authoritarianism was so complete that when the regime collapsed in the 1990s, no one knew what to do. It was a case of nation-wide post-traumatic stress syndrome.

According to the UN's Economic Commission for Europe, the post-Hoxha communists had initiated reform measures in 1989. These came too late and were never fully implemented. By the summer of 1990 unemployment was rising. A drought reduced electricity supplies and plants were forced to shut down. Anti-government riots broke out in April 1991 and tens of thousands of Albanians fled to Italy, Germany, and Greece.

By summer, only a quarter of Albania's production capacity was functioning. Inflation was fed by the government's decision to pay idle workers 80 percent of their salaries. The prolonged shutdown of the production lines caused damage to equipment and the breakdown of the rule of law resulted in widespread theft of state-owned property.

Albania thus began its transition towards a capitalist economy from a difficult starting point. All production sectors except agriculture were at a standstill, and agriculture was severely contracted. In 1992, inflation was 226 percent and almost 30 percent of the workforce was officially unemployed, with the real number much higher. According to the International Monetary Fund, the country's real Gross Domestic Product (GDP) fell by 10 percent in 1990, 28 percent in 1991 and 7.2 percent in 1992.

And then something very strange happened. Desperate, one sixth of the population naively bought into a bizarre national pyramid investment plan. By 1997, the economy was just beginning to show signs of recovery when the Ponzi scheme collapsed, bringing further economic ruin. People responded by launching a widespread revolt that led to the ransacking of military and police depots. Some 640,000 small arms were stolen.

Thousands of people were impoverished either by the loss of their investments or by the destruction of their property during the rioting. The economic consequences were severe. GDP again contracted, by 7 percent in 1997. Inflation returned, exports decreased by 27 percent and imports by 25 percent. Remittances from abroad, a major source of income, dropped from US$425 million to $250 million. External debt rose from 27 to 33 percent of GDP. Even foreign aid and investment flows came to a halt.

Albania's agrifood system continued to languish. Agriculture accounted for over half of employment but only about one-fifth of GDP. Although Albania had more agricultural land per capita than Italy, it was importing Italian food; with a similar terrain and climate, Italy enjoyed grain yields 40 percent higher than those in Albania.

Another casualty of the turmoil of the 1990s was the country's forests. In antiquity, Albania had been 92 percent forested. Under the succession of imperial powers they had been gradually plundered, leaving just 34 percent of the land with some form of forest and only 10 percent as solid forest (compared to 41 percent for all of Europe.) During my travel I noted extensive deforestation and accelerated erosion on the mainly mountainous land. And from 1990-2000, forest cover declined another 7 percent, three and a half times the average global rate of deforestation, mainly as a result of illegal logging.[212]

Both people and land languished together. Soil fertility declined even further and some 200,000 hectares, most of it in the potentially highly productive coastal zones, were seriously degraded. Pasture was converted to crops resulting in further degradation of marginal land. Soil erosion also increased on the less fertile soils and in the hilly and mountainous areas. A study by the Albanian Research Institute of Soil estimates than 70 percent of the land was eroding at 30 tonnes/ha/year. In 2002, about 100,000 hectares of agricultural land was in the process of desertification, according to the World Bank and FAO.[213]

The new government that took office after the July 1997 election re-established macroeconomic and fiscal controls, but in early 1999, the Kosovo conflict created a new crisis. War threatened internal security and stretched Albania's administrative capacity as Kosovar refugees swelled Albania's population by 14 percent. Albania was now even worse off than under the communist regime.

REVIVING FAILED STATES

The Albania trip in 1995 was my first experience of a failed state. Common indicators are a central government so weak or ineffective it has little control over much of its territory; the inability to provide public services; widespread corruption and criminality; high numbers of refugees and involuntary movement of populations; and sharp economic declines.

According to the 2012 Failed States Index[214] of 177 countries, 33 were in the worst "alert" category and another 44 in the next worst "warning" category, indicating the high level of disorder in the world. Just 13 countries were in the best "sustainable" category.

Perhaps the most interesting and unexpected thing about a failed state is—and this is an important lesson I'll come back to later—that day-to-day life somehow carries on despite a lack of structure or any semblance of normal economic activity. For those who expect that ecological catastrophe, peak oil, or economic collapse could spell the end of civilization, it is instructive to visit a failed state and see how resilient people can be under extreme duress.

During my 1995 visit to Albania, the social contract was holding and a flexible, undemanding visitor could get by with few problems. But the Albanian people seemed to me to be suspended in time, without meaning or purpose or ambition. And this was before things really fell apart.

Despite what my travel agent might think about them, there was nothing wrong with Albanians, no inherent, built-in flaw that got them into their predicament. Given a few propitious twists of fate, Albanians might have been more like their Italian neighbours, living *la dolce vita*. Albania was stricken by economic and ecological poverty as a result of a long history of oppression, injustice, and exploitation that had bankrupted the country, undermined the integrity of its culture, and demoralized, even traumatized its people, leaving them with limited will and capacity to take hold of their destiny.

Albania's predicament is, in many respects, analogous to that of the world. In fact, large parts of the world are quite like Albania was at that time—and many parts are much poorer, with even more degraded ecosystems. And the high-income consumer countries with their heavy ecological footprints are unwittingly mired in another potentially more serious predicament. They are, in a sense, another type of failed state.

If we think of Albania as a microcosm, its plight illustrates a crucial point about the future of civilization. We worry that the world may not have the capacity to carry 11 billion of us, but the real problem we face in meeting the needs of a full world have less to do with physical carrying capacity and more to do with human capacity.

Albania, like the world, has sufficient resources; the underlying problem is the disarray of the social-economic order and, consequently, the ecological order. Population pressure and ecological carrying capacity are critical, to be sure; the larger issue, however, is the state of the relationships that bind a society together and the inner condition of its people, which in many ways determines the quality of those relationships. I have argued that if we can get our relationships right, if we can build a global culture based on the highest human values, if we can work out our inner conflicts and traumas, we can make the world work beautifully for 11 billion.

> *The real problem we face in meeting the needs of a full world have less to do with physical capacity and more to do with human moral capacity.*

HISTORICAL TRAUMA

The Albanian experience exemplifies the issue of historical trauma, defined by Maria Yellow Horse Braveheart as "cumulative emotional and psychological wounding over the lifespan and across generations, emanating from massive group trauma." Such trauma is a significant factor in the strange passivity that can derail the process of change even when its necessity is painfully obvious.[215]

Unfortunately, the historical trauma experienced by Albanians may be more the norm than an exception. A long list of horrors is too readily available. Whole continents have been affected.

A particularly egregious example is the physical, emotional, social, and spiritual oppression of the indigenous people of the Americas by colonial powers over a 500-year period. Genocide, slavery, imprisonment, forced assimilation, various forms of abuse, rejection, and injustice have resulted in a loss of culture and identity, leading to entrenched problems, from unemployment, poverty, and high rates of illness to substance abuse, depression, and despair.

The emotional, psychological, social, and biological impacts of trauma on the individual are well documented. Trauma can even alter the structure of the brain: brain imaging of traumatized individuals shows the shrinking of the cortex, decreased volume of the amygdala, and atrophy of the hippocampus. This can compromise an individual's ability to process information in the rational or reflective part of the brain, as context and understanding are sacrificed for the speed and survival functions of the reflexive brain.

The research also shows that trauma can be passed from one generation to the next, even though the succeeding generation has not itself experienced the same trauma. The children of Holocaust survivors, for example, are known to have recurrent dreams of being chased, persecuted, and tortured. It seems these individuals, who are now adults, have somehow absorbed the repressed and insufficiently worked-through Holocaust trauma of their parents.

How does this occur? Children are of course influenced by their parents in a variety of ways. It may be that the parents or other relatives have shared their traumatic stories or the children may have heard stories that have become part of the historical record. In addition, the parenting styles of traumatized individuals may inadvertently perpetuate trauma.

Another factor is epigenetics, defined as the study of heritable changes in gene *expression*. Changes in gene expression often occur as a result of environmental influences, including major emotional trauma. Traumatic experiences leave marks on the chemical coating, or *methylation*, of the chromosomes. The coating becomes a sort of "memory" of the cell and since all cells carry this kind of memory, it becomes a constant physical reminder of past events, our own and those of our parents, grandparents, and beyond. "The body keeps the score" not only in the first generation of trauma survivors but even in subsequent ones. Because of their neurobiological susceptibility to stress, children of Holocaust survivors may imagine the physical suffering of their parents and almost "remember" the hunger, the frozen limbs, the smell of burned bodies, and the sounds that scared them.

Trauma is more common than we may think, even in relatively stable affluent societies. Post-Traumatic Stress Disorder (PTSD) rates in the general population in the United States, for example, have been estimated at 8-14 percent. Among certain disadvantaged groups, such as Native or African Americans, the proportion is higher. And if we take into account the idea of historical trauma, or Transgenerational Transmission of Trauma (TTT), the overall rate of at least some degree trauma is likely very high.

As a white male living in one of the most privileged and peaceful countries in the world (particularly for white males) I have never experienced any substantial trauma or abuse that could in any way be compared to the experience of, say, the aboriginal people of Canada. However, as a person of Irish Catholic ancestry I carry certain baggage. My great grandparents left Ireland for North America in the aftermath to the potato famine of the mid-19th century. The "Great Famine" is viewed today by many historians as a genocide perpetrated by the British, who had colonized Ireland. As a result of the imposed famine, a million people died and another million emigrated, reducing Ireland's population by as much as one quarter. The parallels between the treatment of the Irish and the First Nations and Métis people of Canada or the United States—by the same imperial power—are remarkable from the imposed starvation to the suppression of culture and language. Is it any wonder that many Irish "took to the drink" to numb the pain, and that stereotypes of "drunken Irishmen" parallel those of "drunken Indians"?

Sadly, the mistreatment of Irish Catholics continued in North America. Family lore has it that my grandfather changed his name from "O'Byrne" to the Scots-sounding "Burns" to avoid job discrimination. Well into the 20th century, my uncle was openly told by his superiors that he would never be promoted as a municipal employee due to his heritage. Like his father, he started his own business.

Discrimination against Irish Catholics in Canada is a thing of the past, but one wonders how the trauma experienced by our ancestors has manifested in my generation.

Would it be reasonable to say that most people are affected by historical trauma? In addition to its aboriginal population, who were subjected to centuries of abuse, Canada is composed of immigrants and their descendants, a very large proportion coming here to escape oppression, often of a very brutal nature. If we trace their histories back to their countries of origin—every country in the world—would we not conclude that most peoples have been oppressed by the elites of their country or colonizers or both?

We might also speculate that even the oppressors have experienced a type of trauma incurred from mistreating other human beings, leading on some level of consciousness to a sense of shame for what they or their ancestors have perpetrated. And might their mistreatment of others be traced back to their own abuse, suffered at the hands of some historical enemy, part of the long train of human injustices fading back into prehistory?

Would it be far off to speculate that the numbing use of alcohol and drugs, discussed at length in a previous chapter, or the mass obsession with mindless entertainment or insatiable consumption, may have at least some connection to the phenomenon of current and historical trauma?

Personal or intergenerational trauma can become a significant block in our ability to fully acknowledge and understand our reality, or the implications and consequences of our behaviour, or the capacity to change it.

Trauma is known to foster despair and passivity, given the overwhelming nature of the power imbalance that resulted in its occurrence. Is it not plausible that our inability to respond to the social-ecological trauma currently afflicting the planet can be traced, in part, to the traumatic stresses that have undermined humanity's will throughout its history? Could our adherence to materialism be a response to a fatalism that results from the colossal moral failures that made these injustices possible? Have these traumas disillusioned us of the hope that we have the capacity to create a more ideal reality?

Research indicates that people can be relieved of the burden of trauma, including historical trauma, through interventions such as: education to increase the awareness of trauma; providing safe spaces to share the experiences and effects of trauma; grief resolution through collective mourning and healing in order to foster positive group identity and commitment to community; efforts to address grievances and resolve longstanding injustices; building interior resources through psychotherapy or spiritual practices; and the development of authentic relationships—a transformative process that will be described in more detail in subsequent chapters.

IS THE WORLD GETTING BETTER?

No matter how traumatized, people can and do turn their world around. Human resilience is astonishing. People who fear the future of the planet is slipping out of control need to understand that anything is possible if people pull together.

The more recent history of Albania is a case in point. Shaking off the trauma from several millennia of imperialism, 45 years of Stalinist isolation, and 10 more years of utter disarray at all levels of society, Albanians gathered their wits, rejoined the global community, established a more ethical government, and got back to work.

As a result of the Kosovo conflict, Albania obtained much-needed international assistance so that, in spite of this tragedy, the macroeconomic performance of the country picked up. GDP grew at a fast 7.3 percent in 1999 and an even faster 7.8 percent in 2000. (GDP may be a grossly inadequate metric of well-being, but in the case of a poverty-stricken country that actually needs economic development, it is a useful one.)

Tight monetary policies and international aid brought inflation to zero and strengthened the national currency, the *lek*. With a steady currency and growing GDP, Albania's economy stabilized, despite the country's ongoing dependency on international aid.

According to UNDP statistics the situation continues to improve; 12.4 percent of the population was poor in 2008 compared to 18.5 percent in 2005 and 25.4 percent in 2002. Albania's high GDP growth from 1998-2010, averaging 7.1 percent per year, along with an average wage increase (in real terms) of 36.5 percent between 2005 and 2008, and of 17.5 percent for pensions between 2005 and 2007, contributed to these results. Meanwhile, Albania's ecological performance also improved, with the country rising on indices of sustainability.[216]

Of course, Albania still has a long way to go to achieve a prosperous, resilient, sustainable, and equitable society, but the transformation of the culture and institutions has begun to bring positive results in the day-to-day life of the average person.

The Albanian example shows that—even in a failed state—people can overcome mind-boggling, age-old limitations and seemingly unbearable traumas to initiate positive change in social values and institutions, resulting in improved conditions. The nation is experiencing a welcome reprieve, yet the free market growth model on which Albania has hitched its wagon is itself deeply flawed and likely dooms the country to another set of crises in the future, crises it will share with the rest of the world.

The ultimate resolution for Albania, and for the rest of us, will not come until a new model of social-ecological transformation is adopted. And given the growth in population anticipated during this century, this transformation must be of a deeper nature than anything so far conceived.

We do not have an *environmental* problem or an *economic* problem, we have a *human* problem, one that can only be resolved as people engage in transforming their inner and outer realities. What is required is what many believe impossible: that the people of the planet—as individuals and organized as communities, organization, and institutions—will learn to act out of their highest ideals and aspirations. We will have to become socially unified; to govern ourselves in a new, non-partisan way; to be more egalitarian and service-oriented; to be less materialistic; to adopt a vision that is global, not confined to ourselves or our class, religion, or nation; and to learn how to mobilize for change. And as we will see, a further extension of these inclusive, holistic ideals to encompass the ecosphere will be necessary to support the gradual regeneration of ecosystems and the resiliency they provide.

This is not only possible, it is happening on the local and in some cases the national and international levels already, giving reason to hope. Progress is being made, leading some prominent thinkers to advance a very hopeful prognosis for the future.

"By almost any measure, the world is better than it has ever been." That's the optimistic opening sentence from Bill and Melinda Gates' 2014 annual letter for the Gates Foundation, the globally-minded aid organization they started.[217] With the help of friends like Warren Buffet, the foundation has a $40 billion endowment and has given away $28.3 billion to date.

The 2014 letter addresses "Three Myths that Block Progress for the Poor." The first is that "Poor Countries are Doomed to Stay Poor." Not so says Mr. Gates, and the proof is that incomes are rising everywhere. Gates points out, for example, that per-person incomes in Turkey and Chile are where those in the United States were in 1960. Malaysia is nearly there, as is Gabon. Since 1960, China's real income per person has gone up eightfold. India's has quadrupled, Brazil's has almost quintupled, and the small country of Botswana has seen a 30-fold increase. Contrary to popular perception, incomes are up in much of Africa. Seven of the 10 fastest-growing economies of the past half-decade are African.

Given the world-wide rise in incomes, Gates predicts that "By 2035, there will be almost no poor countries left in the world."

The second myth addressed is that "Foreign Aid is a Big Waste." To counter this perception, Gates points to the role of donor aid in providing vaccines that save children's lives. Since 1988, the Global Polio Eradication Initiative has immunized 2.5 billion children. Since 1988, the number of countries where polio is found has gone from 125 to three and new cases of polio have fallen from 350,000 a year to fewer than 400. By 2035, due in part to aid of this type, it is quite likely that child mortality in nearly all countries will be as low it was in the United States in 1980.

Myth three—"Saving Lives Leads to Overpopulation"—is addressed by Melinda Gates. According to this myth, saving the lives of poor kids will increase overpopulation, resulting in more stress on the environment. The opposite is the case, says Gates. Whenever you improve infant mortality rates, couples have fewer kids. In fact, any measure that reduces poverty generally leads to lower reproductive rates. So with poverty declining in most places, population is starting to stabilize. In fact, "The amount of children in the world today is probably the most there will be! We are entering into the age of the Peak Child!"

This good news from Bill and Melinda Gates is welcome and quite accurate, as far as it goes. It shows people can make a difference, that they can—and are—making the world a better place. Having said that, the Gates' analysis does not show the full picture.

First, rising incomes around the world could be very bad news for the ecosphere. If low-income countries adopt the consumerism of high-income countries like Canada every dollar of income will bring a corresponding increase in energy and resource consumption, leading to more pollution, ecological stress, and more destructive climate change.

Second, poverty is a relational issue. The social impacts of poverty are not so much related to low income as *relative* income: how little one has compared to those around you. And the disparity between the poor and the affluent is growing. Early in 2014, for instance, Oxfam released a report showing that the 85 richest people in the world, including Bill and Melinda, have greater wealth than the 3.5 billion poorest people combined.[218]

Thirdly, though population is stabilizing in the middle- and high-income countries, it will take until century's end for that process to filter down to the low-income countries. By that time, there will be 3.7 billion additional people on the planet, almost all in low-income areas. If each of these people is better off, and begins to consume more goods and services, the human ecological footprint would overwhelm the planet.

To make the world work for 11 billion people in 2100, we have to reduce our ecological footprint dramatically, starting with the wealthiest 85 and working our way down. In the long term, the problem we face may not be poverty, but too much wealth of the wrong kind. Shedding the inclination to accumulate rather than share our wealth would signal a sea change in the nature of humankind.

CHAPTER 11
CHANGING INSCAPES

The landscapes of our making match and reflect
society's cultural inscapes. – Stan Rowe

"All through my young life I had a recurrent dream," wrote the late, great ecologist Stan Rowe at the outset of *Home Place*, his collection of essays on ecology. "In sleep, I came into a lovely land, somewhere off to the east in a soft light, with rounded hills and waving grass and the smell of wild flowers in the wind.... and all the secrets of this primeval prairie, all its mysteries and beauties, lay unspoiled before me."[219]

Rowe spent decades in the waking world searching for this perfect place. "The few localities that came close to fitting my dream—like the flowery meadows on the top of the Cypress Hills—had already been preempted by others and showed too many signs of use." Then one morning while conducting an ecological survey in Riding Mountain in Manitoba he sensed an opening in the forest: "Something strange lay ahead, under the sunshine and the blue sky. I plunged through the trees, pushed aside the fringing bushes and, heart pounding with excitement, entered as close a match to dreams as reality can ever afford, a wonderful prairie island in the forest, little hills and valleys bright with wild flowers, grasses waving in the breeze, sweet meadow smells. Mixed with the elation of discovery and all the first joyful impressions, a strong sense of affection, of coming home to my grasslands-in-the-trees and belonging there."

It was not that long ago that an influx of European settlers supplanted the flower-lands of Rowe's dreamtime with monocultures of grain. Flying over the prairie today, should one look up from the video screen and out the window, the dominant impression would be the endless rectangular grid superimposed on the land's gentle curves.

Rowe described with sad eloquence how the prairie landscape has been transformed by a set of ideas carried here by incoming colonizers just over a century ago. For the invaders, a place belonged to them rather than them to place.

"As we look out from the rectangular lots and fields that enclose us today in towns and country—the legacy of the grid surveys of the 1870s and 1880s—we find it difficult to imagine the curvilinear sights, sounds and smells of the primeval grasslands, now reduced to a few forlorn and untypical fragments." He notes for example that just one percent of the Tall Grass Prairie biome remains, reduced to a few isolated remnants. "Incongruously, the largest protected fragment—the Living Prairie Museum of 12 hectares—carries a city address: 2795 Ness Avenue, Winnipeg. Under our feet a miniature 'Amazon forest,' of which we knew little, has disappeared."

The rapid shift from diverse prairie, the product of 10,000 years of adaptation, to industrial monocultures corresponded with the shift from indigenous to European worldviews, from belonging to owning.

"The ways that we use and exploit the earth's surface," writes Rowe, "are direct and visible measures of sensitivity to our source. The landscapes of our making match and reflect society's cultural inscapes. Land use, mirroring our North American minds, cries out for changes in attitudes toward what surrounds us."

The incoming Europeans saw the prairie as a vast empty space, virgin territory waiting for the plough, an as yet untapped resource to supply grain for Europe's and eastern America's growing industrial working class. The new prairie would both sustain and expand the industrial revolution and be modeled on it. Surveyors divided it into a million half-mile squares. The buffalo herds that interfered with farming were eliminated, barely surviving total extinction. Chinese labourers were imported to build the railroads needed to bring in the military and police and then the settlers, and later take their grain back east. Those who had occupied the land for millennia were first dehumanized and then herded onto remnant reservations. Thousands were allowed to starve and succumb to disease.[220] Settlers, most escaping oppression and poverty in industrializing Europe, poured in to claim their homesteads, seemingly oblivious that what they were now doing had been done to them. Farming here was a commercial enterprise: there would be no farm villages, just isolated equidistant plots for independent producers. Towns were situated at intervals determined by how far horses could haul grain and return home in a day.

With little regard to people or place, a model of industrial efficiency was imposed on an area more than 10 times that of England. Farms were food factories for the factories of eastern North America and Europe. The benefit accrued largely to the industrialists. Today, even the small family enterprises that once dotted the prairies have given way to large capital, energy, and chemical intensive enterprises. The rural schools and churches are closed. The towns are dying out. The wooden grain elevators, once emblematic of small Prairie towns, have been replaced with high-tech, high-throughput terminals. The farmer's cooperatives have been privatized and bought out by vertically integrated global firms.

The contemporary prairie landscape is a clear reflection of the cultural inscape—ideas, values, emotions—of the plutocrats who created it, of those who still control it, and of all those who buy into their worldview. They came to make money and made the land a money making machine.

CHANGING INSCAPES, CHANGING LANDSCAPES

The transformation of the Canadian prairie—one of the most thorough alterations of landscape in recorded history—shows, quite literally, that *inscape generates landscape*. While its consequences are typically destructive, understanding this maxim offers us this corollary: *degraded landscapes can be regenerated by changing our inscapes*.

A case in point is the remarkable restoration of part of China's Loess Plateau, described in a previous chapter. Collaboration by Chinese government institutions, individual farmers, and local communities, with support from a major global institution, resulted in the rehabilitation of an area the size of Belgium.

> Degraded landscapes can be regenerated by changing inscapes.

As John Liu, the filmmaker who recorded the transition from desert to productive agroecosystem put it, "ideas transform landscapes." In this case, the transformative idea *putting ecosystem function first* resulted in long-term social, economic, and ecological benefits. Once it was understood and accepted, mobilization of the local population became possible. And, as predicted, as ecological functions were restored farm incomes on the Loess Plateau doubled.

The mobilization was a response to the unifying vision that resulted from a meritorious idea. Even more important than the conceptual framework, however, was the spirit of unity that brought about mass collective action. The new cultural inscape—ideas, feeling, spirit, volition—transformed the landscape; the new outer world reflected the new inner world.

The world is full of sad illustrations of the influence of bad ideas on landscape. But fortunately we can now look to many instances of positive changes that manifest good ideas. Following are a few notable examples:

Cheonggyecheon Stream Restoration – Of particular interest, given rapid urbanization, is ecological restoration *within* cities. The Cheonggyecheon, a major stream that runs through central Seoul, was an important factor in choosing the site for a new Korean capital 600 years ago. Over time the stream deteriorated into an open sewer, bordered by slums. A blight on the city, the stream was covered over with concrete following the Korean War of the 1950s and in the 1970s became the site of a heavily used multilevel freeway.

In 2002, Lee Myung-bak was elected Seoul's mayor based largely on his promise to revive the historic stream as part of an urban renewal project. Ironically, as a former leader of construction companies operated by the giant Hyundai Corporation, the mayor had helped build the freeway. He was able to redeploy his skills to launch and quickly complete a $384 million restoration project.

As the following before and after pictures show, the restoration of the Cheonggyecheon has changed the urban landscape in fundamental ways. Tens of thousands soon flocked to the restored waterway. "We've basically gone from a car-oriented city to a human-oriented city," according to Lee In-keun, Seoul's assistant mayor for infrastructure. Today, picnickers cool their feet in the reed-filtered water and carp swim in tranquil pools where thousands of cars and trucks once roared overhead.

Seoul's central waterway is buried under concrete and cars.

Seoul's restored waterway revitalizes the urban core.

"The restoration of the Cheonggyecheon is part of an expanding environmental effort in cities around the world to 'daylight' rivers and streams by peeling back pavement that was built to bolster commerce and serve automobile traffic decades ago," comments journalist Andrew Revkin.[221] "Open watercourses handle flooding rains better than buried sewers do, a big consideration as global warming leads to heavier downpours. The streams also tend to cool areas overheated by sunbaked asphalt and to nourish greenery that lures wildlife as well as pedestrians."

The ecosystem along the Cheonggyecheon has been greatly enriched: the number of fish species increased to 25 from 4, bird species to 36 from 6, and insect species to 192 from 15. The highway removal reduced small particle air pollution by 40 percent and, by reducing the heat island effect, temperatures were lowered an average of 5° compared to other parts of the city.

Ironically, traffic flow has improved because of expanded bus service, restrictions on cars, and higher parking fees. And today Seoul's mayor is the President of South Korea.

Urban Culture in Northern Europe - In the post war period, cities in Denmark and the Netherlands succumbed for a time to the lure of American-style car culture. However, when the accidental death toll mounted and the 1970s energy crisis hit, the population rose in protest against car dominated cities and governments readjusted their thinking. Today, over half of trips in places like Copenhagen and Amsterdam are taken on foot, bicycle, or public transit, making these cities what urban planner Jahn Gehl calls "sweet places for people." Sweet places for people also have lighter ecological footprints.

Declining deforestation in the Brazilian Amazon - Deforestation of the Amazon has been a major concern for several decades, but more recently new thinking by Brazil's government has resulted in impressive progress in forest protection.[222] Brazil's National Institute for Space Research has pioneered the use of satellite data to prevent illegal logging and the forest sector uses a sophisticated electronic system to track wood flow throughout the supply chain. While illegal logging remains a major concern, deforestation had declined from a high of 27,770 km^2 in 2004 to 5,843 km^2 in 2012-13.

Reforestation in Germany - Deforestation is a major problem, but some nations have altered their course and adopted large-scale sustainable forestry practices. Germany for instance, ranks among the most densely wooded countries in Europe, with 11 million hectares of forest covering one third of the nation. Forests increased by some 1 million hectares in Germany over the past four decades. The percentage of stands over 80-years old also rose from one quarter to one third of the forest area. This is largely a result of the efforts to restore high-yielding and ecologically valuable forests following the destruction of large forest tracts over the past centuries and, more recently, after clear-cutting during both world wars.[223]

German Energiewende – Germany is also the first major industrial country to substantially shift its energy policy, replacing an emphasis on growth with conservation and renewable sources. Between 1990 and 2013, primary energy use decreased 11 percent and CO_2 emissions went down 25.5 percent, yet the economy continued to grow. Renewable sources supplied 23 percent of electricity in 2013, but Germany aims for 35 percent by 2020 and 80 percent by 2050. Plans are to reduce energy consumption by another 20 percent by 2020 from 2008 levels and 50 percent by 2050. CO_2 emissions are expected to fall to 80 percent below 1990 levels by 2050. The new thinking (and action) on energy will have substantive impacts on pollution abatement, with positive outcomes for ecosystems.

Gross National Happiness - The nation of Bhutan originated the concept of Gross National Happiness in 1972 as a lead indicator of national wellbeing, eschewing the standard GDP metric that measures only material production. In 2011, the United Nations approved the Bhutan-sponsored resolution *Happiness: Towards a Holistic Approach to Development*. It stated that "happiness is a fundamental human goal and universal aspiration; that GDP by its nature does not reflect that goal; that unsustainable patterns of production and consumption impede sustainable development; and that a more inclusive, equitable, and balanced approach is needed to promote sustainability, eradicate poverty, and enhance wellbeing and profound happiness."

While Prime Minister Tshering Tobgay later backed away from efforts by his predecessor to promote GNH internationally, he has announced plans to leapfrog oil-dependent mobility in favour of zero-emission electric transport. Bhutan produces hydropower that is exported to purchase oil for vehicles; electric vehicles would utilize domestic power and circumvent the need to import oil, reducing costs and pollution. Bhutan hopes to increase employment by assembling electric vehicles in the country.[224] Tobgay has also dropped the use of personal limousines and luxury accommodations and set modest development goals such as making a rototiller available for use in every village.

OUR THOUGHT IS OUR REALITY

Thousands of similar examples of enlightened practices and policies from around the world could be cited, many flowing through such organizations as the Global Restoration Network, the Society for Ecological Restoration, and the Global Partnership on Forest Landscape Restoration

As a writer focused on environmental issues since the 1970s, I have concluded that *everything that needs to be done to make the world just and sustainable is being done somewhere, successfully, already*. But while there are many hopeful signs, they are nevertheless overshadowed by a tsunami of foolishness and complacency. The dominant world culture is expanding and intensifying its campaign to increase material wealth regardless of cost.

> *Everything that needs to be done to make the world just and sustainable is being done somewhere, successfully, already.*

Though the social-ecological worldview that results in growing inequality and declining ecological resilience has been exposed as fundamentally flawed and outdated, it is clung to tenaciously. People in positions of power talk sustainability and human rights, but the way they *really* perceive the world—demonstrated in the way they behave most of the time—is that human beings and the ecosphere exist to be exploited. They hold to the belief that by exploiting people and the planet sufficient wealth will be generated that some of it will trickle down to the middle and even the bottom of the pecking order. This perspective is backstopped by beliefs, traditions, and values that are cleverly spun to win compliance from even the most exploited. In fact, those who are most exploited are often the most conservative element in society, the most committed to a system carefully crafted to screw them at every turn, all because the system offers a faint hope that they themselves could conceivably strike it rich.

If we trace the roots of the dominant worldview it leads us to the conception that human beings are *essentially* animals engaged in a competitive struggle for survival, in which only the fittest succeed. Herbert Spencer, for example, compared society to a living organism and argues that, just as biological organisms evolve through natural selection, society evolves and increases in complexity through analogous processes. Darwin's theories of evolution by natural selection influenced this conception of humanity, but were also influenced by the harsh socio-economic conditions of his time.

This conception of human beings supports a hierarchical view of society, justifying domination by elites. After all, the will to power is the "law of nature." The fact that someone dominates proves he or she is the fittest to do so. This conception also supports the view that the human species should dominate other species to gain the control over the ecosphere it needs to survive and thrive. The fact that we are able to do it justifies doing it.

The deep-rooted belief that the so-called "law of the jungle" underlies the social-ecological order favours values such as competitiveness, individualism, personal initiative, and hard work, all necessary in the struggle to get ahead, to gain the things that support our material existence, and therefore confer status. As a top predator, we also value a kind of pack mentality, working together at the level of family or community or nation, building alliances that offer security, creating the conditions within which we may be able to move up the ladder of success.

The point has now been made repeatedly that the inner world generates the outer world. But the outer world we create also affects our inscapes: our beliefs are verified every time we observe the world we have created. Our belief in the value of competition, for example, generates a competitive world; the fact that the world appears to be highly competitive reinforces our belief. It's a self-referencing loop.

Given the law of the jungle concept with its dominance hierarchy is a primary value, it is little wonder unethical behaviour is so common in the struggle for power. In fact, it has become a requirement of that struggle. Power is its own justification: by this logic, what is normally considered *unethical* is deemed *ethical* in that it supports one's achieving and maintaining power, which is a kind of ultimate, self-justifying value. Anyone high on the pecking order deserves to be there because they *are* there, so they can do what they want to stay there.

Over the past 300 years, science and its philosophical offshoot materialism have greatly reinforced the idea that people are merely animals, though of above average intelligence. Evolutionary biology shows that our most sophisticated cultural activities are all rooted in biology: we exhibit the same behaviors as animals, with the same motivations: food, status, power, sex. The finest soprano, for instance, is little different from a songbird staking out territory or calling in mates. A CEO is no different form an alpha male in a pack of wolves.

With the rise and apparent success of materialism, the notion that there is a spiritual aspect to reality fades into anachronism. By eliminating the notion of the noble human soul with intrinsic capacity to rise above animal instinct, human beings, like the rest of life, could be defined merely as biological machines ultimately controlled by the laws of physics. Orthodox science says ours is a *deterministic* universe and we are just cogs in its machinery. In fact, science informs us that our impression that humans have a will is illusory: in reality people have no free will at all, we are merely subjects of our selfish genes which are in turn controlled by the laws of physics. Our consciousness and sense of freedom are therefore illusions, mechanisms employed by mindless gene machines to get ahead in the world.

In essence, it would seem science, and the worldview it generates, says we can't *really* change anything, whatever happens will just happen as a result of physical processes. Nor does it matter, because fundamentally *nothing really matters*, given that, in the view of orthodox science, existence is absurd.

If we choose the kind of sustainable society exemplified in the six examples listed above, it would not really be due to conscious choices people made, though it may appear that way. It would just happen that way due to the immutable laws of physics manifest in evolutionary biology. But a benign, altruistic future is unlikely because of the fundamentally selfish nature of biological organisms. Indeed, many of our greatest scientific minds—such as Martin Rees and Stephan Hawking—are predicting the imminent end of civilization, if not human annihilation.[225]

Obviously, if this nihilistic worldview were true it would invalidate what is being proposed in this book: that human beings can choose to move against the flow of history and do what it takes to make the world work for 11 billion people—and that it matters that we do.

CAN WE DO ANYTHING? AND DOES IT MATTER?

If the outer world reflects the inner world, it is no surprise that materialistic beliefs have remade our social-ecological reality. Indeed, the rise of materialism as a dominant philosophy corresponds with the growing preoccupation with and appetite for material things and a decline of attention to our interior world and its spiritual qualities. Ironically—but logically—the steady rise of materialism as a way of thinking corresponds with a steady decline in the integrity of the material world, the ecosphere we inhabit.

Is this just the natural course of things, or is there another way forward?

Materialism, defined as the belief that only matter exists and that all phenomena, including consciousness, result from material interactions, has been around for millennia as a sub-current in human thought. Over the past 300 years, however, it has become increasingly accepted. Gradually, it has extinguished notions of the sacredness of the physical world, or that of human beings. Billions may still hold to religious ideas—the sense of the sacred, the existence of an immaterial spirit and the human soul, a greater purpose and meaning to existence, free will, divine authority, and revelation—but these are viewed as anachronisms by the intelligentsia, especially the vocal and influential group of "evangelical atheists" who aim to banish religious faith altogether.

But how solid are these beliefs? Are they true? Their acceptance by the scientific establishment argues in their favour. Scientific enquiry shows no empirical evidence for God, for any form of spiritual reality, or for any special purpose for existence. Such things are seen to be mere superstitions that were proposed in an attempt to explain reality before the methods of modern science and reason were available. The weight of science now demands that we reexamine these outdated and unsupported beliefs and confine them to the dustbin of history.

Science having led us to this materialistic understanding of reality, we have no choice but to accept that life has no meaning that would give it purpose, that it is absurd. Orthodox science holds that human beings are automatons determined by all past events. We could precisely predict everything any of us is about to do if we had the computational power to analyze all the factors that led up to our present state. (To do this, Stephen Hawking notes that one would need a knowledge of the initial state of each of the thousand trillion trillion molecules in the human body and the capacity to solve something like that number of equations.)

"The classical-physics-based claim that science has shown us to be essentially mechanical automata has had a large impact upon our lives," comments physicist Henry Stapp. "Our teacher's teach it: our courts uphold it; our governmental and official agencies accept it; and our pundits proclaim it. Consequently, we are incessantly being told that we are physically equivalent to mindless robots, and are treated as such. Even we ourselves are confused, and disempowered, by this supposed verdict of science, which renders our lives meaningless."[226]

Having arrived in the universe purely by chance with no meaning or purpose, science has concluded, as our most celebrated contemporary scientist Stephen Hawking put it: "The human race is just a chemical scum on a moderate-sized planet, orbiting around a very average star in the outer suburb of one among a hundred billion galaxies. We are so insignificant that I can't believe the whole universe exists for our benefit."[227] Astrophysicist and science writer David

Lindley, author of *Uncertainty: Einstein, Heisenberg, Bohr, and the Struggle for the Soul of Science*, takes is a bit further saying, "we humans are just crumbs of organic matter clinging to the surface of one tiny rock. Cosmically, we are no more significant than mold on a shower curtain."[228]

The idea of the insignificance of human life, of an absurd universe, "is probably the majority view among scientists," according to the physicist Paul Davies.[229] The celebrated physicist Richard Feynman said, for instance, "the great accumulation of understanding of how the physical universe behaves only convinces one that this behaviour has a kind of meaninglessness about it." Or as the theoretical physicist Steven Weinberg put it, "The more the universe seems comprehensible the more it also seems pointless."

It's all pointless. And what is more, consciousness and free will are not *real.* "Hard determinists are highly skeptical of the idea that the human mind can consist of anything but—or is not reducible to—the activity of the atoms and energy (nature) that constitute the human animal," observes Timothy McGettigan in his discussion of *The Grand Design*, a book by Hawking and Leonard Mlodinow. "Hawking and Mlodinow emphasize their 'exclusively nature' position by asserting that the human experience is entirely reducible to, and determined by the physical properties of the human animal's constituent elements: 'It is hard to imagine how free will can operate if our behavior is determined by physical law, so it seems that we are no more than biological machines and that free will is just an illusion.'"[230]

The logical next step is to ask what point there is in doing anything? If will is merely an illusion, why get up in the morning? Without free will, or even a belief that there is free will, let alone meaning or purpose, where is the impetus to even attempt to radically alter our way of life, indeed to sacrifice a degree of self-interest in order that humanity can live on? The materialism now widely accepted and taught by the intelligentsia perhaps underlines our passivity in the face of the social-ecological crisis.

In light of the idea that our outer world reflects our inner world of thought, values, and emotions, is it any wonder the world is being overloaded with chemical pollution given the notion that human beings are themselves merely chemical scum? Or that we have so threatened the integrity of the ecosphere that there is a very real risk that "we will becoming nothing," as E.O. Wilson puts it, thus actualizing the very insignificance assigned to us by our most brilliant scientists.[231] In fact, Hawking expects this to happen: he believes human civilization will not survive, unless perhaps human colonies can be established elsewhere in the galaxy.

The orthodox interpretation of science is widely but not universally accepted. For example, Henry Stapp, who worked on quantum mechanics with Wolfgang Pauli and Werner Heisenberg, argues that empirical evidence upends the orthodox notion that human beings are insignificant automatons whose actions are entirely predetermined by previous events.[232] He contends that quantum theory, "basically a theory of the mind-brain connection," elevates our conscious experiences from passive witnesses to active participants in the creation of our common physical future.

"It is important to us," Stapp asserts, "both as individuals and collectively, that we correct the currently widespread notion that science shows us to be mechanical automata. Classical mechanics grew out of our observations of large astronomical and terrestrial bodies. In such cases, our choice of what to attend to has little or no effect on the system being observed. Quantum mechanics is technically far better suited than classical mechanics to deal with the causal effects of our probing minds on what they are probing. It explains the big difference between our perceptions of the planets and our perceptions of ourselves. That idea is based on empirically invalidated classical mechanics. Its successor, empirical valid quantum mechanics, represents us as psycho-physical beings whose conscious intentions are not determined by the physical aspects of nature, yet causally influence the course of physical events."

> It is important to us, both as individuals and collectively, that we correct the currently widespread notion that science shows us to be mechanical automata.

Brains should be understood quantum mechanically, thereby permitting the behavior of a person's brain to be significantly influenced by the free choices made by that person's conscious mind. Stapp understands human beings as psycho-physical beings that can form value-based intentions about how best to act and to then act in accord with those mentally-chosen intentions. Thus the mind is not simply a product of the physical brain, but an entity in relationship with the brain.

Weird as this quantum feature might seem to scientists steeped in classical physics, it is where quantum mechanics rationally leads. It is completely concordant with all human experience, including our experience-based understanding of ourselves. And it is in line with a certain idea of parsimony that would not allow nature to encumber itself with a highly developed consciousness that can make no difference in what actually happens.

The failure of classical mechanics at the level of the atom led to its replacement by quantum mechanics. But that change alters the behaviors of all systems composed of atoms. This includes our brains, which, according to the atomic laws, generally become mixtures of states corresponding to different perceptions. That mind-brain disparity caused the founders of quantum mechanics to bring our conscious experiences into the theory as independent variables, not mere restatements or reformulations of the physical properties.

Stapp says prevailing descriptions of quantum theory tend to emphasize "quantum weirdness" in a way that prevents philosophers or scientists using the theory to understand human beings. "It is the 300 years of indoctrination with basically false ideas about how nature works that now makes puzzling a process that is completely in line with normal human intuition."[233]

In classical physics, all observers and their acts of observation are parts of the evolving, fully predetermined, physically described universe. The present or future is entirely determined by the past. Quantum mechanics contradicts this, introducing the idea that the course of events is an "objective tendency" or *potentia* for psycho-physical events to occur, which can be influenced by human minds (which is what the world seems to be like.)

Reality, according to Heisenberg, is built not out of matter as matter was conceived of in classical physics, but out of psycho-physical events—events with certain aspects that are described in the language of psychology and with other aspects that are described in the mathematical language of physics—and out of objective tendencies for such events to occur. The transition from the *possible* to the *actual* takes place during the act of observation. The probability function combines objective and subjective elements.

Stapp says that the physically described world is not a world of material substances, often compared in classical physics to billiard balls bouncing around, but rather a world of potentialities for future experiences. The conception of the physical world is changed from one made out of tiny-rock-like entities to a holistic global informational structure that represents tendencies for real events to occur and in which the choice of which potentiality will be actualized in various places in the hands of human agents. Human observers can alter the course of things and not only at the experimental level but in the world of normal human actions. As Stephen Hawking and Leonard Mlodinow succinctly put it in *The Grand Design*: "We create history by our observations, rather than history creating us."[234] (Oddly, this statement seems entirely at odds with a previous Hawking quote describing human beings as automata.)

In a quantum universe, information can be transferred instantly at any distance, which is often described as "spooky," but only because it is being judged on the basis of classical physics which can only account for direct connections between inanimate things. In fact, and this is empirically evident says Stapp, it is the classical notion that is counterintuitive because it denies the causal efficacy of our intentional efforts; is problematic because it provides no logical foundation upon which a rational understanding of the occurrence of subjective experience could be built; and is weird because it leaves out the mental aspect of nature while chopping nature's body into microscopic, ontologically separate parts that can communicate and interact only with immediate neighbours, thereby robbing both conglomerates and the whole of any possibility of fundamental wholeness or meaningfulness.

It is only conscious free choices taken by conscious beings that inject the wholeness and meaning into the quantum universe: without these acts there is nothing but a continuous smear of meaningless un-actualized possibilities.

CONSCIOUSNESS AS A CREATIVE FORCE

Consciousness then is not merely a product of the universe, and an illusory one at that. Rather, it is a creative force. Possessing a relatively high level of consciousness makes human beings entirely unlike chemical scum. Even some of Hawking's peers look on humans as marvelous beings. David Deutsch, a pioneer of quantum computation, points out for instance that human beings must be at a minimum a very extraordinary type of chemical scum given our capacity to build accurate mental models of the universe.[235]

The physics of the human brain could hardly be more unlike that of a quasar, says Deutsch. Quasars are quasi-stellar objects with the illumination of a trillion suns, which escaped from black holes. Yet that quasar happened in precisely such a way that billions of years later on the other side of the universe a "chemical scum" accurately described, modeled, and explained what was happening there and then in reality. He notes that the brain contains an accurate working model of the quasar, not just a superficial image of it, but an explanatory model embodying the same mathematical relationships and the same causal structure as the distant quasar itself. That is knowledge. What is more, the faithfulness with which the one structure resembles the other is increasing with time. That is the growth of knowledge.

The laws of physics have this special property that physical objects as unlike each other as they can be can nevertheless embody the same mathematical and causal structure and more so over time.

"So we are a chemical scum that is different," says Deutsch. "This chemical scum has universality, its structure contains with ever increasing precision the structure of everything. This place, and not other places in the universe, is a hub that contains within itself the structural and causal essence of the whole of the rest of physical reality. And so far from being insignificant, the fact that the laws of physics allow this, or even mandate that this can happen, is one of the most important things about the physical world."

Deutsch points to the specialness of locations like Earth, of life, and of its human inhabitants, and to our ability to secure our own future through the application of knowledge. He places knowledge alongside mass and electrical charge as a fundamental physical quality and suggests there is no reason theoretically why human beings could not at some point in the future use that knowledge to undertake "cosmic engineering," to, for example, reengineer the sun to prolong its lifespan. There is, in fact, no reason in principle why life and mind cannot, over eons, transform the structure of the universe on a very large scale.[236] (And logically, then, there is no reason why we cannot transform ourselves and this planet.)

Life is not simply just another physical system like rocks or clouds or glue or quasars, as physicist Paul Davies puts it. "When it comes to the mental realm, the characteristic qualities are even more distinctive and totally unlike anything else found in nature. Now we are dealing with thoughts, beliefs, purposes, feelings—the inner, subjective world of the human observer who experiences external reality through the senses." We may be able to model material objects like quasars, but human beings "do not even exist on the same level of description as material objects and bear no obvious relationship to them whatever."

Although "non-material" in the usual sense, the inner world of thought, beliefs, values, purposes, and feelings not only exists, it is essential to the existence of material things. In fact, it may be, as the physicist John Wheeler proposed, that "the physical universe is fundamentally informational, and matter is a derived phenomenon [the reverse of the orthodox arrangement]."[237] Wheeler "thought of observers as participants in shaping physical reality, and not as mere spectators."

This gives "life and mind a type of creative role in physics, making them an indispensible part of the entire cosmological story. Yet life and mind are products of the universe. So there is a logical as well as a temporal loop here. Conventional science assumes a linear logical sequence: cosmos > life > mind. Wheeler suggested closing this chain into a loop: cosmos > life> mind > cosmos. He expressed it this way: "Physics gives rise to observer-participant; observer-participant gives rise to information; information gives rise to physics." Thus the universe explains observers and observers explain the universe. Wheeler thereby rejected the notion of the universe as a machine subject to fixed a priori laws, rather describing it as a self-synthesizing world he called "the participatory universe."

Given that according to quantum mechanics reality is a psycho-physical event, and that the central point of quantum mechanics, as Wheeler put it, is that "the only real phenomenon is an observed phenomenon," this question arises: "How is it that things existed before there were observers to observe them?" After all, it took billions of years for the universe to generate sentient beings able to observe anything. Also, most events are not observed at all.

As strange as it may seem, Wheeler and others have proposed "the possibility of observers today, and in the future, shaping the nature of physical reality in the past, including the far past when no observers existed."[238] This *backwards-in-time* aspect of quantum mechanics means "the past can be shaped by observation at any stage in the cosmological future."[239]

This can be verified theoretically and through observation, according to Henry Stapp. "A large number of experiments have revealed the existence of various retro-actions directly at the macro-level of perceivable-sized effects. One kind of example consists of a change in the size of the pupil of the eyes of human subjects slightly before a randomly-timed shocking stimulus! Another kind of example is a sudden increase in skin-conductance before a shocking visual stimulus is shown to a human subject. These retro-effects are incompatible with a material world governed by the principles of classical physics."

Assuming that life and mind continue to exist for billions if not trillions of years, says Stapp, over time "a progressively larger fraction of the universe will be brought under intelligent control. More and more matter will be used to process information and create a rich mental world, perhaps without limit.... As the timeline stretches toward infinity, so an emerging distributed super-intelligence will become more and more godlike, so that in the final stage the supermind will merge with the universe: mind and cosmos will be one. It is a vision sometimes referred to as the final anthropic principle." According to this principle, then, as David Deutsch has put it, "the universe is heading toward something that might be called omniscience."

The laws of physics and the states of matter in this universe, states Paul Davies, have the special property that they permit physical systems (brains, genes, computers) to construct an internal representation of the world, that is, to know the world. But the model goes beyond knowledge to include interpretation and understanding. We are not only observers but gain some understanding of how the universe is put together and works as a coherent system. The "cosmic scheme" has not only created life and consciousness, it has also constructed an understanding of the cosmic scheme.

The final state of the universe, infused with mind, would have the power to bring into being the pathways of evolution that lead to the same final state. In this way the universe could create itself and steer itself toward its destiny. Observer-participancy would allow humanity—or rather all sentient beings in the cosmos—to build the universe, past, present, and future.

Interestingly, Henry Stapp says that the everyday processes of choosing by human players are in some way analogous to the processes involved in choosing the initial boundary conditions and laws of the universe. That is, the free choices made by human players can be seen as miniature versions of the choices that appear to be needed at the creation of the universe. Quantum theory opens the door to, indeed demands, the making of these later free choices.

This situation, according to Stapp, is concordant with the idea of a powerful Being that creates the universe and its laws to get things started, but then bequeaths part of this power to beings created in it's own image, at least with regard to their power to make physically efficacious decisions of the basis of reasons and evaluations.

"I see no way for contemporary science to disprove, or even render highly unlikely, this religious interpretation of quantum theory, or to provide strong evidence in support of an alternative picture of the nature of these 'free choices.' These choices seem to be rooted in reasons that are rooted in feelings pertaining to value or worth. Thus it can be argued that quantum theory provides an opening for an idea of nature and of our role within it that is in general accord with certain religious concepts, but that, by contrast, is quite incompatible with the precepts of mechanistic deterministic classical physics. Thus the replacement of classical mechanics by quantum mechanics opens the door to religious possibilities that formerly were rationally excluded."

This conception of nature, in which the consequences of our choices impact not only directly our immediate neighbourhood but also indirectly and immediately far-flung places, alters the image of the human being relative to the one spawned by classical physics. It changes this image in a way that reduces a sense of powerlessness, separateness, and isolation, instead enhancing a sense of belonging and of responsibility. Each person who understands his or herself in this way, as a spark of the divine, with some small part of the divine power, integrally interwoven into the process of the creation of the psycho-physical universe, will be encouraged to participate in the process of plumbing the potentialities of, and shaping the form of, the unfolding quantum reality that it is his or her birthright to help create.

Stapp goes on to say that quantum choices are built into human brain processes and consciousness. The evaluations that guide our actions "appear to come from an experiential or spiritual realm, and are certainly allowed by quantum theory to have the effects they seem to have."

WE *CAN* CHANGE THE WORLD

The reason for this lengthy foray into the mysterious world of quantum mechanics and its possible spiritual implications is to demonstrate on a deeper level than the obvious one that our interior world affects our exterior world. And that, contrary to classical physics on which much of the orthodox materialistic worldview is built, human beings can play a role in shaping the world based on choices that are freely made, i.e. without being entirely determined by the past. The unfolding of the future may be governed by mathematical laws, but these are laws into which our conscious free choices enter as essential inputs.

We can shape the future. Thus human beings are highly significant beings, much more so than "shower curtain mold". We have choices and these will be made based on reason and feelings that are rooted in what we value. What we value is determined by how we view the world, so whether we view it in a mechanistic, deterministic sense without meaning or purpose and devoid of free will or as a world determined by our choices, which have profound meaning, is highly significant.

To achieve an 11 billion-world we will have to abandon the mechanical self-conception fostered by 19th century physics. Socio-economic structures with severe ecological consequences are built up on conceptual foundations that are fundamentally flawed. To change the social-ecological reality we have to change the conceptual framework.

By adjusting our values and thoughts to more accurately reflect reality, and by entering a process of consulation—action—reflection—correction—action, we *can* alter our inner and outer conditions in ways that support justice and sustainability in an 11 billion-world.

CHAPTER 12

HUMANATURE

The environmental crisis requires not simply rhetoric or cosmetic solutions
but a death and rebirth of modern man and his worldview.
— Seyyed Hossein Nasr

While the iconic daytime image of Earth from space shows no obvious signs of human activity, its nighttime counterpart is a different story.[240] The global light show maps out a human presence that encompasses the planet. Earth emerges from the interplanetary darkness as a *human* reality.

The world has entered the anthropocene.[241] NASA's image of Earth at night provides us with a glimpse of the vast human infrastructure in which the world is wrapped. Brightly lit coastal cities outline the continents and pinpoint islands. Threads of light map connectors such as the United States Interstate Highway system, the Trans-Siberian railroad, and the lower Nile and upper St. Lawrence Rivers.

The ability to photograph the entire planet in itself illustrates the scope and immensity of the human project. NASA's composite nighttime image of the whole earth was assembled from data provided by the Defense Meteorological Satellite Program (DMSP) of the United States Air Force. The program was originally designed to aid navigation for military aircraft by detecting lunar illumination on nighttime clouds. It was later discovered that the equipment was sufficiently sensitive to record illumination from human settlements. Over a period of several months, the satellite data was pieced together to produce a nighttime counterpart to NASA's Blue Marble photograph of the whole Earth.

The DMSP is just one of many satellite programs. The Space Surveillance Network has tracked more than 26,000 man-made orbiting objects, including 8000 currently being tracked. Of these, 560 are operational satellites, the rest presumably space junk. By taking photographs and gathering remote sensing data, the working satellites help us observe, measure, inventory, and navigate Earth, land and sea, and also connect to—and sometimes fight—each other.

NASA's more detailed nighttime photographs and video images of Earth are more spectacular—and more eerie. Taken by the crew of the International Space Station, they must be seen to be believed (and billions now have free access on the Internet to see and believe them.)[242] They reveal light networks which leave no doubt that this is a world encompassed by humankind.

Nighttime photograph of South Asia taken from the International Space Station.

Our satellite system, which provides us with new perspectives of our planet, is part of the apparatus that facilitates the instantaneous communications of a globalized community. The various media using the satellite system add to the connectivity and flow of information, services, and materials that build a truly global civilization.

Some observers have proposed (to much derision), that a *noosphere*, an encompassing layer of human thought, has formed—at least figuratively—around Earth.

Moving closer to the planet's surface, the contrails of 180,000 daily airline flights demarcate another layer of the human network. From above, the two million people that fly every day can look down on an endless grid of fields and roads. Agriculture—farms and grazing land—forms 43 percent of Earth's land surface. A human-nature hybrid, agriculture has all but replaced what we think of as natural ecosystems on those parts of the planet that support it. Between agriculture and urban space, human systems occupy 50 percent of the planet's land surface.

Looking down on the forestland, covering just under a third of Earth's land-mass, the airline passengers would be unable to see the true extent of human influence. How many would realize most of the tropical and temperate forests are already gone, with much of the rest fragmented by highways and logging, oil, gas, power-line, and mining roads? Only 20 percent of the world's original forests remain as large undisturbed tracts. Some five percent of all forestland is plantation. The boreal forest, the taiga, the last of the two great northern biomes largely extant, a vast buffer against climate change, has been studied, mapped, inventoried, and divided among forestry companies, ready for commodification.

Layer upon layer of our engineered systems—from rice paddies and agrofor-ests to parks and gardens to villages and vast metropolises—are now superim-posed on the planet, claiming it for our species. Human beings, one of the esti-mated 8.7 million species that cohabit the planet, now use 20 percent of Earth's Net Primary Production (NPP) capacity on land. NPP, the total plant material produced on Earth, is the primary fuel for the planet's food web. Outnumbering us five to one, our livestock consume an ever-larger portion of NPP.

Whether on the prairies and savannahs or forests, man-made fires, deliberate or accidental, transform ecosystems for human purposes, spewing millions of tonnes of carbon into the atmosphere, steadily increasing the greenhouse effect.

We move about the world on a 70 million kilometre network of roads, another 1.4 million kilometres of train tracks, not to mention countless lengths of streets, lanes, trails, and paths. Rivers, lakes, seas, and canals are also pathways: every year commercial vessels, nearly 35,000 in number, transport more than 7 billion tonnes of cargo, one tonne for each of us. All these pathways are needed to move the 80 tonnes of natural resources currently removed from the ecosphere, per person per year, to produce our goods and services.[243]

What we have called *nature* is becoming, has become, a socio-ecosphere, what we might call *humanature*. Our species has, in a very real sense, taken control of the ecosphere, the dynamic, life-supporting layers of land, water, and air at Earth's surface. This is not to suggest that people are not also subject to ecological systems; we are, and more so all the time. Still, humans have a preponderant influence, with impacts exceeding certain geological forces, sufficiently so that it has been proposed that the current geological epoch be named after us. "Humans," commented Nobel laureate Paul J. Crutzen, "have become a geologic agent comparable to erosion and eruptions. It seems appropriate to emphasize the central role of mankind in geology and ecology by proposing to use the term 'anthropocene' for the current geological epoch."

Most disturbing, perhaps, is our influence on the composition of the atmosphere, which is altering global climate, thus impacting all living things. The world altering emissions issue from billions of our vehicles and furnaces and fires and cattle and power plants and rice paddies and factories. For better or worse, we have a wrap on the world.

The night-dark seas are human places too. In the oceans, the land pattern continues, as shipping lanes and fishing lines and nets transform aquatic ecosystems. Some of us understand that the great fisheries are going or gone; fewer are aware that our commercial fishers are actively dragging the ocean floor with weighted nets, with impacts similar to harrowing farmland.[244] The ocean temperature is up, the water itself expanding. Small island nations, along with the river valleys and deltas where so many live, are threatened. The Pacific gyre is loaded with fine particles of plastic. A film of oil is spread across the seas. The coral beds, marvellous places, are bleached. And great seas and lakes are being turned into sewers—or in some cases drained.

We are also taking control of Earth's crust, tapping ever-greater quantities of its minerals. Our drilling and hydraulic fracturing is busily sucking out the post-peak oil and natural gas. Our world encompassing networks include the continental energy grids, pipelines and other energy distribution systems that are the primary vectors of climate change. There is, for example, a 793,000-kilometre network of oil and natural gas pipelines crisscrossing the continental United States. Water distribution systems are becoming similarly ubiquitous, facilitating our insatiable demand for water, which in some cases taps the entire flow of major rivers and fossil aquifers. The ground beneath any modern city is a warren of pipes and lines and tunnels moving our fluids and gases and electrons.

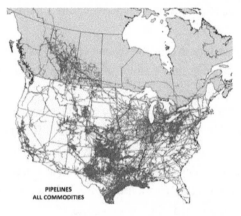

PIPELINES
ALL COMMODITIES

Overhead we see a world-connecting mesh of wire, the local carriers of the intercontinental telecommunication grid. In addition to immeasurable lengths of suspended and buried cables, it includes the wireless communication filling the air with our signals. Transmission towers and receivers of all kinds are everywhere. Handheld computers—with capabilities that exceed the computation available to the manned moon flights—linked to a rapidly expanding Internet, plug us—the two billion of us who can afford to buy in—to the total information accumulated by our species about our universe (another definition of the term *noosphere*.)

The psychiatrist Normal Doidge—in language reminiscent of Marshall McLuhan—proposes that the highly plastic human brain and nervous system have been reshaped by this electronic world, and are, in turn, reshaping the world.

"All electronic devices rewire the brain," he observes. "As we use an electronic medium, our nervous system extends outward, and the medium extends inward.

"Electronic media are so effective at altering the nervous system because they both work in similar ways and are basically compatible and thus easily linked. Both involve the instantaneous transmission of electric signals to make linkages. Because our nervous system is plastic, it can take advantage of this compatibility and merge with the electronic media, making a single, larger system. Indeed, it is the nature of such systems to merge whether they are biological or manmade.

The nervous system is an internal medium, communicating messages from one area of the body to another, and it evolved to do, for multi-celled organisms such as ourselves, what the electronic media do for humanity—connect disparate parts. McLuhan expressed this electronic extension of the nervous system and the self in comic terms: 'Now man is beginning to wear his brain outside his skull, and his nerves outside his skin.' In a famous formulation, he said, 'Today, after more than a century of electric technology, we have extended our central nervous system in a global embrace, abolishing both space and time as far as our planet is concerned.'"[245]

Or as novelist Douglas Coupland puts it, vindicating in a sense de Chardin's concept of a noosphere, we are "turning into a cloud of data that circles the planet like a thin gauze."[246]

Our trace is everywhere. Twenty years ago, I flew into a wilderness area in far northern Saskatchewan accessible only by boat or float plane. The spectacular Athabasca sand dunes are the most northerly active dunes in the world. Standing on the south shore of Lake Athabasca contemplating what I thought was my first true wilderness experience, I noticed a little figure bobbing on the waves: Ernie from Sesame Street. Untouched wilderness is gone.

Flying to the far side of this great lake, among the world's largest bodies of fresh water, I looked down on the abandoned uranium mines that once yielded fuel for the West's nuclear arsenal. A detectable layer of radioactive material originating from these mines is deposited in the soils of the entire planet, a remnant of weapons testing.

Even more widespread is a film of pesticides and other artificial chemicals, some detectable in the tissues of every living thing—and Antarctic snow. Humanity's invisible emissions and our visible physical infrastructure mark our presence everywhere, their global spread paralleling our conceptualization of *nature*, a concept that also recreates the world as a human place. This world-encompassing man-made infrastructure is a manifestation—and generator—of the even more complete *mental* embrace of the planet: the ways we imagine, conceptualize, name, communicate, describe, and divide it, in whole and in part, and hold its mental model in our individual and collective minds. Our local and planetary cultures make Earth our mental product.

This conceptualization—the sense of the ecosphere as an external environment that surrounds *us,* who are its centre, and which exists to be exploited for maximum economic gain by our species, or more precisely its elites—must and will change as we prepare for an 11 billion future. But not in the way you may think.

CHANGING WORLDVIEWS

"What we do in the world flows from how we interpret the world," said the ecologist Charles Birch. According to Birch and other leading thinkers the crisis that threatens the integrity of the ecosphere can be traced, at least in part, to the worldviews, models, or paradigms that, often unconsciously, guide the way we organize and operate civilization. These worldviews are built from—and also shape—our individual and collective interpretations of the world and humanity's role in it and, if Birch is right, ultimately determine what we *do*.

"Nothing less than the current logic of world civilization," observes Al Gore, runs counter to the well-being of the ecosphere.[247] A literature scan yields hundreds of similar statements, many of which come round to a need to shift "the collection of values and assumptions that determines our basic understanding of how we fit into the universe."[248] The problem, as he sees it, is that "We have misunderstood who we are, how we are related to our place within creation, why our very existence assigns us a duty of moral alertness to the consequences of what we do." So we need to reappraise "who we are and how we are related to creation" in order to come up with new, sustainable modes of behaviour.[249]

> *The current logic of world civilization runs counter to the wellbeing of the ecosphere. We need to reexamine the values and assumptions that determine our basic understanding of how we fit into the universe.*

Seyyed Hossein Nasr sees the present predicament as "primarily the consequence of the loss of 'sapiential' knowledge of nature and an inner spiritual crisis and not simply the result of bad engineering."[250] For Nasr, "The environmental crisis requires not simply rhetoric or cosmetic solutions but a death and rebirth of modern man and his worldview."[251] Along this line, Thomas Berry has said that the time has come to "re-invent the human at the species level."[252]

Many leaders of thought who study the global ecological crisis look to a shift in worldviews, models, or paradigms as key to its resolution. This is critical because worldviews are integral—and formative—parts of all cultures. A socially shared view of reality gives a culture a sense of direction, confidence, and self-worth, making worldviews strongly motivating. An advance in world-views can be both a guide to and a motivator of change.

"Societies, as well as individuals, have always contemplated deep ques-tions relating to their being and becoming, and to the being and becoming of the world," comments one group of thinkers involved in a process to build a worldview that corresponds to the present global reality.[253] "The configuration of answers to these questions forms their worldview." "A worldview is a coherent collection of concepts and theorems that must allow us to construct a global image of the world, and in this way to understand as many elements of our expe-rience as possible."

Worldview has been described as "a map that we use to orient and explain, from which we evaluate and act, and put forward prognoses and visions of the future."[254]

Obviously, a worldview is not the world, just as a map of Beijing is not Beijing. It is not fully accurate, but a "good" worldview helps us understand and navigate our world, just as a map—a good map—can help us figure out Beijing.

We may entertain several worldviews simultaneously. Significantly, it may be that elements of our worldview that are unconscious have more influence on us than conscious ones: a person or society may profess to a Christian world-view, for instance, but may act in an un-Christian way given a more pervasive materialist worldview is functioning in the background. Or we may incorporate the idea of *sustainability* into our worldview, as per the Bruntland report, but continue to act unsustainably because a more entrenched worldview has more influence on our behaviour.

Our *full* world is infinitely complex in comparison to earlier periods of history. Everything has changed in our relationship to the world except our understanding of it: '…we all operate," comments Edward O. Wilson, "by a worldview distorted by the residues of hereditary human nature. We exist in a bizarre combination of Stone Age emotions, medieval beliefs and god-like technology."[255] This combination is particularly jarring as we try to navigate our social-ecological reality, the more so as population pressure mounts.

THE DOMINANCE CONTINUUM

What are the worldviews or models that govern our relationship with the ecosphere?

Though they vary from place to place and over time, there appear to be two main models of human-nature relations: ecocentrism and anthropocentrism. We might sum up ecocentrism in the expression "We are the world's" (i.e. we belong to it) and anthropocentrism in the expression "We own the world."

The currently dominant anthropocentric worldview boils down to the notion that the earth exists primarily to support human development. We are the most important species, having established ourselves as such in the struggle for existence. Since our needs supersede those of all other species, humankind can assign to itself whatever portion of the ecosphere it needs to survive and prosper. (Of course, it is not so much *humanity's* interests that prevail as those of its elites.)

This model is rooted in the agricultural and industrial revolutions, which provided the means for people to populate and subdue the earth. Over the past 300 years, the worldview has been entrenched by philosophical notions and scientism. The idea that the fittest survive, for example, reinforced the human-centric worldview: our species survived and dominated other species because it was fit to do so. The success of our species, aided by science and technology and especially the harnessing of fossil fuels, allowed people to win—for the most part—the struggle with nature and dominate the ecosphere. Our ability to dominate became its own justification, our success further supporting the notion than humans were indeed a species above ecological limits.

This model is often seen as a product of certain influential religious ideas, such as the mandate given by God to "god-like" human beings in the Judeo-Christian tradition (Genesis 26-28) to "people and subdue the earth." While it may be reinforced by interpretations of the Judeo-Christian worldview, places as religiously divergent as Japan, China, Indonesia, and India have adopted the same perspective without being primarily Christian. And to be fair, Christianity and other religions are also primary sources of conservationist thinking.

Capitalism, "a machine for demolishing limits," is a lubricant that quickens human exploitation of the planet, though experiments with communism in many ways proved even more brutal ecologically. The rise of materialism and consumerism clearly accelerated the impacts of the human-centric model, which might be better characterized as *human-centric materialism*. This worldview exerts a strong gravitational influence, drawing all peoples and cultures to it.

Ecocentrism is also considered a product of religious ideas. Many indigenous traditions support a worldview that sees human beings as encompassed by the world, like a child in the womb of its mother. We are children of Mother Earth, one of her myriad offspring, each according to some variants of this view endowed with spirit and intelligence. Our mandate is to inhabit our world as members of a family of living things—and all things are alive. The priority is to do nothing to upset nature's equilibrium.

For all the criticism of the Judeo-Christian tradition, it too is replete with conservationist ideas, such as stewardship, and figures, such as St. Francis, who championed compassion for other species. Modern variants of ecocentrism were developed in reaction to the Industrial Revolution by religious thinkers such as William Blake and Gilbert White, forerunners of modern conservationists. Conservation is a global phenomenon not restricted to any culture or religious tradition.

Ecocentrism today is informed by the science of ecology, which places more value on eco*systems* than the organisms living within them; the ecosphere, as the largest whole system, has ultimate value rather than any subsystem or species, including human beings. This being the case, the human species has no right to overburden the Earth.

Either worldview can be materialistic or religious. Anthropocentrism corresponds with materialism, but it also fits with a hierarchical view of religious cosmology. Ecocentrism is often associated with certain religious traditions, but is also advocated by secularists. People freely choose whatever connections they want to make or break.

While anthropocentrism and ecocentrism seem diametrically opposed, both views can be seen as ends of a *dominance continuum*. On one end we see humanity dominated by an all-powerful and encompassing nature, submissive, fearful, or defiant. On the other we see humanity triumphant in its dominance over nature. Interestingly, the two views in a sense *need* each other. Earth's powers—from geological forces and extreme weather to the rhythm of the seasons and parsimony or extravagance when it comes to rain and warmth—are constantly unleashed on us, attempting to destroy what we have built. They seem to demand a constant battle to subdue them. The confrontation between the two worldviews—to protect or control nature—is ongoing.

THE DOMINANCE CONTINUUM

ECOCENTRISM	STRUGGLE FOR SURVIVAL	ANTHROPOCENTRISM
SUBMISSION	*RESPONSE TO VIOLENCE*	*HUBRIS*

The two poles also resemble each other. Through anthropocentrism humankind looks at nature the way it sees itself: as a competitive arena where the players strive for power. Class structure is *natural*. Just as we justify classism, we justify human domination of nature. At the other end of the scale, ecocentrism often takes the form of a struggle against elites intent on exploiting nature, modelling certain characteristics of the human-centric model it opposes.

All manner of variations and thought hybrids fall along the continuum. On the far end of anthropocentrism, for example, is extreme human triumphalism, which sees no significant value in conserving ecosystems. Moving to the left, we see the more benign variant sustainable development, the management of the ecosphere to ensure continuous production of goods and services into the future. Modern environmentalism, conservation, and stewardship are either subsets or hybrids of the human-centric or ecocentric models, rather than distinct models. The goal of conservation is either to moderate the negative or accommodate the positive aspects of the economy built on the anthropocentric model, or to imbue civilization with a measure of ecocentrism that does not entirely limit socio-economic development. Ecocentrism also has strong variants, which call for the radical reduction of human population or which justify eco-terrorism, even rationalizing murder to protect other species. At the far end are those who would wish to see humankind largely eliminated to ensure the success of the ecosphere.

I imagine these worldviews to be on a dominance continuum because they are closely associated with the notion that all life is motivated and dominated by a self-interested struggle for survival. This notion involves a measure of truth or it would never have come into existence: the struggle for survival is a factor in humanity's evolution. Yet contemporary evolutionary theory presents a counterbalance to "the traditional take on Darwin, which condemns all life to a protracted and bloody struggle for survival and reproduction."[256] As stated earlier, this aspect of Darwin's theory has been seized upon as a justification for cut throat competition that dominates our social and economic space, and justifies the many forms of violence, direct and subtle, which the "strong" use to justify their dominance over the "weak."

History *has* involved a struggle to eke out a living through hunting, gathering, and later agriculture and industry, allowing us to build and sustain a progression of social units from family and tribe to nation states, often involving a degree of violence. Today, we continue to compete to make our way in the world. But this does not mean that the fundamental nature of the world is defined by natural selection through competitive struggle for survival of the fittest.

> *Cooperation was the principal architect of four billion years of evolution. Cooperation constructed humanity. Cooperation makes evolution constructive and open-ended.*

"Mutation and natural selection are not in themselves enough to understand life," says Martin Nowak, director of the Program for Evolutionary Dynamics at Harvard University and author of *SuperCooperators*. "Cooperation was the principal architect of 4 billion years of evolution. Cooperation built the first bacterial cell, the higher cells, then complex multicellular life and insect superorganisms. Finally cooperation constructed humanity. I propose that 'natural cooperation" be included as a fundamental principle to bolster those laid down by Darwin.... Cooperation makes evolution constructive and open-ended."

FULL WORLD VIEWS

The weakness of the human-centric model has become obvious with the emergence of increasingly complex local and global ecological problems. Climate change would seem to deliver the *coup de grâce* to anthropocentric hubris as a guiding worldview, and seemingly calls for an ecocentric perspective.

Certainly, it becomes obvious to most reasonable observers that in a *full world* the present way of doing things is ultimately unsustainable.[257] While a few may believe, with conservative environmental commentator Peter Huber, that "Humanity can survive just fine in a planet-covering crypt of concrete and computers," most would now agree that the days of our species' pursuit of world domination are temporary at best.[258] Without acknowledging and accommodating the rights, needs, and intrinsic value of the other players in the ecosphere, its ecological balance will be destabilized to the point where it is incapable of supporting civilization in anything like its present form. An 11 billion world operating under the anthropocentric view is unthinkable.

It is important to point out that this model is not really *anthrop*-centric at all, but centered on the interests of some *anthrops*. It would be one thing if a cost-benefit analysis of the outcomes of the human-centric model led at least to the welfare of humanity as a whole, but it really supports the development of certain favoured individuals, classes, and nations. The model contributes to excess accumulation of wealth in the hands of relatively few, while billions live on their table scraps, figuratively speaking. A new model is needed for social as well as environmental reasons.

Having said that, we should not discount certain strengths of or positive outcomes from the antropocentric model. This way of seeing ourselves in relation to the world has allowed humanity to separate out from its environment to the extent that it can identify itself as a distinct entity, dissatisfied with its lot and hungry for and capable of development.[259] This allows a new form of consciousness conducive to rapid *cultural evolution*,[260] including the development of philosophies, arts, sciences, religions, ethics, and technologies that have allowed our species to form complex and diverse cultures that support human development in myriad ways.

Civilization may have outstripped the bounds of moderation, but who among us would opt for a world without the benefits of civilization, such as tools, mechanization, agriculture, literacy, communications and information technology, education, health care, travel, cultural amenities, political and administrative structures, public institutions, human rights, or social services agencies? These exist in large measure because we have made use of the human-centric model.

Ecocentrism also has its strengths and shortcomings. On the plus side, ecocentrism rightly acknowledges that human civilization is built on an ecological foundation. Without respecting these sources, we gradually undermine the resilience needed to support an ever-advancing civilization. Ecocentrism recognizes the threat of continuous growth and rightly demands the development of a stable state economy that limits resource consumption.

Certain iterations of ecocentrism seem on the surface to be the only sensible way to view human-nature relations, but ecocentrism also has fatal flaws.

Chiefly, the model does not accommodate the contemporary human reality. On a purely physical level, our species is part of the ecosphere, but humanity is not entirely confined by physical limitations. In one sense, we have broken free of many of nature's limitations and now operate in another sphere, a new kind of constructed reality of which the ecosphere is the foundation but not the encompassing whole. An 11-billion worldview has to accommodate this reality.

A proof of this assertion is the "environmental crisis" itself. A case can now be made that it is the ecosphere that exists in a matrix of our making. Human beings already control more than 20 percent of the primary productivity, or plant growth, on the planet's surface;[261] we have changed the global climate, the atmosphere, the land, the ecosystems, and the oceans in ways equivalent only to geological or cosmic forces. Yes civilization exists in the ecosphere, but the ecosphere now depends on what we make of civilization.

Consequently, we can no longer operate from a point of view embedded in or encompassed by the ecosphere. We cannot exist without extreme manipulations of our environment. Less than 1 percent of the human diet, for example, comes from hunting and gathering activities associated with traditional ecocentric worldviews. Even if we develop sustainable systems they will no longer be *natural* in the true sense of the word, but human-contrived systems that mimic what we know of natural systems. Wilderness does not even exist to return to.

Contemporary ecocentrism is informed by a scientific view of ecology and systems theory. It recognizes that natural systems, the largest and most encompassing of which is the ecosphere, have a limited carrying capacity. When a species exceeds that capacity it is in jeopardy, along with its environment. People have figured out how to get around this problem in the short term by drawing down the planet's *natural capital* when we should be living primarily on its *interest*, the annual accumulation of renewable resources made possible by energy coming into the system from sunshine. Living strictly by the limits of the earth's carrying capacity implies that we need to drastically reduce our ecological footprint. Much can be achieved through conservation, efficiency, and harnessing renewable forms of power, but to live by the ethics of an ecocentric worldview—which values the ecosphere above humanity—we would have to radically reduce our population, to 1 billion or less.[262] The ethical implications of that ecocentric agenda would appear to make this approach impossible.

We cannot go back to an ecocentric world. The way forward seems equally challenging. We would therefore benefit from a new model of human-nature interaction that facilitates both further human development and the healthy, sustainable functioning of the ecosphere.

But can we be neither the masters of our world nor its subjects?

HUMANATURE

A new model or worldview has to protect the ecological balance of the planet but it also has to accommodate 11 billion people in the near future. Such a model will have to leave behind the *eco-anthro continuum* entirely. It must recognize human welfare and healthy ecosystems as identical concerns. It must resolve our current notion of power, moving away from the *desire for power* toward the *desire to serve*. It must jettison the very notion of *environment*, as a thing separate from the people it surrounds.

A more fitting model or worldview can be summed up in the expression, "We are the world." This model is built on the initially strange notion that the human reality encompasses and contains the physical world. Accordingly, we literally view the world as the extended human body and, logically, assume the responsibility to care for the health and integrity of the ecosphere as we would our bodies. By this way of thinking, the interests of humanity and the ecosphere, their mutual sustainability and well-being, are one and the same. The environment disappears as object and reemerges as subject (or perhaps more accurately as a verb.) *Human* and *nature* become *humanature*.

What does this mean? How can humanity, just one species of millions, be said to encompass the world? And is this not just another form of anthropocentrism, with humans again on top of the pyramid?

The encompassing model does not reject other models entirely, but transforms them into something new through a different understanding of the nature of power. Power in this model is not about dominance or subservience, it is about the capacity to collaborate and serve.

To help understand the humanature model, consider the house/home as an analogy. Seemingly, the house encompasses or contains its residents. However, it may be more accurate to say that the residents or family—the household— actually encompass the house, given the house is a product of the family's intention to create a home. The house is obtained or made by the family as a critical element of homemaking. It is there to facilitate the lives of those living in it. It is the staging ground for everything that a family does: making a living to sustain itself, educating the children, building a web of social relationships, etc. Although the physical house contains the people, the people encompass the house mentally, emotionally, and spiritually, and even physically they imagine, conceive of, design, plan, build, execute, finance, and maintain it. Focused human attention, not only on the part of the family but also their larger social-economic network, created the house.

So we can say the family encompasses the house or even that the family *is* the house, thus the word *household*. Of course, the family must also look after their house, pay the rent or mortgage, do repairs, maintain the property, and so on if it wants to sustain the home over time. If it fails to do so, the house eventually ceases to serve its function and the home cannot be maintained. So, while the house exists for the family, which *encompasses* the house, the family is in a position of service to the house. It is a reciprocal relationship. House and family make a home; it is one system. To have a home the house must be maintained.

A second analogy is the human being's body. The body in some way contains or encompasses the human reality, the mind, personality, character, or as some would say the soul of the person. However, we can also say the mind encompasses the body, in that the mind is its driver and caregiver, as well as its purpose: what would be the point of the body without the mind? The body exists to manifest the mind, which then manages the body, looking out for its shelter, clothing, nutrition, exercise, and so on. The body has less value than the mind: a person can lose much of their body and many of its physical functions without damaging the mind or interfering with the person's mental, emotional, or spiritual capacities. One is no less human without legs and arms, or sight or hearing, for example. People can communicate and interact without ever encountering each other bodily. So it is possible to say that the human reality— the mind, soul, character, personality, emotions—actually contains or encompasses the body. Yet we see that the mind, or the full human reality, must also be embodied, making the mind and body one system. Nevertheless, the mind is in the position of serving its body.

Both analogies deal with the idea of *part* and *whole* in similar ways. Are the residents simply a part of the house? Or is the house a part of the resident's reality?

We can look at it this way: Something that is a *part* cannot have qualities not evident in the *whole*. The residents have qualities and capabilities that are much more complex and sophisticated than the house, such as vision, intelligence, imagination, foresight, and so on. The residents are not *part* of the house because they have qualities of which the house is deprived. So the residents can be said to be the *whole* and the house the *part*. Similarly, the body lacks the range of qualities and capacities of the whole person—thinking, creativity, model making, relationships, communication, intuition, and so on. So we can say the person is not *part* of the body, but the body a part of the larger human reality.

Clearly, humanity as a species is in one sense a part of the world and physical laws and limitations apply to it as to other species. Yet the human reality has qualities of the mind that do not exist elsewhere in the physical world which facilitate the manipulation and control of the natural world, allowing humans to overcome limitations insurmountable to other species, to, for example, make meaning, to plan, to organize, to act collectively, to use technology, as well as disrupt and even destroy the order of the physical world. While all other things conform to physical law, humanity has—uniquely—free will that can be used to shape the physical world in the ways described earlier in this chapter. We can therefore say the world is actually a part of a larger human reality.

Humanity may be in a superior position to other species, yet the only intelligent way it can express this power is to assume a position of service.

If we were merely part of nature, equal to other creatures, there would be no ecological crisis; we would have long since been eliminated or brought back into balance given we have exceeded Earth's carrying capacity.

As is the analogy of the house or body, while humanity may be in a superior position, the only intelligent way that it can express this power is to assume a position of service. Just as the family must serve the house (or the mind the body) to sustain it, so that in turn it can maintain the family's (or the mind's) capabilities, as humanity assumes an increasingly more significant role in the ecosphere, it must learn to serve the ecosphere if it hopes to continue to develop and exercise its capabilities in an 11 billion world.

CORRESPONDENCE WITH SCIENTIFIC THEORIES

Is an encompassing model a better model of reality, a better worldview, than previous models? It is better if it does two things: first, if it provides a more accurate description of the human-nature relationship than ecocentrism or anthropo-centrism and second, if it is more useful in helping us order our thoughts and actions such that we can carry forward an ever-advancing civilization.

How accurate is the model? The idea that humanity encompasses nature corresponds with certain scientific and philosophic interpretations of reality.

The Anthropocene "Designation of the Anthropocene as a geologic epoch provides a formal scientific framework for the increasingly obvious fact that human activities interact strongly with environmental, ecological, and social changes at local to global scales," observes biologist Stuart Chapin.[263] "The time is past when ecologists can study 'pristine' ecosystems, ignore human roles in the dynamics of those systems, and expect their results to be broadly applicable. Ecology must be part of an interdisciplinary suite of disciplines that embraces the linkages between social and ecological components of social-ecological systems, often focusing on those linkages as aspects where scientific study is likely to provide the most novel insights."

Terms like *social-ecological systems* or *human-earth system* and other varia-tions have become common descriptors of our reality.[264] Increasingly, the ecosphere itself is seen as an *artifact*, i.e. an object made by humans. The field of Earth Systems Engineering (ESE) recognizes that humanity has unwittingly reengineered planetary systems, such as climate and the nitrogen and carbon cycles, and that being a fact, proposed that we now have no choice but to adopt that role wittingly.[265]

The Noosphere The Ukrainian geochemist Vladimir Vernadsky popularized the concept *biosphere*—first proposed by Austrian geologist Eduard Suess—in the book *Biosfera,* published in 1926. Vernadsky conceived of the biosphere "as the Earth envelope in which living matter exists and which is comprised of the whole atmospheric troposphere, the oceans, and a thin layer of the continental regions inhabited by living matter, which reveals itself as a geological force of immense proportions, completely remaking the Biosphere and changing its physical, chemical and mechanical properties." Vernadsky was among the first scientists to identify biogeochemical cycles and the growing human influence on those cycles. He put forward the notion that the human transformation of Earth that is taking place "is a change of a new kind which, with time, acceler-ates with an extraordinary rapidity" because "the increase, in the course of time, of machinery in the structure of human society also proceeds in geometrical progression."

This later led Vernadsky to speculate that human activities were modifying biogeochemical cycles to such an extent that the biosphere was undergoing transformation into a new configuration that had been described by Teilhard de Chardin as the noosphere (*noos* being Greek for mind). For Vernadsky, the term noosphere was a name for the transformation of the biosphere through human interference in biogeochemical cycles. To that point, the transformation was occurring unwittingly, but Vernadsky looked to the growth of science and technology, coupled with social and economic planning, to make inadvertent human intervention in biogeochemical cycles more deliberate, and so bring about a smooth transition from biosphere to noosphere. According to Vernadsky, the noosphere would enhance human development through respect and management of biogeochemical cycles. De Chardin added another dimension to the concept, seeing it as a stage in a movement toward planetary spiritual enlightenment.[266]

The scientific establishment has generally looked on this notion as nonsense, but more recently the concept has gone through something of a revival as a model for understanding the role of human beings and their technologies, especially the global web of information and communication technologies. The impact of social-economic systems on the planet has now been substantiated thorough large-scale collaborative assessments such as the reports of the International Panel on Climate Change and the Millennium Ecosystem Assessment.[267]

Richard Doyle tells the story of how Vernadsky first conceived of the noosphere. During World War 1, Vernadsky was waiting in a railway station and found himself counting passing rail cars. He began to think about what was moving them. Obviously, it was the locomotive, which was in turn moved by steam produced by burning coal. But beyond the obvious, Vernadsky determined that it was really *focused human attention* that was moving the rail cars: people had invented the technology, put the infrastructure in place, developed the economy and markets, discovered and produced the energy, manufactured the products being moved, provided the capital and labour. From this rumination, Vernadsky identified what we would now call a feedback loop between what we think and what happens on the planet.

Doyle says the term noosphere names the biological reality of our thought: not only that biology supports thought, but that our thought, our collective attention, feeds back to the biosphere. Part of the output of our mental system returns to the biosphere, or more precisely the ecosphere, in a way that affects its performance. What we think or imagine to be true—our worldview—impacts the ecosphere.

For Doyle, noosphere is the collective attention not just of humans but of all semiotic actors in the ecosphere, i.e. all organism that use signs and symbols to communicate. Bacteria swap DNA, flowers use scent and colour to attract insects to outsource reproduction, birds use songs and plumage to attract mates: the world swarms with management of attention.

The term noosphere puts a word to the feedback between our inner and outer worlds, between worldview and world. It is not just our thoughts but also our thought about thought, the way we view and model ourselves and the world, that impacts the planet.

The participatory universe The idea of humanity encompassing nature has some parallels with the idea of a "life principle" or a "self-explaining universe" as described by physicist Paul Davies in his book *Cosmic Jackpot*. Davies sees possible validity to the idea that purpose, life, and consciousness is built into the workings of the cosmos at a fundamental level. He points, for example, to the "participatory universe" model described by John Wheeler, the physicist who coined the term 'black hole.'

As stated in the last chapter, Wheeler said that, "The central point of quantum theory...can be put in a single, simple sentence. "No elementary phenomenon is a phenomenon until it is a registered (observed) phenomenon." In one sense, nothing exists until we know it exists. "We are inescapably involved in bringing about that which appears to be happening."[268] He describes the universe as a self-excited system brought into being by self-reference. "The universe gives birth to communicating participators. Communicating participators give meaning to the universe."[269] In this participatory universe, the mind is a necessary player in the concrete nature of reality. Paul Davies considers the possibility of life and mind expanding to saturate the universe over an immense duration of time, with consciousness literally encompassing everything.[270] According to this theory, then, the human reality encompasses not just the ecosphere but ultimately the entirety of physical reality.

WE GET THE FUTURE WE IMAGINE

Consciousness is the organized effort to model reality. Physical reality without consciousness would be a soup of particles and waves, a "smear of possibilities." Consciousness uses mental maps/models to make the physical world intelligible and choice to sufficiently limit possibilities to create a concrete subjective experience.

Our maps are not the world, they are not perfect, but they are necessary for an intelligible experience of self and world. The concepts 'inner' and 'outer,' for instance "are models for aspects of reality—words that map the world only imperfectly," says Richard Doyle.[271]

> Our 'inner world'—subjective experience—is all we ever experience, so if we change it obviously we will see a change in what we label 'external' reality that it is of course part of and not separable from. The notions inner and outer are artificial, since the real world is one, but they are required to create a personal reality with which one can know about and play a role in the larger reality, that is, this dichotomy is needed to form intention and take action.

> Maps of 'continuity' are crucial and urgently needed. We can model the world as either 'discrete'—made up of parts—or 'continuous'—composing a whole—to powerful effect. Both are in this sense true. This is not relativism but a corollary of that creative freedom to choose our models that seems to be an attribute of consciousness. The mechanistic worldview extracts, separates and reconnects raw materials, labour, and energy in ways that produce astonishing order as well as disorder (entropy). By mapping the world as discrete—such as the difference between one second and another—and uniform— to a clock, there is no difference between one second and another—we have transformed the planet. Consciousness informed by discrete maps of reality has been an actual geological force in a tiny sliver of time. In so doing, we have transformed the biosphere. So you can see just how actual this relation between consciousness, its maps, and earthly reality

is. This is why Vernadksy, a geophysicist, thought we needed a new term for the way consciousness functions as a geological force: noosphere.

These discrete maps of reality are so powerful that we forget that they are maps. Now if the world can be cut up into parts, it is only because it forms a unity. A Sufi author commented that the unity of the world was both the most obvious and obscure fact. It is obvious because our own lives and the world we inhabit can be seen to continue without any experienced interruption—neither the world nor our lives truly stops and starts. This unity can be obscure because in a literal sense we can't perceive it with our senses—this unity can only be 'perceived' by our minds.

We are so effective as separate beings that we forget the whole for the part. The world is more than a collection of parts, and we can quote Carl Sagan: 'The beauty of a living thing is not the atoms that go into it, but the way those atoms are put together.' Equally beautiful is what Sagan follows up with: 'The cosmos is also within us. We are made of star stuff.' We are an aspect of something unfathomably grand, beautiful, complex and unbroken. This is perhaps the 'grandeur' Darwin was discussing. And when we experience that grandeur it can help us think and act in ways appropriate to a geological force.

Our capacity to encompass the cosmos makes human beings particularly important. "… It turns out that we are central, after all," says Doyle. "Our ability to create models—virtual realities—in our brains, combined with our modest-looking thumbs, has been sufficient to usher in another form of evolution: technology. That development enabled the persistence of the accelerating pace that started with biological evolution. It will continue until the entire universe is at our fingertips."

By making maps/models we derive meaning and purpose, generate an understanding of self and whole, and, in addition to being observers, become actors that shape the objective world. By changing our consciousness (the awareness of awareness) by changing our maps (the interpretation of subjective experience of the world), we change the world.

As Doyle points out, our maps are so effective that we forget they are just maps, and not the world itself. Now that we are beginning to understand the extent to which our maps or worldviews exist as powerful forces that affect the world, we also recognize that we can choose how we view the world and therefore how we shape it. Finding the worldviews, maps, and models that most accurately conform to reality, based on the broadest possible understanding of reality, supports a worldview that can help us transform the world so that it can work for 11 billion people. The humanature model—*humanity encompassing the world*—has utility in helping us to manage our thought and behaviour, individually and collectively.

The consciousness of semiotic life forms has played a profound role in creating an ecosphere fit for life, as Vernadsky realized. The evolutionary process was gradual, resulting in a balanced, global *Gaian* system with feedback loops that protected the whole over the part. If, for example, the population of any species moved out of balance by exceeding carrying capacity, its growth would be checked by predation or disease.

Although the level of attention the human collective has focused on the ecosphere has only been around for a few millenniums—a split second in geological time—we already see the effects it has, and the speed at which its impacts are felt. The Gaian feedback mechanisms have been disrupted by human intentions; one species has not only disrupted the whole, it has in a certain sense taken control of the processes that maintain the balance of the ecosphere. The only way to stop us, according to the Gaian model, is to cause a collapse that reduces our numbers, but human ingenuity allows us to avoid or delay this correction—to maintain the growth and conservation stage of the adaptive cycle as in panarchy theory—resulting in an ever more palpable threat to the ecosphere. This brings into clear relief the need to attend to the right things lest we destroy the unity of planetary life and bring down civilization with it.

The thing is, humanity cannot retreat into a previous, animal state where we are just another species with limited global impact. There are too many of us and we know too much. The solution is not to relinquish our power but to learn to use it wisely. What we need to do is *to be more of what we are, not less*; not more like animals but more fully human, more intelligent, wiser, more morally sensitive agents for the transformation of reality.

So as much as we are—and should be—skeptical that we have the information or understanding or ethical capacity to undertake planetary engineering, the fact is, we are doing just that. We have to shift the focus of collective human attention from either a human-centric or ecocentric approach to an encompassing approach. We have to recognize the powerful influence of human consciousness and learn to adjust our influence on the outer world by shaping our inner world in new ways. We must form a model of the world in which the planet is identical with our selves.

We get the future we imagine. The solution begins by seeing ourselves as who we are: an interconnected human reality whose inner, subjective experience transforms our outer world. Our inner world must develop the qualities that we want to see in the outer world. If we want the outer world, the ecosphere, to be a harmonious, balanced, well functioning system we have to become whole, harmonious, balanced individuals who are participants in whole, harmonious, balanced communities and institutions. If we want the global ecosphere to function harmoniously, *humanity* has to function harmoniously at a global scale.

We will get the future we imagine. We bring about a sustainable future by seeing ourselves as an interconnected human reality whose inner experience transforms the outer world. Our inner world must manifest the qualities we want in the outer world.

An ethic modelled on the struggle for survival through a competition for power is now clearly counterproductive. The alternative is to reimagine power in terms of service. We become truly free human agents by imagining ourselves as servants rather than masters of the ecosphere.

We are free beings, potentially. But the fact is we are perpetually imprisoned by limiting thoughts and desires. As has been fully discussed in previous chapters, materialism, power seeking, status seeking, competitiveness, addictions, traumas, and other preoccupations have taken over our inner and outer realms, rendering us destructive. Our preoccupations are not worthy of a human being, who should be a free actor who uses her or his unique freedom to serve the welfare of the world. We are obliged to set aside counterproductive thoughts, worldviews, programming, and habits and seek out new worldviews, models, and corresponding behaviours that will make us new human beings fit for life in a 11 billion world.

WHAT IS A HUMAN BEING?

We have looked at the idea that humans are meaning makers; that we use models and maps and metaphors to make meaning; that the meaning we make affects the world; and that the notion that human beings encompass the world is a meaningful model that can assist us to carry forward an ever advancing civilization by helping us protect the ecological balance of the planet.

We can look at this idea of encompassing from another viewpoint: Human beings are themselves a model or microcosm of the world—quite likely the best model. The universe is folded within us. By reading our own reality we see the structure of the world and can ultimately learn how we must think and act to make the world work for 11 billion people.

In a previous chapter it was mentioned that some of our leading scientists have adopted a very limited view of the human reality, comparing the human race, for example, to "mold on a shower curtain." Perhaps this serves some constructive purpose by undercutting human hubris. Yet it clearly misses the point, since the human being, with its large brain, is the most complex and sophisticated being known—the more so when we consider humanity collectively.

A typical healthy human brain contains about 200 billion nerve cells, or neurons, linked to one another via hundreds of trillions of tiny contacts or synapses. It is at these synapses that an electrical impulse travelling along one neuron is relayed to other neurons. Each neuron may make tens of thousands of synaptic contacts with other neurons.

Researchers at the Stanford University School of Medicine[272] have used state-of-the-art imaging in brain-tissue samples to quickly and accurately locate and count the myriad connections between nerve cells in unprecedented detail, as well as to capture and catalogue those connections' surprising variety. Observed in this manner, the brain's overall complexity is almost beyond comprehension, says Stephen Smith, a professor of molecular and cellular physiology. "One synapse, by itself, is more like a microprocessor—with both memory-storage and information-processing elements—than a mere on/off switch. In fact, one synapse may contain on the order of 1,000 molecular-scale switches. A single human brain has more switches than all the computers and routers and Internet connections on Earth."

In particular, the cerebral cortex—a thin layer of tissue on the brain's surface—is a thicket of prolifically branching neurons. "In a human, there are more than 125 trillion synapses just in the cerebral cortex alone," says Smith. That's roughly equal to the number of stars in 1500 Milky Way galaxies. Collectively, we have more synapses than there are stars in the known universe (and there are a lot of stars, some 70 sextillion.). Our computational power allows us to make ever more sophisticated models of the universe, projecting back to the Big Bang and forward to the Big Crunch—virtually encompassing the universe.

Beyond this mental mapping, the factors that unite humanity and the physical world are equally remarkable. Our separateness from the world is merely an idea; we are intimately connected with everything. And while we can say that humanity encompasses the world, we must also say that the world inhabits us. Our inner world shapes the outer world and the outer world deeply affects our 'inscapes.'

Respiration provides an apt example of this unity. According to biologist Tyler Volk, a person exhales roughly 5×10^{20} [500 million trillion] molecules of CO_2 per breath. "When these new CO_2 molecules leave your mouth, they begin dispersing in the air. The entire atmosphere, from the North Pole to the South Pole, is stirred in about a year, so within that year the molecules you added from each exhalation are evenly distributed into the very air you will later breathe back in. To put the number 5×10^{20} in perspective, assume that you live in the mid latitudes of the northern hemisphere and that you exhaled at the end of the summer's growing season, say in October. By the start of the next spring, the mixing in the atmosphere is essentially complete within the hemisphere. The green leaves that grow in the spring draw on CO_2 from the atmosphere as their source of carbon for the organic molecules they make, including cellulose and thousands of other kinds of molecules. Each and every leaf that grows will incorporate into its body a few dozen atoms of carbon that came from one particular exhalation you made during the previous fall."[273]

Our common genetic heritage with other living things reinforces this unity. It is perhaps not that surprising that we share about 90-95 percent of our DNA with chimpanzees, but certainly surprising that 88 percent is shared with mice,

73 percent with zebra fish, 47 percent with fruit flies, 25 percent with rice, and 18 percent with baker's yeast.[274]

Genomes overlap to the extent that to understand the human genome, researchers collect genomic data not just from humans and their closest relatives but also from every far-flung branch of the tree of life.[275] Genetic research has shown, for example, that certain segments of 'ultraconserved' DNA in humans—sections that have stayed exactly the same throughout recent vertebrate evolution and are identical in humans, rats, and mice—can be traced back to a group of ancient fishes. Efforts to understand the mechanisms of evolution benefit from getting as much genetic information on as many diverse organisms as possible. As scientists learn more about the extent of DNA conservation throughout the living world they are teasing out a deeper comprehension of the human genome. That's why the US National Human Genome Research Institute added, for example, a fly and a worm to its ENCODE project, which is cataloguing all functional parts of the human genome.

Human beings might also be thought of as communities of species. It has been estimated that only 10 percent of the cells in our bodies are actual human cells. We are made up of 10 trillion cells but we carry about 10 times as many microorganisms inside our bodies as our own human cells. Most of these are bacteria found in our gut; they take some of our energy but protect their host from harmful, pathogenic bacteria and produce vitamins and hormones that are crucial to our well-being.[276]

The powerhouses of our cells, mitochondria, are organelles that retain their own small genome, which shows substantial similarity to bacterial genomes. Mitochondria reproduce independently of the human cell cycle. The fact that our bodies are powered at the cellular level by something that is not exactly *us* generates some profound questions about human identity. In *Lives of a Cell* the physician Lewis Thomas ponders the fact that his own cells are occupied by "strangers." "My mitochondria comprise a large proportion of me…. I suppose there is almost as much of them in sheer dry bulk as there is the rest of me…. They feel like strangers, but the thought comes that the same creatures, precisely the same, are out there in the cells of sea gulls, and whales, and dune grass, and seaweed…. Through them, I am connected; I have close relatives, once removed, all over the place."

The cosmos, as Carl Sagan put it, is quite literally within us. When *we* think of ourselves, of humanity as a whole, it is necessary to ask the question who or what this pronoun *we* really refers to?

The anthropologist Gregory Bateson was a gifted teacher who challenged students of various kinds, artists or engineers for instance, to look deeply at the nature of reality and to identify patterns. In *Mind and Nature: A Necessary Unity*—the title says it all—he argues that the mental system that governs how we humans think and learn is the very same sort of system that governs the evolution and ecology of all life on earth. Insofar as we are a mental process, he says, we must expect the natural world to show similar characteristics of mentality. Thus, the human reality, i.e. thought, can be found throughout the natural world.

How is it that *we* can know anything, asks Bateson? "In the pronoun *we,* I of course included the starfish and the redwood forest, the segmented egg, and the Senate of the United States." The *knowing* we humans are self-consciously aware of is active everywhere, in all creatures. "In the anything which these creatures variously know, I included 'how to grow into five-way symmetry,' 'how to survive a forest fire,' 'how to grow and still stay the same shape,' 'how to learn,' 'how to write a constitution,' 'how to invent and drive a car,' 'how to count to seven,' and above all, 'how to evolve,' because it seemed to me that both evolution and learning must fit the same formal regularities or so-called laws."

Bateson was transcending a line supposed to enclose the human being. There is a *wider knowing* which is a glue holding together starfishes and sea anemones and redwood forests and human institutions. "There is a single way of knowing which characterizes evolution as well as *aggregates* of humans.... Mind became, for me, a reflection of large parts and many parts of the natural world outside the thinker.... On the whole, it was not the crudest, the simplest, the most animalistic and primitive aspects of the human species that were reflected in the natural phenomena. It was rather the more complex, the aesthetic, the intricate, and the elegant aspects of people that reflected nature." It was not the greed and so-called animal instincts that Bateson recognized on the other side of that mirror, over there, in nature. He was seeing the roots of human symmetry, beauty, aesthetics, the human being's very aliveness and wisdom. He noted that the theories of man that start from the most animalistic and maladapted psychology turn out to be improbable first premises from which to answer the psalmist's question: "Lord, What is man?"

The anthropologist Wade Davis points out that there are thousands of peoples and thousands of cultural perspectives on what it means to be human. The reflections of Gregory Bateson seem similar to indigenous interpretations that recognize a unity of all life forms, including we human storytellers. For these cultures, people are enfolded in the greater Earth system, like an embryo in its mother. This is in stark contrast to the dominant worldview today that, as Lewis Thomas put it, "the earth is man's personal property, a combination of garden, zoo, bank vault, and energy source, placed at our disposal to be consumed, ornamented, or pulled apart as we wished. Mastery over nature, mystery and all, was a moral duty and social obligation."

In more recent times, as this approach to living on this planet played out, Thomas points out that "we have been wrenched away from this point of view, recognizing instead that we are as dependent on the rest of life as are the leaves or midges or fish. We are part of the system." But even more recently, with each report of the International Panel on Climate Change, it seems that that eco-centric view isn't right either. "The degree to which we are all involved in the control of the earth's life is just beginning to dawn on most of us," says Thomas, "and it means another revolution in human thought...The truth is, we have become more deeply involved than we ever dreamed. The fact that we sit around as we do, worrying seriously about how best to preserve the life of the earth, is itself the sharpest measure of our involvement. It is not human arrogance that has taken us in this direction, but the most natural of natural events. We developed this way, we grow this way, we are this kind of species. We have become, in a painful, un-wished for way, nature itself."

These and perhaps other progressions in our models, our worldviews, call for "some quite fundamental changes in our attitudes toward each other, if we are really to think of ourselves as indispensable elements of nature we would surely become the environment to worry about the most."

What our understanding of ourselves leads to, then, is the realization of an essential unity within and without us. The human being is a highly complex system with unique capacity to model, understand, and transform itself and the world. Our sense of unity allows us to mentally, emotionally, spiritually, and even physically encompass our extended body, the ecosphere, Earth—which is very much like us. The lesson we learn from looking at ourselves reinforces the notion that unity should be our guiding principle. We need to be inwardly and outwardly united, knowing that this unity will be reflected in the ecosphere, the thin life zone that envelops Earth, our extended body. And just as we must learn how to look after ourselves to remain whole and healthy, we must now tend to the ecological balance of our planet. To do this, in a full world of 11 billion, we must become, essentially, a new type of human being, a new human race.

CHAPTER 13
CHANGING CHANGE

*You never change things by fighting the existing reality. To change some-
thing, build a new model that makes the existing model obsolete.*
— R. Buckminster Fuller

"You see before you, talking of the past, the academician Vavilov, but now
according to the opinion of the investigators, nothing but dung." On January 24,
1943, after two years of starvation rations and torturous interrogations, Nikolai
Vavilov muttered these words to his guards as he was admitted to the infirmary
of Saratov prison. Two days later, the Soviet scientist who had dedicated his life
to feeding the world died of starvation, one more victim of Stalin's purges.

"You would have to have no love whatever for your country," wrote
Aleksander Solzhenitsyn in *The Gulag Archipelago*. "You would have to be hostile
to it, to shoot the pride of the nation—its concentrated knowledge, energy and
talent! And wasn't it exactly the same … in the case of Nikolai Ivanivich Vavilov."

It has been said that every visit to every grocery store and farmer's market in
the world owes a debt to this man. Within the world's scientific community, in
his day, Vavilov was renowned for his tireless efforts to preserve the world's crop
diversity. Yet within the Soviet Union—as the chief scapegoat for the failure of
agricultural reforms—his efforts were rewarded with imprisonment and death.

Born in 1887 to a bourgeois family, as a youth Vavilov was infected by the
idealism of the times. While a student at the Petrovskaya Agricultural Academy
in Moscow, he wrote in his diary that he had decided to "commit his life to

understanding nature for the betterment of humankind." He pledged to "work for the benefit of the poor, the enslaved class of my country, to raise their level of knowledge." He believed science had to be used as a progressive social force, to be constantly verified and vigorously applied in the service of humankind. While a patriot, his world-embracing vision was evident through his international travels and collaborations, and his guiding vision of "a common bowl from which everyone could feed."

Valilov was among the first scientists to fully appreciate the importance of conserving humanity's agricultural heritage. What is more, he was a man of action. The leading plant geographer of the 20th century, Vavilov organized and took part in over 100 collecting missions from 1916-1941 in the major agricultural areas of the world, at times risking his life to find samples. He collected 50,000 wild plants and 31,000 wheat specimens for the seed bank of the Bureau of Applied Botany in Leningrad, now the Vavilov Institute (VIR). It was Vavilov who developed the theory that food crops were not domesticated at random but had originated from eight centres of high plant diversity.

By the time of his death, Vavilov and his colleagues at the Bureau had painstakingly assembled the world's largest plant genetic bank, a collection of 380,000 samples of 2500 species. Under the leadership of Vavilov, the Bureau had become an essential resource for plant breeders around the world. Ironically, this "enemy of the people" had done more for the reputation of the Soviet Union in scientific circles than any other.

Vavilov's "crime" was to defend Gregor Mendel's principles of genetics. Soviet scientists were forced to promote the notion that environmental conditions, not inherited qualities, were the sole determinant of plant—and human—traits. Vavilov's chief opponent was the strange figure Trofim Lysenko, a peasant who had ruthlessly climbed the ladder of Soviet scientific establishment. A pseudo scientist with little aptitude or training, and a lackey of Stalin, he ultimately rose to become head of Soviet agriculture with disastrous consequences. These he managed to blame on Vavilov, with the full support of the upper echelons of the Communist Party. With his forced victory over Vavilov, who rotted in prison, Lysenko attained cult status. His portrait hung in all scientific institutions. Art stores sold busts and cities erected monuments.

The inspirational quality of Vavilov's leadership is most clearly evidenced in what occurred after his imprisonment. The outbreak of WWII provoked a crisis at the Bureau. The capture of Leningrad was among Hitler's foremost preoccupations. With its director in prison and most of its top scientists jailed or murdered, and with most of its staff at the front or working on the construction of fortifications around Leningrad, those remaining faced an unprecedented challenge. As the city came under siege in 1941, the food supply ran out, as did fuel to heat the Bureau. When the bombardment commenced, the windows of the former Tsarist palace were smashed and had to be boarded up. This left the institute dark, damp, and cold, the worst conditions for seed preservation.

While Stalin moved decisively to relocate the massive art collection of the Hermitage, one of two great prizes sought by Hitler in Russia, he neglected the even more important seed collection of the Bureau, apparently unaware of Hitler's plan to relocate it to Germany.

Keeping the seeds viable under siege conditions was difficult, but preserving the 6000 potato varieties was near impossible. The potatoes had to be regrown yearly, but in 1941 the Bureau's potato fields were under bombardment. The winter of 1941-42 saw record low temperatures. Preventing the potatoes from freezing required round the clock vigils. The staff burned boxes, cardboard, paper, and debris from shelled buildings. Though numb from the cold and starving, they refused to eat the irreplaceable tubers.

The Bureau, with its tonnes of edible seeds and tubers, was surrounded by a starving population. To protect the collection, each sample was divided into duplicate parts. Some were trucked across frozen Lake Lagoda, the last route out of Leningrad, to safekeeping in the Urals. Other samples were divided and spread around 16 rooms. The rooms were sealed and the keys locked in a safe. To avoid the temptation to eat the seeds, no one was allowed to be alone.

The troubles did not end with the cold. An invasion of rats meant everything had to be transferred to metal boxes. Then in the spring of 1942, because of the cold and damp, the collection had to be regrown immediately. Despite the danger of shelling and bombing, several hectares of land were found and additional planting areas were created by removing paving stones from city sidewalks. These areas were dug, seeded, and harvested by hand, and the collection was saved.

Hunger was killing Leningrad's citizens by the thousands. The Bureau's scientists were no exception. Nine died after they refused to consume their collections. When the rice specialist died, his co-workers discovered thousands of packs of seeds he had preserved while succumbing to hunger.

Without the sacrifice of these scientists thousands of varieties of food crops, part of the common heritage of humankind, might have disappeared forever. It took 10 years after the war to return the VIR to full working capacity. Following the death of Stalin, Vavilov's reputation was rehabilitated and the Bureau was renamed in his honour.

Vavilov's 1926 essay *Centres of Origin of Cultivated Plants* was a landmark. Today's scientists have modified the Vavilov centres, but three were "bull's-eyes" according to a leading expert, Jack Harlan.

"The world of N.I. Vavilov is vanishing," said Harlan, "and the sources of genetic variability he knew are drying up. The pattern of variation may no longer be discernible in a few decades and the living traces of the long co-evolution of cultivated plants may disappear forever." Vavilov's world collection is his enduring legacy. The seeds in Leningrad, again St. Petersburg, are still in demand by plant breeders and those who would preserve the genetic diversity of the world's food plants from catastrophe, natural or man-made.

"Baked bread is savoury and satisfying for a single day," wrote Goethe, "but flour cannot be sown, and seed-corn ought not to be ground." Humankind has generally failed to follow this aphorism, which encapsulates the conservation ethic. Occasionally, some among us—like Vavilov—rise heroically to the challenge. The future hinges on our ability to foster the ethos of selfless service he exemplified.

THE PURSUIT OF POWER CORRUPTS

As the story of Vavilov and his institute illustrates, two opposing tendencies coexist in the human psyche: self-interest and an altruistic desire to serve others. Which of these we allow to dominate will determine the future.

Making our way toward a just and sustainable world of 11 billion will be a complex and difficult journey, even with an other-focused spirit of service as a core motivation. But as Vavilov discovered, that journey is that much harder when the road is mined with self-interest, greed, power seeking, and at times sheer malevolence. To move forward, we will have to muster the "better angels" of our nature and root out its dark side.

Among the chief obstacles that will have to be rooted out as we move forward is corruption, which has been described as "the single greatest obstacle to economic and social development around the world," as well as a major impediment to protecting the ecosphere.[277] Behind the political machinations that destroy heroes such as Vavilov and exalt crooks like Lysenko is a lust for power and money.

It has been estimated that $1 trillion is paid in bribes and an estimated $2.6 trillion is stolen through corrupt practices every year, equivalent to more than 5 percent of Gross World Product (GWP). According to the United Nations Development Programme, funds lost to corruption in developing countries are estimated at 10 times the amount of official international development assistance (ODA).

> *Corruption is the single greatest obstacle to economic and social development around the world and as a major impediment to protecting the ecosphere.*

Corruption is widespread. Nearly three quarters of 178 countries listed on the Corruption Perceptions Index score below five on the corruption scale, where 10 is very honest and zero very corrupt.

Corruption can reach to the highest levels of government. The value of assets stolen by corrupt leaders is staggering: former Indonesian president Suharto is thought to have embezzled up to US$35 billion; former Egyptian President Mubarak's personal fortune has been estimated as high as $70 billion. Trustworthiness alone might have transformed their nations.

Beyond the theft of public and private funds, corruption weakens governance and leads to a cascade of problems, from the proliferation of organized crime to human trafficking, arms and migrant smuggling, counterfeiting, and the trade in endangered species.

Corruption has a substantial impact on the ecosphere. Sectors particularly vulnerable include forestry, supplying water, oil, fisheries, and hazardous waste management. From embezzlement during the implementation of environmental programs, to corruption when permits and licenses for natural resources exploitation are issued, to the petty bribery of officials, corruption occurs at any and every level. Corruption also makes it possible for environmental and social safeguards to be ignored or bypassed.

Tax evasion can be another barrier to social-ecological progress. The world's shadow economy and legal economic activities that go untaxed now account for 16 percent of the global economy by one estimate. Greece, for example, loses

€15 billion a year to tax evasion. Its shadow economy is twice the size of its budget deficit. Tax evasion cost the US economy $3 trillion over the last decade.

Corruption affects average citizens indirectly and directly. In one survey covering 86 countries, over a 12-month period one in four people reported they had paid a bribe when they came into contact with at least one institution or service provider, from healthcare to education to tax authorities.

Corporate corruption is also rife. In a survey conducted by Ernst & Young, more than 40 percent of employees at the board or senior management level said sales or cost numbers had been manipulated by their company. This included reporting revenue early to meet short-term financial targets, under-reporting costs to meet budget targets, and requiring customers to buy unnecessary stock to meet sales targets.

Though often associated with low-income countries, corruption is universal. An estimated €120 billion is lost to corruption each year throughout the 27 EU member states. Out of more than 250 companies on the World Banks's running list of firms blacklisted from bidding on its global projects under its fraud and corruption policy, 117 are from Canada, with one company, SNC-Lavalin and its affiliates, representing 115 of those entries.[278] The United States was second with 44 companies on the debarment list.

Corrupt practices are often aided and abetted by "legitimate" corporations and governments. According to Global Witness, "Corrupt politicians, terrorists, arms traffickers, drug smugglers, tax evaders, and other criminals cannot commit their crimes if they can't move and launder their money." All rely on two tools to do this. The first is anonymous companies and trusts—the global getaway cars for crime, corruption, and tax evasion—which allow them to hide their identity. The second is banks and other professionals willing to do business with them. Shady practices by banks, and the governments that regulate them, aid and abet corruption and state looting.[279]

According to the Tax Justice Network, approximately US$11.5 trillion of assets were held offshore by high net-worth individuals, circa 2004; the annual income that these assets could earn amounts to approximately $860 billion annually; and taxes not paid are thought to exceed $255 billion each year.[280]

Secrecy in the oil, gas, and mining sectors allows the corrupt to steal billions. Nigeria, for example, has been in the midst of an oil boom for over 50 years; an estimated $400 billion has gone missing from oil revenues while the vast majority of Nigerians still live on less than US$2 a day. This was possible because the secrecy in which oil, gas, and mining deals are conducted allows corruption to flourish.

"Big oil and gas companies like Shell, Exxon, and Chevron are fighting hard to gut transparency laws and keep their business secret," according to Global Witness.

At the same time, companies and governments are routinely striking secretive deals for large areas of land and forests to grow the cash crops that feed soaring consumption in high-income countries. Over the past 50 years, the tropical logging industry has made a fortune but failed to deliver on decades of promises to log sustainably and bring economic development to the people living in and around the forests. Huge land deals are routinely made behind closed doors without the consent of local communities in Africa, Asia, and Latin America.

Global Witness also reports that multinational companies benefit from sourcing minerals from conflict-affected and high-risk areas around the world, resulting in misery for affected populations. These "conflict resources" enter global supply chains where they are traded, processed, and manufactured into a wide variety of consumer and industrial products such as laptops, cell phones, and jewelry.

Once again, we see how moral laxity undermines the social-ecological order. Efforts to build moral capacity will be required to shore it up.

THE FAILURE OF PARTISAN POLITICS

Governments are particularly prone to corrupt and unethical practices, in a variety of forms. A toxic mix of inflated egos, self-interest, vested interests, high stakes, and suspect ideologies fuels a highly partisan pursuit of power that is inimical to the public interest. While dictatorial regimes are particularly prone to corruption, liberal democracies are also at risk. A 2012 study at the University of Illinois calculated, for example, that 31 of the approximately 100 Chicago aldermen who had served since 1973 and four of the seven state governors had been convicted of corruption.[281] But corruption is not restricted to overt, criminal behaviour; it can be subtle.

Just under half the world's population live in what are considered democracies, including 11.3 percent in full democracies and 37.2 percent in flawed democracies. Over half live under authoritarian regimes (37.1 percent) or hybrid regimes (14.4) that have limited democratic characteristics.[282] But even in full democracies, vested interests often have undue influence over decisions. This happens because the democratic political systems that have evolved around the world are based on a competitive, partisan approach. Such systems can only work in the interest of those with the capacity to finance and mount campaigns to win over an often-gullible electorate—and the inflated egos to pull it off.

Even in the most democratic nations, the electoral systems are deeply flawed. Canada is considered among the most democratic countries in the world—it's ranked 8th on The Economist's Democracy Index. But the reality is that its apathy-inducing, first-past-the-post electoral system means that swaying a small minority of votes can translate into a majority government that can do essentially whatever it wants, regardless of public opinion.

In Canada's 2011 federal election, for example, just 61 percent of eligible voters voted. The winning party received 39.6 percent of the vote, which resulted in the formation of a strong majority government. In other words, the government's mandate is based on the support of just 24 percent of the adult population. With this mandate the government proceeded to gut Canada's environmental policies and legislation, including withdrawal from its international climate change commitments—actions that were counter to public opinion. The national government has since been rocked with a series of scandals reaching to the highest offices of the land.

Why don't more Canadians vote? The fact is that more and more people, and particularly young people, are disengaging from a partisan political process that seems irrelevant. When asked why they didn't participate in the 2011 election, 28 percent of non-voters said they just weren't interested. Another 23 percent were simply too busy. The rest said they were out of town, ill, or didn't like any of the candidates.

There must be better forms of governance, but how can we identify and establish a more effective alternative when the governments that would have to make the change are dominated by self-interested political parties? There's the rub.

The partisan electoral system also has negative impacts on politicians who may start out as idealists. They quickly find they have to adapt to a system that requires them to court interest groups, respond to lobbyists, continuously raise campaign funds, and participate in an intensely competitive system with another election always looming. It is a recipe that dampens idealism and fosters corruption.

Partisan systems favour vested interests. In the United States, for example, political partisanship has become so toxic that governments are dysfunctional. The partisanship is fuelled by vested interests that stand to gain from policies that favour low taxation and resource exploitation. Between 2008 and 2010, 30 big corporations paid more to lobby Congress than they paid in federal income taxes. Despite combined profits totalling $164 billion in that three-year period, the companies actually received tax rebates totalling $11 billion. Altogether, these companies spent nearly half a billion dollars over three years to lobby Congress—about $400,000 per day.[283]

The power of political lobbying in the US has historically been balanced against a ban on corporate campaign contributions and on corporate involvement in Political Action Committees. Now, however, Supreme Court rulings allow corporations to spend unlimited money to advocate for or detract from political candidates. In combination with lobbying efforts, the rulings give profit-driven entities substantial influence over the democratic electoral process. These developments have seemingly contributed to the intense partisanship that contributes to government dysfunction. Nevertheless, the United States is considered to be a "full democracy."

There is nothing wrong with corporations participating in the democratic process. Why fault them for looking out for their own interests? But short-term corporate and long-term public interests may not mesh. Government must represent everyone, including the vast majority who are not part of corporate elites, and always champion the public interest. Yet it would appear that in many jurisdictions dedication to the public interest is dwindling.

Corruption and partisanship are factors that undermine the ability of governments to respond effectively—or at all—to issues such as climate change where public and private interest are deemed to be different.

Climate change was first identified as a potential problem in the 19th century. US President Lyndon Johnson included an emphatic warning about climate change in a message to Congress in February 1965. That the highest levels of the government of the world's most prominent nation were aware of the global threat from anthropogenic climate change almost 50 years ago and little meaningful action has been taken since is profoundly disturbing.

In 1965, the concentration of carbon dioxide in the atmosphere was 320 parts per million, already well above pre-industrial levels. Almost 30 years later, in 1992, as CO_2 concentrations reached 355 ppm, 154 nations signed the United Nations Framework Convention on Climate Change (UNFCCC), which upon ratification would commit signatories' governments to a voluntary "non-binding aim" to reduce atmospheric concentrations of greenhouse gases.

These actions were aimed primarily at industrialized countries, with the intention of stabilizing their emissions of GHGs at 1990 levels by the year 2000. One early signatory was President George H.W. Bush, who called on world leaders to translate the written document into "concrete action to protect the planet." Three months later, the US Senate unanimously ratified the treaty.

According to terms of the UNFCCC, having received over 50 countries' instruments of ratification, it entered into force March 21, 1994, as CO_2 concentrations approached 360 ppm.

Perceiving a threat to the status quo, deniers of climate change financed by the fossil fuel industry shifted into high gear. Three large American industry groups set to work on strategies to cast doubt on climate science. Even though oil industry scientists had declared, as early as 1995, that human-induced climate change was undeniable, the American Petroleum Institute, the Western Fuels Association, and a Philip Morris-sponsored anti-science group called TASSC all drafted and promoted campaigns of climate change disinformation. From 1992-2002, another group called the Global Climate Coalition—funded by ExxonMobil, Royal Dutch Shell, British Petroleum, Texaco, General Motors, Ford, DaimlerChrysler, the Aluminum Association, the National Association of Manufacturers, the American Petroleum Institute, and others major emitters of GHGs—spent millions to spread confusion on this issue.

By the end of 2009 the Convention had been signed by 192 nations, but most were now backtracking on commitments and vigourously avoiding meaningful action. Atmospheric CO_2 reached 390 ppm in 2010 with no progress of any kind being made on emissions reductions, despite overwhelming evidence supporting climate change theory and the fact that almost every nation had openly professed their concern and entered conventions to reduce emissions.

According to the Global Carbon Project, CO_2 emissions from fossil fuel combustion and cement production reached 9.7 gigatons in 2012, the highest annual total ever. While international agreements called for emissions to be reduced below 1990 levels, emissions were in fact 58 percent higher than in 1990.[284]

One reason for inaction was the reemergence of a pattern of denial that can be seen throughout the history of climate change science. More recently, however, the deniers were not motivated by ignorance. These were the deliberate efforts of vested interests—corporate and political—who were prepared to disregard the general welfare of humankind in order to protect their perceived interests.

The inability or unwillingness of most governments to act on climate change is a sad illustration of the ineffectiveness of contemporary political arrangements. The reality is that governments cannot deal with climate change because changing the practices that cause it—like burning fossil fuels—would be contrary to the interests of their backers, the plutocrats who own and operate the coal, oil, gas, transportation, and other energy intensive industries. Governments of course are complicit because their revenues depend on income from the exploitation of fossil fuel resources and all areas of the economy energized by fossil fuels. But the vast majority, especially those in the middle and upper income brackets, are also complicit having bought in to a political order that is morally bankrupt.

REJECTING THE PURSUIT OF POWER

The current socioeconomic order rewards and reinforces complacency, since doing nothing serves the status quo. At some point, however, demand for change will outweigh complacency as real world impacts from climate change and other major problems intensify. At that late hour, we will have to act, on a global scale, simultaneously in every community, as one united world community, to radically alter our behaviour, including the way that we govern ourselves.

Of course, no one knows how to achieve such a monumental task, given we have never done it before. Having said that, humanity has developed an array of principles and tools that at the very least point us in the right direction, that give us a place to start. The way forward involves identifying principles and processes to guide transformation at the levels of the individual, of communities, and of institutions, and, starting small, with a humble posture of learning, to move forward, reflect on what we have done, and adapt the processes as we go.

While the transformation may take decades or centuries to complete, any quick solution would not go deep enough.

Certainly, new forms of governance are needed to foster a new ethos, but what political approach will help achieve this?

The ineffectiveness of government in dealing with the big issues facing an 11 billion world makes it increasingly apparent that we cannot hope to achieve a just and sustainable world by employing the methods and models that generate the present dysfunctional order. We cannot hope to replace an order that is defective due to its power-seeking dynamic using the dynamic that makes it defective.

Transformation cannot be achieved using traditional political means that feed on the inclination to pursue power, rather than rewarding humble public service. In the future, leadership will be synonymous with service, not power. In an 11 billion world new forms of governance—and new means of selecting governments—will ensure that the commonweal is valued above private interests.

> *Transformation cannot be achieved using traditional political means that feed on the pursuit of power. In the future, leadership will be synonymous with service, not power.*

While the global dilemma presented in this book may appear to call for revolutionary political change, history informs us that a revolutionary power shift typically results in a new order resembling the one that was overthrown: kill the tsar and raise up a Stalin. Violent change is utterly contrary to the goal of achieving a peaceful and harmonious civilization. But democratic political change through electoral politics, through political parties that are no more than alliances for power, is also antithetical to our objective. We need more sophisticated approaches to change than conventional political models can provide, approaches that move beyond a culture of contest. Substantive change will not come until the underlying paradigm of power is replaced.

"You never change things by fighting the existing reality," as systems theorist R. Buckminster Fuller famously put it. "To change something, build a new model that makes the existing model obsolete." I said at the outset of this book that adding another 3.7 billion to an already overburdened world will force everyone to change everything. We will even have to change *change*, because the *way* we make change influences the outcome of the change process.

Critically, new models, including our change model, must break with conventional approaches that revolve around a self-interested pursuit of power and the accumulation of wealth, motivations that are a critical defect in the current model. To be clear, power itself is not the problem. Nor is wealth. We need power and wealth—more than ever before—to transform society. Our new social-ecological model must, however, reject the notion of *pursuing* power over others. Similarly, it must reject the desire to amass wealth at the expense of others or of ecological sustainability.

Instead, we need a model that aims to release the power of individuals, of communities, and of institutions by building their capacity, especially their moral capacity, to contribute to an ever-advancing civilization. The new model will also address the capacity to generate wealth in ways that genuinely contribute to the commonweal, including increased ecological resilience. And to do this, we will need to redefine our understanding of wealth itself.

In brief, the new model must reject inordinate self-interest. It will focus instead around a set of values that include humility, service, self-sacrifice, self-control, moderation, detachment, generosity, trustworthiness, compassion, cooperation, and truth seeking—values that can only be fostered through effective moral education.

Building a model focusing on these higher ideals is not utopian. It is the only realistic way forward in a world of 11 billion.

CHAPTER 14
INTELLIGENT IDEALISM

First the thing is impossible, then improbable, then unsatisfactorily achieved, then quietly improved, until one day it is actual and uncontroversial. It starts off impossible and it ends up done. - Adam Gopnik

Idealism, a belief in the pursuit of perfection as an attainable goal, is often scoffed at and associated with utopian thinking or naiveté. But people differ from animals in their ability to use the elements of culture—from language, shared tools, and institutions to philosophical enquiry and the scientific method—to shape a reality partly of their making. We are human because we do not entirely accept the fate of animals, to live immersed in an environment to which they merely adapt. We are human because we change our environments to suit us. In other words, idealism makes humans a unique order of being.

People use two forces to shape their reality: intelligence—their capacity to understand reality, the world as it is—and idealism—their capacity to imagine something thought to be better, the world as it should be. Positive transformation occurs when people come to an accurate understanding of the nature of some part of their reality, envision an ideal, and take effective action to change the current reality to something closer to that ideal. This is a continuous loop, as reflection on change becomes part of the new understanding of what is. To use a simple example: We are cold; we build a fire; we assess how we feel; we adjust the size of the fire.

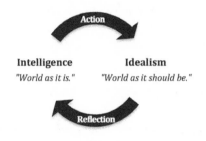

Action

Intelligence   Idealism
"World as it is."   *"World as it should be."*

Reflection

Of course, there are all kinds of obstacles to smooth transitions from reality to ideal. What may limit us—and this is nowhere more evident than in the current global social-ecological crisis—is that our understanding of the world as it is is not complete. Reality is not so obvious that we all easily agree on what it is. We do not have a consensus on what is known to be true or how to interpret what we do know, at least with certainty. Neither do we have agreement about what an ideal condition would be.

Ironically, the more we learn about reality, the more we find it to be more complex than imagined; and since everything we do has unexpected consequences, the realization of ideals is a tricky business. Back to the example of fire: it may solve the problem of being cold but we soon realize it requires continuous efforts to supply fuel, plus it's smoky, which calls for a new set of actions.

So, how do we come to an accurate, collective understanding of our current reality? And how do we agree on a more ideal reality to move toward? And once we do, how do we initiate action?

Any significant advance in transforming reality will be marked by an increase in the capacity to think in terms of process. Too much focus is often placed on events (such as a protest march) or projects (such as political campaign) based on a mindset that derives satisfaction from the sense of expectation and excitement they generate. But authentic transformation involves a radical change of culture requiring sustained effort over decades.

A sustained transformation encompasses a number of interacting processes, each of which contributes its share to the movement of humanity towards a more ideal state. The lines of action associated with any given process provide occasion for events and from time to time activities take the shape of a project with a clear beginning and a definite end. However, if events and projects are not subordinate to the explicit needs of the processes unfolding, or if they are not consonant with its underlying values, they will yield little fruit over the long term.

A sustainable civilization will be one wherein the participants—individuals, institutions, communities—have developed the capacity and skills to think in terms of a sustained transformational process: continuously assessing reality, envisioning a better future, acting to achieve it, and reflecting on results, with ever-increasing sophistication.

UNDERSTANDING REALITY: THE FIRST STAGE OF TRANSFORMATION

In *Love, Power and Justice*, the philosopher William Hatcher elaborated a transformational process model based on his study of multiple approaches to change.[285] He outlined some basic elements of a process that might be employed at any level of society, from the arena of the individual to that of institutions and communities of all sizes. The process has four stages:

1. Developing a clear conception of the present reality: where we now stand.

2. Developing a clear conception of the goal or ideal condition we seek to obtain: where we want to go.

3. Developing a well conceived, staged process that if properly implemented will lead us from here to there.

4. Developing motivation strong enough to sustain this transitional process and overcome obstacles in the path.

The four stages of Hatcher's change model incorporate a six-step virtuous cycle of continuous movement from the current reality to a more ideal state. Before presenting these steps, Hatcher's notion of authenticity, which is critical for understanding the change model he proposed, should be explained.

Hatcher sees transformation as fundamentally a moral process since it requires movement from a set of relationships characterized by systematic injustices resulting from the pursuit of power (the current reality) to authentic relationships (a more ideal state.)

Authentic relationships between people are characterized by reciprocal connections based on a mutual recognition of the universal value that each shares as a human being, a value inherent in their essential nature. This value is based on their uniquely human capacities of consciousness, intellect, feeling, and will. The mark of authenticity in human relations is the presence of self-sacrificial love, or altruism. Moral qualities, including altruism, are products and generators of authentic relationships.

A relationship with any given category of existence is authentic to the degree that it is based on an accurate perception of a shared reality. Authentic relationships between people are based on the perception that each has high and equal value. An authentic relationship with the ecosphere would flow from an accurate conception of the reality of the ecosphere—of its values—and of the relationship between it and us.

In the process of change, we seek to apply the moral principles required to achieve authenticity. Parents for instance would apply principles such as love, justice, compassion, and forgiveness as required to raise their child, in ways that help the child achieve her full potential and become a contributing member of the family and community. Institutional leaders would apply a similar set of principles to build capacity in personnel and allow them to play an effective role within the context of the institution. In relation to their land, farmers would value and sustain ecological functions while also achieving their economic goals.

> *A relationship with any given category of existence is authentic to the degree that it is based on an accurate perception of a shared reality.*

An authentic relationship is true and trustworthy, not merely an imitation of social norms but understood and felt genuinely, and it generates constructive action. As a father, for instance, I understand my role and responsibility in my familial relationship and take concrete action to lovingly support the growth and development of my children.

Authentic relationships derive from an accurate perception of the reality of that relationship coupled with a conscious will to act on the basis of that perception. Action is proof of the accuracy of the perception (if you don't do anything constructive it is likely you didn't really understand yourself and the relationship.) Although no one can ever fully understand the reality of any relationship, authentic relationships evolve progressively toward a fuller understanding. An ever-advancing civilization would be one that promotes the continuous search for truth about the nature of reality.

A SIX-STEP VIRTUOUS CYCLE

With the concept of authenticity in mind, let us consider the six steps in Hatcher's change process model. While primarily aimed at the level of individual relationships, the model applies to their role in institutional or community change as well.

Step 1 - Investigating the Present Reality – We make efforts to increase our awareness of the present condition of our self and the relationships we find ourselves in. This involves an investigation of the reality of our and others' perceptions, thoughts, and feelings about a situation. We can also look at our current motivations, desires, and actions. We attempt to gather factual information, making an effort to avoid bias. In this initial step, we ask *what* questions:

- What am I (or others) currently thinking or feeling about a situation?

- What are our goals? What is being done to achieve them?

- How am I (or others) behaving? Is this part of an entrenched pattern?

- Do we really want change?

Step 2 – Gaining Insight and Understanding – We now seek explanations, interpretations, and causes for the facts found in Step 1 and uncover patterns of relationships between and among these facts. As we move from perceptions to conceptions, from descriptions to theories, and attempt to understand the inner models underlying observed fact, *why* and *how* questions are asked:

- What are the most reasonable explanations for why we act the way we do?

- What are the assumptions we are working on?

- Are these reasonable, conscious, unconscious, known unknowns, etc.?

- What are the possibly unconscious feelings and attitudes most likely to have produced the observed behaviour?

- What ends do the observed behaviour really tend to serve (regardless of stated or presumed intentions)? What is the payoff or reward sought?

- What desires appear to motivate the behaviour?

- What needs and desires are fulfilled by the behaviour?

Step 3 - Envisioning What Could and Should Be – Now we envision the ideal, both the possible and the desirable, and compare our understanding of the current reality with it. We now ask *value* questions, *which* questions. We morally evaluate the current reality, judging and assessing it in the light of an ideal standard.

- Which values/virtues are present and absent in the current situation?

- If the situation were ideal, what characteristics would it have?

- How would my point of view/inner model be different if I were functioning in an ideal manner?

- Which elements of the current situation represent an authentic relationship to self and others (including the ecosphere), i.e. a relationship based on an accurate understanding of reality and a genuine concern for human well-being and the ecosphere?

- Any given pathological (inauthentic) condition involves some combination of ignorance (lack of understanding), immaturity (lack of development), or sickness (improper development). Which of these factors predominates in the current situation?

- Now, how would I/we feel in the ideal situation? Are we attracted to these ideal feelings? Are we capable of giving ourselves to such feeling and, if not, what fears might we need to face?

Step 4 – Selecting a Plan of Action - From among these various possible ideal configurations we formulate a plan of action that will help us move concretely, practically, and incrementally toward that ideal. We consider which values we should choose to implement with regard to this situation.

- Among the virtues and values lacking in the present situation, which are most needed?

- Which virtue, if implemented, has the greatest potential for affecting constructive change?

- Which virtues or values are the most reliable in the light of, first, the need of the current situation and second, the inner resources we possess or can acquire within a reasonable length of time?

- What practical steps can I/we take toward implementing the values and virtues chosen?

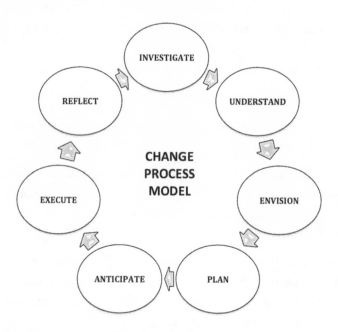

It is unrealistic to think we can move, in one step, from a relatively low level to a high level of authentic functioning. It is better to be realistic about our expectations and make some genuine progress than to pursue an unrealistically high ideal and fail completely. In fact, it is better not to think in terms of success or failure, but to consider learning the goal.

Step 5 - Identifying and Anticipating Barriers to Change – We now strive to anticipate those conditions of our lives most likely to challenge our intent to change. We ask mainly *how* questions.

How can I/we prepare to face and overcome our own and others resistance?

- What perceptions of self and others might I/we have to relinquish?

- What reactions to my/our changed behaviour do I/we anticipate?

- How can the degree of love and unity necessary to accomplish the action and sustain the resulting change be generated?

- How much resistance do I/we feel to making this change?

- Do I/we have the courage to actualize the given virtue?

- What kind of internal or external supports do I/we need to help sustain change?

Step 6 – Executing the Action, then Evaluating the Reaction – We now execute the contemplated action with as much awareness, deliberateness, and naturalness as possible and then evaluate the results of having done this. Now we ask:

- How effective was I/were we in accomplishing the intention?

- How did people react?

- What went through my mind as I acted? What about others?

- What emotions were felt? Do I/we feel good or bad and why?

- Has the situation moved closer to the ideal?

- What is the new situation as a result of the action?

As we evaluate we come to an understanding of the new reality, which may call for a return to Step 1.

Of course, in a larger–scale process we would be working on various aspects of change on a number of fronts simultaneously, at different speeds, and multiple cycles would be in place. Such a process would require spaces to be created to foster ever-wider participation by individual, institutions, and communities.

MULTIPLE WAYS OF UNDERSTANDING REALITY

This change model begins with efforts made to understand the world as it is. The problem that immediately arises is the immense difficulty in understanding the true nature of the reality in which we find ourselves, and especially coming to a collective understanding.

Few of us fully understand the reality we find ourselves in. Our systems of education, public discourse, media, and governance are not designed to help us gain an accurate understanding. In fact, as described in previous chapters, obfuscation is often actively promoted. Similarly, it is difficult to envision a more ideal future, especially one that most of us agree is worth striving for. In fact, social pressures often have us pursuing a future inimical to our authentic needs in order to meet those of some vested interest.

Public discourse is also biased and unbalanced in part because is does not validate a wide variety of ways of understanding our reality. To gain an accurate understanding we will have to be open to multiple ways of knowing. Observation of facts, using the scientific approach, is obviously important, but as the questions above suggest, an effective change process will have to account for factors such as emotions, values, or experiences that may lie at least partly outside the purview of sense perception.

Following is a brief overview of ways of knowing that can help build a common, authentic understanding of reality.

The Empirical Method – The empirical method, using sense-derived observation and experiment, not theory, to accumulate knowledge, is usually considered the most accurate and credible

> To gain an accurate understanding of reality and to form authentic, common ideals, we have to be open to multiple ways of knowing.

means of coming to an understanding of reality. Empiricists consider sense perception so important that they say that all authentic knowledge comes from the senses (aided by instrumentation.)

While the value of the empirical method is clear and does not require further elaboration, it offers an incomplete understanding of reality. Its limitations include simple ignorance: First, we don't and probably can't know everything there is to know; second, it is impossible to say with certainty that what we know is accurate given we don't know what we don't know. Science always provides an incomplete understanding of reality because, by its nature, its interpretation of reality is never static. We see current scientific theories and paradigms as *true*, when the best we can actually do is to say that the current understanding is simply the way things appear to be and accept that this too is likely to change. Attachment to what is currently understood through the empirical approach can be a significant obstacle to the ongoing evolution of our understanding.

Another limitation of science is that it has little to offer in providing a sense of meaning and purpose, two things that fuel the movement toward ideals. In fact, the scientific establishment has determined that there is no meaning or purpose to reality beyond that which we arbitrarily assign to it.

What is more, science can only make a limited contribution, at least at this point in its development, to forming ideals since these involve fundamental moral questions dealing with complex choices of future states. Science is, at some fundamental level, indifferent in the area of morality. This is not to say scientists are amoral or unethical—though that can be another obstacle to achieving an accurate understanding or reality—but that science is about observation of what is and not what should be. Even where it can contribute to ideals, it lacks moral authority to do so.[286]

Another major obstacle to an accurate understanding of reality through science is bias. An observer always interprets. Whether you are rich or poor, male or female, Portuguese or Kenyan can affect your perceptions of reality. Our efforts to understand reality must include an investigation of the bias that led to our current understanding, including the bias that comes from being an expert. This implies that our movement to a more ideal reality will include efforts to identify bias and limit it to the extent possible while accepting that one bias is always replaced by another.

Yet another limitation of the scientific approach is that it is biased toward technological solutions. People who are good at doing science generally have a certain bent that involves applying technical solutions to problems. Designating scientists as the experts inclines us to technological solutions when workable solutions may lie elsewhere. Maybe a better solution is to change oneself, the way one thinks or feels, rather than the outer world.

Reason – Knowledge of anything is a product of both the thing observed (the object) and our mind (the subject), which smoothly completes our partial and limited experience of the world through a multitude of mostly unconscious simplifying assumptions. This is the inescapable human condition. As suggested in the previous paragraphs, our knowledge is always partially subjective (i.e. accompanied by mental constructs) no matter how exhaustive and precise may be the observations on which that knowledge is based.

Reason is the ongoing and deliberate attempt to become as aware as possible of our underlying assumptions. The goal of reason is to make our assumptions totally explicit. Reason explicitly acknowledges the relativity of one's point of view. Indeed, in making our own assumptions explicit, we become aware of other possible assumptions and the rationale for them. Moreover, making our assumptions explicit gives us greater autonomy and control over life processes. For once we have clearly identified our operational assumptions, we can apply logic to them and thereby predict their long-term consequences. With this knowledge, we can proceed to modify our assumptions in the light of the longer term, rather than just the short term, thereby optimizing our autonomy and functionality.[287]

Reason also has its limitations. We may err in our reasoning due to ignorance, bias or emotion, for example. It is also possible to overemphasize the value of reason, thus excluding other ways of knowing, resulting in an unbalanced view. Other values can trump reason: it may be reasonable to do something but some other value, such as love or hate, could override a reasonable approach.

Emotion and Intuition – What many would agree are the most important aspects of life, such as personal relationships, cannot always be understood intellectually, but have to be experienced emotionally. Love, for instance, may not be reasonable but it can guide us to a higher level of understanding of self and the world—or lead us into error.

Akin to emotion, intuition can be an important way of understanding reality; people have a highly developed intuition about cheating, for example, which is essential to forming relationships. Often one knows that certain things are not right ethically by way of gut feelings or intuition. Some problems are so complicated that other sources of knowledge are insufficient and one has to rely on feelings or intuition to make decisions. Of course, overreliance on emotions and intuition also present a danger of being overly subjective and must be balanced by appeal to additional ways of knowing.

Authority – We may gain an understanding of reality directly or indirectly from an authority understood to know more about something than we do. This can be an important shortcut. However, legitimacy is a key issue: is the source really authoritative or merely influential? Given the above comments about reason and objectivity, the status of an authority is always temporary at best. A political leader, eminent scientist, religious leader, or village elder may or may not possess true knowledge or wisdom. Authority can be bestowed through an illegitimate system of designation.

Cultural Knowledge/Language – Traditional knowledge transferred through culture provides another way of knowing. Wade Davis sees the world's cultural or language groups as unique and profound responses to a fundamental question: What does it mean to be human and alive?

"When asked that question," says Davis, "the peoples of the world respond with 7,000 sources of knowledge and wisdom, history and intuition which collectively comprise humanity's repertoire for dealing with all the challenges that we'll face as a species in the coming centuries." Together, these cultures convey "a vast archive of knowledge and expertise, a catalogue of the imagination, an oral and written language composed of the memories of countless elders and healers, warriors, farmers, fishermen, midwives, poets, and saints. In short, the artistic, intellectual, and spiritual expression of the full complexity and diversity of the human experience."[288]

The telling and appreciation of stories and myths appears to be a formative element in human consciousness since the development of narrative skills plays a pivotal role in the process of building the human brain.[289] The ability to develop and use symbols and metaphor is among the things that make us human. While myths may be seen as a primitive attempt to explain the cosmos, they typically convey sophisticated concepts, which may explain their ongoing presence in art, literature, and psychology. Knowledge of myth can make an important contribution to our understanding of reality, so long as it is not confused with scientific explanation.

Many cultures use dreams and images produced through sensory and sleep deprivation, fasting, trance states derived through prayer and meditation, or perhaps hallucinogens, to gain an understanding of reality. Science may 'pooh-pooh' such notions, but is it scientific to reject the subjective experience of billions of people over thousands of years because the mechanism is not evident?

Cultural knowledge is subject to the same limitations as other forms of understanding. All knowledge evolves. Where cultural understanding no longer evolves in relationship to the variety of ways of knowing it loses value.

Art – The power and efficacy of art as a way of knowing has been proven by an array of models and exemplars drawn from different cultures and historical contexts. Art has potency for identifying, penetrating, synthesizing, and representing both natural and cultural phenomena.

Some of our most important insights and understandings are not transmissible through standard language or text. Consequently, art can be an essential tool for conveying subtle meaning. Art simultaneously addresses the mind and emotions, contributing to transformational processes and motivation. Art is a way of knowing reality as it is and as it should be through creative modelling of existing or newly imagined entities.[290]

Beauty is a fundamental goal of transformation to an ideal state, but a sense of what is beautiful is not entirely rational. It operates on multiple levels. Architecture, for example, operates in the realm of science and technology but also in ineffable qualities of artistic creativity.

Art's limitations are in many ways similar to those of other ways of knowing. As well, its particularly subjective quality can make it difficult to communicate the artist's interpretation of reality.

Contemplation/Meditation/Prayer – Contemplatives of various faiths have been engaged in the study of the impacts of meditation and prayer and recording observations over a period of several millennia. Contemporary science has studied these states of mind and corroborated aspects of the influence these practices can have on brain and body functioning.

Meditation can be seen in a materialistic way, as a method of focusing concentration and developing the capacities of the brain, or as a spiritual experience, in which attention in the here and now reduces sensory inputs, making it possible to connect with one's soul or with the divine. Prayer and meditation are means of detaching from mundane emotions such as anger or anxiety and elevating human consciousness.

Prayer is sometimes described as our effort to communicate with God and meditation as listening to God. These practices can inform the practitioner's understanding of reality thorough insights, thoughts, and imagery.

Because of the highly subjective nature of these ways of knowing, insights must be balanced or corroborated with other ways of knowing if they are to contribute with any certainty in our understanding of reality.

Non-rational knowing – Factors that cannot be easily explained by science or reason may nevertheless contribute to an understanding of reality. Chance favours the prepared mind, but dreams, serendipity, and intuition have played a role in many scientific discoveries, from the periodic table, the chemical transition of nerve impulses, and the theory of relativity to inventions like insulin, the sewing machine needle, and the Google search engine. "Mysticism and science meet in dreams," said E.O. Wilson. About the process of discovery Max Planck said, "the pure rationalist has no place here." Einstein said: "There is no logical way to the discovery of these elemental laws [such as relativity.] There is only the way of intuition, which is helped by a feeling for the order lying behind the appearance."

Rational and non-rational ways of knowing work well together in the creative process. As with the other modes of knowing, non-rational modalities must be tested against other modalities to avoid collapse into pure fantasy.

Religion – Religion is the idea that a non-material supreme being who created the universe communicates with humankind to assist us to understand and change our reality. Divine communication is thought to occur mainly through the revealed word of God, i.e. religious scripture; the oral teachings and example of the divine manifestations and other religious teachers; as well as inspiration received directly by individuals.

While some see religion as complementary to other means of understanding reality, such as science, the fact that prominent scientists are vigorously attacking the validity of religion as a way of knowing, while some religionists are attacking accepted scientific theories, brings the notion of complementarity into question.

God's reality or non-reality is not conditioned on the belief or non-belief of scientists, yet it is perhaps useful to know that the idea of God and religious belief is not as ludicrous as the "evangelical atheists" would have us believe— if the opinion of the scientific academy has credibility. While the activism of celebrity scientists has created an impression that scientists on whole have rejected faith, surveys show that belief in God among scientists is actually on the rise. The first survey that asked scientists about their religious views was conducted in 1914. At that time only 42 percent of those surveyed said they believed in God. According to a survey of 2500 members of the American Association for the Advancement of Science, published by the Pew Research Center in 2009,[291] a majority (51 percent) believed in God or a higher power. And belief in God was significantly higher among younger scientists, with about 66 percent of those under 35 believing in God.

In many cases, scientists accommodate religion via the principle of non-overlapping magisteria (NOMA) popularized by Stephen J. Gould. Gould defined a magisterium as "a domain where one form of teaching holds the appropriate tools for meaningful discourse and resolution." He describes NOMA as follows: "the magisterium of science covers the empirical realm: what the Universe is made of (fact) and why does it work in this way (theory). The magisterium of religion extends over questions of ultimate meaning and moral value. The two magisteria do not overlap, nor do they encompass all inquiry (consider, for example, the magisterium of art and the meaning of beauty)."

While Gould identified science and religion as too different realms of understanding he conceded that "the two magisteria bump right up against each other, interdigitating in wondrously complex ways along their joint border. Many of our deepest questions call upon aspects of both for different parts of a full answer—and the sorting of legitimate domains can become quite complex and difficult."

There is a great deal of revelation that offers tremendous insight into the nature of reality, not just an inner spiritual reality, but also social relationships and the natural order. Books such as the Bible, the Qur'an, or the Hindu and Buddhist scriptures are distinguished by their profound influence on human culture, from the arts to legal codes to everyday mores. While primarily metaphoric, these books are not without influence on scientific enquiry. Many scientific discoveries from the principles of physics to those of ecology were inspired or influenced by interpretations of scripture.

There are many things unexplainable through scientific enquiry alone, given there are many nonmaterial things. In fact, the things that are most important to us are intangible properties of human relationships, such as love, trust, and compassion. Even if we discover the biochemical or genetic origins of a force such as love, love remains a nonmaterial product of these processes that has to be understood in part by other methods of knowing than science can provide.

While it reveals an orderliness to the world at certain levels of organization, at another level science shows us that the material reality is itself a product of intangibles, those insubstantial, mysterious quantum possibilities which display indeterminate qualities in time and space. The world of quantum mechanics in fact creates an interesting possibility for the interaction of science and religion. Religious understanding is built on the idea that there is a nonmaterial, spiritual reality; science has disputed this idea, proposing that only material things that can be perceived by the senses exist. Along comes quantum mechanics which calls into question the very notion of materialism in the classical sense.

Werner Heisenberg, one of the founders of quantum mechanics said, for instance: "The ontology of materialism rested upon the illusion that the kind of existence, the direct 'actuality' of the world around us, can be extrapolated into the atomic range. This extrapolation, however, is impossible...atoms are not things."

Max Planck put it this way: "As a man who has devoted his whole life to the most clear headed science, to the study of matter, I can tell you as a result of my research about atoms this much: There is no matter as such. All matter originates and exists only by virtue of a force which brings the particle of an atom to vibration and holds this most minute solar system of the atom together. We must assume behind this force the existence of a conscious and intelligent Mind. This Mind is the matrix of all matter." Such concepts are compatible with religious understanding of a spiritual foundation of reality.

Religion's supposed resistance to the theory of evolution is much discussed, but the evolution of religion is not. Too often religious people become attached to a particular set of religious dogma and close their minds to other possibilities. However, if we think of religion as a whole, as an ongoing, evolving effort to understand reality, it is a much richer phenomenon.

One of the great stumbling blocks in the appreciation of religion is the often blatant contradictions between scripture and science. The idea of religion as an evolving understanding of reality can eliminate this contradiction. Scripture such as the Bible provided a sense of cosmic order for societies in an early stage of scientific enquiry; this is done through metaphor and myth that are nonsense when taken literally but profound when considered metaphorically. We may think, for example, of the genesis story as primitive and ridiculous by contemporary standards, but as a mythic tale it introduces the concept that the world was created in stages, providing a rudimentary concept of evolution.

Much of scripture is instructive in the area of spiritual or social mores and can be drawn on as a source of guidance in one's inner or social life. Religion provided an original source for legal codes, but few today would accept biblical law, for example, in its entirety, even those who say they are biblical literalists. Stoning people for blasphemy or adultery would be unimaginable in most contemporary Jewish or Christian societies. Religion evolves like every other aspect of life and a contemporary understanding of religious laws respects the notion of inalienable human rights.

The problem of religious fanaticism stems largely from the rejection of the notion that religion evolves, and that it develops in ways complementary to other modes of understanding reality. The very real problem of fanaticism can be eliminated by acknowledging this complementarity.

Consultation – Consultation combines the knowledge and insights of a range of participants, and potentially a wide range of perspectives, to shed light on any subject, helping to turn conjecture into certainty. It relies not only on the combined knowledge of the consultative group's members, but seems also to have a synergistic quality, where the whole is more than the sum of the parts. Depending on the range of participants, it can include all modes of knowing.

The main limitation of consultation comes when the range of participants lacks diversity, in which case the participants may merely reinforce each other's limited point of view. Consultation is also limited when the pursuit of power interferes with open participation and an unfettered dedication to seeking truth.

SCIENCE, RELIGION, AND MORALITY

Given the emphasis placed in this book on morality as an antidote to many of the problems that undermine an ever-advancing civilization, a few more words on the relationship of science and religion are in order.

Science and religion can be seen as complementary approaches to understanding reality. Science operates by identifying order—patterns, systems—in the otherwise spontaneous experience of concrete reality. Without a scientific perspective it would seem that "stuff just happens."

Science builds generalizations based on systematic observation coupled with creative interpretation or conceptualization of a series of observations, leading to the emergence of abstract general principles or laws. These are then tested using verification procedures.

The language of science is deliberately linear, progressively eliminating multiple meanings and metaphor. It is also minimalist, preferring whenever possible to reject non-observable factors to achieve explanations of observable configurations.

The strengths of the scientific approach to understanding reality are clarity, precision, and applicability to meeting needs (or fulfilling desires). Its weaknesses derive primarily from partialness and incompleteness, that is, it can lack a global vision of reality since it is necessarily focuses on those things that can be fully understood by its methods. For example, it cannot explain why anything should exist at all.

Modernity is built around the idea that it is possible to use the tools of science to generate a complete description of reality in exact, mathematical terms. The work of such figures as Newton, Maxwell, and Darwin at first suggested that this program might be successful. However, Heisenberg's uncertainty principle in physics, Godel's incompleteness theorem in mathematics and logic, and Penrose's strong thesis regarding the indeterminacy of the human brain dashed this hope. Hatcher points out that there is an inescapable trade-off between exactness, on the one hand, and completeness, on the other. In choosing exactness, science has thereby renounced completeness.

This observation brings us to the other way of knowing, the study of religious revelation, which has been universally employed throughout history to understand reality. Revelation refers to the teaching of spiritual educators carried in the wisdom traditions and religious texts of all cultures. Like science, this method of investigating reality aims to achieve an ever-increasing understanding of reality and to apply that understanding in pursuit of an ever-advancing civilization.

Unlike science, revelation begins with general, universal principles and then moves toward specific applications to human experiences. Its language is nonlinear (it makes extensive use of metaphor and multiple meanings) and maximalist (it is rich, with free reference to non-observables.) It offers a complete (though nonlinear and inexhaustible) description of the structure and dynamics of reality through metaphoric modelling. It can answer questions such as "why does anything exist at all?" Thus, its strengths are its adequacy and completeness—its ability to provide vision and offer moral direction; its limitations are its complexity, lack of clarity, and lack of exactness; it may be difficult to understand and thus to achieve agreement on meanings of stories and texts.

The study of science, said Hatcher, is about verification. It consists of confronting our experience of some aspect of objective reality, formulating propositions whose meaning is based on something that is clearly known, and then applying methods to verify the truth or falsity of the proposition. The study of revelation is about explication. We confront portions of texts, focusing on certain statements whose truths are clearly known, and then try to determine various linear meanings of these statements. For science, clarity of meaning is given *a priori* but truth is determined *a posteriori*. For revealed religion, truth is given *a priori*, but meaning is determined *a posteriori*. As opposites, the two are complementary ways of knowing.

In a general way, how would we apply these processes to the question, "how do we know if something is conducive to an ever advancing civilization?"

(which as previously proposed should determine if it is moral.) How are they complementary?

Let's take the issue of climate change. Science would provide us with the understanding of climate change and what its implications are likely to be. It could also help us to determine appropriate responses, such as reducing our emissions of greenhouse gases. Science then tells us that reducing emissions is conducive to achieving a sustainable social-ecological system, and that the lion's share of the adjustment must occur in wealthier, energy-intensive, consumer societies. As a rational, verifiable approach it is truthful. This can offer a type of motivation, which involves self-interest.

Religion would start by identifying a fundamental truth: the purpose of human life is to carry forward a civilization that supports people materially so they can pursue their investigation of reality, including their spiritual reality. Anything that undermines sustainability is immoral, since it ultimately limits human development. What is more, it is understood that all people share God-given value as equal members of the human family; in this light, since climate change will disproportionately affect the poor, it is immoral on that additional ground. Religion would then call on people, in particular the rich, to moderate their consumption in order to preserve the ecosphere and ensure continued development opportunities for the poor. Authentic faith provides another kind of motivation: to sacrifice self for the common good.

> *Together, authentic religion and authentic science can be conducive to human progress in ways neither could alone.*

Although starting from different perspectives, the two approaches come to similar conclusions, are highly complementary, and mutually reinforcing. The persistent, conjoint application of scientific verification on the one hand and careful, prayerful explication of revelation on the other yields the very thing we need for the successful prosecution of the human enterprise: truth, i.e. an accurate, useful, and adequate knowledge of reality.

Together, religion and science can be conducive to human progress in ways neither could alone. A proviso is that we are talking about authentic religion, not superstition, fanaticism, or dogmatism. Authentic religion can be seen as based in its texts but with the understanding of these texts evolving in dialogue with science. It is best to look on religions as part of a progressive continuum of spiritual thought rather than competing brands.

By the same token, there is authentic and inauthentic science. Science is often prostituted to vested interests, dominated by elites, dogmatic, and resistant to change. Science must be undertaken in the service of truth and for the betterment of humanity and the ecosphere to be considered authentic.

COMMON, AUTHENTIC IDEALS

To truly understand our current reality—the first step in the transformative process—we must employ a variety of ways of knowing; while all are prone to error, together they can yield a more reliable model of reality, particularly when they are honed through consultation.

Once we come to an understanding of our current situation, we can begin to form a picture of a more ideal state. The fact that we have developed a better understanding of the present reality is itself a step toward a more ideal state, since one of the most important objectives for any person, community, or institution is to attain a clearer understanding of the reality in which they operate.

Employing various ways of knowing to gain a deeper understanding of reality, where more of the assumptions we make have been made explicit, is likely to lead to a critique of that reality. That critique will naturally suggest some ideals to work toward. When we assess our situation as a community we may identify, for example, a high infant mortality rate; this is likely to result in a desire to reduce infant mortality. We then have to figure out how to achieve that. The action plan will again be informed by our analysis of reality, that high infant mortality is linked to poverty and low educational attainment. Thus, the means for achieving our goal is to reduce poverty, which is in turn linked to improved access to education. Now the task becomes mobilizing people to make this happen—often the most difficult step in the transformational process.

The planning and action stages of the change process will also be informed by our open pursuit of multiple ways of knowing. This does not mean that everyone has to fully subscribe to each way of knowing, that the strict empiricist must necessarily embrace religion, for example. It does require a willingness to respect and draw from all points of view in an open consultative process.

As previously stated, this transformation process must be applied at the level of the individual, the community, and institutions, such as institutions of governance. Using the various ways of knowing described above will generate a set of ideals that apply at each of these levels.

There is a high degree of complementarity in the process and, I believe, our multiple ways of knowing point to three overarching ideals or objectives for humankind:

- To achieve a complete understanding of reality.

- To carry forward an ever advancing civilization.

- To develop the capacities required to achieve these objectives.

These objectives are tightly linked in the following way:

- It is the nature of human consciousness to strive to understand reality.

- Building this understanding is necessarily collaborative: we cannot achieve this understanding alone but only in the context of an ever-advancing civilization.

- If our ultimate objective is to achieve a complete understanding of reality—enlightenment in religious terms—we must sustain civilization until this understanding is achieved.

- We must therefore develop certain capacities needed to sustain civilization. These capacities are both material and spiritual in nature.

- Among these capacities are moral qualities—virtues in religious terms—conducive to the functioning of a highly complex, diverse, and global social-ecological system.

- Developing these capacities requires that we understand ourselves.

- Understanding ourselves is a key to understanding reality.

- Understanding ourselves and the universe and developing the capacities, including moral capacities, needed to sustain civilization can only be achieved through education: we have innate capacities but they are merely potential unless they are developed through educational processes.

- Education is the means by which we develop capacity to understand ourselves and the universe and foster the qualities of character needed to sustain this process in perpetuity.

- Our educational process must help us balance the material and spiritual aspects of civilization.

- The educational process evolves in response to our growing understanding of reality and through its response to the needs of an ever-advancing civilization.

To understand the nature of the interacting processes that, in their totality, engender progress toward an ideal we must bear in mind that progress is achieved through the development of three protagonists in the change process—the individual, institutions, and communities. The implications of these common ideals for the three proponents might be summarized as follows:

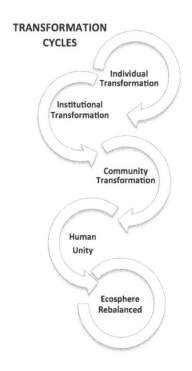

TRANSFORMATION CYCLES

Individual Transformation

Institutional Transformation

Community Transformation

Human Unity

Ecosphere Rebalanced

- This set of objectives and processes draws the individual into an investigation of her or his outer and inner reality. While material well-being for self and immediate family is a continuous concern, the adoption of higher ideals allows the individual to balance material requirements with the development of the inner world of the mind, heart, and soul. For the individual, the highest level of attainment becomes development of self with the aim of service to the community, which is where one engages with the process of supporting the advancement of civilization.

- For the community, creating an environment that fosters the material and spiritual development of its citizens becomes paramount. In addition to promoting equitable access to basic material requirements, the community creates spaces that facilitate education, consultation, action, and reflection, with sustainability—the understanding that future citizens are equal members of community—as a key consideration in its discourse.

- Institutions foster and channel individual and collective capacities to efficiently and fairly organize material and human resources. They facilitate public discourse and consultation in order to advance ongoing education for all ages and segments of the community, aiming to promote the goals of enlightenment and sustainability.

The next chapters will consider several examples of holistic educational and community development models that address the issues raised in this book by animating individuals, institutions, and communities to better understand their reality and to move toward a more ideal world.

CHAPTER 15
HOMO MORALIS

If you are planning for a year, sow rice; if you are planning for a decade, plant trees; if you are planning for a lifetime, educate people.
– Chinese Proverb

This book began with the disquieting observation that 11 billion people will populate this planet by century's end. Given that 7.2 billion of us are already overshooting Earth's capacity by 60 percent, it was predicted that increasing the population by 50 percent would force everyone to change everything.

Although I said pressures from a rising population and increasing affluence would bring down the current social-ecological order, I also argued this would awaken humanity from its "strange slumber." This awakening would necessarily lead to an ethical revolution that will help emerging generations build a new social-ecological order on a sustainable foundation. I stated that the sweeping changes that result from this revolution would wholly transform humankind, reshaping its inner life and external conditions. This process will result in the emergence of a new culture, a new agriculture, and ultimately a new morally mature human race. *Homo sapiens* will transform itself into *Homo sapiens moralis*.

The vast increase in population combined with rising affluence poses an unparalleled threat to civilization but also an unprecedented opportunity to build a just and sustainable world. Why do I believe we will survive the threat and seize the opportunity? In the course of the book I made 15 observations that support this idea:

1. It's not how many but what kind of people – An 11 billion world peopled by rampant consumers has no future. A full world peopled with morally-advanced individuals like Yacouba Sawadogo, the farmer from Burkina Faso who fought back the desert to restore his farm and went on to help farmers in his area reforest theirs, would be a good world to live in. While the dominant trend may be toward rampant consumption and unchecked growth, a less visible movement of people involved in creative, restorative ventures, large and small, is taking root throughout the world. Future conditions will leave us no choice but to abandon the shopping malls and join the ranks of the altruists and Earth healers.

2. We are waking up – The socio-economic superstructure is constructed on an illusion that accumulating material things and sensations brings happiness. Trillions are spent maintaining this illusion through an immense accumulation of spectacles that reduce human beings to passive consumers. But as affluence increases and happiness remains illusive, as ecological impacts grow and as deep social inequalities are exposed, the illusion is losing its grip on more and more of us. Consequently, the movement for social and environmental change, "the largest movement in the world," is raising a fundamental challenge to the materialistic myths we live by.[292]

3. We can re-model our minds – The creation of the consumer culture was not an inevitable progression in civilization. It was and is a deliberate, orchestrated, global campaign to reinvent culture—and our mental infrastructures—to serve vested interests. The understanding that the current social-ecological model is not natural but constructed helps us understand that it can be reconstructed. We can build new mental models that will help us to live equitably and sustainably.

4. Consciousness is a powerful force – Human beings are not automatons entirely controlled by physical laws and selfish genes. We have free will to causally influence the course of physical events. Human consciousness is a creative force that will allow us to shape a future of our choosing. Taking advantage of multiple ways of knowing we can develop a common understanding of our current reality, agree on *authentic* ideals to work toward and establish a systematic process to get us there.

5. The outer world reflects the inner world (which we can change) – Changing our inner world can literally change the outer world, the ecosphere. If changing the world is a matter of first changing our minds, then that change is

PAUL HANLEY

within our power. By changing their inscapes—their perceptions, values, world-views—people are already changing villages, neighbourhoods, institutions, cities, and even countries for the better.

6. Human unity is a powerful force that will change the world – Cynicism about the human race is unfounded. Self-interest is not the fixed expressions of human nature. In fact, most human interactions are cooperative, even altruistic. We are noble beings, super-cooperators, not merely clever animals locked in a struggle for survival. History shows a gradual movement toward the recognition of the oneness of humanity, as people progressively discard prejudices and move to wider circles of inclusion. The principle of human unity is pivotal. Unity is, for example, the rationale for social equity, which has been shown to improve every aspect of a society. Given that landscape reflects inscape, universal adherence to the principle of human unity would result in a cohesive ecosphere.

7. Ethics are everything – Ultimately, ethical choices, not technical problems or solutions, determine what happens—and ethics are something we can change. Currently, a materialistic, self-centred ethos untempered by higher values is limiting human potential to understand and change our reality. Seeking values such as humility, self-sacrifice, self-control, moderation, detachment, service, generosity, trustworthiness, compassion, cooperation, and truth-seeking has been a sub-current in every culture. These intrinsic values latent in each of us are developed through moral education.

8. Ecosystem function first – Looking after ecosystem functions as a first priority produces more wealth than resource extraction. The wide application of this principle would mitigate the ecological deterioration that has spread to an area the size of South America. Alongside measures such as energy conservation, efficiencies, and renewables, soft geoengineering through plant and soil restoration could substantially mitigate climate change. Agroecology and other methods have proven effective in restoring ecosystem functions while increasing production and reducing poverty. Relatively small investments in agriculture, rather than paternalistic aid, would make this possible. Such investments have a high internal rate of return.

9. Uneconomic growth – Economic growth is becoming *uneconomic* growth. Growth that results in a deteriorating ecosphere, a hostile climate, skyrocketing health care costs, extreme inequality, and $223 trillion in debt is not so attractive as its mythology suggests. Economies obsessed with concentrating wealth at the top by avoiding taxation are losing their ability to deliver public goods. As the costs of maintaining the massive public infrastructure—roads, bridges, sewers, etc.—overwhelm us and services deteriorate, dissatisfaction and demand for alternatives will mount.

10. Alternatives work – Evidence is mounting that social equity and ecosystem protection enhances the commonweal. Consumerism and the growth imperative are modern inventions; until recently a relatively stable state economy was the norm. Creating a modern stable state economy can occur rapidly due to the high level of connectivity in society. Avoid and shift policies, demand-side management, resource efficiencies, full cost accounting, carbon charges, renewable energy, sustainable farming, urban agriculture, land reclamation, cooperative ventures, social investing, progressive taxation—all the elements of a fair and sustainable society—reduce costs and increase public goods.

11. The meaning deficit – The myth of affluence is being exposed. What was initially alluring turns out to be of limited value when we acquire it. Ultimately, people want something more profound from life, something with more meaning than chasing the chimera *more*. Research is also helping us discover the veritable sources of happiness, which are found mainly within ourselves and in authentic relationships.

12. Illth can become regenerative wealth – Much of what we do as a society lies on a continuum between unnecessary and destructive. Therein lies an opportunity. Not only would we be happier and healthier if we gave up these anti-social activities, letting go would free up "unhealthy wealth" (illth) that could help transform the world. The top 20 percent of consumers can reduce consumption and waste substantially without being reduced to poverty; reorienting their priorities around authentic relationships would increase their happiness. The highly connected global economy hinges on the actions of relatively few superrich individuals and companies. As their worldviews shift, the plutocrats could facilitate solutions to many of the world's problems by making pro-social investments. Governments could eliminate extreme poverty by shifting perverse subsidies for fossil fuels and agriculture to pro-social spending.

13. Change triggers virtuous circles - Most problems conceal a solution: the rural poor, for example, can be seen as a massive human resource to rally behind a global campaign to regenerate a billion hectares of degraded land, an effort which could help mitigate climate change. Helping small farmers adopt sustainable methods also increases productivity, improves nutrition, lowers health care costs, creates rural employment, and slows migration to urban slums. When we abandon junk food, we feel happier, educational attainment improves, we are more able to use active transportation, pollution decreases, health care costs decline, and more money is available for public goods. Most things that are good for the ecosphere are pro-social and vice versa; addressing problems effectively triggers virtuous circles of social-ecological renewal.

14. Progress is evident – Humanity is gradually shedding debilitating prejudices and embracing progressive concepts such as human rights and gender equality. Warfare and violence are declining; the last decade was the least violent in recorded history. The proportion of people in extreme poverty is declining, as is the rate of population growth. Ecological awareness (if not always action) is expanding. The economy is becoming more energy and resource efficient. Everything that we need to do to make the world work for 11 billion has been done somewhere successfully already. Inertia retards action, but our knowledge of effective alternatives will provide a basis for action as population pressures mount. Buckminster Fuller's wry comment bears repeating: "Humans beings always do the most intelligent thing ... after they've tried every stupid alternative and none of them have worked." Ultimately, we do the right thing.

15. Change is inevitable – Panarchy theory shows every living system moves through a cycle involving traumatic but necessary stages of release and reorganization. The living global social-ecological system will inevitably experience a pulse of transformation. During times of change, new ideas and behaviours can emerge and grow rapidly. The future is being seeded by the creative experiments people are undertaking today.

MAKING IT HAPPEN

As stated at the outset of this book, the transformation that will ultimately bring about a new and better world order will occur concurrently with a terrifying disintegration of the old one, making the 21st century a precarious period. The assertion that change is inevitable and humankind will do the right thing when it comes does not imply that this process is going to be automatic or easy. The twelve interconnected global problems and potential solutions presented in this book are summarized in the following table; the nature of both the problems and the solutions shows just how challenging getting to an 11 billion world will be.

PROBLEM	SOLUTION
Misplaced Priorities Much of what we do is unnecessary, frivolous, useless or destructive	**Value Management** Revaluate priorities from full world perspective
Overconsumption Already excessive human ecological footprint increases as population grows to 11 billion	**Demand Management** Top 20% of consumers reduce demand; avoid/shift policies to reduce resource consumption
Inefficiencies Resources undervalued	**Measure and Manage** Full cost accounting, proper valuation of resources: "what gets measured gets managed"
Chrematistics Economy maximizes corporate wealth, inequity makes everything worse for everyone	**Unity Ethos** Human unity principle leads to reorientation of economy to serve public interest and eliminate extreme wealth/poverty
Uneconomic Growth Growth imperative makes social-ecological system brittle	**Qualitative Growth** Value quality of relationships over quantity of things
Pursuit of Power Pursuing power over others corrupts organizations, institutions, individuals	**Service Ethic** Adopt service-oriented values, non–partisan governance
Spectacular Materialism Extreme focus on spectacle, celebrity, sensation generates illusory world, alienation, addictions	**Elevate Relationships** Cultivate inner space, build direct relationships at neighbourhood, village level
Toxic Inscapes Oppression, abuse result in intergenerational trauma that is projected onto surroundings	**Authenticity** Resolve through authentic inner life and relationships based on love, justice
Erroneous Worldviews Dominant worldviews generate sense of meaninglessness/emptiness, result is social-ecological deterioration	**Accurate Worldviews** Thorough investigation of reality results in more accurate worldviews that empower people to serve community, ecosphere
Erosion of Biocapacity Above problems drive loss of biocapacity, climate change	**Ecological Function First** Prioritizing ecological function serves human needs best
Cascading Impacts Above problems trigger cascade of negative impacts	**Virtuous Cycles** Above solutions initiate cycles of positive impacts
Moral Deficit Above problems evidence of moral deficit	**Moral Capacity Building** Moral education/community building process initiates social-ecological transformation on sound foundation

We cannot pretend that these are simple solutions. Suggesting there is a simple approach to solving the world's problems would trivialize their nature and undermine an authentic transformative process, which is necessarily highly complex and long term. There is no easy way out, through nuclear power or solar power, through revolutions or Green Party politics, through genetic engineering or organic gardens. Achieving the solutions outlined above will require not just a new culture and agriculture but a very different kind of human being, with a deeply moral character focused on serving the commonweal and the welfare of the ecosphere.

That is all well and good as a vision, but how can it be achieved? How can we learn how to form a new culture and a new agriculture? How can we become new human beings, a new human race?

What else but education can make this happen? Just as we have been trained in current norms by our families, schools, peers, workplaces, the media, and other environmental influences, we need to be trained to live in a new world of 11 billion. We will have to replace conventional education modelled on the current, defective worldview, which is focused mainly on turning out a new crop of passive, self-interested consumers. We need an educational approach built around the true sense of the word educate, an approach that will *educe* the innate moral capacity of human beings and guide them toward thoughtful and effective involvement in the process of carrying forward an ever-advancing civilization.

The education we need would engage children, youth, and adults in understanding and changing their reality, in rethinking and reorganizing their communities and institutions. It would engage the whole community at the neighbourhood and village level, where real grassroots change can occur.

There is no faster or surer way to make the needed changes than through a grassroots participatory educational program that actively engages its participants in community development. My sense is that beyond a few broad strokes no one really knows how to do this kind of education—and it may be better that way. The danger in well-formed theories is that they are derived from and correspond too closely to outmoded worldviews rather than building from the experience of people grappling with understanding and changing *their* realities.

The new education/community development model will have to be fleshed out in the doing. While the impetus must come mainly from people at the local level, initiating the model may require input from the broader community operating at the regional, national, or even international levels.

While millions throughout the world are engaged in efforts to bring about positive change—many of which successfully demonstrate the effectiveness of elements of the change model proposed—there are relatively few examples of comprehensive approaches of the kind required to shift global culture. Two prominent examples that provide a more holistic model are summarized below. Both have received substantial support and shown a degree of success.

MAYANGE MILLENNIUM VILLAGE, RWANDA

The Mayange cluster, located 40km south of Kigali, Rwanda, includes 23,000 people living mainly in four villages. The area suffers from sporadic rainfall and declining soil fertility, leading to endemic poverty, illness, and a lack of economic opportunity. While the villagers have traditionally grown maize and beans, the land, which is flatter and drier than the rest of the country, has largely been used for grazing.[293]

When the Millennium Villages Project (MVP) started there in January 2006, the community was struggling to recover from a devastating drought. The only health centre serving the four villages had no running water, electricity, or medicine. Nearly one in five children died before the age of five. Primary schools were overcrowded, with classes of up to 80 children. Teachers lacked books, supplies, and training. Most parents were unable to pay for their children to attend past the primary level.

By applying targeted, science-based interventions and maximizing community leadership and participation, the villagers of Mayange went from chronic hunger to a bumper harvest in 2006. Agriculture yields tripled and the villagers set up a cereal bank to store grain and help curb the risk of food insecurity. Farmers have also made great progress in terracing, which is proving to be highly effective in combating soil erosion and harvesting rainwater. The villagers are diversifying into high-value crops and are planting fruit trees such as avocado, mango, and pomegranate.

The lack of basic infrastructure and electricity is a recurring problem in poor, remote areas of sub-Saharan Africa. In its multi-sectoral approach, the MVP puts an emphasis on grid extension and road construction. In Mayange, the MVP has spent about $280,000 to connect four out of five primary schools and the only secondary school, two trading centres, two government offices, and about a third of all households to the grid as of 2011.

For Janvier Nzanywayimana, connection to the electricity grid allowed him to go to university. "I finished high school in 2007 but couldn't afford to continue my education. Then the MVP facilitated the connection of my house to the power grid. I took a loan, started an Internet cafe and a photo lab and made enough money to put me through university."

Access to improved drinking water has also tripled.

Education is a key component of the development process. Spending has increased, with three computer laboratories and two libraries added to school facilities. Through the "Buy a Cow, Feed a School" program, cows are donated to schools to provide milk for students, generate income, and teach animal husbandry.

The health centre has been connected to the grid and its facilities were improved and expanded with X-ray equipment, stocks of medicines, and an ambulance service. It also boasts a maternity ward, electronic check-in system, computer database of Community Health Worker visits, and labs testing for HIV, malaria, and other diseases. Immunization coverage is now above 90 percent.

Malaria incidence has declined dramatically thanks to a mass distribution of insecticide-treated bed nets and malaria testing and treatment at the health center. Maternal and child mortality rates are improving as well. The number of pregnant women now coming to the clinic to deliver has quadrupled due to improved health facilities that are helping to ensure safe births.

Contraceptive use has increased dramatically since the health center introduced routine counselling on contraception for all patients, male and female, regardless of the nature of the health center visit.

An important new feature is a center specifically for teenage girls located near the school. With flush toilets, showers, and beds, the centre provides an important cultural accommodation that ensures that menstruating girls need not miss school.

More than 25 cooperatives have been established, with businesses ranging from poultry production to soap making to tourism. The goal is to build on existing successes and earn more cash so that families and the community can go beyond meeting their basic needs and begin to build wealth through savings and investment.

One example is the women's basket weaving cooperative. "In 2012, the women worked outside in the shade on the ground, surrounded by children and roaming goats," reports Nina Sharma, who revisited the project two years later. "On this visit, I found the cooperative located in an industrial craft complex alongside other cooperatives. The women have a dedicated section to showcase their wares and negotiate wholesale prices to buyers. The complex also houses welders, furniture makers, bicycle repairmen, and more. Each industry has its masters and apprentices, the latter mostly high-school aged boys learning a trade that will ultimately raise their incomes and help pull them out of extreme poverty."

In 2012, the community's cassava plant had a small washing station, a hand-pressing station, and a few drying beds. Today, the cooperative has built a new commercial washing and pressing unit and numerous drying beds. Farmers now sell commercially as well as locally.

For the beekeepers' co-op members, their personal investment, supplemented by a loan from the MVP, is already paying off. Their new income allows them to pay back 60 percent of the loan after the first season. The remaining profit is used to buy additional equipment to improve production for the second season. The cooperative will also progressively produce more beehives for members who have not received one.

In the past, beekeeping in Mayange was constrained by the lack of rainfall and resulting lack of pasture for the bees. Thanks to efforts by the community and assistance from the MVP, Mayange has been intensively reforested and is now as green as other regions where bees have traditionally done well.

In Mayange, single women make up one of the most vulnerable groups of society. The MVP helped establish a pig cooperative for single women. Initially, 12 women joined the cooperative and obtained loans to start raising pigs. The new income will help the women pay for daily expenses and their children's school fees.

In 2008, a group of 74 women received training and equipment to start a machine-knitting cooperative. Today, it supplies sweaters for four large schools in the district and has also won a contract to supply Rwanda Knits, the country's leading exporter of knitted products. Knitters who belong to the cooperative can earn more than they could through casual labour.

Mayange is also successfully producing and distributing energy efficient cook stoves.

MILLENNIUM VILLAGES

The Millennium Development Goals (MDGs), endorsed by all member states of the United Nations in 2000, are considered "the world's shared framework for development." The MDGs reflect an understanding of the interconnected factors that contribute to extreme poverty and include time-bound and measurable targets to address low income, hunger, disease, lack of adequate shelter, and exclusion while promoting gender equality, education, and ecological sustainability.

The Mayange Millennium Village is one of 15 village clusters in Africa that are part of the The Millennium Villages Project. The MVP attempts to "address the root causes of extreme poverty by taking a holistic, community-led approach to sustainable development." The MVP contends that, "No single intervention is enough. In order to affect lasting change in any one sphere, we must improve them all."

The MVP aims to spur broad scaling up of integrated rural investments for achieving the MDGs by focusing on 15 village pilot projects where the best ways to achieve the MDGs can be tried and evaluated.

Currently more than 500,000 people in 10 countries are involved. Each cluster site is located in a distinct agro-ecological zone. Together, they represent the farming systems used by 90 percent of the agricultural population of sub-Saharan Africa.

Offering an innovative integrated approach to rural development, the MVP simultaneously addresses the challenges of extreme poverty in many overlapping areas: agriculture, education, health, infrastructure, gender equality, and business development. To meet the many different challenges each region faces, the villages use multiple tools such as community health workers, diversified local food production, commercial farming, malaria control, piped water, solar electricity, and increased connectivity. The goal is to assist communities to escape their "poverty trap" and to achieve self-sustaining economic growth.

Providing high-yield seeds, fertilizers, medicines, drinking wells, and materials to build schools and clinics helps to combat extreme poverty. Improved science and technology such as agroforestry, insecticide-treated bed nets, antiretroviral drugs, the Internet, remote sensing, and geographic information systems are also employed. Over a 10-year period spanning two five-year phases, community committees and local governments aim to build capacity to continue these initiatives and develop a solid foundation for sustainable growth thereafter.

The Millennium Village financing model is built on the premise that, with modest support, rural economies can transition from subsistence farming to self-sustaining commercial activity. Funding and implementing a Millennium Village is a shared effort among the MVP, donors, NGOs, local and national governments, and the village community itself. Each Millennium Village budgets an investment of $120 per person per year. Half of this is mobilized directly through the MVP and the other half comes from partners, including the community itself ($10), the national government ($30), and NGOs ($20).

The guiding principle of the MVP budget framework does not imply a top-down set of fixed interventions across every community. Instead, it offers a basic approach to multi-sector budgeting that ensures communities have access to a minimum set of basic goods and services, including agricultural inputs, primary health services, functioning schools with school meals, clean drinking water, sanitation, and simple infrastructure like roads.

Critical to the sustainability of the Millennium Villages is the need to empower the entire community, including women and vulnerable groups, by building local technical, administrative, and entrepreneurial capacity. In conjunction with improved health and education, this transformation encourages women and men to establish their own businesses, to take advantage of microfinance and micro-enterprise opportunities, and to explore income-earning possibilities beyond farming.

Participatory, community-led decision-making is central to the way Millennium Villages work and is also fundamental to sustainability.

Establishing community agreement to become one of the Millennium Villages sites takes place through a series of discussions with elected and appointed officials, community committees, and open forums at the local level. Once agreement is established, specific committees and community members begin the process of identifying and evaluating project possibilities with the support of a scientific team and local partners. Together they create a package of village-specific project initiatives that are deemed most appropriate and cost effective. They also produce a community action plan for implementing and managing these projects. All along, Millennium Villages foster and empower democratic practices, and actively promote gender equality in decision-making and allocation of resources.

National government participation is also a key to success. Villages are initiated only in countries where national leadership supports and engages with the program. Agreeing on cost sharing from the outset and making sure the program is consistent with broader national development plans ensures that governments are full partners in the project in both the short- and long-term.

The MVP will be considered successful if it: (1) demonstrates the feasibility of integrated investments to achieve the MDGs in impoverished rural Africa;

(2) helps to create new models for community-based delivery, monitoring, and measurement; (3) plays a constructive role in helping global aid commitments come to pass by making the MVP lessons widely known within Africa and internationally; and (4) helps to encourage increased global public financial flows towards more practical and effective ground-level investments rather than low quality aid.

Successful interventions from the MVP can be taken to a broader scale since the financing needs of the Millennium Villages are fully in line with commitments made by high-income countries to increase their official development assistance (ODA) to 0.7% of Gross National Income. A scale-up would only be possible if ODA promises are met.

Although a full independent evaluation of the project will not be available until 2015, the MVP reports that since the project began in 2005/06, substantial progress has been observed in a number of areas related to reducing child hunger, promoting gender equality in access to primary education, reducing child mortality, and providing access to safer drinking water. Good though less pervasive progress has also been made in improving maternal health, combating malaria, and enhancing access to improved sanitation, however the pace of progress in these areas will need to increase in order to achieve the MDG targets by 2015. Not enough progress has been made in achieving universal access to primary education overall due in part to low baseline levels. Progress also varies across the sites, with some showing substantial progress across all the MDGs and a couple of sites lagging behind the others on some education and health outcomes.

Some critics of the MVP counter that there is little evidence of success and point to fundamental problems with the projects' evaluation processes. Others say that results to date show improvement but do not prove that it was the project activities that achieved these results, as opposed to other factors such as a general upswing in economic development in the regions. Still others say that early successes in previous projects of this type were not sustainable once project funding ended.

Progress has been considered sufficient, however, that donors are increasing contributions. The Islamic Development Bank agreed, for example, to provide $104 million in long term, zero interest loans to fund an expansion of the MVP to new areas. The government of Uganda has also decided to expand the program in that country.[294]

THE HARLEM CHILDREN'S ZONE

Holistic development projects are also occurring in high-income countries. Founded in 1970 as the Rheedlen Centers for Children and Families, the Harlem Children's Zone, Inc. is a pioneering community organization dedicated to improving the quality of life for children in one of America's poorest neighbourhoods.

Over 40 years, the HCZ has developed a network of neighbourhood-based poverty prevention programs in New York City's Central Harlem, Upper West Side, and Chelsea/Clinton communities. The programs address the critical needs of children and their families and, in so doing, support the revitalization of their communities.

Under its second President, Geoffrey Canada, the number of programs and initiatives has increased from 6 to 30; the number of children receiving services from 1,500 to over 10,000.

Originally focused on truancy, HCZ identified a correlation between young children out of school, abuse and neglect, and a later life of dependency. Through experience it was determined that this cycle could only be broken through the development of a community of support that provides family stability, opportunities for employment, decent and affordable housing, a quality education, and youth development activities.

The HCZ spends approximately $40 million a year, about $3500 per year per child served. Funding from public sources covers 29 percent of costs and private donors 61 percent, with the remainder made up with fees and endowment income.

The HCZ initially focused its activities over just one city block. In 1997, it began the Harlem Children Zone Project, a seven-year, comprehensive community building initiative in Central Harlem that took the initiative to a 100-block area. The comprehensive program to end child poverty involves a holistic community building approach, including a spectrum of some 30 ongoing initiatives to address everything from pre-natal care to asthma to after school activities.

The HCZ has created a new paradigm for fighting poverty intended to overcome the limits of traditional approaches. The model focuses primarily and intensively on the social, physical, and educational development of children. To help support that development, it also provides wrap-around programs that improve the children's family and neighbourhood environments. The theory of change underlying the HCZ model requires the coordinated application of its five core principles. To create change it is necessary to:

- *Select a specific neighbourhood and work comprehensively within it.* This helps to achieve three goals: It reaches children in sufficient numbers (about 65 percent of a population) to affect the culture of a community; it transforms the physical and social environments that impact the children's development; and it creates programs at a scale large enough to meet the local need.

- *Create a pipeline of support.* Develop excellent, accessible programs and schools and link them to one another so that they provide uninterrupted support for children's healthy growth, starting with pre-natal programs for parents and finishing when young people graduate from college. The HCZ continuum of services provides children and families with a seamless series of free, coordinated, best-practice programs focused on the needs of children at every developmental age, including specific programs addressing pre-natal care, infants, toddlers, elementary school, middle school, adolescence, and college. Academic excellence is a principal goal of the HCZ pipeline, but high-quality schools are only one of the means to achieve it. Others include nurturing stable families, supporting youth development, improving health through fitness and nutrition, and cultivating engaged and involved adults and community stakeholders.

- *Surround the pipeline with additional programs that support families and the larger community.* Build community among residents, institutions, and stakeholders who help to create the environment necessary for children's healthy development.

- *Evaluate program outcomes* and create a feedback loop that cycles data back to management for use in improving and refining program offerings.

- *Cultivate a culture of success* rooted in passion, accountability, leadership, and teamwork.

Based on its program experience, HCZ has found that:

- It takes at least 7 years to create an effective project. Without adequate time to develop, quality may suffer.

- A community-based organization, not government, must be the lead entity, with full accountability for the program.

- Sufficient, secure, and sustainable funding is needed to build capacity, plan strategically, and execute high-quality programs.

- It is critical to begin strategic planning at the outset and plan for the long term. Proper planning will help transform a vision into a blueprint for success.

Although some critiques of the program argue that there is insufficient evidence of benefits from the wrap-around service approach provided by HCZ,[295] judging from academic improvement, it appears that the HCZ program has been effective. Over 98 percent of Promise Academy students scored at or above grade level on math exams, for example, outperforming their counterparts throughout New York State; over 84 percent of students scored at or above grade level in language arts, outperforming on average their counterparts throughout New York State; 97 percent of media and fitness program seniors graduated from high school; 100 percent of seniors applied to college and all of these students were accepted into at least one school; 100 percent of high school after-school program participants stayed in school; the initiative organized or rejuvenated 39 block associations in the Harlem neighbourhood.

Despite its apparent success, and its catching the eye of the Obama administration—which has announced a pilot program to replicate the success of the HCZ in poverty-stricken areas of other US cities—it has not proven easy to replicate. This may be because the HCZ has been propelled by the passionate commitment and skill set of a visionary leader and has emerged from and responded to the realities of a particular neighbourhood. This vision, passion and skill set is not easy to find, or to insert into another place.[296]

UNIVERSAL EDUCATION

The development projects described above are promising experiments that we can learn from as we shape a new educational/community development model. However, they do not address the full set of fundamental problems facing an 11 billion world.

While holistic educational programs like the HCZ are helping youth to escape inequity and poverty, unless such programs begin to address the deeper questions raised in this book, might such successes merely replace one set of problems with another? Would helping more people achieve the American dream of affluence really help them to achieve a meaningful life or contribute to an ever-advancing civilization? Obviously, projects that help eliminate barriers that have held back the poor, including racial minorities, are very positive, but are they enough to safeguard an 11 billion world?

By the same token, would the efforts by the MVP or similar projects to raise people out of poverty really address the issues of an 11 billion world? Eliminating extreme poverty is clearly one of the key goals of civilization building, but a development process that aims to bring those living in poverty into the fold of materialistic consumer culture, into the illusion that material possessions bring happiness, would ultimately be counterproductive. If the emergence of the poor from poverty results in their assuming the way of life—and the ecological footprint—of the middle classes, the ultimate result could be even more poverty as a result of ecological collapse.

Furthermore, the assumption that it is only the poor that need development is fundamentally wrong. A transformational model for the affluent is needed at least as urgently as for the poor and disadvantaged. An effective transformational model must confront the materialistic worldview, the problem of overconsumption and resource depletion, the privilege of the plutocracy, and the myths of eternal growth. We need a model of education and community development for the whole world, a model that addresses the material and spiritual development of every human being and builds a universal ethic of service.

CHAPTER 16
A TRANSFORMATIONAL MODEL

Civilization is a race between education and catastrophe.
– H.G. Wells

Bodh Gaya in the Indian state of Bihar is said to be the place where Gautama Buddha achieved enlightenment. Today, thousands of people in Bihar are engaged in a comprehensive community development program that aims to actualize the enlightened society envisioned by Buddha 2500 years ago.

The Regional Training Institute of Bihar, which animates the program, is modelled on the Ruhi Institute, a popular education movement started in rural Columbia in the 1970s.[297] The educational model has now spread to thousands of communities throughout the world. It aims to build the capacity of its participants—children, youth, and adults—to transform their lives, communities, and institutions in ways that will contribute to an ever-advancing civilization.

The Bihar institute's impact has been remarkable, particularly around the town of Bihar Sharif.[298] After a decade working with the model, substantive changes at the level of culture were apparent. While cultural strengths were being reinforced, longstanding prejudices were falling away and more inclusive values taking hold. Significantly, the transformation was happening without political upheaval, violence, or even significant confrontation.

A core principle of the institute training is an appreciation for the oneness of humankind. As a natural consequence of adopting this principle, a deeply ingrained caste system, which entrenches social exclusion and poverty, is gradually being set aside. Participants from different castes are associating, visiting each other's homes, and sharing meals. Some parents report they no longer tell their children what caste they belong to so they have no reason to feel either inferior or superior to others.

Traditionally, women in the region are under the control of their husbands and families and not allowed to be active outside the home. The institute training emphasizes the equality of women and men, which has led to the wider participation of girls and women in education and community affairs. Restrictions on women leaving the home are disappearing and their active participation in the institute as animators and coordinators has become the norm. The number of girls receiving an education is increasing and the practice of having girls as young as 12 marry is decreasing. Some girls now delay marriage and choose a husband themselves.

The dowry system is also being revised. Previously, parents of girls often had to sell land or other assets to pay dowries and finance elaborate weddings, which contributed to their poverty. Now, some participants in the institute are opting to waive the dowry and have simple wedding ceremonies that do not burden their parents. This contributes to economic security.

Traditionally, elders made all the decisions in the community. While elders retain due respect, youth, adults, and elders now consult on community affairs and unilateral decisions are avoided.

The movement in Bahir Sharif—and in other communities around the world using the Ruhi approach—is still in its early stages, yet its potential to contribute to social transformation is increasingly evident. Change at this level is not easy, however. While there are many obstacles to progress, as participants learn to read their reality and understand the scientific and spiritual principles that support positive change, they become active agents in the development of their villages and neighbourhoods.

This approach is an example of a deep-change process that can address the underlying cultural causes of the social-ecological problems described in this book. The program fosters a rich inner life and a vibrant social experience; cultivates a commitment to service; replaces passivity with a sense of empowerment and engagement; and builds a set of values and capacities in citizens that allow communities to address increasingly complex problems, from inequity to degraded ecosystems. By generating new cultural experiences that are ultimately more meaningful and compelling than consumer culture, the institute program creates an attractive alternative to materialism. Ultimately, it helps to shape a new kind of human being.

This chapter offers an example of how the change model outlined in Chapter 14 can be put into practice simultaneously at the individual, community, and institutional levels. The example also shows how the change model can be implemented in real world situations at the village or neighbourhood level, but also coordinated on a regional, national, and even international basis. The Ruhi approach thus provides a glimpse of an emerging process aimed at global transformation.

COMPONENTS OF THE INSTITUTE PROCESS

What does this transformational process look like in Bihar? The institute is an inclusive, grassroots educational movement that is free or low-cost for participants. This is particularly attractive in places like Bihar, where more than 50 percent of the population lives on an income below US$1.25 a day. The illiteracy rate, at 60 percent, is one of the highest in India. Village schools typically have one teacher per 100 students spread across eight grades. The strong influence of caste and religious prejudice often leads to social tension and violence and women are particularly disadvantaged and at risk. Such conditions result in receptivity to constructive change and openness to opportunities for learning.

As of 2012, 6000 people in Bahir Sharif were participating in the four core components of the institute's program. The first three are educative processes:

- Some 500 adults and older youth were engaged in *study circles* that investigate and immediately apply specific skills in community building including: the exploration of ethical values; the development of moral capacities such as truthfulness; attitudes such as respect for women and girls; practices such as daily reading of inspirational writings to reinforce learning; the art of elevating conversation in order to broaden community interest in transformative education; and building community connections by, for example, visiting each other's homes to discuss important principles and issues.

The training follows a sequence of courses that call on participants to gradually increase their level of service. The courses and related activities foster an ethos of community service by creating an environment conducive to the spiritual empowerment of individuals, who come to see themselves as active agents of their own learning and protagonists in a constant effort to apply knowledge to affect individual and collective transformation.

As new skills are learned, participants in the courses gain confidence in expressing themselves and articulating their needs and aspirations. Many begin to reorient their lives to include service components. Emphasis is placed on finding a path of service and then accompanying others in finding and pursuing their path. Specifically, the courses include training in teaching children, animating junior youth groups, or facilitating additional study circles. This way, the institute continuously develops new human resources able to facilitate the movement of an ever-increasing number of people, of all ages, through the capacity-building process.

- Close to 1000 children under the age of 11 were attending *children's classes* that focus on the development of attitudes and habits that are conducive to both personal and community transformation. The classes seek, for example, to develop essential virtues such as truthfulness, trustworthiness, honesty, and justice. They aim to build a strong moral framework that will assist children to achieve excellence in material, intellectual, and spiritual aspects of life. Resource materials gauged to each age level focus around inspirational stories and quotations and classes include arts activities and sports. Literacy and numeracy are important components of the program, especially where formal schooling is not available or is inadequate. The training is action oriented; learning is reinforced by engaging in simple acts of service, such as beautifying the community by picking up trash.

- Another 1000 children aged 11-14 are involved in the *junior youth empowerment program*. This age group is beginning to build an independent identity and to consider what they want to do with their lives. Consequently, they are especially open to meaningful exploration. Youth and young adults play an important role in animating this process. The junior youth program follows its own sequence of courses, which help the participants to understand their reality, including the changes they are going through at this formative stage in their life, and to articulate their thoughts. The training aims to engage the youth in adopting a two-fold moral purpose: the betterment of self and participation in the betterment of society. The youth immediately engage in action through service projects that are somewhat more sophisticated than those undertaken by the younger children, such as tree planting or gardening. The use of music and other art forms, created by the youth, is a key to the success of this program.

Many of those who go through the children's and junior youth programs go on to teach children's classes themselves, to animate junior youth programs, or to start study circles for youth, leading to constructive engagement in community development.

A fourth component of the community building process brings friends and neighbours together in informal *devotional gatherings* to share inspirational writings and prayers which can provide a deep source of motivation. In Bihar Sharif, study circle participants organized some 60 of these spiritual meetings in their homes or outdoors. Open to people of all faiths or none, the simple, inclusive approach avoids ritual and typically includes music, singing, simple refreshments, and fellowship. The prayers and readings provide inspiration and spiritual rejuvenation and renew the participants' sense of purpose. Participants are encouraged to meditate on the themes presented in the devotions and gain insight on how these can be applied in their day-to-day lives. When people from diverse backgrounds pray together, it creates bonds of love and

Educating the mind without educating the heart is no educational all. - Aristotle

unity and engenders an atmosphere of free and open discussion on matters of import to the life of each individual.

Experience has shown that the synergistic combination of all four components of the institute process reinforces the movement for individual and community renewal. Parents attending devotional gatherings, for example, learn about classes for their children; children in classes invite their parents or siblings to attend activities; families seeing the maturity that is developing in the junior youth become attracted to study themselves; home visits to study prayers and learn about spiritual principles build bonds of friendship between neighbours and turn strangers into friends. Multiple points of connection increase a sense of community and social engagement.

Also critical to the success of the process is the involvement of institute participants in a range of consultative activities that help them shape and adapt the training institute's program. Regular *reflection meetings* assess progress over the past few months, make adjustments, set new priorities, and coordinate new initiatives. The use of the arts is an important feature of these gatherings and other festivals for children, youth, and the whole community designed to inspire and encourage ever-wider participation and process refinement.

While the institute is non-political, it makes efforts to form cordial relationships with existing community institutions such as schools or local and regional governments. Collaboration with parallel community institutions can enhance the capacities of everyone working for community development. Institute participants gain ethical skills that equip them to be effective public servants, teachers, or administrators and this can influence the moral tone of community institutions.

INITIATING THE INSTITUTE PROCESS

The movement underway in Bihar shows promise as a model for addressing the key issues that face an 11 billion world. But how does such a process get underway? How does it maintain momentum? And how can it be replicated? To answer these questions, let's look at the history of the Ruhi Institute.

The Ruhi approach emerged in rural Columbia in response to development activities undertaken by that country's Bahá'í community. Bahá'ís are members of the Bahá'í Faith, a religion started by the spiritual educator Bahá'u'lláh in the 19th century, which has now spread throughout the world. Its goal is to engage all the peoples of the world in a universal cause that endeavours to unify humanity and establish justice, equity, and peace, thereby laying a strong foundation for an ever-advancing civilization. While affirming the core values of all religions, Bahá'ís promote the unity of science and religion, universal education, gender equality, and the coherence of material and spiritual forms of development.

By 1960, 100 years after the faith's inception, small Bahá'í communities could be found in every country and some Bahá'ís were beginning to promote its teachings on a broader scale. While many people joined the Bahá'í community in Columbia, a decade or more of experience with large-scale promotional activities demonstrated that merely transferring knowledge—no matter how progressive and attractive that knowledge may be—is not an effective means of helping people or communities transform. While initially attractive to many people, the movement was not generating the human resources needed to serve the multiple needs of growing communities. The most active members were becoming exhausted and new members were losing interest before they could develop independent motivation.

The lack of success in truly affecting and improving people's lives led the Columbian Bahá'ís to reflect deeply on their purpose and goals. What really is the purpose of their religion? Was its objective merely to gain converts to a different religious "brand"? To build a congregation of followers who attend religious events? Or was its object to affect a transformation in individuals and society so that the just, equitable, and peaceful world anticipated by all world religions could finally be achieved?

With these thoughts in mind, the Columbian Baha'is began to experiment with practical community-building approaches intended to empower people to change their lives and their communities in positive ways. The learning from these efforts gradually led to a participatory study-action-reflection process that became formalized as the Ruhi Institute. The vision of the institute was defined as "the development of human resources for the spiritual, social, and cultural development of the Colombian people."[299]

As it continued to develop, the potential of this approach was recognized by the Bahá'í International Community, which ultimately adopted the model worldwide (with appropriate local adaptations, such as translation of the resource materials into local languages.) Regional institutes were established in a number of countries and began to share experiences and lessons learned.

Importantly, Ruhi is a process model. It is not exported or imported as a kind of *fait accompli*, to be superimposed on local communities. It is an organic, grassroots process of cultural transformation and community building that local people can learn from and apply according to their needs and capacities. They then contribute to its further development by sharing what they have learned. Learning from local experience is accumulated at the regional, national, and global level and reflected back to communities to assist further study, action, and reflection.

Currently, the learning from communities around the world is compiled and assessed at the Bahá'í World Centre. Thus, the model is continuously updated based on the lived experience of participants everywhere, as part of a systematic global effort to carry forward an ever-advancing civilization.

As far as I am aware, this is the only initiative where learning from grassroots experience in cultural transformation, from tens of thousands of communities, is being pooled on a global scale.

While the Ruhi-inspired training institutes are administered by Bahá'í institutions, participants are not required to be Bahá'ís or, for that matter, to subscribe to any religion. In fact, most institute participants are typically not Bahá'ís. The process is freely available: anyone who can recognize in its methods and instruments potent means for movement towards a better society is welcome to participate.

The model is presented in this context because it has already achieved some success in addressing the issues addressed in this book. People everywhere are welcome to join the process if it already exists in their community or simply to learn from it and adopt elements of the program as they see fit. But be warned that applying this change model is not easy. However, as the pressures from rising population and a heavier ecological footprint mount, we will find that staying the same is not easy either. At some point, change will become more compelling than sticking with the status quo. At that point, the rate of change will become exponential.

Changing a village or neighbourhood, let alone the world, requires a compelling vision and tremendous capacity for self-sacrifice, including countless hours of volunteer time. Regardless of the models used, making the world work for 11 billion will be the most difficult task humanity has ever undertaken. And it is likely to be even more difficult to effect change in communities in wealthy nations than in the poor ones, where people at least know that the present social order is defective. But what better way to spend a lifetime?

The formation of the regional training institute in Bihar was a response to conditions similar to those found in Columbia. The Bahá'í community in Bihar was formed in the 1950s and was an early site of large-scale expansion through the 1960s and 70s. As in Columbia, the community in Bihar did not possess a means to sustain the participation of a large group of new members and interest eventually flagged.

The Ruhi approach was introduced in 2005. One of the first lessons learned was that initiating change is difficult, particularly at the initial stages when few people in a community are aware of the inherent potential of the process. In Bihar Sharif, for example, the thriving programs which grew to include thousands of participants were started by a few individuals who had to overcome indifference or even hostility.

Launching the institute in new areas at times required near heroic efforts, as one participant discovered.[300] Responding to an appeal for people to assist communities to inaugurate the institute process in new localities, a man named Shravan decided to devote his attention to Palni, about four kilometres from his home in Tetrawan. Already actively serving as a tutor for a study circle in his own community, Shravan began visiting Palni weekly, but he met with a cold response. The people were suspicious of his intentions, asking him, "What do you get from this?" and "How will we benefit from doing what you are asking us to do?" Still, he persevered and eventually was able to establish a study circle. Though he continued to be treated with mistrust, he visited the village regularly and worked with the study circle participants.

Then the monsoon season arrived. The stream separating Tetrawan from Palni flooded. The only way to cross it was to wade through dangerous chest-deep water, which Shravan did. When the people from Palni saw the degree of his commitment and sacrifice, their attitude softened. His spirit of devotion and service facilitated the success of the study circle, which attracted many people to the institute. It went on to develop a vibrant local program with five devotional gatherings and two children's classes. Shravan's efforts also inspired other friends in his home village to become more involved. Such sacrificial and active participation stood in marked contrast to the apathy that pervaded the area a decade before.

The community in Bihar Sharif has been transformed through countless efforts of individuals such as Shravan, who are in turn empowered through the unified efforts of the regional institute. With a great deal of concerted effort, the community has developed the capacity to administer large numbers of activities and to welcome into its warm embrace thousands of participants who have begun to transform their culture to achieve a balance of material and spiritual values.

GETTING STARTED

There are many wonderful examples of constructive change happening everywhere in the world, many with more immediate impact in specific areas than the Ruhi model presented here. However, the sustained village and neighbourhood level educational process prescribed in the Ruhi approach, which aims for a comprehensive transformation of individuals, communities, and institutions based on moral principles, would appear to have significant potential to truly transform cultures everywhere—not just in low-income countries—and to begin to transform humanity as a whole.

The proposed transformational model is outlined in the illustration in this chapter. Typically, it begins through conversation and follows this pattern:

Elevating Conversations Someone familiar with the methodology of the institute initiates a meaningful conversation with some residents in a village or urban neighbourhood. Those involved in the discussion begin to "read their reality," that is, to assess their current situation as individuals or community members and consider where changes are needed, along the lines outlined in the transformative model explained in Chapter 14.

What are the conditions they are experiencing and what do they need to bring about some positive change? Perhaps they are concerned about the well-being of the children as they deal with the materialistic influences of consumer culture or media? In that case, they may wish that there was a children's or youth program, and that can be started on a small scale, perhaps in their home. They may wish for ways to increase the unity of their community, which may call for a neighbourhood devotional meeting, where residents can come together for inspiration and fellowship. And some will want to study the change process itself, by joining a study circle.

A key to success is to train new human resources within the community that can carry the process forward. At first it may require support from another community more familiar with the process, but a group of friends, family members, co-workers, or neighbours will eventually want to form a study circle and move through the sequence of institute courses.

Study Circles The study circle follows a sequence of courses that consider the basic elements of community development. The current set of courses look at the following themes and practices:

- **Personal study and behaviour change** – The study begins with an exploration of basic moral values, such as being truthful and trustworthy, that must be developed to build a unified community. It engages people in reflection of such profound issues as the meaning of life and death. It considers the elements of personal transformation that help build moral capacity, such as daily prayer, meditation, and study of spiritual writings. It also invites participants to immediately take some first steps in the process of community building by connecting with friends, family, and neighbours to study prayers and hold small devotional meetings.

- **Service** – The study next focuses on the idea of service to humanity, where the good of the community is placed above personal desires. The study reinforces community values through engaging in visits to the homes of friends, family, and neighbours where the understanding of spiritual principles can be deepened and developed through conversations that are elevated above the mundane.

- **Children's classes** – One branch of the learning is a set of courses that assist participants in establishing moral development classes for children. The classes do not aim at religious indoctrination; they use stories, example, and the arts to awaken the child's spiritual nature and learn the principles and practices that contribute to a happy, healthy life and a thriving community. Especially during the early years of childhood, great emphasis is placed on the development of spiritual qualities and on those beliefs, habits, and patterns of conduct that constitute the essential attributes of a spiritual being. Developing the moral capacity of children is essential for the long-term development of the community; children trained in this way are well prepared to enter into more sophisticated spiritual enquiry as they reach adolescence.

- **Modeling** – The Ruhi training also looks at the lives of the spiritual educators who are the source of the spiritual teachings promoted by the Ruhi program, and their self-sacrificial example.

- **Junior youth empowerment** - The Ruhi program offers a course for training animators of junior youth empowerment programs. Anyone can benefit from this course, but it is often older youth and young adults who have the greatest rapport with the junior youth (ages 11-14). Here the Ruhi training branches but providing a full curriculum for the youth to follow in these formative years.

- The JY resource books are concerned with developing language skills and the power of expression. Some also address mathematical concepts and social issues, while others seek to prepare young people to approach the investigation of physical, social, and spiritual reality in a scientific manner. Though the moral concepts in the materials are drawn from spiritual teachings, they are not overtly religious in nature. Many kinds of organizations, including secular academic institutions, therefore find them useful for their educational programs with junior youth.

- **Spreading the message** – The training assists groups of participants to learn how to effectively bring larger numbers of people into the institute program. The goal is to bring its healing message to an ever-wider circle of the community, and also to take it to new communities that have not yet been exposed to it.

- **Tutoring study circles** – The training process next assists people to themselves become the tutors of new study circles so that they can contribute to a self-sustaining system for the development of a growing pool of human resources.

The Ruhi institute is coordinated at the local, regional, and international levels by persons who emerge from the training program with strong administrative skills. As mentioned, the learning from the efforts at the local level is shared widely, ultimately internationally, and systematically studied to determine the most effective community development approaches. The information generated by the world community of participants is then shared with everyone and the model is continuously refined.

In addition to moving ever-larger numbers of people through the institute courses, the world has been divided into geographical clusters. The aim is to see the program of spiritual growth develop in each cluster and for the enthusiasm to spread among clusters until the impact is felt worldwide. The current goal of the Bahá'í International Community is to sustain or initiate an intensive program of growth using these methods in 5000 geographic clusters around the world by 2016. By early 2014, programs were already underway in 3000 clusters.

The resources for the Ruhi Institute are available on line at www.ruhi.org.

CIVILIZATION BUILDING

The Ruhi program is a method of developing human resources for the spiritual and social development of communities. As human resources develop, the ripples move out to affect the three protagonists in the civilization building process: individuals, institutions, and communities.

Throughout history, these three protagonists have often been at odds, the individual seeking freedom, the institutions submission, and the community collective rights. Balancing these interests in different ways, societies have achieved greater and lesser degrees of peace and turmoil. Today, for example, the authority of institutions is increasingly drawn into question as a result of abuses of that authority, including widespread corruption. Individuals seek extreme freedom, economically and socially; freedom from taxation, for example, may contribute to the economic disparity that weakens community ties. And communities seek to sort out their collective rights and responsibilities as distinct from those of their individual members.

The model suggests roles for each proponent. The individual's focus on moral development and service allows that person to exercise the freedom to take initiatives for his/her personal development, in a manner suited to his/her interests, talents, and capacities, but in a manner that is also conducive to the advancement of the commonweal. Institutions, themselves made up of individuals who are in the process of developing their moral capacity, are able to nurture that development and harness it in collective action that is systematic and well coordinated, bringing to bear the resources required to facilitate movement. The community, the collective that is more than the sum of its individual participants, creates spaces for consultation and collective action, all reinforced through the ties of true friendships based on sharing a collective vision.

Together, the three proponents can begin to engage in public discourse and social action that can begin to transform whole villages, towns and cities, as has been shown in the example of Bihar Sharif.

DEVELOPING NEW GOVERNANCE MODELS

One area that can be addressed early in the development of the change model is the formation of administrative institutions that can contribute to the broader welfare of the community. The Bahá'í system of administration offers an attractive model that can be emulated to improve the character of governing institutions, from the local to national to international levels.

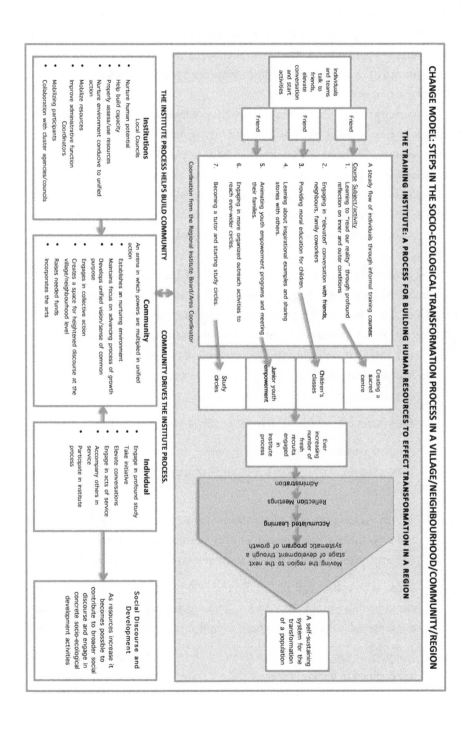

In this model, local assemblies are elected to administer certain aspects of local affairs using a unique electoral process that eschews nominations, campaigning, and partisanship. The assemblies begin to carry out community development activities of a more complex nature than the acts of service conceived by the participants of the institute.

Returning to the Bihar region, we see the potential of these new institutions, which operate parallel to local government (without usurping its authority.) In Hargaman, for example, a village of 2000 in the Bahir Sharif cluster, 1600 citizens are involved in institute activities. The community-elected assembly consulted on local needs and identified that eye care was an important issue for elders. They were able to organize an eye clinic for 10-12 surrounding villages, bringing in doctors who treated 400 people. A needs assessment also resulted in opening a new community school.

As previously discussed, a critical source of the failure of contemporary political institutions is the competitive model upon which they are established, in which individuals vie for power by forming alliances based on general ideological categories, such as conservative, liberal, green, or socialist. As previously discussed, this approach lends itself to corruption on several fronts:

- It attracts persons who have a desire for power and the types of personality that wish to have authority over others.

- The system often fosters the worst qualities of inflated ego.

- Political parties are alliances for power, not principled organizations. They often do what it takes to obtain power, even if this involves unethical behaviour.

- Politicians and parties require substantial resources to succeed in elections and in gathering these resources they become indebted to contributors and may be required to serve their interests rather than that of the public.

- Those with substantial resources, such as corporations and the wealthy, can contribute more than others, creating a powerful lobby to advance their interests. These lobbies have an inordinate power between elections.

- The pool of candidates is very small and leaves out many talented people not inclined to vie for power.

- In many electoral systems, a relatively small percentage of people participate in elections and parties may win power with a small minority of support.

- Candidates campaign for power using sophisticated techniques to influence public opinion that are often untruthful.

- Partisanship means that opposing forces in society are entrenched in opposition; instead of fostering a dialogue aimed at finding the truth on any issue, the objective is merely to win.

The governance model being proposed is quite different. There are no parties or nominations. There are no individual positions of leadership.

- In a local election, every adult is eligible to vote and be voted for. There are no nominations and no campaigns. Anyone attempting to campaign surreptitiously would essentially disqualify themselves in the mind of the electorate.

- The voting is for an assembly in which no individual has any authority. Electors vote for a set number of people they believe would do a good job among those who have mature experience, a well-trained mind, and exhibit moral capacity.

- The voting is by secret ballot.

- The elected assembly meets every month with the community members to obtain their views and recommendations.

- Consultation follows a unique format. The facts of every situation are obtained and the spiritual principles required for a decision identified. The participants frankly and lovingly make their contributions to the consultation and then step away from them, that is, they merely contribute to the pool of options and no longer lobby for their point of view.

- All assembly decisions are made by consensus following consultation. Only if no clear consensus is achieved will a majority vote prevail. All members are then asked to support the majority decision. Appeal of decisions is allowed.

The same format can be used in electing national assemblies, which oversee national affairs. Local or area conventions elect delegates using the same electoral procedure described above. These gather at a national convention to elect a national assembly, again without nomination or campaigning. The delegates are also a consultative body that advises the national assembly on the views of the national community.

All the members of the national assemblies are also delegates to an international convention, which elects an international governing council according to the same process.

In this way, the main obstacles to authentic democratic governance are eliminated, ensuring the formation of governing institutions that are as impartial as possible and not subjected to the influence of vested interests.

Applying this model of governance at the local, regional, national, or global levels moves decision making processes out of the realm of self-interest, creating consultative spaces that support just and equitable decision making—marking a clear departure from current models that are evidently subject to corruption.

This model of political authority is obviously more suited to the needs of a diverse world. A system with these characteristics will be required to make the world work for 11 billion people.

RESTORING THE ECOSPHERE

How would such an approach impact the needed adjustments to the human ecological footprint, which is a key concern of this book?

A case has been made that the condition of the outer world, i.e. ecosystems and the ecosphere as a whole, is a reflection of people's inner world and the set of relationships between people (that also reflect their inner conditions.) As we adjust our inner world and social conditions to reflect the values of unity, justice, compassion, and so on, the change will be reflected in the physical world. Logically, by fostering a sense of unity within and among people, the Ruhi approach and others like it will gradually influence behaviours that affect the ecosphere at the local level and beyond.

Importantly, for example, the model of development is not exclusively focused on material progress, being moderated by the understanding that veritable happiness comes from a rich inner life and harmonious relationships among people and with the natural world. Material and spiritual progress go hand in hand, thus de-emphasizing the material side of human development. This addresses the most serious threat to our future, overconsumption.

The case has also been made in previous chapters that inequality and the deterioration of ecosystems are closely linked. The Ruhi study materials raise the principle of the elimination of extremes of wealth and poverty, the importance of living simply, and the value of service. Inculcating such values is another key to reducing ecological footprint.

The model proposed also discourages power vested in interest groups by proposing an alternative governance model that disallows partisanship and political influence. This is another key to building social cohesion and lowering ecological impacts.

Over the long term, the collective process of reading one's reality i.e. understanding conditions in one's community and identifying their root causes and solutions, guarantees that ecological considerations will receive due regard. As issues such as climate change come to a head, and impact them at the local level, participants in resilient communities built around these principles will have developed the capacity to respond effectively. The collective learning at the local level, aggregated by national and global institutions, will contribute to grassroots solutions that can be put into effect everywhere.

A NEW HUMAN RACE, A NEW WORLD

This book began with the statement that the issues raised by peak population would cause "everyone to change everything." An argument has been presented that we need a new culture, a new agriculture, and even a transformation in the nature of the human race. The model described in this chapter begins to address the deep level of change needed to make the world work for 11 billion people.

How do we begin to bring about such as profound change? We begin within ourselves, exploring our inner and outer reality and learning how to change by trying new behaviours, seeing what happens, and making adjustments.

We begin by working with others in our neighbourhoods and villages by studying our collective reality, by imagining improvements, by trying to make small changes that will move us toward our goals, by reflecting on what happened, and by trying again and again to improve our lives.

While change will come from individual action and at the level of the neighbourhood and village, a grassroots process will not be enough. We will need to assemble our learning on the regional, national, and international levels to identify the most effective approaches and provide feedback to the local level to perfect and accelerate the transformative process. We will have to build a new, enlightened social-ecological order at a global as well as the personal and local levels. And this will require moral as much as a scientific and technical approaches.

There is no easy way to change the world. It may take decades to figure out how to make change effective and get everyone on board. It will be a frustrating, difficult, and amazing process, but not so difficult as doing nothing.

Initially, progress will appear to be minimal or even nonexistent. For half the journey we will be closer to and look more like what we are leaving behind than what we are headed toward. Only in the latter part of the transformative process will we begin to realize how much has changed.

Ultimately, we will achieve a united, just, and sustainable civilization that encompasses everyone, including our extended human body the ecosphere. We must all be prisoners of that hope.

ENDNOTES

1   Population figures in this chapter are from World Population Prospects, The 2012 Revision, Highlights and Advance Tables, Economic and Social Affairs, United Nations, 2013. Available at esa.un.org/unpd/wpp/Documentation/pdf/WPP2012_ HIGHLIGHTS.pdf.

2   See for example Hans Rosling's talk on shifting global demographics at www.ted.com/talks/hans_rosling_on_global_population_growth. html.

3   Anup Shah, Poverty Facts and Stats. available at www.globalissues. org/article/26/poverty-facts-and-stats.

4   Bruce Campion-Smith, Donuts over diplomacy, The Toronto Star, September 24, 2009, available at www.thestar.com/busi- ness/2009/09/24/doughnuts_over_diplomacy.html.

5   Dale Allen Pfeiffer, Eating Fossil Fuels, New Society Publishers, 2006, p.21.

6   Michael E. Weber, More Food, Less Energy, Scientific American, January 2012, p.76; B. Grace and R.P. Zentner, Energy Consumption in the Canadian Food Sector, The Canadian Agricultural Energy End-Use Data Analysis Center (CAEEDAC), 1998 available at www. usask.ca/agriculture/caedac/PDF/energy_95.PDF.

7   Tim Hortons 2012 Sustainability and Responsibility Summary Report, available at sustainabilityreport.timhortons.com.

8   Tralee Pearce, "Sugar, salt, fat: How the food industry got us hooked on an 'unholy trinity'", an interview with Michael Moss, The Globe and Mail, February 24, 2013.

9   Congressional Budget Office, The Long Term Outlook for Health
     Care Spending, November 2007, www.cbo.gov/ftpdocs/87xx/
     doc8758/intro.shtml.

10   Joseph Schnurr, Functional Medicine: A Comprehensive Strategy for
     Addressing the Root Causes of Chronic Illness, Sixth Annual Betty-
     Ann and Wade Heggie Lecture in Integrative Medicine, Medicine
     Alumni Conference, University of Saskatchewan, 2013.

11   Mark Lemstra, Seek rationale for poor Sask. Health outcomes,
     Saskatoon StarPhoenix, Sept 22, 2011, p.A11.

12   Joseph Schnurr, Functional Medicine: A Comprehensive Strategy for
     Addressing the Root Causes of Chronic Illness, Sixth Annual Betty-
     Ann and Wade Heggie Lecture in Integrative Medicine, Medicine
     Alumni Conference, University of Saskatchewan, 2013.

13   The Worldwatch Institute, Getting to One-Planet Living, State of the
     World 2013, available at www.worldwatch.org/node/12813.

14   Robert Goodland and Jeff Anhang, Livestock and Climate Change,
     Worldwatch, November/December 2009, available at www.world-
     watch.org/files/pdf/Livestock%20and%20Climate%20Change.
     pdf. The authors attribute 50 percent of GHG emission to livestock
     agriculture by including factors such as deforestation for farming and
     livestock production.

15   Transport Canada, The Cost of Urban Congestion in Canada, 2006.

16   ibid.

17   INRX Traffic Scorecard 2012-2013, available at www.inrix.com/
     scorecard/summary.asp.

18   Herman Daly, Full Employment Versus Jobless Growth, July 16, 2013,
     available at steadystate.org/full-employment-versus-jobless-growth.

19   Danielle Nierenberg and Hitesh Pant, Information on China's dietary
     transition is based on higher income versus better health, China Daily,
     February 11, 2012, p.9.

20   The Associated Press, Chinese premier promotes consumer-driven
     economy, posted Mar 5, 2013 at www.cbc.ca/m/touch/world/
     story/2013/03/05/china-legislative-session.html.

21   Dariush Mozaffarian et al. (2011-06-23), Changes in Diet and Lifestyle and Long-Term Weight Gain in Women and Men, New England Magazine. Retrieved 2011-07-15.

22   Centers for Disease Control and Prevention, Americans Consume Too Much Sodium (Salt), accessed at www.cdc.gov/features/dssodium.

23   USDA Economic Research Service, Historical Food Sales, available at www.ers.usda.gov/data-products/food-expenditures.aspx#26636.

24   New Directions in Global Food Markets (AIB-794), Economic Research Service, USDA, available at www.ers.usda.gov/media/872111/aib794_002.pdf.

25   New brain imaging study provides support for the notion of food addiction, Boston Children's Hospital website, available at www.childrenshospital.org/newsroom/Site1339/mainpageS1339P960.html. The study published in the June 26, 2013 edition of The American Journal of Clinical Nutrition.

26   Economic Research Service, USDA, Dietary Assessment of Major Trends in U.S. Food Consumption, 1970-2005, March 2008, available at www.ers.usda.gov/media/210677/eib33_reportsummary_1_.pdf.

27   Centers for Disease Control and Prevention, Americans Consume Too Much Sodium (Salt), available at www.cdc.gov/features/dssodium.

28   Economic Research Service, USDA, Dietary Assessment of Major Trends in U.S. Food Consumption, 1970-2005, March 2008, accessed at www.ers.usda.gov/media/210677/eib33_reportsummary_1_.pdf.

29   Andrew Nikiforuk, The Energy of Slaves: Oil and the New Servitude, Greystone Books, 2012.

30   The Real Cost of Vehicle Ownership, American Automobile Associations, 2013, available at http://newsroom.aaa.com/wp-content/uploads/2013/04/Your-Driving-Costs-infographic.jpg.

31   Maria Cook, A Suburban Nation, The Saskatoon StarPhoenix, September 7, 2013, accessed at www.thestarphoenix.com/suburban+nation/8882601/story.html.

32   Michael Renner and Maaz Gardeziin, Vital Signs Online, The
        Worldwatch Institute, available at www.worldwatch.org.

33   CBC Television, The Secret World of Gold, available at www.cbc.ca/
        doczone/episode/the-secret-world-of-gold.html.

34   Lois R. Lupica, The Consumer Debt Crisis and the Reinforcement
        of Class Position, Loyola University Chicago Law Journal [Vol.
        40, 2009), available at http://mainelaw.maine.edu/news/pdf/
        blog_lupica_credit.pdf.

35   ibid.

36   See www.usdebtclock.org.

37   Sudeep Reddy, Number of the Week: Total World Debt Load
        at 313% of GDP, The Wall Street Journal, May 11, 2013,
        available at http://blogs.wsj.com/economics/2013/05/11/
        number-of-the-week-total-world-debt-load-at-313-of-gdp.

38   Herman Daly, Rio+20 Needs to Address the Downsides of Growth,
        The Natural Resources Forum (vol. 35, no. 4)

39   Tim Jackson, Prosperity Without Growth, Earthscan 2009, p 98-102.

40   ibid.

41   Robert Welsch and Luis Vivanco, quoted in The Worldwatch
        Institute, State of the World 2010, p.8, available at www.worldwatch.
        org.

42   Erik Assadourian, in State of the World 2010, the Worldwatch
        Institute, available at www.worldwatch.org.

43   John Dulac, Global Land Transport Infrastructure Requirements:
        Estimating road and railway infrastructure capacity and costs to 2050,
        OECD/IEA 2013. Available at www.iea.org/publications/freepubli-
        cations/publication/TransportInfrastructureInsights_FINAL_WEB.
        pdf.

44   World Bank, Global Purchasing Power Parities and Real
        Expenditures, 2005, International Comparison Program, 2008,
        available at http://siteresources.worldbank.org/ICPINT/Resources/
        icp-final.pdf.

45   Omar El Akkad, Apple shows signs of losing steam, The Globe and Mail, January 23, 2013; Channtal Fleischfresser, Apple's Q1 revenue misses the mark, shares tumble 10 percent, SmartPlanet, January 24, 2013.

46   Herman Daly, A Liberating (but Damned Uncomfortable) Conversation, available at http://steadystate.org/foreword-to-wendell-berry-what-matters.

47   See She-conomy: A guy's guide to marketing to women at www.she-conomy.com/facts-on-women.

48   Victor Lebow, Price Competition in 1955, Journal of Retailing, Spring 1955, available at http://ablemesh.co.uk/PDFs/journal-of-retailing1955.pdf.

49   Harald Welzer, Mental Infrastructures: How Growth Entered the World and Our Souls, Publication Series on Ecology, Volume 14, edited by the Heinrich Böll Foundation, 2011, available at www.boell.de/publications/publications-mental-infrastructures-12600.html.

50   Data is available at http://data.worldbank.org/indicator/NE.CON.PETC.ZS/countries?display=default. The figure excludes purchases of dwellings but includes imputed rent for owner-occupied dwellings. It includes payments and fees to governments to obtain permits and licenses. Here, household consumption expenditure includes the expenditures of nonprofit institutions serving households, even when reported separately by the country. This item also includes any statistical discrepancy in the use of resources relative to the supply of resources.

51   Bree Barbeau, Global Footprint Network, e-mail to J. Matthew Roney, Earth Policy Institute, 10 November 2010. More information about the Ecological Footprint concept available at the GFN Web site, www.footprintnetwork.org.

52   Thomas Homer-Dixon, The Ingenuity Gap, Knopf 2000, p. 53-4

53   ibid.

54   Getting to One-Planet Living, State of the World 2013, p. 42, www.worldwatch.org/node/12813.

55   A summary of this study is available at www.atkearney.
      com/paper/-/asset_publisher/dVxv4Hz2h8bS/content/
      consumer-wealth-and-spending-the-12-trillion-opportunity/10192.

56   Eric Zuesse, Global inequality is much greater than inequality
      within any country, The Tyee, available at http://thetyee.ca/
      News/2013/05/29/Income-Inequality.

57   Vitali S, Glattfelder JB, Battiston S (2011), The Network of Global
      Corporate Control, PLoS ONE 6(10): e25995. doi:10.1371/journal.
      pone.0025995

58   Working for the Few, Oxfam Briefing Paper 178, January 20, 2014
      available at www.oxfam.org/sites/www.oxfam.org/files/bp-working-
      for-few-political-capture-economic-inequality-200114-en.pdf.

59   Getting to One-Planet Living, State of the World 2013, www.world-
      watch.org/node/12813.

60   How Cubans' Health Improved When Their Economy Collapsed,
      Richard Schiffman, The Atlantic, April 18, 2013, www.theatlantic.
      com/health/archive/2013/04/how-cubans-health-improved-when-
      their-economy-collapsed/275080; Population-wide weight loss and
      regain in relation to diabetes burden and cardiovascular mortality
      in Cuba 1980-2010: repeated cross sectional surveys and ecological
      comparison of secular trends, BMJ 9 April 2013; 346 doi: http://
      dx.doi.org/10.1136/bmj.f1515.

61   Information on The Society of the Spectacle is taken from www.
      marxists.org/reference/archive/debord/society.htm, http://www.
      bopsecrets.org/SI/debord/ and http://culturalstudiesnow.blogspot.
      ca/2011/05/guy-debord-society-of-spectacle-summary.html.

62   Many of the figures in this section come from Elliott Morss, The
      Economics of the Global Entertainment Industry, available at www.
      morssglobalfinance.com.

63   Fathima Ahmed and Leon Pretorius, Mega-events and Environmental
      Impacts: The 2010 FIFA World Cup in South Africa, http://alterna-
      tion.ukzn.ac.za/docs/17.2/11percent20Ahmpercent20FIN.pdf.

64   Figures in this section from List of sports attendance figures, December 1, 2010, Wikipedia, http://en.wikipedia.org/wiki/ List_of_sports_attendance_figures.

65   Tyler Falk, Fantasy sports, billion-dollar industry, Smart Planet Daily, September 11, 2013, available at www.smartplanet.com.

66   Elliott Morss, The Economics of the Global Entertainment Industry, available at www.morssglobalfinance.com

67   Giuditta De Prato and Jean-Paul Simon, The Book Industry, European Commission MCI Workshop 2, IPTS Seville, October 27-28, 2011, available at http://is.jrc.ec.europa.eu/pages/ISG/MCI/docu- ments/09.GDepratoMCI271111bookv32.pdf.

68   PriceWaterhouseCooper, Internet access: wired and mobile, Global entertainment and media outlook: 2012-2016, available at www.pwc. com/gx/en/global-entertainment-media-outlook/segment-insights/ internet-access.jhtml.

69   Global Textiles, Apparel and Luxury Goods, MarketLine, May 2012 available at http://www.reportlinker.com/p016087-summary/ Global-Textiles-Apparel-Luxury-Goods.html.

70   Make-up Industry: Market Research Reports, Statistics and Analysis, Marketline, November 2011 available at www.reportlinker.com/ ci02147/Make-up.html.

71   Global Hair Care Products Industry, Marketline, available at www. reportlinker.com/ci02138/Hair-Care-Products.html.

72   Beauty Salon 2012, SBDCNet available at http://www.sbdcnet.org/ small-business-research-reports/beauty-salon-2012.

73   See www.statisticbrain.com/perfume-industry-statistics.

74   PR Newswire, Worldwide Plastic Surgery Statistics Available for the First Time available at www.prnewswire.com/news-releases/world- wide-plastic-surgery-statistics-available-for-the-first-time-100248404. html.

75   Available at www.unodc.org/documents/wdr/WDR_2008/ WDR_2008_eng_web.pdf.

76   Sources for this section include Simon Bowers, Global profits for
       tobacco trade total $35bn as smoking deaths top 6 million, The
       Guardian, Thursday 22 March 2012; The global tobacco crisis, www.
       who.int/tobacco/mpower/mpower_report_tobacco_crisis_2008.
       pdf; The Tobacco Atlas, World Lung Foundation and the American
       Cancer Society, published in Singapore at the World Conference on
       Tobacco or Health available at www.tobaccoatlas.org.

77   World Health Organization, Global Status Report on Alcohol and
       Health, 2011.

78   ibid.

79   European Commission, Alcohol, Work and Productivity: Scientific
       Opinion of the Science Group of the European Alcohol and Health
       Forum, September 2011 available at ec.europa.eu/health/alcohol/
       docs/science_02_en.pdf.

80   World Health Organization, Global Status Report on Alcohol and
       Health, 2011.

81   Information in this section is derived from UNODC, World Drug
       Report 2012.

82   National Institute on Drug Abuse available at www.drugabuse.gov/
       publications/addiction-science/introduction/drug-abuse-costs-
       united-states-economy-hundreds-billions-dollars-in-increased-heath-
       costs.

83   See www.freecaliforniadrugrehab.com/blog/drug-alcohol-abuse-
       definitely-increase-incarceration-rates-261.html.

84   Costs of Police Services available at http://what-when-how.com/
       police-science/costs-of-police-services.

85   See http://what-when-how.com/police-science/
       costs-of-police-services/.

86   Farrell, G. and Clark, K., 2004. What does the world spend on crimi-
       nal justice? HEUNI Paper 20. Helsinki, Finland: Helsinki European
       United Nations Institute for Crime Prevention and Control available
       at https://dspace.lboro.ac.uk/dspace-jspui/handle/2134/783.

87   Billions Behind Bars: Inside America's Prison Industry available awww.cnbc.com/id/44762286.

88   John Schmitt, Kris Warner and Sarika Gupta, The High Budgetary Cost of Incarceration, Center for Economic and Policy Research, June 2010 available at www.cepr.net/documents/publications/incarceration-2010-06.pdf.

89   Fareed Zakaria, Incarceration nation, Time Magazine, Apr. 02, 2012 available at www.time.com/time/magazine/article/0,9171,2109777,00.html.

90   The Tobacco Atlas, World Lung Foundation and the American Cancer Society, published in Singapore at the World Conference on Tobacco or Health available at www.tobaccoatlas.org.

91   See www.alcoholpolicymd.com/alcohol_and_health/costs.htm.

92   Sports events leave a giant 'ecological footprint', New Scientist, 16 April 2005 available at www.newscientist.com/article/dn7274-sports-events-leave-a-giant-ecological-footprint.html.

93   What's the carbon footprint of ... a pint of beer? available at www.theguardian.com/environment/green-living-blog/2010/jun/04/carbon-footprint-beer.

94   Hilary Osborne, Stern Report: The Key Points available at www.theguardian.com/politics/2006/oct/30/economy.uk.

95   Source: World Drug Report 2009, United Nations Office on Drugs and Crime, Vienna available at www.unodc.org/documents/wdr/WDR_2009/WDR2009_eng_web.pdf.

96   J. N. Pretty, et al., An Assessment of the total external costs of UK agriculture, Agricultural Systems 65, 2000, p 113-136.

97   Liz Kimbrough, Illegal marijuana cultivation threatens Nigeria's forests and chimps available at http://news.mongabay.com/2013/0726-kimbrough-marijuana-nigera.html.

98   Melissa Breyer, 25 Shocking Fashion Industry Statistics, September 11, 2012 available at http://www.treehugger.com/sustainable-fashion/25-shocking-fashion-industry-statistics.html.

99   William S. Hatcher, Love, Power and Justice: The Dynamics of
        Authentic Morality, Bahá'í Publishing Trust, 2002.

100   Anthony Arnold, The Fateful Pebble: Afghanistan's Role in the Fall of
        the Soviet Empire, Presidio Press 1993; Anthony Arnold, The Fateful
        Pebble: Afghanistan's Role in the Fall of the Soviet Empire, review
        published May 1993, IC Publications Ltd available at http://findar-
        ticles.com/p/articles/mi_m2742/is_n223/ai_n25022095.

101   Rupert Smith, The Utility of Force: The Art of War in the Modern
        World, New York: Knopf 2007.

102   An M1 Abrams tank produced for the US army, for example, costs
        $6.2 million per unit, while a Russian T-72 costs $1-2 million.

103   Stockholm International Peace Research Institute (SIPRI), Yearbook
        2010, available at www.sipri.org.

104   ibid.

105   Robert Higgs, Defence Spending Is Much Greater than
        You Think, The Beacon, Saturday April 17, 2010, avail-
        able at http://blog.independent.org/2010/04/17/
        defence-spending-is-much-greater-than-you-think/.

106   ibid.

107   Sean Kennedy, National Debt Reaching Critical Mass, Military
        Spending Bloats Budget, June 24, 2010 available at http://business.
        gather.com/viewArticle.action?articleId=281474978325767);
        Where Your Income Tax Money Really Goes, War Resisters League
        pamphlet available at www.warresisters.org.

108   Joshua S. Goldstein, The Real Price of War: How You Pay for the War
        on Terror, New York University Press, 2004.

109   See for example http://inflationdata.com/inflation/Inflation_
        Articles/Inflation_War.asp

110   David Pugliese, Post-9/11 security tab tops $92B: report, The
        Ottawa Citizen, September 7, 2011, available at http://www2.
        canada.com/health/post+security+tops+report/5361387/story.
        html?id=5361387.

111 Linda Bilmes and Joseph E. Stiglitz, The Economic Costs of the Iraq War: An Appraisal Three Years After the Beginning of the Conflict, paper prepared for presentation at the ASSA meetings, Boston, January 2006 available at http://www.informationclearinghouse. info/article11495.htm#_ftn7.

112 See http://www.iraqbodycount.org/database. Figure cover the period from 2003-2011.

113 Material from this section is taken from Coleen Kivlahan and Nate Ewigman, Rape as a weapon of war in modern conflicts, British Medical Journal, 24 June 2010. BMJ 2010; 340:c3270. Additional information from http://en.wikipedia.org/wiki/War_rape.

114 Information in this section is taken from Silja Halle (Editor), From Conflict to Peacebuilding: The Role of Natural Resources and the Environment, United Nations Environment Programme, Nairobi 2009.

115 Nature 476, 371 (25 August 2011) doi:10.1038/476371a, published online 24 August 2011.

116 David Pugliese, Canada's F-35s: Engines not included, The Ottawa Citizen, April 17, 2011.

117 Richard Sanders, Canada's Military Industrial Complex, Global Research, April 21, 2011, available at www.globalresearch.ca/canada-s-military-industrial-complex/24447.

118 Eric J. Hobsbawm, reported in Anthropology Today (Feb. 1992), lecture to the American Anthropological Association.

119 BBC poll: Germany most popular country in the world, 23 May 2013, available at BBC.co.uk.

120 See http://violentdeathproject.com/countries/germany.

121 Information in this section is taken from Lance Gunderson and C. S. Holling, Panarchy: Understanding Transformations in Systems of Humans and Nature, Island Press, 2001 and Thomas Homer-Dixon, The Upside of Down, 2006, p.225-234.

122 Bill Rees, Big Picture: The Jekyll and Hyde of "Resilience", in Resiliency: Cool Ideas for Locally Elected Leaders, Centre for Civic Governance, 2011, available at www.civicgovernance.ca.

123 E.O. Wilson, Consilience, The Unity of Knowledge, Knopf, New York, 1998, p.297.

124 The Ruhi Institute is an educational institution, operating under the guidance of the National Spiritual Assembly of the Baha'is of Columbia, which dedicates its efforts to the development of human resources for the spiritual, social, and cultural development of the Colombian people. Its programs are open to all, regardless of religious affiliation (if any.) In recent years its educational programs have been adopted by an increasing number of agencies worldwide. See www.ruhi.org for more information.

125 E.O. Wilson, Consilience, The Unity of Knowledge, Knopf, New York, 1998, p.277.

126 Leonid Sharashkin, Michael Gold and Elizabeth Barham, Ecofarming and Agroforestry for Self-reliance, Association for Temperate Agroforestry, Conference proceedings 2005; the Statistical Yearbook of the Russian Federation 2007, Rosstat-Federal State Statistical Service, 2008, p. 445 available at http://www.gks.ru/.

127 United States Agency for International Development, Farm Reference Handbook for Ukraine, 2005, available at www.lol.org.ua/eng/docs/Farm%20Handbook%20ENG.pdf.

128 Figures in this section refer to cereal yield in 2008, measured in kilograms per hectare of harvested land, including wheat, rice, maize, barley, oats, rye, millet, sorghum, buckwheat, and mixed grains. Production data on cereals relate to crops harvested for dry grain only. Cereal crops harvested for hay or harvested green for food, feed, or silage and those used for grazing are excluded. Source: Food and Agriculture Organization of the United Nations, available at www.nationmaster.com/graph/agr_cer_yie_kg_per_hec-cereal-yield-kg-per-hectare#source.

129   Information available at www.tradingeconomics.com/ukraine/cereal-yield-kg-per-hectare-wb-data.html.

130   Vaclav Smil, How Many People Can the Earth Feed?, Population and Development Review, Vol. 20, No. 2 (Jun., 1994), pp. 255-292.

131   Vaclav Smil, Feeding the World: A Challenge for the Twenty-First Century, Cambridge: The MIT Press, 2000.

132   Paillard, S., Treyer, S. and Dorin, B., Agrimonde: Scenarios and Challenges for Feeding the World in 2050, Editions Quae, 2011.

133   Thomas Homer-Dixon, The Ingenuity Gap, Knopf 2000, p.35.

134   Stanley Wood et. al., Pilot Analysis of Global Ecosystems: Agroecosystems, World Resources Institute, 2000, p.5, 48.

135   Sandra Postel, Pillar of Sand: Can the Irrigation Miracle Last? Worldwatch Institute, 1999.

136   Thomas Homer-Dixon, The Ingenuity Gap, Knopf 2000, p. 66.

137   Thomas Homer-Dixon, The Ingenuity Gap, Knopf 2000, p. 55.

138   FAO, Statistical Yearbook 2013, p. 130, available at www.fao.org/docrep/018/i3107e/i3107e03.pdf.

139   FAO Committee on World Food Security, Fostering the Political Will to Fight Hunger, 25th Session, Rome, 28 May – 1 June 2001, #15.

140   Paul Mozur, Lessons of the Loess, New York Times, December 9, 2009.

141   The film can be seen at www.youtube.com/watch?v=kK8z0qDtE2g.

142   The Worldwatch Institute, State of the World 2011, W.W. Norton, p. 21, available at www.worldwatch.org.

143   Loess Plateau benefits from World Bank aid, People's Daily Online, March 11, 2006.

144   Further information about the film is available at www.1080films.co.uk/project-mwsd.htm.

145   Chris Reij, Investing in Trees to Mitigate Climate Change, in State of the World 2011, W.W. Norton, available at www.worldwatch.org.

146   Stan Rowe, Home Place: Essays on Ecology, NeWest Publishers, 1990, p.172.

147   Ratan Lal, Soil carbon sequestration to mitigate climate change, Geoderma, Volume 123, Issues 1-2, November 2004, p. 1-22; Rattan Lal, Managing Soils and Ecosystems for Mitigating Anthropogenic Carbon Emissions and Advancing Global Food Security, BioScience: Vol. 60 No. 9, October 2010.

148   Read more at www.environmentalgraffiti.com/news-micro-financing-carbon-farming-solution#eVIYfI4MU0WRFoXl.99.

149   Forest management techniques for mitigation (REDD+) available at http://climatetechwiki.org/technology/jiqweb-ar.

150   Information from the National Institute of Space Research available at www.inpe.br/ingles/news/news.php?Cod_Noticia=271.

151   Albert Bates, The Biochar Solution, Carbon Farming and Climate Change, New Society Publishers, 2010.

152   Buildings and Climate Change: Summary for Decision-Makers, United Nations Environment Program, 2009, available at www.unep.org/sbci/pdfs/sbci-bccsummary.pdf.

153   Robert A. Dull et al., The Columbian Encounter and the Little Ice Age: Abrupt Land Use Change, Fire, and Greenhouse Forcing, Annals of the Association of American Geographers, Volume 100, Issue 4 October 2010, pages 755 – 771.

154   Jennifer A. Burney et al., Greenhouse gas mitigation by agricultural intensification, Proceedings of the National Academy of Sciences (PNAS) June 29, 2010 vol. 107 no. 26 12052-12057.

155   Olivier De Schutter, Agroecology and the Right to Food, a report submitted by the Special Rapporteur on the Right to Food, to the United Nations General Assembly 20 December 2010, available at www.srfood.org/images/stories/pdf/officialreports/20110308_a-hrc-16-49_agroecology_en.pdf.

156   Stephen Leahy, Save Climate and Double Food Production With Eco-Farming, IPS News Agency, Mar 8, 2011, available at http://www.ipsnews.net/2011/03/save-climate-and-double-food-production-with-eco-farming.

157   Sustainable Farm Practices Improve Third World Food Production, ScienceDaily, January 24, 2006, report on an article in the Feb. 15, 2006 issue of the American Chemical Society journal Environmental Science & Technology.

158   Organic Farming Can Feed The World, Study Suggests, ScienceDaily, July 13, 2007.

159   See http://rodaleinstitute.org/our-work/farming-systems-trial.

160   Olivier De Schutter, Report submitted by the Special Rapporteur on the right to food, 2010. United Nations, General Assembly, Human Rights Council, Sixteenth session, Agenda item 3: Promotion and protection of all human rights, civil, political, economic, social and cultural rights, including the right to development, available at www2. ohchr.org/english/issues/food/docs/A-HRC-16-49.pdf.

161   Six et al. 2004, quoted in Rattan Lal, Managing Soils and Ecosystems for Mitigating Anthropogenic Carbon Emissions and Advancing Global Food Security, BioScience: Vol. 60 No. 9, October 2010.

162   Steinbach and Alvarez 2006, quoted in Rattan Lal, Managing Soils and Ecosystems for Mitigating Anthropogenic Carbon Emissions and Advancing Global Food Security, BioScience: Vol. 60 No. 9, October 2010.

163   For example, see Albert Bates, The Biochar Solution, Carbon Farming and Climate Change, New Society Publishers, 2010.

164   Information from Dave Levitan, Refilling the Carbon Sink: Biochar's Potential and Pitfalls, December 9, 2010, Yale Environment 3060 available at http://e360.yale.edu/feature/ refilling_the_carbon_sink_biochars_potential_and_pitfalls_/2349.

165   See www.holisticmanagement.org for additional information.

166   Paul Hanley, Holistic Animal Care Improves Health and Biodiversity, Saskatoon StarPhoenix, March 1, 2005.

167   The subject of a popular article in the Atlantic Magazine, available at www.theatlantic.com/life/archive/2011/09/the-brown-revolution-increasing-agricultural-productivity-naturally/245748.

168   Available at www.achmonline.org/Resource/A%20Global%20
       Strategy%20for%20Addressing%20Global%20Climate%20Change.
       pdf.

169   Sandra Postel, Getting More Crop Per Drop, State of the World 2011,
       The Worldwatch Institute, W.W.Norton 2011.

170   For additional information see www.johnjeavons.info/index.html.

171   Brian Halweil and Danielle Nierenberg, Farming the Cities, State
       of the World 2007, The Worldwatch Institute, W.W, Norton 2007;
       Nancy Karanaji and Mary Njenga, Feeding the Cities, State of the
       World 2011, The Worldwatch Institute, 2011.

172   Statistic from www.nationmaster.com/graph/
       env_pol_mun_was_per_cap-pollution-municipal-waste-per-capita.

173   Information for this section from Richard St. Bare Baker, I Planted
       Trees, Lutterworth Press, 1944; Nigeria, Mongabay website at
       http://rainforests.mongabay.com/20nigeria.htm; and UNICEF, The
       Nigerian Situation, available at www.unicef.org/nigeria/1971_2199.
       html.

174   Food and Agriculture Organization of the United Nations, Fostering
       the Political Will to Fight Hunger, Committee on World Food
       Security, Twenty Seventh Session, Rome, 2001, #30.

175   Food and Agriculture Organization of the United Nations, New
       Challenges to the Achievement of the World Food Summit Goals,
       Committee on World Food Security, Twenty Seventh Session, Rome,
       2001, #58.

176   Food and Agriculture Organization of the United Nations, Fostering
       the Political Will to Fight Hunger, Committee on World Food
       Security, Twenty Seventh Session, Rome, 2001, #30.

177   Jonathan A. Foley et al., Solutions for a cultivated planet, Nature,
       October 2011.

178   Edward O. Wilson, Consilience: The Unity of Knowledge, Knopf,
       1998, p.276-277.

179   E.F. Schumacher, Small is Beautiful, ABACUS, 1974, p. 86.

180   Edward O. Wilson, Consilience: The Unity of Knowledge, Knopf, 1998, p. 277.

181   ibid. p. 264.

182   ibid. p. 261.

183   Masanobu Fukuoka, One Straw Revolution, Rodale Press, 1978, p xii.

184   Eric Hobsbawm, On History, The New Press, 1998, p.157.

185   Martin Nowak, Super Cooperators: Altruism, Evolution, and Why We Need Each Other to Succeed, Free Press, 2011.

186   Colin Duncan, The Centrality of Agriculture—Between Humankind and the Rest of Nature, McGill-Queen's University Press, 1996, p.xv.

187   Information in this section from The International Assessment of Agricultural Knowledge, Science and Technology for Development (IAASTD), Industrial Agriculture and Small-scale Farming, Island Press 2009, available at www.globalagriculture.org/report-topics/industrial-agriculture-and-small-scale-farming.html.

188   Information for this section was adapted from Olivier De Schutter, Report of the Special Rapporteur on the right to food, Olivier De Schutter, Final report: The transformative potential of the right to food, Human Rights Council, United Nations, 24 January 2014, available at www.srfood.org/images/stories/pdf/officialreports/20140310_finalreport_en.pdf.

189   Stan Rowe, Home Place, NeWest, 1990, p. 173.

190   Information for this section comes from Rattan Lal, Marginal Soils, Tropentag "Development on the margin" Conference 2011, Bonn, available at www.tropentag.de/2011/abstracts/links/Lal_P74l25nK.php; Rattan Lal, Beyond Copenhagen: mitigating climate change and achieving food security through soil carbon sequestration, Food Sec. (2010) 2:169–177; Rattan Lal, Managing Soils and Ecosystems for Mitigating Anthropogenic Carbon Emissions and Advancing Global Food Security, RATTAN LAL, BioScience: Vol. 60 No. 9, October 2010.

191   The Worldwatch Institute, Hefty Subsidies Prop Up Unsustainable Energy System, press release dated January 22, 2014, available at www.worldwatch.org/hefty-subsidies-prop-unsustainable-energy-system.

192   Vaclav Smil, Feeding the World, The MIT Press, 2000, p.ix.

193   Information from www.uihealthcare.com/topics/nutrition/nutr3176.html.

194   Christian J. Peters, Jennifer L. Wilkins and Gary W. Fick (2007). Testing a complete-diet model for estimating the land resource requirements of food consumption and agricultural carrying capacity: The New York State example, Renewable Agriculture and Food Systems, 22, pp.145-153 doi:10.1017/S1742170507001767.

195   U.S. could feed 800 million people with grain that livestock eat, Cornell ecologist advises animal scientists, Cornell University, Science News, August 7, 1997, based on David Pimentel, "Livestock Production: Energy Inputs and the Environment."

196   From World Resources Institute, Earth Trends Online Database, available at www.wri.org.

197   Information from this section is taken from Tristram Stuart, Post-harvest Losses: A Neglected Field, State of the World 2011, Worldwatch Institute, W.W. Norton, 2011.

198   From World Drug Report 2009, United Nations Office on Drugs and Crime, Vienna available from www.unodc.org/documents/wdr/WDR_2009/WDR2009_eng_web.pdf.

199   Information from Food and Agriculture Organization of the United Nations (FAOSTAT), available at http://faostat.fao.org.

200   Solveig Torvik, Norway's economic riddle, May 13, 2011 available at www.newsinenglish.no/2011/05/13/norway's-economic-riddle.

201   Deloite Monitor Group, Braving the New World: Sovereign Wealth Fund Investment in the Uncertain Times of 2010, June 7, 2011, available at www.monitor.com. Deloitte ranks Norway SWF as the largest in the world at US$560.5 billion, significantly downsizing its assessment of the value of the Abu Dhabi Investment Authority to $342 billion.

202   The new lords of global finance, The Week, July 12, 2008, available at www.thefirstpost.co.uk/44862,news-comment,news-politics,the-new-lords-of-global-finance,²#ixzz1Q8AlxYr1.

203   Alister Doyle, Norway puts a value on nature, Oslo-Reuters, Thursday, Oct. 21, 2010.

204   Jeffery Sachs, Common Wealth: Economics for a Crowded Planet, New York: Penguin Press 2008, p.264.

205   Alberto Alesina, Why Doesn't the United States Have a European-Style Welfare State? Brookings Paper on Economics Activity, Fall 2001, 187-278; Fairness and Redistribution: US vs. Europe, American Economic Review, September 2005, 95: 913-35 Available at www.economics.harvard.edu/faculty/alesina/recently_published_alesina.

206   Richard Wilkinson and Kate Pickett, The Spirit Level, Why Equality is Better for Everyone, Penguin, 2010, p.233

207   E.O. Wilson, Consilience: The Unity of Knowledge, Knopf 1998, p.297.

208   ibid. p.297-298.

209   Murder rates from http://en.wikipedia.org/wiki/List_of_countries_by_intentional_homicide_rate.

210   Information about the Albanian economy is taken from Index Mundi available at www.indexmundi.com; United Nations Development Programme, Albania, available at www.undp.org.al/index.php?page=detail&id=123); Economic Commission for Europe, Committee on Environmental Policy, Environmental Performance Review: Albania; Government of Albania, Albania National Report on Progress Toward Achieving the Millennium Development Goals, Special Edition, July 2010.

211   Source cited in www.bankofalbania.org/web/pub/speech_Governor_Bank_of_Albania_EBRD_London_september_2_1221_1.pdf

212   World Resources Institute, Earth Trends 2003: Country Profiles: Albania, available at http://earthtrends.wri.org.

213   Andrea Shundi, Country Pasture Profiles: Albania, FAO, revised 2006, available at www.fao.org/ag/AGP/AGPC/doc/Counprof/Albania/albania.htm.

214   See www.fundforpeace.org for more information on the Failed State Index.

215   Background information from this section from Brian R. Sims, Understanding the Biopsychosocial Impact of Trauma, National Association of State Mental Health Program Directors, available at http://cabhp.asu.edu/files/professional-development/trauma-informed-care-summit/understanding-the-biopsychosocial-impact-of-trauma-brian-sims-m.d/view; Maria Yellow Horse Braveheart, Welcome to Takini's Historical Trauma website, available at www.historicaltrauma.com; Natan Kellerman, Epigenetic Transmission of Holocaust Trauma: Can Nightmares Be Inherited? Israel Journal of Psychiatry Related Science, Vol. 50 - No 1 (2013), available at http://doctorsonly.co.il/wp-content/uploads/2013/07/08_Epigenetic-Transmission.pdf; Amy Bombay et al., Intergenerational Trauma: Convergence of Multiple Processes among First Nations peoples in Canada, Journal of Aboriginal Health, November 2009, available at http://www.naho.ca/jah/english/jah05_03/V5_I3_Intergenerational_01.pdf.

216   Wikipedia, Environmental Performance Index, available at http://en.wikipedia.org/wiki/Environmental_Performance_Index.

217   Bill and Melinda Gates, Annual Letter 2014, available at annualletter.gatesfoundation.org.

218   Oxfam Briefing Paper, Working for the Few, January 20, 2014, available at www.oxfam.org/sites/www.oxfam.org/files/bp-working-for-few-political-capture-economic-inequality-200114-en.pdf.

219   Stan Rowe, Homeplace: Essays on Ecology, NeWest Publishers, 1990, pp.11-12.

220   James Daschuk, Clearing the Plains: Disease, Politics of Starvation, and the Loss of Aboriginal Life, University of Regina Press, 2013.

221　Information sourced from Andrew C. Revkin, Peeling Back Pavement to Expose Watery Havens, The New York Times, July 17, 2009 available at www.nytimes.com/2009/07/17/world/asia/17daylight. html?pagewanted=all.

222　Information from the National Institute of Space Research, available at www.inpe.br/ingles/news/news.php?Cod_Noticia=271.

223　Information sourced from Federal Ministry of Food, Agriculture and Consumer Protection, German Forests, available at www.bmelv. de/SharedDocs/Downloads/EN/Publications/GermanForests. pdf?__blob=publicationFile.

224　Information from Gardiner Harris, Index of Happiness? Bhutan's New Leader Prefers More Concrete Goals, New York Times, October 4, 2013 available at www.nytimes.com/2013/10/05/world/asia/ index-of-happiness-bhutans-new-leader-prefers-more-concrete-goals. html?pagewanted=1&_r=0 and Charlie Osborne, Bhutan aims to transform capital into all-electric vehicle playground, on Smart Planet available at www.smartplanet.com/blog/bulletin/bhutan-aims-to-transform-capital-into-all-electric-vehicle-playground/?tag=nl. e660&s_cid=e660&ttag=e660&ftag=TRE4eb29b5.

225　See for example Our Final Century, Martin Rees, Arrow Books, 2004 or Stephen Emmott, Ten Billion, Penguin, 2013.

226　Henry P. Stapp, Quantum Theory of Consciousness, Paris Talk 2013 available at www-physics.lbl.gov/~stapp/stappfiles.html.

227　From Wikiquotes http://en.wikiquote.org/wiki/Stephen_Hawking.

228　Quoted in Brett Smith, Biocentrism: Are Life, Death And The Universe Just Constructs Of The Human Mind? from redOrbit, available at www.redorbit.com/news/science/1113004811/ is-the-universe-a-creation-of-the-human-mind-111513/.

229　Paul Davies, Cosmic Jackpot, Houghton Mifflin, 2007, p. 261.

230　Timothy McGettigan, Stephen Hawking's God: A Stubbornly Persistent Illusion, The Scojournal, November 2013, available at www.sociology.org/featured/stephen-hawkings-god-a-stubbornly-persistent-illusion.

231 E.O. Wilson, Consilience: The Unity of Knowledge, Knopf 1998, p. 298.

232 Information in these paragraphs from Henry Stapp. Mind and Values in the Quantum Universe, in Paul Davies and Neis Henrik Gregersin (Eds., Information and the Nature of Reality, Cambridge University Press, 2010; Henry P. Stapp, Quantum Theory of Consciousness, Paris Talk 2013 available at www-physics.lbl.gov/~stapp/stappfiles.html.

233 Paul Davies and Neis Henrik Gregersin (Eds.), Information and the Nature of Reality, Cambridge University Press, 2010, p.105.

234 Stephen Hawking and Leonard Mlodinow, The Grand Design, Bantam, 2012, p.140.

235 The talk is available at www.ted.com/talks/david_deutsch_on_our_place_in_the_cosmos.html. A full transcript is available at http://news.rapgenius.com/David-deutsch-chemical-scum-that-dream-of-distant-quasars-lyrics.

236 Paul Davies, Cosmic Jackpot, Houghton Mifflin, 2007, p. 226.

237 ibid p228.

238 ibid p. 237.

239 ibid p.249.

240 The nighttime image of Earth is from http://cdn.theatlantic.com/static/mt/assets/international/earthatnightLG.jpg.

241 Joseph Stromberg, What is the Anthropocene and Are We in It?, Smithsonian, January 2013 available at www.smithsonianmag.com/science-nature/What-is-the-Anthropocene-and-Are-We-in-It-183828201.html.

242 Aerial images of Earth are available from http://eol.jsc.nasa.gov/Videos/CrewEarthObservationsVideos.

243 Homer-Dixon, The Ingenuity Gap, Knopf, 2000, p.53-54

244 See for example National Oceanography Centre, Southampton (UK): Human impacts on the deep seafloor, September 14, 2010 available at www.eurekalert.org/pub_releases/2010-09/nocs-hio091410.php.

245 Norman Doidge, The Culturally Modified Brain in The Brain That Changes Itself, Viking Penguin, 2007, p. 311.

246 Douglas Coupland, A radical pessimist's guide to the next 10 years, The Globe and Mail, Oct. 08, 2010.

247 Quoted in Larry L. Rasmussen, Cosmology and Ethics, in Bucknell Review: Worldviews and Ecology, edited by Mary Evelyn Tucker and John A. Grim, Toronto: Associated University Press, 1993, pp. 173-174.

248 ibid, p.175.

249 ibid.

250 Seyyed Hossein Nasr, Religion and the Order of Nature, Oxford: Oxford University Press, 1996, p. 5.

251 ibid., p. 6.

252 Quoted in Ralph Metzner, The Emerging Ecological Worldview, in Bucknell Review: Worldviews and Ecology, edited by Mary Evelyn Tucker and John A. Grim, Toronto: Associated University Press, 1993, p. 163.

253 Clément Vidal and Alexander Riegler, World Views: From Fragmentation to Integration, Internet Edition 2007, available at http://pespmc1.vub.ac.be/clea/reports/worldviewsbook.html. The definition and elaboration on worldviews in this section is derived from this document.

254 Ibid.

255 Edward O. Wilson quoted in Jeffrey Sacks, Common Wealth: Economics for a Crowded Planet, Penguin Press, 2008, p. xii.

256 Martin Nowak, SuperCooperators, Free Press, 2011, p. 280.

257 For an explanation see Herman E. Daly, Economics in a Full World, Scientific American, September 2005, Vol. 293, Issue 3.

258 Thomas Homer-Dixon, The Up Side of Down, Catastrophe, Creativity, and the Renewal of Civilization Knopf 2006 p. 201.

259 For an interesting discussion of this idea see Jacques Cauvin, The Birth of the Gods and the Origins of Agriculture, Trans. Trevor Watkins, Cambridge University Press, 2000.

260   See Thomas Homer-Dixon, The Ingenuity Gap: How Can We Solve
       the Problems of the Future?, Knopf, 2000, p. 205.

261   Evan Eisenberg, The Ecology of Eden, Random House Canada, 1998,
       p. 22.

262   See Stan Rowe and Ted Mosquin, A Manifesto for Earth, available at
       www.ecospherics.net.

263   F. Stuart Chapin III and Erica Fernandez, Proactive ecology for
       the Anthropocene, December 4, 2013. DOI 10.12952/journal.
       elementa.000013 available at http://elementascience.org/article/
       info:doi/10.12952/journal.elementa.000013#sthash.NdhqPMEq.
       dpuf.

264   See for example Chapin FS III, Power ME, Pickett STA, Freitag A,
       Reynolds JA, Earth stewardship: Science for action to sustain the
       human-earth system, Ecosphere 2: art89. 2011.

265   Brad R. Allenby, Earth Systems Engineering: The World As Human
       Artifact, The Bridge, Journal of the National Academy of Engineering,
       Spring 2000.

266   Rafel Serafin, Vernadsky's Biosphere, Teilhard's Noosphere, and
       Lovelock's Gaia: Perspectives on Human Intervention in Global
       Biogeochemical Cycles, International Institute for Applied Systems
       Analysis (IIASA) Working Paper WP-87-096, 1987 available at www.
       iiasa.ac.at/publication/more_WP-87-096.php.

267   See www.unep.org/maweb/en/About.aspx.

268   For a full explanation see John Archibald Wheeler, Law Without Law,
       available at www.forizslaszlo.com/tudomany/wheeler_law_without_
       law.html.

269   John Wheeler, in Isham et al., eds, Quantum Gravity.
       Oxford: Clarendon, 1975, pp. 564-565.

270   Paul Davies, Cosmic Jackpot, Why Our Universe Is Just Right for
       Life, New York: Houghton Mifflin Company, 2007, p.258.

271   Quotations from Jason Silva and Richard Doyle, An Ecstatic
       Dialogue between Jason Silva and Richard Doyle, author of Darwin's
       Pharmacy: Sex, Plants and the Evolution of the Noosphere, H+
       Magazine, June 24, 2011 available at http://hplusmagazine.
       com/2011/06/24/an-ecstatic-dialogue.

272   Stunning Details of Brain Connections Revealed, Science Daily, Nov.
       17, 2010, www.sciencedaily.com/releases/2010/11/101117121803.
       htm.

273   Tyler Volk, CO_2 Rising, The MIT Press, 2008 available at http://
       mitpress2.mit.edu/books/chapters/0262515210chap1.pdf.

274   See http://ngm.nationalgeographic.com/2013/07/125-explore/
       shared-genes.

275   See Life as we know it, Nature, Vol. 449, Issue 7158, 6 September
       2007.

276   Ina Damm Muri, The appendix mystery might be solved,
       SmartPlanet, March 11, 2012, available at www.smartplanet.com/
       blog/smart-takes/the-appendix-mystery-might-be-solved.

277   Information in this section from United Nations Office on Drugs
       and Crime, Corruption and Development and Corruption and
       the Environment, available at www.actagainstcorruption.org/
       actagainstcorruption/en/factsheets.html; Transparency International
       UK, Corruption Statistics, www.transparency.org.uk/corruption/
       statistics-and-quotes.

278   Armina Ligaya, Canada now dominates World Bank corruption list,
       thanks to SNC-Lavalin, Financial Post, September 18, 2013, available
       at http://business.financialpost.com/2013/09/18/canada-now-
       dominates-world-bank-corruption-list-thanks-to-snc-lavalin.

279   Information in these paragraphs was obtained from the website of
       Global Witness, http://new.globalwitness.org.

280   Tax Justice Network, Briefing Paper: The Price of Offshore, March
       2005, available at www.taxjustice.net/cms/upload/pdf/Price_of_
       Offshore.pdf.

281 Dick Simpson et al., Chicago and Illinois, Leading the Pack in Corruption, Anti-Corruption Report Number 5, University of Illinois, February 15, 2012 available at www.uic.edu/depts/pols/ChicagoPolitics/leadingthepack.pdf.

282 Information in this paragraph from the website of The Economist Intelligence Unit, available at www.eiu.com/public/topical_report.aspx?campaignid=DemocracyIndex12.

283 Public Campaign, For Hire: Lobbyists or the 99%? How Corporations Pay More for Lobbyists Than in Taxes, December 2011, available at http://publicampaign.org/sites/default/files/ReportTaxDodgerLobbyingDec6.pdf.

284 Katie Auth, Record High for Global Greenhouse Gas Emissions, Vital Signs, The Worldwatch Institute, November 27, 2013, available at http://vitalsigns.worldwatch.org/vs-trend/record-high-global-greenhouse-gas-emissions.

285 William Hatcher, Love, Power, and Justice, Bahá'í Publishing Trust, 2002.

286 See E.O. Wilson's discussion of this topic in Consilience. Wilson's view is that science will eventually be able to contribute substantially to moral questions.

287 These points are taken from William S. Hatcher, Minimalism, Juxta Publishing, 2002.

288 Wade Davis, The Wayfinders: Why Ancient Wisdom Matters in the Modern World, The 2009 CBC Massey Lectures, available ar www.cbc.ca/ideas/episodes/massey-lectures/2009/11/02/massey-lectures-2009-the-wayfinders-why-ancient-wisdom-matters-in-the-modern-world.

289 See for example Terrence W. Deacon, The Symbolic Species: The co-evolution of language and the brain, W.W.Norton, 1997.

290 Ideas for this section were drawn from the report of the conference Art as a Way of Knowing, March 3-4, 2011 available at macaulay.cuny.edu/eportfolios/adams2013/files/2013/08/ARTSci_ConferenceReport.pdf.

291   David Masci, What do scientists think about religion? The Los
       Angeles Times, November 24, 2009, available at http://articles
       .latimes.com/2009/nov/24/opinion/la-oe-masci24-2009nov24.

292   Paul Hawken, Blessed Unrest: How the Largest Social Movement in
       History Is Restoring Grace, Justice, and Beauty to the World, Penguin
       Books, 2008.

293   Information on Mayange was accessed from the Millenium Villages
       website at http://millenniumvillages.org/tag/mayange and Nina
       Sharma, Going Back to Mayange, available at http://millenniumvil-
       lages.org/field-notes/going-back-to-mayange.

294   The description of this project is taken from the Millennium Villages
       website at http://millenniumvillages.org and the 2012 Millennium
       Promise Annual Report on the Millennium Villages Project, available
       at http://millenniumvillages.org/wp-content/uploads/2013/11/
       MP2012AnnualReport-FINAL.pdf. An overview of criticisms
       of the project can be found in Tom Murphy, Learning from
       mistakes made: The Millennium Villages Project, Humanosphere,
       October 2, 2013, available at www.humanosphere.org/2013/10/
       learning-from-the-millennium-villages-project.

295   Danielle Hanson, Assessing the Harlem Children's Zone, Center for
       Policy Innovation, March 6, 2013 available at www.heritage.org/
       research/reports/2013/03/assessing-the-harlem-childrens-zone

296   Amanda Erickson, Why Hasn't the Harlem Children's Zone Been
       Replicated Even Without Obama's Help?, Atlantic Cities, August
       16, 2012, available at www.theatlanticcities.com/politics/2012/08/
       why-hasnt-harlem-childrens-zone-been-replicated-even-without-
       obamas-help/2968.

297   Information about the Ruhi Institute is available from www.ruhi.org.

298 For additional information see the video Frontiers of Learning at www.bahai.org/frontiers. This video shows the activities of the institute process underway in Bihar Sharif, as well as Toronto, Canada, Norte de Bolivar, Columbia, and Lubumbashi, Democratic Republic of Congo. Additional explication is available in Insights from the Frontiers of Learning, prepared by The International Teaching Centre, Bahá'í World Centre, April 2013 and available at www.scribd. com/doc/143639671/Insights-From-the-Frontiers-of-Learning.

299 The early history of the Ruhi Institute can be found in Learning About Growth, The Ruhi Institute, Palabara Purlications, 1991. See www.papabrapublications.com.

300 This story and other history of the institute process in different areas is available in Attaining the Dynamics of Growth: Glimpses from five continents, International Teaching Centre, Bahá'í World Centre, April 2008.

CPSIA information can be obtained
at www.ICGtesting.com
Printed in the USA
LVHW031252160720
660842LV00001B/34